D0992131

The Sinister Way

The Sinister Way

*The Divine and the Demonic
in Chinese Religious Culture*

Richard von Glahn

UNIVERSITY OF CALIFORNIA PRESS
Berkeley · Los Angeles · London

University of California Press
Berkeley and Los Angeles, California

University of California Press, Ltd.
London, England

Library of Congress Cataloging-in-Publication Data

von Glahn, Richard
    The sinister way : the divine and the demonic in
Chinese religious culture / Richard von Glahn.
       p. cm.
    Includes bibliographical references and index.
    ISBN 0-520-23408-1 (cloth : alk. paper)
    1. China—Religion—History. 2. Demonology—
China—History. I. Title.

BL1800 .V66   2004
299.5'1121—dc22   2003016068

Manufactured in the United States of America

13 12 11 10 09 08 07 06 05 04
10 9 8 7 6 5 4 3 2 1

For Hitomi

Contents

Illustrations

Acknowledgments

This book is an outgrowth of research I conducted during my tenure as a visiting fellow at the Institute of Oriental Culture, Tokyo University, in 1988–89, which was supported by a fellowship from the American Council of Learned Societies. Subsequently I continued my research in China in 1991–92 with the aid of a grant from the Committee for Scholarly Communication with China, and I also received a grant from the National Endowment for the Humanities for research and writing during the 1996–97 academic year. In addition, throughout the life of this project I received financial support from the Academic Senate of the University of California, Los Angeles. I am deeply grateful for the support of all of these benefactors.

I owe a special debt of gratitude to Ursula-Angelika Cedzich, who pioneered scholarly study of the Wutong cult and has generously shared her findings and thoughts with me. Barend ter Haar also provided me with insight and guidance in addition to sharing his own research on the Wutong cult. I have benefited over many years from the wisdom of Terry Kleeman, who was present at the birth of this project when we were sharing an office at the Institute of Oriental Culture. Lothar von Falkenhausen and Stephen Bokenkamp read substantial portions of the book manuscript, which has been much improved by their criticism and advice. Wang Ch'iu-kuei's painstaking reading of previously published portions of this study has likewise rescued me from error. I also wish to thank anonymous readers for the University of California Press for their evaluations and criticism. Liao Hsien-huei made an enormous contribution to this book in her multiple roles as assiduous research assistant, inquiring student, and accomplished scholar. Finally, it will be clear to readers that this book rests upon the work of many scholars without which this enterprise would not have been possible.

Shiba Yoshinobu, Wang Chunyu, and Li Bozhong have been extraordinarily helpful in facilitating my access to various archives and libraries. For unstinting courtesy and assistance I wish to thank the librarians and staff at the Institute of Oriental Culture, Tokyo University; Tōyō Bunko; National Diet Library; National Archives of Japan; Seikadō Library; Institute of History, Chinese Academy of Social Sciences; Beijing Library; Beijing University Library; Nanjing Library; Nanjing University Library; Shanghai Library; Library of Congress; and the Young Research Library, University of California, Los Angeles.

I also wish to thank the editors of the *Harvard Journal of Asiatic Studies* for permission to reproduce (in much changed form) two essays that first appeared in that journal's pages: my article "The Enchantment of Wealth," published in volume 51, number 2 (1991), and a review article that appeared in volume 53, number 2 (1993).

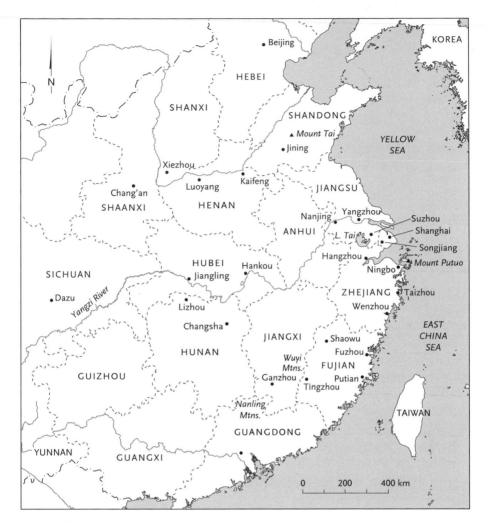

Map 1. China

Introduction

This book at heart is a study of stories told and retold; thus it is fitting that it begins with a story. The following anecdote was published in 1194 by the prolific chronicler of the strange and miraculous, Hong Mai, in the eleventh installment of his *Tales of the Listener*. Hong informed his readers that the story was passed on to him by Zhu Conglong, an otherwise unknown figure who apparently was a refugee from the Jin kingdom then ruling north China. The story is undated, but the rest of the anecdotes attributed by Hong to Zhu date from the 1140s and 1150s, and this one probably does as well.

Liu Xiang, a shopkeeper, had the good fortune of marrying a beautiful wife née Zheng, but his business fared poorly. Wretched and haggard, the disheartened Liu would spend his days drinking with rather unsavory companions in the tavern. Zheng, abandoned to suffer hunger and privation alone, bitterly resented her husband's absence. One day Zheng contracted a feverish illness. After a few days she recovered somewhat, but she withdrew to her bedchamber, where she would sit and stare without uttering a word. Whenever her husband approached, Zheng scowled and sneered at him. Liu, more despondent than ever, left home altogether. His wife sealed herself in the house, admitting no visitors, yet it often seemed as if she were whispering with some invisible guest. Family members spied on her through a crack in the wall, but they never saw anyone.

Some time passed, and Liu Xiang eventually returned home. Upon entering his house he was amazed to discover that it was filled with gold coins and richly worked silks. When he asked his wife how she came to possess all of these treasures, she replied, "For several months a young man has come every night after the midnight watch has sounded. He calls himself Sir Wulang. He shares my bed and has given me everything you see. I dare not hide this from you." Liu was outraged at his wife's infidelity, but he had endured poverty for so long that, finally seeing some relief at hand, he could not bring himself to rebuke her. Subsequently the stranger appeared before Liu in broad daylight, admonishing him never again to spend the night with his wife. Frightened, Liu heeded this warning and moved to another lodging.

Awed by the riches the strange spirit had brought to his wife, Liu himself cast a bronze image of Wulang and paid homage to it morning and night. Soon the spirit procured a new wife for Liu. Not having any sons, Liu prayed to Wulang for assistance. Wulang thereupon kidnapped the ninth son of Marshal Xi, the local governor, and presented the child to Liu so that he could continue his family line. The governor offered a lavish reward for the return of his missing child. A woman in Liu's neighborhood happened to catch sight of an infant dressed in fine silk swaddling in Liu's house. Suspecting that the child could not have been raised in the household of a poor shopkeeper, she ran to the constables to make a report and collect the reward. Liu and Zheng were arrested, and all of their goods were confiscated.

Incensed, the Wulang spirit summoned a host of demons and specters who threw open the gates of the prison, releasing Liu and his wife and at the same time allowing all the other prisoners to escape. Enraged in turn, the governor had Liu and his wife seized the next day and ordered that they be beaten mercilessly. That same night the spirit once again freed the couple and then set fire to the governor's compound, which burned to the ground. Bricks and tiles streamed down like rain, preventing anyone from drawing near enough to extinguish the blaze. Conceding defeat, Marshal Xi consented to allow worship of the spirit to continue and foreswore any further prosecution of Liu and Zheng. Sir Wulang in the end kept possession of Zheng.[1]

Wulang, more commonly known by the name Wutong, was a familiar figure in the religious culture of Hong Mai's day. The diabolical spirit appears in no fewer than two dozen stories in the surviving portions of *Tales of the Listener*. Custodians of public order, like Marshal Xi in the anecdote recounted here, were aghast at the tenacity of popular devotion to such phantom spirits who flagrantly violated the cherished values of fidelity, chastity, and deference to imperial officers. Though Hong

Mai himself was deeply versed in classical learning, his tale, which concludes with the triumph of the wanton spirit over the forces of order, contradicted the fundamental Confucian tenet that righteousness inevitably prevails over evil. Many Confucians scoffed at the kind of supernatural accounts recorded by Hong, dismissing them as wild confabulations of credulous bumpkins, but the imperial state kept vigilant watch on those who would exploit "sinister doctrines" *(zuodao)* to enthrall its subjects.[2]

Zuodao—the "sinister way," as opposed to the "correct way" *(zhengdao)* necessary to the governing of a well-ordered society—had commonly been used to describe the heretical teachings of sorcerers and conjurers since the beginning of the imperial era. The "Regulations of the King" chapter of the *Canon of Ritual,* composed during the Han dynasty (202 B.C.E.–220 C.E.), deemed recourse to "sinister doctrines" a heinous crime:

> Those who use clever speech to violate the law, subvert or circumscribe the statutes by exceeding their proper duties, or resort to sinister doctrines in order to disrupt imperial governance, shall be put to death. Those who create lewd music, strange costumes, and mysterious devices or perform outlandish stunts in order to delude the masses shall be put to death. Those who persevere in evil conduct, engage in specious sophistry, spread false learning, or hide their evildoing behind a beguiling countenance in order to delude the masses shall be put to death. Those who falsely claim to conjure ghosts and spirits, predict lucky or ill-omened days, or practice divination in order to delude the masses shall be put to death. No appeals shall be allowed for these four capital crimes.[3]

The word *zuodao* appears in the first of the four crimes enumerated in this passage, which seems to refer strictly to political machinations, specifically the self-serving cant of unscrupulous officials seeking to deceive the emperor. In contrast, the other three sets of criminal acts all concerned various kinds of sorcery, soothsaying, and mantic arts intended "to delude the masses." Over time, *zuodao* too came to be associated with sorcery and malediction. In the first century B.C.E., the language used in this passage, "resort to sinister doctrines," was on several occasions cited in indictments that charged ministers of state with the broadly insidious crime of impiety *(budao)*.[4] In other cases *zuodao* referred to the extravagant claims of soothsayers and fortune-tellers seeking to curry favor with the emperor.[5] Especially noteworthy was the allegation of "resort to sinister doctrines" in memorials seeking the death sentence for palace women accused of engaging in witchcraft—more precisely, "spells and curses" *(zhouzu)*—to harm or kill the emperor or other members of the impe-rial family.[6] In 18 B.C.E., when Xu Mi, sister of the disowned consort of Emperor Cheng, was condemned to death for using witchcraft against the emperor's new favorite, she was specifically charged with "resorting to sinister doctrines."[7] By the end of the Han *zuodao* had become synony-mous with sorcery.[8] In 224, Emperor Wen of Wei, successor to the Han, decreed that those accused of sorcery and offering improper sacrifices to spirits should be tried on the basis of the statute against "resort to sinis-ter doctrines."[9] In subsequent legal codes "resort to sinister doctrines" was invariably linked to witchcraft and sorcery.[10]

In Hong Mai's day, local magistrates continued to invoke the statute outlawing "resort to sinister doctrines" to prosecute sorcery and illicit forms of worship.[11] A century earlier, in 1023, a prefect by the name of Xia Song serving in Hong Mai's native province of Jiangxi called the court's attention to the prevalence of self-anointed "spirit-masters" es-pousing "sinister doctrines" in his jurisdiction and throughout south China.[12] These charlatan thaumaturges, Xia reported, smugly claimed to be able to conjure spirits and heal the sick, yet they forbade family members from giving food or medicine to, or even remaining in the house with, sick persons. Instead, the spirit-masters set up altars on which they placed graven or painted images of "goblins and fairies" *(chimei)*—as Xia called them—and tried to exorcise the demons afflicting the ill by means of charms and talismans. Most abominable of all in Xia's eyes, local people often entrusted newborn infants to these sorcerers, who raised their wards as acolytes, training them in diabolical arts with the expectation that the youths would eventually succeed them. Xia claimed to have arrested and defrocked more than nineteen hundred such sor-cerers within his jurisdiction, and he called upon the imperial govern-ment to enforce the strict laws against "sinister doctrines," "spells and curses," and "wanton practice of heretical rites." Hong Mai's account of the Wulang spirit shows that, despite such periodic persecutions, civil officials failed to shake popular faith in the abiding presence of ghosts and demons in the people's lives.[13]

Although historians of Chinese religion have devoted considerable at-tention to the origin and development of cults centered on individual gods, less attention has been paid to the demonic aspect of the super-natural realm.[14] No single figure in Chinese religious culture embodied evil like the Satan of Christian religion, nor did the Chinese imagine a divine world starkly divided between forces of good and evil. Misfor-tune could be attributed to the inexorable workings of an inscrutable

destiny, but it was most commonly blamed on a host of demonic entities. Almanacs from the third century B.C.E. detail inauspicious days for
particular activities (because of the presence or activity of malicious spirits), taboos (often based on the fear of offending spirits), sources of illness (including disgruntled ancestors as well as demonic attack), and the
causes of dozens of forms of affliction (ranging from spirits inhering in
animal forms and inanimate objects to natural phenomena).[15] Later anecdotes and folklore suggest that beings best described as specters,
fairies, and goblins populated the most intimate sphere of the supernatural and had the greatest impact on the daily lives of ordinary people.
Yet historical documentation for such figures is scant. Most unsavory gods
and demonic spirits lacked shrines, or their shrines were excluded from
official records, and their cults were typically described in a highly stereo-
typical fashion that sheds little light on actual beliefs and worship.[16] This
study seeks to repair this omission in the study of Chinese religion by
examining the remarkable history of the cult of Wutong within the larger
context of China's evolving religious culture.

Chinese religion, past and present, has functioned above all as a means
of invoking supernatural powers to gain some measure of control over
one's mortal existence. It has also provided moral injunctions; explanations for sin, suffering, and the disposition of the dead; symbols and
metaphors for structuring social order and temporal authority; and spiritual, ritual, and physical disciplines for the attainment of immortality.
But Chinese religion never produced a conception of the divine that stood
apart from the cosmos, and the mundane world human beings inhabited
was not governed by laws fashioned by a transcendent creator god. Thus
the divine and the mundane remained organically connected, each subject to powers of change and transformation inherent in the physical universe. These "powers" were often represented as gods, although Chinese
civilization also produced philosophic traditions that conceived of the
cosmos as spontaneously self-generating, a product of insuperable mystical processes unbeholden to any god or divine will external to itself. In
both the grand organized religious traditions like Daoism and Buddhism
and the multitude of local religious traditions without church or scripture, the sacred was wedded to the ability to wield divine power in pursuit of human aspirations. Powers of miraculous intervention *(ling)*
demonstrated the efficacy of the gods, the sacrifices employed to propitiate them, and the intercessors who mediated between the mundane and
the divine.

Chinese religious culture not only admitted a vast number of gods but also acknowledged the involvement of lesser spirits, especially the ghosts of the dead, in human affairs. Indeed, the ghosts of the dead often loomed larger in the popular religious imagination than the heavenly gods. While exalted deities remained distant and aloof from the mortal realm, the spirits of the dead, both one's own ancestors and the anonymous legions of wandering ghosts, were vivid presences in everyday life. In his classic study of religion in modern Taiwan, Arthur Wolf has drawn attention to the marked correspondences between popular images of supernatural beings and the categories of social identity and interaction. The tripartite division of the spirits into gods, ancestors, and ghosts mirrored popular perceptions of the principal divisions of social life: officialdom, family, and the amorphous mass of "strangers" with whom one had no kinship ties.[17] This congruence between the supernatural world and lived social experience extended to relations of power and the reciprocal obligations incumbent upon mortals and spirits. Though the exalted but remote gods possessed great power, they encroached only slightly on everyday social existence. The ancestors, in contrast, commanded constant attention in the form of worship and sacrifice, and they closely supervised the moral conduct of their descendants. Yet the ancestors were no more powerful in death than they had been in life. Ghosts, the spirits of unrelated dead, remained resolutely alien. Whether envisioned as hapless and beggarly souls or predatory bandits, ghosts were shrouded with a fell aura of malignancy that evoked fear and aversion.

This map of the spiritual landscape thus provided the necessary guideposts for safely navigating social life on both the mundane and supernatural levels. It is especially important to note that this conception of the divine was founded on principles of bureaucratic authority and hierarchy derived from the model of imperial government that prevailed in China for two millennia. The symbols, vocabulary, and rituals that mediated political action were reprised, not simply as metaphors, but as the actual instruments of intercourse between the divine and mundane worlds.[18]

Wolf's model of Chinese religious culture as a reflection of social relations offers important insights into the operation of religious ideas and practices and is especially helpful in understanding Chinese religion not simply as an inventory of beliefs and rituals but as a product of social and historical experience. Yet the functionalist logic of the model, and especially its implication of rigid categorical distinctions among divine beings corresponding to sharp differences in social status, fails to capture the complex and fluid dynamics of the relationships between Chinese gods and their worshipers. As many scholars have noted, there are numerous gods and spirits—and indeed whole categories of divine beings, for example the Buddhist pantheon, or female deities—that do not fit easily into Wolf's tripartite model of the supernatural world.[19] The most important qualification to the tripartite model is that the categories themselves of god, ghost, and ancestor were unstable over time; many gods, especially local tutelary deities, originated as ghosts; ancestors, too, might be transformed into gods; and in some cases the images of the ancestors scarcely differed from those of other ghosts. Finally, the tripartite model offers only limited insight into the nature of evil, and the problems of theodicy posed by morally ambivalent gods like Wutong.

While anthropologists have constructed models of Chinese religion based on contemporary behavior (above all ritual practice), historians have tended to categorize religion in terms of the dominant hieratic traditions, the Three Teachings (Sanjiao) of Daoism, Buddhism, and Confucianism (or state religion). Each of these traditions can be identified in terms of a distinct theology, a body of sacred writings, ritual practices and precepts for the conduct of daily life, a cadre of learned men (and, in rare cases, women) who authorized the teachings and practices of the tradition, and enduring institutions that served to reproduce it. Recently, historians have begun to give ample consideration to "popular religion" as a fourth distinct religious tradition. Despite the secular ethos of Confucian education and socialization, the religious practices of the ruling elite of imperial China shared much in common with the "folk" religion of the peasantry.[20] Instead of distinguishing "popular religion" from a sublime elite religion, historians of China have typically defined "popular religion" as a body of beliefs and practices common to laypersons of all social classes, in contradistinction to the religious world of scriptural traditions and ecclesiastic authority. This notion of popular religion essentially reprises the binary structure postulated by C. K. Yang in his landmark study of Chinese religion. Yang delineated two structural forms in Chinese religion: 1) institutional religion (primarily understood as denoting Buddhism and Daoism, but also including a wide range of practitioners of mantic arts and congregational groups), systems of theology, rituals, and organization independent of secular social institutions; and 2) diffused religion, whose beliefs, practices, and organization were embedded in and inseparable from secular life.[21] Yang emphasized the relative importance of the latter, which in his view derived from the classical religion of ancient China, rather than the former in Chinese religious life. Yang also claimed that diffused religion was crucial to reinforcing the social and economic cohesion of secular institutions (family, lineage, guild, village, fraternities and other associations) and in justifying the normative political order of the imperial state.

Although scholars today abjure the Weberian and Parsonian sociological precepts underpinning Yang's analysis, his basic premise that this diffused religion constituted the principal form of Chinese religious life has gained broad acceptance. In a groundbreaking study Valerie Hansen has sought to show how this diffused religion (what she refers to as "secular" beliefs and rituals), rather than being vestiges of an archaic religion, emerged out of the social and economic changes of the pivotal Song dynasty (960–1276).[22] Patricia Ebrey and Peter Gregory likewise have described popular religion as "diffuse," centered on family and community rather than congregational and ecclesiastic institutions. Like Hansen, Ebrey and Gregory insist that popular religion should not be opposed to "elite" practices, invoking once again Yang's distinction between the diffused religion of laypersons of all social classes and the doctrinal and ritual traditions of organized religion. In their view, popular religion comprised a distinct tradition alongside the Three Teachings of Buddhism, Daoism, and Confucianism. Yet all four of these traditions evolved through mutual interaction and influence. Following an analogy first drawn by Eric Zürcher, Ebrey and Gregory suggest that the popular tradition formed the bedrock of all Chinese religious practice.[23] This popular religion proved remarkably pliant and amenable to the needs of its practitioners, precisely because it was unencumbered by the doctrinal and theological rigidities of organized religion. Because popular religion lacked canonical scriptures and an established priesthood, its heterogeneous beliefs and values were reproduced and transmitted in the forms of symbol, myth, and ritual primarily through the agency of folklore, performance arts, and family culture.[24]

Anthropologists have also underscored the distinction between the lay/secular/diffused religious practice of ordinary laypersons and the hieratic theology and liturgy of Buddhism and Daoism. Anthropological studies of modern Chinese popular religion to a large degree have been dominated by the question of whether religious ideas and practices promoted unity or difference in society and cultural values.[25] C. K. Yang and Maurice Freedman, for example, maintain that the manifold variations in Chinese religious practice were subsumed under an all-encompassing structure that bound Chinese culture together.[26] James Watson, in contrast, contends that the superficial uniformity of religious beliefs disguised wide divergence in the meaning of these beliefs among discrete social groups; worship of a given deity ramified into distinctive social identities fractured along lines of status, class, and gender.[27] Recent scholarship on religion in contemporary Taiwan has stressed the ways in which religion simultaneously creates both ideological coherence and social differentiation. Steven Sangren, for example, argues that a consistent symbolic logic pervades the "structures of value" in Chinese culture, but the contingent histories of individual communities generate variations in institutions and social behavior that mask this essential cultural continuity. Rather than seeing the divine world as a projection of social categories in the style of Wolf and Yang, Sangren views religious symbols as multivocal, subject to conflicting interpretation precisely because of the inherent tensions in social relations. Ultimately, though, ritual action serves to reinforce the hegemonic social order. Sangren describes the relationship between social organization and its symbolic representations as "recursive" and concludes that the particularizing tendencies of local communities become sublimated within a universal cosmo-political order.[28] A different sort of dialectic between orthodox sociopolitical norms and religious practice has been proposed by Robert Weller, who contrasts the shared body of basic cultural values with the variety of interpretations and meanings drawn from that common fund. Weller distinguishes between the ideological constructs of formal religion (the state and ecclesiastic authorities) on one hand and the "pragmatic interpretations" derived from them in the course of lived social experience on the other. Different groups utilize a range of styles of pragmatic interpretation, and thus the same sets of general values and ritual structures can engender starkly different meanings. He then illustrates how people in Taiwan in the recent past have adapted hieratic ritual and scriptural "ideologies" to suit their own purposes.[29]

Sangren's emphasis on the recuperative function of ritual coincides with the views of other anthropologists who assert the primacy of ritual action over belief in Chinese religion, arguing that the standardization of ritual substantiates and maintains a unified culture across Chinese society.[30] Weller, while acknowledging that shared social experiences foster ideological as well as social unity, instead stresses the potential for social change to undermine the unity of interpretation and values: "Seeing beliefs as mechanical correlates of class or society hides the flexibility of interpretation in light of ongoing historical experience. People use, manipulate, and create culture (including religion) as part of everyday life within a system of social relations."[31] The formulations proposed by Sangren and Weller certainly improve upon Yang's institutionalized/

diffused dichotomy. Both recognize the importance of "history" (lived social experience) in forming religious values and practices; they avoid the pitfalls of marking a stark disjuncture between great and little traditions, whether conceived in sociological (elite/commoner) or religious (lay/clerical) terms; and they recognize that Buddhism, Daoism, state religion, and popular religion are all part of a single cultural system.

Although anthropologists generally have endorsed Yang's basic distinction between institutional and diffused religion, in one major respect they have turned it on its head. Yang believed that diffused religion, because it pervaded—and thus was dependent upon—secular institutions, lacked the autonomy to challenge social convention and hierarchy. At the same time, the alienation of the Buddhist and Daoist clergy (to say nothing of covert religious sects) from the rest of the social body placed them in a position to become a dissenting force.[32] Sangren concurs that the ritual process acts to disguise or mystify the ways in which the prevailing "structure of values" legitimates and reproduces existing social institutions. But Weller disputes the notion that popular religion inevitably reinforces the prevailing structures of power and dominance that undergird the status quo and suggests that it has greater potential for generating alternative ideologies than the already ideologized traditions of clerical religion.[33] Emily Martin Ahern has gone even farther, arguing that religious ritual, far from mystifying the true nature of authority or concealing it from the ruled, instead provides the lower classes with the means to access divine power and to manipulate it for their own purposes.[34]

The heterogeneity of both "ideologies" and "interpretations" (in Weller's sense of the words) tends to affirm the view that Chinese religion is not a system of beliefs, but rather a set of purposeful actions (ritual in the broadest sense) undertaken to effect some transformation upon the world and the place of the individual in it. This conception of Chinese religion has gained broad acceptance among anthropologists, and even some historians of religion. James Watson explains the apparent uniformity of funerary rites across China as a consequence of the essentially performative nature of the ritual process: cultural identity inhered in ritual "orthopraxy" (correct performance of ritual), not beliefs and values. This ritual orthopraxy thus acted as a powerful force for cultural homogenization.[35] Jordan Paper concludes that Chinese religion, founded on a core of ritual action (in his view, the communal meal shared with the spirits), has been singular and relatively homogeneous since ancient times.[36] In a similar vein, Sangren asserts that it is not a deity or shrine but rather communal ritual that constitutes a cult in Chinese religion.[37] In contrast to the anthropologists who emphasize ritual action, historians have focused their attention on belief, and especially on the cults of prominent deities.[38]

My own approach to the study of Chinese religion is deeply indebted to these models but also diverges from them in important ways. On one hand, I emphatically stress the diversity of Chinese religious culture. The apparent uniformity of myth, symbol, and ritual in Chinese religion conceals wide variations in "pragmatic interpretations," to use Weller's term, that inform social ideology and action. In an important sense, in China all religion is local. Only by examining the histories of local communities can we truly appreciate the dialectical relationship between religion and society. (Here I diverge from Sangren's sense of "history" as a process of authenticating cultural norms and social categories and allow greater scope for "history" as an open-ended process whereby social order and values are reinterpreted and reconstructed.) Nor do I find satisfying definitions of Chinese religion grounded in notions of ritual practice to the exclusion of belief and values. Ritual forms no less than "ideologies" were flexible practices subject to pragmatic interpretation and adaptation. As instruments of power, rituals could be deployed in manifold ways.

On the other hand, I believe we can define the religious culture of China in terms of certain basic orientations regarding the role of divine power and human agency in shaping the course of human life. I take exception to Yang's dichotomy of institutionalized and diffused religion, and to the sharp distinctions drawn between hieratic and lay religion in recent studies. Nor do I find it helpful to define Chinese religion in terms of distinct traditions such as Buddhism, Daoism, and popular religion. As Weller's concept of pragmatic interpretation suggests, Buddhist or Daoist beliefs and rituals could be utilized in more or less ideological forms to achieve ends quite different from those canonically authorized. Similarly, the distinction between hieratic/institutionalized religion defined by "canonical scriptures" and "professional clergies," and lay/secular religion that lacked either, is overdrawn. We cannot separate out a body of popular or secular religious values and practices from the larger social and institutional matrix in which those values and practices appear. Although there is a certain utility to the notion of "secular religion" as Valerie Hansen defines the concept—religious practices unmediated by clergy—I think Hansen underestimates the importance of scripture and clergy in the formation of this "secular" religious culture. In addition, I strongly disagree with Yang's contention that this secular religion (or "diffused religion," to use Yang's own term) was so deeply embedded in the institutions of secular society that it inevitably served to reinforce existing social identities and relationships.

Consequently, I have chosen to avoid some of the misleading connotations of "secular" by describing the common religious culture of China as its "vernacular" religion. "Vernacular" suggests a demotic idiom, but one that is rooted in local and regional history. Vernacular language of course is closer to common speech than classical language, yet the vernacular language is as much a literary as an oral tradition. Contrasting vernacular language or religion with classical language or religion runs the risk of merely replicating Yang's dichotomy between diffused and institutionalized religion. Instead, we must recognize that Buddhism, Daoism, and state religion were all integrally related to vernacular religion. Hence, in this study vernacular religion denotes local and common discourse, expressed in belief and ritual, for interpreting and expressing ideas that derive from complex and shifting sets of religious ideologies and practices. While vernacular religion shared certain salient orientations that make it possible for us to speak of a common Chinese religious culture, the meaning of vernacular religion diverged across space and time. It is in the instantiation of this religious culture in manifold forms in history, rather than in an overarching, hegemonic "structure," that we will find its meaning and significance. The striking mutations of the Wutong cult over its thousand-year history epitomize the workings of vernacular religion.

My formulation of "vernacular religion" as a local and demotic idiom in some respects corresponds to the distinction between "vernacular" and "classical" delineated by Kristof Schipper in his studies on Daoist liturgical traditions.[39] Schipper portrays the vernacular ritual tradition as exclusively local, pared down in form and substance from the classical tradition of ordained priests while at the same time saturated with local myths, orally transmitted ritual traditions, and ecstatic performances. He rejects the reductionist opposition of diffused versus institutionalized religion, contending that Daoism always remained vitally integrated into local religious cultures. Masters of classical ritual borrowed from vernacular rites, and the two traditions often converged in ritual practice at the community level. Yet Schipper still gives priority to the classical tradition, which he describes as "a literate, refined, elegant, and sophisticated expression of Chinese religion," the "superstructure" that imparts unity and coherence to "more ordinary local cults."[40] In historical terms, Schipper sees the Tang-Song transitional era (the eighth to twelfth centuries), when the Daoist ritual repertoire became deeply ingrained in local cults, as the formative era of vernacular Daoism. While I agree that the Tang-Song transition witnessed an unprecedented vernacularization of ritual, it was also characterized, as Hansen has shown, by the spread of secular (again, in Hansen's sense of unmediated by religious specialists) techniques of ritual action. For Schipper, ritual always requires hieratic mediation, and thus he overlooks the equally important contributions of ordinary believers and their cults to the creation of vernacular religion. Proper understanding of vernacular religion must also give consideration to the distinct social contexts (individual, familial, and communal) in which it operates.

It is my contention that Chinese religious culture throughout its history has manifested two fundamental orientations: 1) eudaemonistic regimes of propitiation and exorcism that regulated relationships between the human and spirit worlds; and 2) an abiding belief in a moral equilibrium inhering in the cosmos itself (though frequently mediated through the agency of divine powers).[41] Both of these orientations can be traced back to the earliest literate civilizations of the Bronze Age: the former is well attested in the court religion of the Shang dynasty (ca. 1700–1045 B.C.E.), and the latter was central to the cult of Heaven developed under the succeeding Zhou dynasty (1045–256 B.C.E.). Both orientations were incorporated into the later hieratic traditions of the Three Teachings. However, there was an irreducible tension between the two. While Chinese (in the imperial era, at least) did not adhere to one orientation to the exclusion of the other, the two could not be embraced equally.

Mu-chou Poo observes that the most enduring substrate of religious mentality in ancient China (the Shang-Zhou era) was fundamentally concerned with securing one's personal welfare through acquisition of mantic knowledge and powers.[42] In Poo's view, the religion of the common people primarily consisted of transactions with the divine mediated by divination and sacrifice lacking any moral component. Misery and mischance, the perennial afflictions of human existence, were attributed to the actions of supernatural beings. Yet suffering was caused not only by evil spirits, but also by intemperate ancestors, unfortunate ghosts, and vengeful gods. Poo thus concludes that "in everyday religious attitudes there was little difference between gods, ghosts, and spirits."[43] Although the idea that supernatural beings judge the worthiness of sacrifices chiefly according to the moral character of the supplicant attained some currency among intellectuals like Confucius, the most "potent" *(ling)* supernatural beings—in terms of their effect on human lives—often were demons. The mantic regimens and exorcistic therapies devised to fend off their afflictions rarely obtained any moral dimension. From the beginning of the imperial era, the calendar of religious ritual and festival was constructed above all around the necessity of purging baleful spirits and appeasing capricious ancestors at regular intervals.

The introduction of a moral ethos into the vernacular religious culture (as opposed to court religion) accompanied the spread of "correlative cosmology," a worldview grounded in belief in the organic nature of a cosmos in which the individual, society, and the natural world were subject to homologous cycles of change and mutation (see chapter 1). This worldview emphasized the harmonious equilibrium and coherence that underlay all phenomena and forces, seen and unseen, at work in the world. From the fourth century B.C.E., virtually every facet of knowledge—philosophy, government, religion, medicine, natural science, and military strategy— and the application of each to human life was deeply colored by the precepts of correlative cosmology. On the level of the individual, correlative cosmology produced mantic practices to halt the entropic decay of the body and human life through regimens of personal discipline (physical and moral) and gnosis. In the social and political realm, the taxonomies of correlative cosmology enabled the ruler to adapt human behavior—especially as manifested in ritual and institutions—to patterns of cosmic structure and change. Although initially devoid of moral ethos, correlative cosmology was infused with ethical significance over the course of the Han dynasty, and this notion of moral equilibrium was subsequently strengthened and elaborated by Daoist and Buddhist doctrines. Robert Campany has referred to this belief in a moral equilibrium governing relations between the human and divine/cosmic worlds as the "doctrine of Heaven and Humanity" *(tianren shuo)*.[44]

Correlative cosmology, and the "doctrine of Heaven and Humanity" that issued from it, was based on a fundamental belief in the "resonance" *(ganying)* that mediated between different orders of reality. In correlative cosmology, events in the human world stimulate *(gan)* responses *(ying)* in the cosmos. Similarly, human actions (all human actions, moral and ritual, not just those of rulers and priests) evoke responses from the divine world and the gods and spirits that inhabit it. Human misdeeds would provoke signs of divine opprobrium (omens and portents) and invite punishment (personal or general calamity). As Campany observes, the "doctrine of Heaven and Humanity" asserts that "morality and piety—no matter of what kind—are unfailingly rewarded; immorality

and impiety are unfailingly punished."[45] The specifically moral character of this resonance between the human and the divine orders becomes
especially clear in the concept of "retribution" (*baoying,* a word that initially referred specifically to portents, and was later employed to trans-
late the Buddhist concept of *karma*), which becomes fundamental to religious discourse from the Han dynasty onward.

Yet *ganying* did not necessarily imply a moral order. The idea that the
spirits respond in predictable ways to ritual propitiation long antedated
the emergence of correlative cosmology. The power possessed by gods
and spirits to intervene in mundane affairs *(ling)* was amenable to human manipulation through sacrifice and mantic arts. Thus, gods were es-
teemed in proportion to their responsiveness to human entreaties, a qual-
ity referred to as "potency of resonance" *(linggan).* This potency cannot
be understood simply in terms of belief in the efficacy of the powers of
a given god or spirit, however. As Sangren emphasizes, the *ling,* or miraculous power, of any entity is "defined or constrained by both general cultural logic and by a historically unfolding logic of social relations in particular contexts."[46] The manifestations of divine power *(lingyan)* in the
forms of the miracles a god performs or boons a god grants not only
testified to the god's ability to affect human destiny, but also defined and
authenticated social relations among its worshipers. As social relations
changed, so did the power wielded by the gods. The bond between a god
and its worshipers was based not on a moral covenant, but rather on the
transactions between them: a circular exchange of sacrifice and devotion
on one hand and protection and aid on the other. Indeed, many gods appeared to be morally ambivalent or even demonic in nature, prone to resort to violence as much as moral power.

The history of Chinese religious culture presented in this study pro-
ceeds from analysis of these fundamental orientations of eudaemonistic
entreaty and moral equilibrium since antiquity, and treats the development of the distinctive religious traditions of state religion, Daoism, and
Buddhism as derivations of these basic orientations. I propose that there
were two major moments in the transformation of Chinese religion during the imperial era. First, in the Han dynasty, new ideas about death
and the afterlife emerged that coalesced in a much-changed cult of the
dead that in turn became the touchstone for the formation of salvific religions, both the indigenous tradition of Daoism and the imported Buddhist religion (see chapter 2). Second, in the Song dynasty, the religious
culture was transformed by a vernacularization of ritual practice and

mantic arts that rendered the divine more accessible to ordinary human beings (see chapter 5). This vernacularization of ritual established the framework of modern Chinese religion.

Demons and demonic forces were cardinal features of both of the basic orientations that I have identified. In the final chapters of this book I turn to a case study of the cult of the god Wutong, which cogently symbolizes the interpenetration of the divine and the demonic in Chinese religious culture. The Wutong cult represents an instance of the near total eclipse of the moral equilibrium orientation by the eudaemonistic orientation, and in this respect it diverges markedly from the apparent trend toward a greater integration of the two. The successive transformations of the Wutong cult, from its origins in the tenth century down to the twentieth century, reflected the continuous evolution of vernacular conceptions of both the divine world and the human social order. Throughout this period the state, ecclesiastic authorities, devout laity, and secular critics each sought to recast the deity in a form that suited their own moral and religious sensibilities. Although their efforts failed to eradicate the demonic aspect of Wutong, they did influence vernacular perceptions of the deity.

In archaic Greece, the word *daimon* described not a category of gods, but rather "an occult power, a force that drives man forward when no agent can be named." The mood and temperament of the individual person were determined by the indwelling presence of either the "happy demon" *(eudaimon)* or the "unhappy demon" *(kakodaimon)*. *Daimon* also referred to the spirits of dead heroes who became guardians over mortals, and "imaginary apparitions" that drove people to desperate acts.[47] In the late Greco-Roman period, *daimon* (like the Latin *genius*) commonly referred to lesser spirits and demigods, especially patron or guardian spirits joined to a person at birth that would protect the homestead and family. Only with Plato's disciple Xenocrates was the word systematically applied to evil spirits filled with lust for blood and sex.[48] In Chinese religious culture, as in archaic Greece, it would be more appropriate to think of the "demonic" as a propensity of gods, spirits, and humans toward hostility and malevolence, rather than a specific category of divine beings. Certain spirits, such as the mountain goblins discussed in chapter 3, were inveterately demonic. Others, like the plague demons discussed in chapter 4, could be construed as demonic in character but were also conceived as emissaries of the august gods who exacted just punishment on sinful mortals. The god Wutong shared some traits with these demonic spirits, but Wutong was also recognized as a deity who manifested potent responsiveness *(linggan)* in his relations with mortal votaries.

In his earliest forms Wutong appeared in a variety of guises, both good and evil, sometimes as a healer of the sick, at other times as a noxious demon. During the Southern Song period (twelfth to thirteenth centuries) Wutong was inducted into the pantheon of imperially sanctioned cults and achieved a similar apotheosis in the liturgical traditions of the newly ascendant Daoist Thunder Magic movements. In the late Ming dynasty (sixteenth to seventeenth centuries) Wutong emerged as the dominant cult figure in Jiangnan, the economic and cultural heartland of China, in the form of a god who governs the dispensation of wealth. The most remarkable feature of Wutong's incarnation as a god of wealth was the deity's diabolical character. Wutong was perceived neither as a culture hero nor as a reification of noble human qualities, but rather as an embodiment of humanity's basest vices, greed and lust, an actively maleficent demon that preyed on the weak and vulnerable. As such, Wutong was very much the antithesis of the modern gods of wealth.

The history of the Wutong cult and the development of Wutong into a god of wealth provide a unique perspective on popular conceptions of the nexus between money and social relations. Many observers have commented on the absence in Chinese culture of religious sanctions against acquisitiveness such as those imposed by the medieval Christian church.[49] Although Chinese religion did not condemn the acquisition of wealth as a motive for invoking the aid of the gods, the popular image of Wutong as a demonic figure reveals a keen awareness of the subversive and potentially dangerous consequences of avarice. Not surprisingly, the cult was often subjected to proscription and repression—sporadically in the mid-Ming, and systematically from the late seventeenth century onwards. Ultimately, although the Wutong cult lingered on into the twentieth century, Wutong's preeminence as the god of wealth was eclipsed by new cult figures that personified positive, "bourgeois" virtues of hard work, modesty, thrift, and moral integrity. Yet the demise of Wutong did not testify to the dominion exercised by the state over popular belief. Instead, the symbolic construction of the modern cult of the god of wealth beginning in the eighteenth century reflected changes in the society, economy, and culture of Jiangnan as profound as those that elevated Wutong to the pinnacle of the popular pantheon two centuries before.

Since this book proposes to study collective popular mentality through the literary record of the dominant patrician *(shidafu)* class, a brief note of explanation about methodology is in order. The variety of sources used here is extremely broad, ranging from Daoist scriptures, religious primers, temple inscriptions, and vernacular fiction to government documents, official memoirs, and local gazetteers. The most important source for the Wutong cult, though, is the vast repertory of anecdotes accumulated over its long history, like the Wulang tale with which this book began. These anecdotes were, of course, written down by men of exalted social class whose book learning distanced them from the mental universe of the cult's nonliterate devotees. To those who insist upon the fundamental autonomy of plebeian culture and belief, reliance upon written anecdote poses substantial risks of misinterpretation or calculated distortion.[50] Yet the utility of studying the mentality of nonliterate classes through an analysis of books they never read has been amply demonstrated by Mikhail Bakhtin's classic work on humor and folk belief in the novels of Rabelais.[51] Close attention to the symbols and metaphors found in anecdotes can reveal the structure of the ideas behind them and how this structure evolves. Indeed, to the extent it preserves the language of concrete experience, the anecdote offers valuable insight into plebeian mentality: "Repetitive stories of this kind are close in form to that of peasant communication, a form which may exist in most communities with 'face-to-face' relationships. This form involves concrete language of symbolic content, which constantly reiterates central aspects of social relationships. Its repetitiveness and its seeming triviality is a pointer to what in fact we want to investigate."[52] The essential congruity of Wutong stories and anecdotes from diverse hands suggests that the written versions preserve much of the oral narrative.

A greater danger perhaps lies in assumptions concerning the essentially classless character of collective mentality and the tendency to abstract "values" out of their social context. Superficial similarities between the ideology of the dominant patrician class and representations of popular mentality in the written record have been read as evidence of a "growing integration" of Chinese culture and "closer congruence" of elite and peasant values in the late imperial period.[53] The present study challenges this view. While recognizing reciprocal influences between the cultures of dominant and subordinate classes, it distinguishes between the culture imposed on the plebeian classes and the vernacular culture that they themselves produce. Only by recognizing this distinction can we begin to hear the authentic popular voices so often elided from patrician discourse about Chinese religious culture.

CHAPTER I

Ancestors, Ghosts, and Gods in Ancient China

Although only dimly perceived before the advent of modern archaeology, the Shang kingdom, which ruled over the North China Plain in the late second millennium B.C.E. (ca. 1700–ca. 1045 B.C.E.), is now recognized as the progenitor of many basic features of Chinese religious culture. The eudaemonistic beliefs and practices that became the foundation for later Chinese vernacular religion were already present in the court religion of the Shang. The subsequent Zhou dynasty (ca. 1045–256 B.C.E.) incorporated many of these practices into its own ritual culture, but the Zhou also departed from the Shang in formulating the earliest version of the moral equilibrium orientation, the cult of Heaven. Wolf's tripartite division of the supernatural realm into gods, ancestors, and ghosts can also be observed in ancient times, but the status and significance of these categories of divine beings differed greatly from their modern counterparts. Indeed, in terms of historical evolution, it would be more proper to invert (as the title of this chapter does) Wolf's ordering of "gods, ghosts, and ancestors" to trace the successive emergence of "ancestors, ghosts, and gods" as epitomes of supernatural power.

The Shang kingdom was a dynastic state encompassing an extensive network of noble domains under the dominion of a paramount king. Each domain was centered on a walled town, the seat of its ruling lineage. The royal clan consisted of ten lineages that alternated succession to kingship. Periodic fission of the royal lineages and award of domains to junior branches impelled aggressive expansion of the Shang realm through war and conquest. The royal and noble lineages who ruled over this polity were above all warriors and sacrificers; conquest and ritual symbiotically nourished each other and swelled the might of the kingdom.

The bonds of royal kinship formed the sinews of military and political power. Ultimately, though, Shang kings derived their authority from powers they could command through the mediation of their deified ancestors. The Shang kings, and indeed the entire noble class, communicated with their deceased ancestors by means of divination. Records of royal divinations were inscribed on the animal bones (cattle scapulae and tortoise plastrons) used to perform the divination. After a king died the archive of inscribed oracle bones accumulated during his lifetime was sometimes interred in the tomb of the deceased or in nearby pits, thus preserved until they were once again brought into the world of light by archaeological excavations. Much of our knowledge about the activities of the Shang ruling class has been obtained from these oracle bones, the oldest literary remains in East Asia.[1]

The Shang projected the social and political hierarchy of the mundane world beyond death and onto the world of the divine.[2] Shang rulers addressed their deceased ancestors as deified spirits, imagining that death only augmented their majesty and power. The divine hierarchy, organized along kinship lines, largely replicated the secular one: the ancestor gods were ranked according to the order of precedence of the royal lineage. Thus the Shang kings ruled by virtue of their *charisma,* in Weber's sense of a special relationship to the divine that endows a mortal being with extraordinary powers.[3] The thaumaturgic powers the Shang kings could exercise through divination and ancestral sacrifices enabled them to obtain bountiful harvests and victory in battle, which in turn enhanced their charismatic authority.

The eclipse of brute force by charismatic authority undoubtedly contributed to the stability of the Shang kingdom. But the divine realm was also subject to the same strife among warring clans that beset the mortal world. The Shang kings did not enjoy exclusive access to divine power; rather, every noble lineage, including the enemies of Shang, could make similar claims based on their intimate relationships with their own exalted ancestors. The exact means by which the ancestor gods aided their mortal descendants remains murky. Prevailing scholarly opinion holds that the Shang believed in a supreme deity known as Di, or Thearch, who was the ultimate arbiter of human fate but stood aloof from ordinary mortals.[4] In contrast to the Yahweh of Abrahamic religions, Di did not impose his moral will on humanity. Di was an impersonal god, indifferent to mortal concerns and largely inaccessible to human supplicants. Living rulers sought to curry favor with Di through the intercession of their deified ancestors, who could communicate directly with the supreme god. A lineage enhanced the potency of its charisma by providing its ancestors with the most munificent sacrifices, thereby magnifying their influence over Di. Shang religion, and indeed the whole Shang social order, revolved around this necromantic propitiation of the ancestor deities.

Thus the Shang kings depended upon the mediation of their ancestors to ensure their political supremacy. The intersecting logic of Shang religion and political legitimation emphasized the mutual interdependence of the living and the dead. Only by receiving rich and regular sacrificial offerings could the ancestors maintain their exalted place within the divine realm. Consequently, the political economy of the Shang state was based on tribute, in the form of sacrifices, offered to the ancestor gods in exchange for their aid in obtaining blessings from Di.[5] In addition to tribute goods submitted to the Shang king by subordinate lords, royal hunts and processions also provided occasions for the king to mobilize the produce of his realm in service to his ancestor cult.[6] Divine blessings more than repaid the copious expenditure of grain, wine, animal and human sacrifices, and ritual objects, especially bronze vessels, consumed by these ancestral rites. The sacrifices also mandated scrupulous attention to the minute details of ritual. The refined bronze-making skills of Shang artisans were concentrated not on the manufacture of weapons or agricultural tools, but rather on the production of ritual vessels that served as the tangible instruments of both sacred and secular power. Shang bronze art is noteworthy for its lack of iconographic representations of gods and mortals. Instead, Shang ritual bronzes featured images of fantastic creatures, either spirits or priests wearing animal masks, who mediated between the living members of the lineage and their deified kin. Chief among them was the enigmatic *taotie,* the most pervasive image in Shang bronze art, a fantastic zoomorph distinguished by prominent eyes, fangs, and horns (figures 1, 2, and 3). In the minds of later Chinese, the striking *taotie* motif of Shang bronzes conjured up demonic images; indeed, the word *taotie,* first applied to this motif in the Warring States period, meant "glutton" and was associated with a monstrous tyrant of insatiable greed and lust.[7] Though the original meaning of the *taotie* is greatly disputed, with many scholars denying that the *taotie* has any iconic meaning at all, there can be little doubt that the fantastic creatures depicted in Shang ritual art metaphorically displayed the union of divine power and temporal authority.[8]

Figures 1–3. *Taotie* motifs from Shang bronzes: *Hu* flagon, Erligang (ca. fifteenth century B.C.E.), from Shanghai bowuguan qingtongqi yanjiuzu 1984: plate 8; *Gui* tureen, early Anyang era (ca. thirteenth century B.C.E.), from Shanghai bowuguan qingtongqi yanjiuzu 1984: plate 26; *Ding* cauldron, late Anyang era (eleventh century B.C.E.), from Shanghai bowuguan qingtongqi yanjiuzu 1984: plate 139.

Communication between Shang rulers and their ancestors via divination was essential to governance, since all important decisions were based on these oracles. Yet the oracles themselves show that the Shang lived not only in awe but also in fear of their deceased kin. Lapses in ritual piety provoked severe punishment. Oracles concerning illnesses suffered by the ruler typically inquired about which ancestors had been roused to anger and how to placate them. Ironically, although distant, more senior ancestors were generally portrayed as powerful and benevolent patrons, the oracles often identified the recent dead—who most likely had personally known the living—as the sources of "curses."

The oracle bones also show that the Shang believed in numerous nature deities (the spirits of mountains, rivers, wind, fire, and rain, for example) associated with particular places. Akatsuka Kiyoshi has argued that these nature deities were totemic tutelary gods of ruling local lineages ("tribes" in Akatsuka's nomenclature) that the Shang, upon subjugating these groups, incorporated into their own pantheon. Akatsuka depicts the Shang polity as a theocratic tribal federation united by a peripatetic king who periodically progressed throughout the entire realm, performing sacrifices to local gods and thereby garnering a common bounty of fruitful harvests and military triumphs. Although many aspects of Akatsuka's portrait of Shang government and religion, especially his conceptions of tribe and totem, are subject to dispute, his overall vision of the sacred nature of kingship is a compelling one.[9] In the late Shang period, sacrifices to nature deities and the more remote Shang ancestors declined markedly.[10] These intermediate divinities were apparently effaced by the late Shang kings' assertion of their direct control over the divine, including Di, an assertion that may have been based on claims that the Shang king himself was a living god.[11] The oracle bones of the last Shang kings also indicate a shift away from heavy reliance on divination and toward systematized, routine administration of sacrifices, reflecting the increasing hubris of kings who no longer dwelled in dread of their ancestors.

Shang religion thus revealed no sharp distinctions between the divine and the mundane worlds, nor between the sacred and the profane. Neither the supreme deity, Di, nor any of the lesser gods of Shang religion imposed any absolute moral standards beyond the ritual obligations binding the living to the dead. The king, through correct performance of ritual acts, could manipulate these spirits and bend them to his will. The charismatic authority wielded by the king inhered not in the king as a heroic individual, however, but in the corporate group, the lineage, that the king represented. Similarly, Shang religion betrays little concern for the fate of the individual (or "soul") after death. The recent dead appear to have retained many of their personal attributes and temperament, but with the passage of time and erasure of memory the ancestors were gradually reduced to the abstractions of rank and title. Depersonalization became congruent with authority: the distant ancestors exercised greater power than the recently deceased, and the supreme deity Di was shorn of any personal qualities whatsoever. Therefore the mortuary ritual of the Shang eschewed veneration of exemplary, "heroic" individuals; instead it concentrated on securing the place of each individual in the eternal hierarchical order of the lineage. The grave goods interred with Shang nobility proclaimed the individual's exalted status, but only in order to confirm and augment the charisma of the lineage as a whole. Shang religion thus allowed little scope for mythology, since it emphasized the prescribed ritual/kinship roles of the ancestors rather than the celebration of their individual traits and life histories.[12]

The divine realm remained a privileged world accessible only to the ruling class. Shang gods never became gods of the masses, nor of the community as a whole. The walled towns that served as political capitals were first and foremost cult centers, sites of the ancestral temples and tombs of royal and noble lineages, the cynosures of sacred as well as secular power.[13] In contrast to cities of the early civilizations of west and south Asia, Shang cities conspicuously lacked monumental architecture glorifying the achievements of the living. Shang cities, reflecting their primary function as ceremonial centers, were defined by walled enclosures and the ancestral temple and tombs of the ruling lineage. Yet the temples devoted to the ancestral cult were dwarfed by the tombs, wherein the greater portion of royal treasure came to rest. The Shang capital was indeed a necropolis, a city of the dead who provided the essential link to divine power. The religious and ceremonial functions of Shang cities thus reinforced rather than mitigated social stratification. Assimilation of local gods into the ancestral cult of the ruling lineage resulted in the exclusion of plebeian urban inhabitants, chiefly artisans and slaves, from religious life.

The intimacy between rulers and their apotheosized ancestors also precluded the rise of a priestly class that might contest the sovereign prerogatives of the ruling lineages. Priestly intercessors had an ancient pedigree dating back to well before the Shang kingdom. The human figures with plumed headdresses conjoined to masklike animal faces that decorate the remarkable jade carvings from the Liangzhu neolithic culture

(third millennium B.C.E.) of the lower Yangzi River valley display striking parallels with the *taotie* and other zoomorphic motifs of Shang ritual
art.[14] The Liangzhu jade tubes were undoubtedly used in hieratic ritual,
and presumably the figures portrayed on them were priests or chieftains
who wielded sacerdotal powers. Although there is no evidence for a direct
filiation between the Liangzhu jades and the high Shang culture more than
a thousand years later, it seems plausible to infer that the Liangzhu culture, like the Shang kingdom, was dominated by a ruling class claiming
the power to marshal divine forces through the mediation of supernatural creatures.[15] We have no way of knowing whether the priests of the
Liangzhu culture exercised temporal power as well. But in Shang times
religious and political authority were inseparable. Since the living king,
or lineage chief, had the closest relationship to his deceased ancestors,
the rulers of secular society retained primary responsibility for communicating with the gods. Given the heavy quotidian schedule of divinations and sacrifices, the Shang rulers employed numerous specialists in
mantic arts, including diviners and priests, to assist them.[16] Yet the king
himself always occupied the position of chief priest, personally conducting
divinations and ancestral rites. In one of the most important Shang ceremonies, the "guest" *(bin)* ritual, the Shang king communed with his ancestors in the divine world, or even with Di.[17] During the final decades of
the Shang, the king's retinue of diviners and priests was almost entirely
superseded by the king himself, who acted as sole intermediary between
the mortal and divine realms.

Shang religion enjoined the ruling class to punctilious performance of
prescribed rituals, but not to laws, or a code of ethics, that transcended
temporal authority. Consequently, Shang religion evinces no sharp separation between good and evil, or between the divine and the demonic.
The *taotie* and other fearsome images found in Shang ritual art convey
some sense of the awe and mystery with which the Shang regarded the
divine, but ultimately the supernatural powers depicted in these images
were subordinated to kingly authority. Through ritual practice grounded
in the logic of lineage solidarity, the Shang rulers gained mastery of the
gods and harnessed divine power in service to their earthly designs.

Around 1045 B.C.E., an upstart rival lineage deposed the Shang and
inaugurated its own Zhou dynasty.[18] The Zhou typically are depicted as
rude barbarians emerging from beyond the pale of Shang civilization, an
image that traces back to the Zhou's own legends, which extol the austere martial vigor of their ancestors in contrast to the effete decadence
of the Shang. But archaeological research has shown that the Zhou, at

least in the century or more before their conquest of the Shang, were part
of the Shang ecumene and shared many cultural traits with the Shang.
The most obvious continuity between Shang and Zhou is found in the
assemblages of sacred bronze ritual vessels central to the royal cults of
each dynasty. Despite similarities in manufacture and style, though, Zhou
bronzes differed from those of the Shang in function. Unlike the Shang,
who buried ritual bronzes with their owners, the Zhou preserved many
bronze vessels in the world of light, passing them down to their descendants. Although Shang bronzes were rarely inscribed with more than the
names of their owners and the ancestors to whom they were dedicated,
Zhou bronzes bear lengthy testaments intended for the edification of the
ancestors and future generations alike. In the minds of the Zhou rulers,
it was the merit accrued by living descendants rather than the charismatic
power of dead ancestors that assured the perpetuation of the lineage and
its patrimony of rank and property. Zhou bronze inscriptions consisted
primarily of announcements to the ancestor spirits proclaiming the meritorious accomplishments of the living kin, especially the honors and gifts
the latter received from the king.[19] Thus, Zhou bronzes bore witness to
the lineage's pedigree and legacy of achievement; their presence in the
ancestral temple constantly reminded the living of the weighty charge
they inherited from their forebears. The changed meaning and use of ritual bronzes in the Zhou ancestral cult betokened a larger transformation in political and religious culture.

Zhou religion departed most significantly from Shang precedents in
its new conception of the supreme deity, whom the Zhou simply named
Tian or "Heaven." In contrast to the distant and inscrutable Di, Tian
was perceived as an immanent god who manifestly intervened in human
affairs. In addition, Tian subordinated the king and all of his subjects to
a universal moral law, and imposed his will on humanity by selecting the
ruler of the mortal realm, the "world under heaven" *(tianxia)*. If the ruler
failed to abide by Tian's decrees (understood not as specific revelations,
like the Shang oracles, but as a general set of moral principles), Tian would
transfer his blessings to a more worthy choice. "Heaven's Mandate"
(Tianming) sacralized royal authority, endowing the king with a moral
sanction none could defy. The Zhou justified their overthrow of the Shang
by insisting that their actions were ordained by Tian, who commanded
the Zhou to vanquish the evil Shang and succeed them as monarchs of
the civilized world. The charter myth of the Zhou dynasty—encapsulated
in the *Odes* and *Documents,* the oldest works in the Chinese literary
heritage[20]—portrayed the Zhou as benevolent agents of a providential

god. Tian, like Di, was an omnipotent but impersonal god, unbeholden to any particular race or lineage. Yet unlike Di, Tian discriminated between righteous rule and mere tyranny. Zhou religion also renounced Shang belief in the charismatic power of the ancestor gods, supplanting the indelible biological bond between the Shang king and his ancestors with a metaphorical kinship between Tian and the earthly monarch. The Zhou king acknowledged his deference to the patriarchal authority of Tian by referring to himself as "Son of Heaven," but his right to rule remained contingent on upholding Heaven's Mandate.[21]

Tian probably originated as a tutelary god of the Zhou people (or, more precisely, the ruling lineage of Zhou). The elevation of Tian to the position of a universal, supreme deity may not have occurred until well after the Zhou had installed themselves as supreme rulers.[22] By eliminating the ancestors as intermediaries between the mortal ruler and the supreme god, the Zhou made the king the sole avenue of access to divine power. Other noble lineages could share in divine blessings only through subordination to the king. Although the Shang kings exalted themselves as paramount rulers over their world, their claims to universal kingship were undermined by the diffusion of charismatic authority among a large number of lineages. The Zhou severed the divine, in the person of Tian, from all human supplicants save the king himself. Unrestricted interaction between gods and humans, such as the practice of divination fostered by Shang belief in the charisma of the ancestors, was deemed inimical to social and political order. Zhou mythology paid scant heed to the narration of theogony and the creation of the mundane world and its mortal subjects, so central to the mythologies of early civilizations in West Asia. Instead, Zhou myths focused on the means whereby a primeval world beset by chaotic commingling of gods, humans, and beasts became civilized and humanized.[23] The ancient sage-kings lionized in Zhou legend and song contributed to the advance of human civilization by inventing useful productive and social technologies (for example, farming, fire, laws, and ritual codes). The sage-kings tamed the natural world, rendering it fit for human habitation; they instilled discipline and harmony in the human community by devising codes of social conduct; and they brought order to the cosmos by establishing boundaries that separated heaven from earth, human from beast, and civilization from barbarism.

Although the Zhou kings reserved to themselves exclusive access to the supreme deity Tian, at the same time they founded a political order based on delegation of sovereign powers among hundreds of vassals.

Through rituals of investiture (known as *fengjian*), the Zhou kings allotted benefices to both kinfolk and their allies against the Shang. The compacts with the vassals were sealed by bestowal of ritual regalia, including bronze vessels—the emblems of royal authority—bearing inscriptions specifying the obligations and rights assigned to the recipients of the king's largesse. Later histories record that most benefices were awarded to men bearing the royal surname, Ji. By subsuming most ruling lineages into the royal clan, the Zhou perhaps sought to obliterate the ancestry of formerly independent noble lineages, yoking their fortunes even more tightly to those of the royal house. The protocols of investiture also included an important rite wherein the vassal received a clod of earth taken from the Soil Altar *(She)* of the royal capital, which then was placed at the Soil Altar of the vassal's own capital. The tangible joining of king and vassal through the Soil Altars, whose role in Zhou ritual life paralleled that of the ancestral temples, no doubt reinforced the vassal's awareness of the derivative nature of his own sovereign powers.[24]

Despite the repudiation of Shang theology implicit in the Zhou cult of Tian, ancestral sacrifices still were central to Zhou religious life. As in Shang times, the cities that served as the seats of noble lineages were primarily ceremonial centers. The very definition of a capital city was based on the presence of a lord's ancestral temple and the Soil Altar (which, because of its crucial place in rituals of investiture, became a synecdoche for sovereignty).[25] It was believed that the ancestors remained sentient spirits, residing "on high" in the company of Tian but also exercising influence over the lives of their descendants. As in Shang times, the ancestors were keenly concerned about the welfare of their living descendants and lent them supernatural support. Ancestral sacrifices took the form of communal feasts celebrated in the physical presence of the ancestors, who descended into the body of an impersonator to partake of the food offerings. The ritual songs preserved in the *Odes* and Zhou bronze inscriptions reaffirm the idea that noble ancestors were powerful spirits who could bring good fortune to their living kin, protecting them from enemies and ensuring that they enjoyed long, ripe lives.[26] The ancestors continued to receive munificent sacrifices, and the main beneficiaries of this ritual exchange, as in Shang times, were the living descendants avidly seeking the blessings of their exalted forebears. But the political meaning of the ancestral cult had changed. To the Zhou, nobility was commensurate with moral excellence and virtuous government. Noble lineages could assure their continued prosperity only through steadfast emulation of their meritorious ancestors.

Within a century following the conquest of Shang, the supreme military power of the Zhou kings waned significantly, and royal authority was challenged from both within and without the Zhou polity.[27] Invasions by hostile peoples to the south and west forced the Zhou to abandon their homeland in the Wei River valley in 771 B.C.E. and reestablish their court in the heartland of the old Shang kingdom. The relocation of the Zhou capital near the modern city of Luoyang marked a crucial shift in dynastic fortunes. During the Eastern Zhou period (771–256 B.C.E.), the attenuation of royal authority allowed the vassals to arrogate to themselves sovereign powers formerly exercised by the Zhou king alone. By the early seventh century B.C.E., the Zhou king had been reduced to an otiose figurehead, easily manipulated by power mongers among his nominally subordinate vassals. Though still acknowledging the Zhou king as supreme monarch in a ritual sense, the vassals—some of who became rulers of great states vastly larger than the royal domain—brooked no interference on the part of the king in the internal affairs of their territories. No ruler wielded sufficient authority to displace the Zhou, however, and the Zhou ecumene became divided among warring camps defined not by ritual protocols but rather by transitory military supremacy and shifting interstate alliances. Deference to lord and king no longer sustained the hierarchical order enacted by the Zhou founders. Constant warfare throughout the so-called Spring and Autumn period (late eighth to fifth centuries B.C.E.) abetted the rise of a warrior culture in which military might outweighed ritual rank. Dissolution of the norms of fealty also strained relations between the rulers and native noble lineages of the now independent states. Many rulers discovered that they had freed themselves from subordination to the Zhou king only to become captive to the increasingly restless and ambitious warrior aristocracies of their own domains.

The rise of the warrior aristocracy and the prevalence of warfare among competing states subtly transformed the meaning of ancestral sacrifices and their relationship to political authority.[28] The ancestors continued to be a powerful and vital presence in the lives of their descendants. Political authority once again was rooted in the ancestral cult, especially through the presentation of "blood sacrifices" *(xueshi)* to the ancestor spirits at the ancestral temple and the Soil Altar.[29] War itself was understood as a sacrificial rite that proved the mettle of the living descendants while winning glory for the ancestral lineage. War, hunting, and animal sacrifice became enshrined as a trinity of homologous liturgies performed in service to the lineage; each was a form of "blood sacrifice" entailing the taking of life to nourish the ancestor spirits.[30] Yet service to the ancestral cult did not imply that the ancestors conferred supernatural powers on their descendants, in the manner of the Shang ancestor gods. In contrast to bronze inscriptions of the early Zhou, which portrayed the ancestors as powerful spirits who blessed their descendants with long life and good fortune, Spring and Autumn bronzes lauded the merits and dignity of the descendants, scarcely mentioning the ancestors at all.[31] The ancestral cult of the Spring and Autumn period thus emphasized the primacy of the living, whose glorious deeds ensured the prosperity of future generations in the name of ancestors who symbolized the eternal legacy of the lineage as a whole.

The impotence of the Zhou dynastic house called into question its logic of legitimation, and the very notion of moral authority itself. Tian's apparent countenance of manifest injustice and the demise of royal power rocked the foundations of Zhou religion.[32] The warrior culture of the Spring and Autumn period equated virtue and honor with martial prowess, not moral pedigree or deference to ritual order. In the absence of any presumption of allegiance to the Zhou or any other sanctioned authority, relationships between states were governed by oaths and covenants sanctified by blood sacrifices.[33] The growing prevalence of oath taking in itself betrayed the lack of trust among aristocratic lineages, even within a single state.[34] These oaths and covenants typically called upon the ancestors and other spirits to bear witness to the compact and punish those who violated their vows. Undergirding these oaths, and the conduct of warfare, was a code of chivalry imbued with the sacred authority of Zhou ritual but no longer constrained by the dictates of Tian's mandate.

During these centuries of endemic warfare and aggressive conquest the relationship between the living and the dead once again underwent a major transformation. Although the ritual aspect of ancestorhood evolved in the direction of ever-greater abstraction and systematization, as individuals the ancestors now were believed to have their own specific existence ("soul") and fate in the afterlife. In the eyes of the living, the dead endured more and more as distinct personalities even as their ritual preeminence diminished. Moreover, the warrior aristocracy's cult of honor fostered vivid images of the ancestors as heroic figures whose robust vitality could not be bound by the coils of mortal existence.

Sometimes the spirits of the dead appeared as awesome titans resplendent in battle dress, but most realized only a pathetic existence as
emaciated ghosts dependent on their descendants for sustenance. This
theme recurs throughout the *Chronicles of Zuo,* a narrative history of the
Spring and Autumn period probably compiled in the fourth century B.C.E.
For example, the *Chronicles* relates that in the year 628 B.C.E. the Lord
of Wei, after being driven from the Wei homeland, set up a new capital
at Diqiu and continued his ancestral sacrifices there. Soon afterward, the
lord had a dream in which the founder of the house of Wei complained
to him that the sacrificial offerings intended for the Wei ancestors had
been stolen by a certain Xiang, an ancient king of the Xia dynasty (legendary predecessors of the Shang) who dwelled at Diqiu long ago. Upon
awakening the lord instructed his officials to prepare sacrifices to Xiang
as well as his ancestors. But an advisor named Ningwu objected, saying
that "unless the spirits of the dead *[guishen]* are members of one's own
lineage, they cannot partake of your sacrificial offerings." The descendants of Xia had forsaken Xiang, Ningwu continued, but Wei bore no
responsibility for Xiang's unfortunate fate, and indeed could do nothing for him.[35] Bereft of ancestral sacrifices, orphan ghosts like Xiang were
condemned to a shadowy existence as restless, perturbed spirits.

Eastern Zhou culture was permeated by fear of ghosts or revenants,
spirits of the dead who linger in the world of the living. One of the principal purposes of ancestor worship was to keep the dead in their place.
If properly cared for, the souls of the dead would remain in the tomb
and not seek to return to the world of the living. The most likely reason
for the ghosts of the dead to remain in the mortal world was that the appointed life span of the deceased had not yet been exhausted, leaving a
residue of liminal vitality in the form of a ghost. This was especially true
of those who died by violence, including victims of suicide, and infants
who died in childbirth. In addition, unfortunates like Xiang, the neglected
king of Xia, who failed to receive proper offerings from their descendants, might return to the mundane realm in search of nourishment. The
morbid touch of these ghosts could harm the life force of the living, causing sickness and death. Moreover, victims of violence were believed to
be actively malevolent, seeking vengeance against those responsible for
their deaths. The culture of violence and the never-ending cycles of
vendetta and bloodshed it inspired, so central to the culture of the Eastern Zhou warrior aristocracy, produced many such ghostly souls, unable
to find peace until the injustices they suffered had been avenged. Another
anecdote from the *Chronicles of Zuo* illustrates the fears aroused by these

"vengeful ghosts." In 534 B.C.E., the aristocratic lineages of the petty state of Zheng were stricken by terror of the ghost of a notorious nobleman named Boyou, who had been accused of treason and slain by his enemies eight years before. Subsequently Boyou's ghost appeared before several witnesses and warned that he would kill specific individuals in certain years. Two of his announced victims indeed died at the prophesied time. The chief minister of Zheng, the renowned statesman Zichan, responded to the ensuing panic by appointing Boyou's son to his father's former office, which allowed the son the privilege of building an ancestral temple and offering sacrifices to his father's spirit. Afterwards Boyou's ghost ceased his hauntings. Asked to explain his actions, Zichan replied, "When the spirit of a dead person has a proper abode to which it can return, it will not engage in evildoing. I simply provided a resting place for Boyou's spirit."[36]

Zichan also attested to the pervasive belief in ghosts shared by his contemporaries. In response to inquiries about whether Boyou had indeed become a ghost capable of inflicting harm upon the living, Zichan answered in the affirmative:

> When a man is born, he is transformed into a corporeal being, which we call *po*. Possessing a body, he thus also is endowed with vitality, his *yang* spirit. Those who command great property and occupy high station are strong both in body and spirit. For this reason [upon their deaths] their pure and sublime *qi* will attain manifest spirithood. If men and women of vulgar station die violent deaths, their somatic [*po*] and psychic [*hun*] souls are capable of possessing the living and causing grievous harm. How much more so is this true of Liangxiao [i.e., Boyou], descendant of our former ruler Lord Ma, grandson of Ziling, son of Zi'er, all nobles of our state, who have served as ministers for three successive generations![37]

Zichan's explanation of the malevolent powers of ghosts reflected the vast differences in social status inherent in the aristocratic society of the Spring and Autumn era. Persons of noble birth were believed to be endowed with greater vital energy and more refined physical substance (expressed by Zichan in terms of *qi*, a concept central to Chinese metaphysics that encompassed both matter and energy; see below, pp. 36–37). The sublime *qi* of the nobility persisted long after death, in contrast to the crude *qi* of the multitude, which quickly dissipated. Yet Zichan also acknowledged that the unspent life force of even a lowborn person who suffered a violent death might remain in the mundane world as a baleful ghost, and even assume another bodily form.

Zichan's reference to *po* and *hun* souls signaled the emergence of a dualistic conception of the postmortem "soul" that became widespread by early Han times. According to this belief, human beings possessed both somatic and psychic identity, in the form of the conjoined *po* and *hun* souls.[38] At the moment of death, these *po* and *hun* souls divided, each seeking its proper place of repose. The *hun* soul, the conscious spirit of the person, fled the body and dissolved. The *po* continued to reside with the body, though eventually it too decayed, much like the corpse itself. Ancestor worship increasingly focused on enabling the deceased to make a successful transition to the afterlife and ensuring that the *po* soul remained securely ensconced within the tomb and not left to wander among the living. In this light, Confucius's famous pronouncement that one should "revere the spirits, but keep one's distance from them" probably reflects the common sentiment of an age in which the souls of the dead were increasingly feared as potentially harmful to the living.[39]

Beginning around the fourth century B.C.E., the noble classes became more and more entranced with the idea of escaping death altogether. Soothsayers beguiled the monarchs of the day with fantastic descriptions of distant yet earthly paradises populated by "immortals" *(xian)*. Once mere mortals themselves, the *xian* had, through arduous regimens of diet and yogic exercises along with ingestion of purifying elixirs, purged their body of its gross properties and transformed it into a light, ethereal form capable of ascending to the cloud-borne paradises.[40] The *xian* thus achieved immortality by escaping death altogether. Fascination with this liberation from death initially developed along the eastern seaboard, in the states of Yan and Qi, whose inhabitants imagined a paradise of the immortals existing beyond the sea's horizon. In the landlocked states of the west and south, however, the immortals were believed to reside in an Olympian paradise atop Mount Kunlun, the *axis mundi* at the center of the world that joined together heaven and earth. Mount Kunlun was thought to be located far to the west, in the twilight where the sun set, and it thus became entwined with a variety of Chinese myths about the afterlife. Mount Kunlun was also said to be the abode of a mysterious monarch, the Queen Mother of the West (Xiwangmu). Perhaps a figure from a vestigial legend from early Zhou times concerning a female ruler at the far western margins of the Zhou polity, the Queen Mother of the West reemerged in Han mythology as the guardian of the secrets of immortality, which she imparted only to the most august princes of the mortal world.[41]

Throughout the Eastern Zhou period, the cult of Tian continued to recede along with the moribund authority of the Zhou king. Rulers of the rising independent states oriented their attention instead to regional cults, particularly the tutelary deities of their own domains. The notion of a supreme being who acted as the arbiter of human fate persisted, though this god now was more commonly referred to as Shangdi (Supreme Thearch) or Tiandi (Celestial Thearch). But like the aloof Di of Shang religion, Shangdi/Tiandi remained distant and inscrutable, seemingly deaf to human cries against tyranny and injustice. With the moral foundations of monarchy in ruins, even Confucians despaired of seeking moral order in the workings of the cosmos.

The obligation to pursue glory through rites of violence led to incessant warfare among states and also provoked civil wars between competing lineages within states, culminating in the annihilation of many of the original vassal domains along with their ruling families. By the fifth century B.C.E., fewer than two dozen of the hundreds of domains established by the early Zhou kings remained in existence. Those that survived did so largely because their rulers had succeeded in subduing their domestic rivals and instituting a more autocratic form of government. Monarchs of the Warring States era (traditionally dated to 403–221 B.C.E.) gained direct control over the land and labor resources of their realms, enabling them to mobilize and maintain the large armies required by escalating warfare, now that massive infantry engagements had superseded chariot duels. Commoners were released from their obligations to the noble lords, whom they once had served as serflike dependents, and instead became direct subordinates to the monarch and his burgeoning bureaucratic state. The monarch awarded land grants to plebeian households in return for military and corvée labor service and tax payments of grain and cloth. The individual household, now responsible for its own economic welfare, became the basic unit of production, consumption, and taxation in Chinese society. The new political and economic relationship between prince and subject established during the Warring States era foreshadowed the imperial system inaugurated by the rulers of Qin in 221 B.C.E.

The new political order of the Warring States era was founded on principles of a *raison d'état*, exemplified above all by the Legalist statesmen-philosophers of Qin, that effected a radical separation of government from ethics. It was Qin that, in the fourth century B.C.E., first deprived its aristocratic lineages of their hereditary offices and benefices and instituted a bureaucratic state under the supreme rule of an autocratic monarch. The Legalist political philosophy admitted no authority except the ruler's decrees, which were codified into elaborate and harshly punitive systems of administrative and penal law. Legalism repudiated the entire charter of Zhou governance, denying any supernatural source of moral or political legitimation. But the constant turmoil of the Warring States period fed rulers' fears and ambitions in equal proportion. Despite their embrace of the austere and uncompromising rationalism of Legalist philosophy, the rulers of Qin and rival states hungered for proof, conveyed through divine omen and prophecy, that they would ultimately triumph in the contest for supremacy. This hunger quickened with the extinction of the house of Zhou at the hands of the rapidly expanding Qin in 256 B.C.E.

Philosophy in this age was dominated by two contrary yet interrelated trends. Growing skepticism of Zhou theology or any belief in a providential supreme being, evident by this time in Confucian as much as Legalist thinking, whetted faith in the power of human reason to govern human affairs. Yet this skeptical rationalism was counterbalanced by an anxious search for consistent meaning and pattern in both human affairs and the cosmos as a whole. Legions of learned men flocked to the courts of powerful monarchs, offering esoteric knowledge and magical formulas that would enable rulers to achieve both personal and political immortality. While these "masters of occult arts" *(fangshi),* as contemporaries dubbed them, professed to wield a wide array of mantic skills, their claims of efficacy rested on a common ontological ground, one perhaps best described as correlative cosmology.[42]

Correlative cosmology asserted a fundamental homology between human affairs and cosmic order, both of which were governed by certain cycles, rhythms, and patterns of change and transformation. The relationship between the human and natural worlds was seen as organic but asymmetric: although changes in one produced corresponding changes in the other, ultimately the human realm was subordinate to the inexorable logic of self-generating metamorphosis imbedded in the cosmos. The *fangshi* claimed exclusive knowledge of the underlying principles of change, knowledge that would enable the ruler to align himself and his government with the ascendant phase of cosmic order and thereby gain mastery of the mundane world.

Some of the theories subsumed under the general rubric of correlative cosmology stemmed from older, holistic notions of cosmic order, such as the dyadic principles of *yin* and *yang,* or female and male essences, frequently invoked as the ineffable ground of reality in the renowned mystical text *Dao De Jing.* Correlative cosmology often is linked to the *Dao De Jing,* but in contrast to the latter, which derogates the human mind as utterly incapable of apprehending the workings of the cosmos (expressed as *Dao,* or "the Way"), correlative cosmology confidently affirmed that the wise ruler could indeed attain such omniscience. Other versions of correlative cosmology were novel inventions conceived by leading *fangshi* of the Warring States period. The best known of them was the theory of Five Phases (Wuxing), espoused most notably by Zou Yan (ca. 305–ca. 240 B.C.E.). One of the most celebrated and successful *fangshi* of the day, Zou believed that human history and cosmic order repeatedly passed through a cycle of five phases or "powers" (*de,* a word also central to the philosophy of the *Dao De Jing* that connotes charismatic sovereignty). Zou linked the Five Phases with their corresponding instantiations in the natural world, beginning with the five elemental forces of nature (water, fire, wood, earth, and metal) and extending to the five cardinal directions (including the center as well as the four points of the compass), the five visible planets, the five primary colors, and innumerable other phenomenological categories. Zou's formula, and the numerous variations it spawned, enjoyed great popularity, especially among the monarchs contending for dominion over the Chinese world.

Given the centrality of the precepts of correlative cosmology in later Chinese thought, it is surprising that we find no real evidence of them prior to the Warring States period. Another concept that enters prominently into Warring States philosophical discourse, and indeed became fundamental to theories of correlative cosmology, is *qi.* We have already seen the term employed by Zichan to express the different gradations of life force that enabled the spirits of the nobility to endure far longer after death than those of common birth. *Qi* defies any simple translation. In its earliest attested form, the word *qi* denoted the vapor of clouds or boiling grains. These meanings suggest on one hand the formless substance or kinetic powers of the universe, and on the other the nourishing energy vital to sustaining life.[43] As a philosophical concept, *qi* came to represent the pervasive "stuff" of the universe, with equal emphasis on what Greek physics distinguished as matter and energy. But *qi* cannot be reduced to a single constituent. Rather, all phenomena possess their own unique *qi,* which in the categorical schemes of Five Phases cosmology ramified into virtually limitless types and permutations. The concept of *qi* assumed an especially important place in the emerging discourse about the human body and how it functioned. *Qi* was applied to both the somatic and psychic dimensions of the body, encompassing a person's emotions, dispositions, and qualities of character as well as the physical self. *Qi* quickly achieved prominence in medical theory, as in correlative cosmology as a whole, because of its utility in giving sublime expression to both the organic unity and the boundless heterogeneity of the cosmos.

The primary impulse behind the Five Phases theories propounded by Zou Yan and others was a prophetic one. The ability to correctly situate the present historical moment within the grand cycles of cosmic change conferred foreknowledge, and thus control, of the future direction of human history. By adapting his government—particularly in its all-important ritual dimension—to prevailing cosmic principles, the prescient monarch could maintain harmony between the cosmic and human orders and thereby preserve his own political supremacy amid the vicissitudes of a constantly changing world. Some *fangshi* interpreted disturbances of nature—such as irregular astral phenomena (comets and eclipses), natural disasters, and other manifestations of discordant *qi*—as omens, issuing prophetic warnings of cosmic imbalance. *Fangshi* also utilized correlative cosmology to devise techniques for maintaining balance and stasis within the body, thereby forestalling the debilitation of aging; their prescriptions for long life and even immortality naturally attracted the rapt attention of contemporary rulers. In many cases the *fangshi* claimed that the esoteric formulas in their possession were imparted by spirits or gods, or by the *xian* immortals.

One monarch captivated by the *fangshi* and their theories was King Zheng of Qin (r. 247–210 B.C.E.), who brought the imperial aspirations of his house to completion by unifying all of China under his iron rule. After vanquishing his last rival in 221 B.C.E., Zheng declared himself First Emperor of the Qin empire. The First Emperor's triumphs seem to have only whetted his megalomaniacal preoccupation with his own mortality, and he readily indulged all manner of soothsayers, prophets, and magicians in his quest to wrest a final victory from death itself. Despite his allegiance to the tenets of Legalism, which denied the existence of a numinous realm beyond mundane sense perception, the First Emperor instituted a state religion that combined the doctrines of correlative cosmology and the exuberant visions of favored *fangshi* with worship of deities long honored by the Qin rulers, most notably Huangdi, or the Yellow Thearch. In part due to Qin patronage, Huangdi became the most vaunted figure in both official and popular pantheons of the gods.

Legends of Warring States provenance relate that the ancient sage-kings had performed sacrifices to the gods of mountains and rivers in addition to Shangdi. The Zhou kings, too, paid homage to sacred mountains and rivers, while their vassals worshiped the mountain and river spirits of their own territories.[44] The systematizing impulse of correlative cosmology prompted incorporation of these sundry local gods into a comprehensive pantheon crowned by the Five Thearchs (Wudi), each of whom symbolized one of the Five Phases of cosmic order. The Five Thearchs also fused with ancient mountain-god cults, assuming alter egos as the presiding deities of the Five Marchmounts (Wuyue), the five sacred mountains of China. Zhou texts often invoked the Four Marchmounts as a metaphor for the ruling lineages of distant regions, especially the foreign peoples around the periphery of the Zhou ecumene. By the Warring States period a fifth marchmount had been added, to conform to the symmetry of Five Phases cosmology, and each of the marchmounts was identified with a particular sage-king of antiquity.[45]

According to the Han historian Sima Qian, veneration of the Five Thearchs dated back at least to Lord Xiang of Qin (r. 776–764 B.C.E.), the first Qin ruler admitted into the collegium of Zhou vassals, who was said to have worshiped the White Thearch (Baidi) as patron of the Qin ruling house.[46] The White Thearch was believed to be the apotheosis of Shaohao, eldest son of Huangdi.[47] Shaohao was associated with the power of metal and hence its corresponding color, white, and direction, the west. Since Qin was located at the extreme western edge of the Zhou polity, it logically followed that the Qin rulers should have adopted Shaohao, in the guise of the White Thearch, as their patron deity. But the claim that Lord Xiang initiated the Qin cult of the White Thearch probably represents a later interpolation that retroactively identified the White Thearch with an ancient god worshiped in the area of the original Qin capital. In any event, the Qin rulers were not exclusively dedicated to the cult of the White Thearch. Lord Ling of Qin (r. 423–413 B.C.E.) built shrines for the worship of Huangdi and the Fiery Thearch (Yandi), two figures depicted in legend as fierce adversaries.[48] By the reign of King Zheng, the future First Emperor of Qin, the cult of Huangdi overshadowed all of its rivals for the attention of the Qin rulers.[49]

In late Warring States texts Huangdi appears as an ancient sage-king, but by Han times Huangdi was regarded as an avatar of the supreme deity (Shangdi/Tiandi). The ruling house of Qi, the dominant state in eastern China, claimed descent from Huangdi, and the prominence of the Qi capital as the main philosophical forum of the day and the hearth of theories of correlative cosmology no doubt burnished Huangdi's image as a paragon of wisdom and leadership.[50] At this time the name Shangdi also was rendered as Huangdi[a51] or "Resplendent Thearch," and it seems likely that as the precepts of correlative cosmology became more deeply entrenched the homonymous Huangdi (Yellow Thearch) gained wide currency as an alternative name for the supreme deity.[52] Huangdi[a] was also the title chosen by King Zheng of Qin (who styled himself Qin Shihuangdi, or "First of the Resplendent Thearchs of Qin") to express his dignity as emperor. (The prosaic English translation of Huangdi[a] as "emperor" obviously fails to capture the implications of theocratic power imbedded in the Chinese word.)

Huangdi emerged in Warring States mythology as the archetypal hero of the autocratic monarchs of the day and the antithesis of the warriors of the Spring and Autumn aristocracy.[53] Legends current in Han times depict Huangdi as an extraordinary mortal named Xuanyuan who lived at the dawn of human civilization, in the declining years of the dynasty established by the first sage-king, Shennong (the Divine Husbandman, reputed to be the inventor of agriculture). Xuanyuan fought righteous wars against the forces of disorder, restoring tranquility to the human world, and in gratitude the multitude elected him as supreme ruler, displacing the lineage of Shennong.[54] Huangdi also figured in Han legend as a god of storms and rain, and thus was the natural adversary of the Fiery Thearch, god of the sun and drought. Huangdi and the Fiery Thearch used their respective "weapons of water and fire" to battle each other for control over the fate of the agricultural cycle and dominion over the mortal world.[55] Virtually all myths emphasize Huangdi's resort to coercion and violence as a necessary expedient to subdue lawless elements and restore civil rule. Consequently, the exaltation of Huangdi as the paragon of sage rule affirmed the sovereign's legitimate use of violence to impose order. As the inventor of the codes of ritual and law by which civil society could be created and sustained, Huangdi provided a compelling precedent for autocratic monarchs seeking to bring to heel the obdurate and fractious warrior nobility.

In legend and myth Huangdi's most formidable opponent was a baleful warrior known as Chiyou.[56] Though scholars differ on the mythic origins of Chiyou,[57] by the Warring States period Chiyou was joined to Huangdi mythology as the archetype of anarchic violence and conflict. In the *Punishments of Lü* (*Lüxing;* now preserved as a chapter of the *Documents*) and other third-century B.C.E. texts, Chiyou is blamed for inventing metallic weapons and using them to sow disorder.[58] A late Han text describes Chiyou as a savage man-beast hybrid: "Chiyou and his eighty-one brothers all possessed the bodies of beasts, but were capable of human speech. They had bronze heads and iron brows, and ate sand

and stones. Armed with the weapons they created, including swords, halberds, and great crossbows, they shook and awed the whole civilized world, attacking and killing without reason or mercy." Unable to restrain Chiyou and his cohorts with suasion and kindness, Huangdi finally launched a punitive campaign against them. Yet Huangdi triumphed only through divine intercession. Heaven dispatched the Dark Woman to bestow magic charms on Huangdi, who used them as weapons to vanquish Chiyou and put him to death.[59]

Popular legends, such as the one just cited, identified Chiyou as the inventor of "the five kinds of weapons" *(wubing)*, though learned authorities, no doubt appalled by Chiyou's outlaw character, instead credited the invention of weapons to Huangdi. Both Huangdi and Chiyou were venerated as gods of war by the Qin and Han emperors. The two represented contrasting faces of violence: whereas Huangdi exemplified the legitimate use of force in defense of the rule of law, Chiyou stood for wanton mayhem. But of course the two aspects of warfare could not be completely differentiated. Following his defeat at the hands of Huangdi, Chiyou was said to have entered the latter's service and earned distinction as Huangdi's loyal lieutenant. Huangdi's defeat of Chiyou thus became a metaphor for the triumph of order over anarchy, a basic motif in Chinese religious culture. Later myth and folklore is replete with fearsome, violent demons who are subjugated by a virtuous ruler and henceforth place their prodigious strength and martial skills at the disposal of the rightful sovereign.

Apart from his mythological role as the chief adversary of Huangdi, Chiyou also appeared in Han religion as a guardian deity who protected travelers from loathsome demons lurking in wild and unfamiliar places. After all, Chiyou's macabre visage was no less terrifying to demons than to human beings. According to a Han legend, after Chiyou died lawless elements once again brazenly defied the law, whereupon Huangdi ordered his subordinates to make images of the fierce warrior and display them throughout the realm to cow any recalcitrant evildoers into submission.[60] The terrifying aspect of Chiyou only enhanced his role as a queller of demons. Priests conducting the exorcisms held during the important midwinter festivals conjured up Chiyou's image to expel noxious demons prior to the arrival of the New Year. Chiyou was also incorporated into funerary ritual as an apotropaic deity warding off evil spirits. In Han tomb iconography Chiyou appears as a fearsome beast brandishing five types of weapons (figure 4). In this guise he represented the terrible majesty of the monarch and the swift hand of imperial justice. Chiyou also became an object of popular worship during the Han. Shrines dedicated to Chiyou in the vicinity of Jizhou (Shandong), reputedly the site of the climactic battle between Chiyou and Huangdi, depicted him in human form but with bovine hooves, four eyes, and six hands. Chiyou was also described as having horns, and forelocks as sharp as the blades of weapons.[61] Chiyou thus became the mythic double of Huangdi: while the latter evolved into a regal sovereign presiding over a tranquil kingdom, Chiyou remained a stark reminder of the harsh punishments meted out to those who flouted the monarch's laws.

The Qin rulers' devotion to Huangdi heralded the rise of a new conception of the ruler as a thaumaturgic king, master of all the elemental powers of the universe. Huangdi quite literally became central to the conceptions of human history that arose from Five Phases cosmology: as the presiding god-king of the Center (linked to the element earth and the color yellow in Five Phases correspondences), Huangdi stood both at the beginning of Chinese civilization and the apex of the celestial pantheon. The august majesty of Huangdi shines through the epiphany described in the *Hanfeizi*, a Legalist treatise of the third century B.C.E.:

> Long ago Huangdi gathered together the ghosts and spirits on the western
> summit of Mount Tai [Taishan, chief of the Five Marchmounts]. He rode
> an ivory chariot pulled by six dragons. Bifang [a fire deity] ran beside him,
> while Chiyou went ahead. The Wind Lord [Fengbo] swept the path, and
> the Rain Master [Yushi] wetted down the dust. Tigers and wolves were
> in front, and ghosts and spirits followed behind. Lizards and snakes were
> beneath, while the phoenix flew overhead. When all the ghosts and spirits
> were gathered together, Huangdi created the pure *jiao* music [which soothes
> the savage beasts and demons].[62]

Here we see Huangdi commanding the awesome powers of nature embodied in spirits like the Wind Lord and Rain Master.[63] Although the ceremonial complex the Qin rulers built at Yong, their capital from 677 to 384 B.C.E., included altars devoted to the other thearchs in addition to Huangdi, the latter ranked as the supreme lord of the divine and mortal realms. In Han dynasty cosmological lore Huangdi was transmogrified into an omnipotent deity and progenitor of the universe. One of the cosmographic works collected into the anthology *Treatises of Huainan* (second century B.C.E.) portrays Huangdi as a star god with power over the fate of mortals. The stellar monarch and his four chamberlains, located in the central constellations of the northern sky, took note of human conduct, rewarding virtue with long life and punishing evildoers by shortening their allotted life span.[64] Elsewhere in the same anthology Huangdi

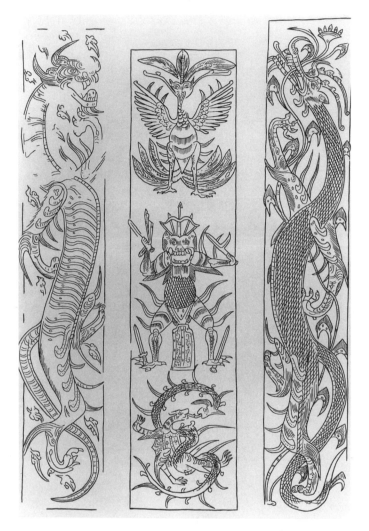

Figure 4. Chiyou and the Four Heraldic Creatures. At the center
of this triptych, taken from the door of a Han tomb, Chiyou
stands bearing the "five weapons" that he was believed to have
invented. Above his head is the vermilion bird representing the
south (and thus the *yang* cosmic principle), and at his feet are
the entwined black snake and tortoise, representing the north
(and *yin*). At the left is the white tiger of the west, to the right
the blue dragon of the east. Chiyou occupies the center, the position of the Yellow Emperor, for whom he serves as a substitute.
Yinan tomb, north wall of chamber no. 1. Shandong, second to
third century C.E. From Hayashi 1989, supplemental plate 1.
Courtesy of Kyoto National Museum.

is said to be the "creator of *yin* and *yang*," the elemental forces of the universe.[65]

The apotheosis of Huangdi perhaps reflects a process of euhemerization, the transformation through myth and legend of an actual person into a god.[66] But it is more likely that Huangdi originated as a god of rain and storms, and only later did philosophers and historians, turning their back on what they regarded as the fanciful caricatures of myth, treat him as a historical figure. The rationalist temper of Warring States–Han thought produced two utterly distinct images of Huangdi. In political philosophy, Huangdi was dressed in the raiment of the sage-king, a paragon of the just use of force, but nevertheless very much a mortal human being. Metaphysicians, in contrast, rendered Huangdi into a wholly depersonalized abstraction, a categorical imperative of Five Phases cosmology, essential to the workings of the cosmos but divorced from mundane life. Yet among the populace at large, as we shall see, these two contrasting images fused into the more vivid person of the awesome lord of the underworld.

Despite its remarkable success in instituting a universal empire, the Qin was unable to sustain its harsh rule. The Qin state collapsed after the First Emperor's death in 210 B.C.E., and a few years later it was replaced by the far longer-lived Han dynasty (202 B.C.E.–220 C.E.). The founder of the Han retained the political infrastructure of the Qin empire, yet at the same time he embraced the nearly defunct tenets of moral sovereignty espoused in Zhou theology. The Han instituted imperial worship of many new gods, such as Houtu, the Lord of the Earth (and terrestrial corollary of the celestial Huangdi), and Taiyi, or Grand Unity,[67] while continuing to pay homage to the Five Thearchs at the old Qin ceremonial center at Yong.[68] By the end of the first century B.C.E., though, these cults had been eclipsed by a reawakened faith in Tian and the political ideals of Zhou championed by the Confucian tradition. Once securely in command of their empire, the Han emperors spurned the Qin state's exclusive reliance on military force and the rule of law in favor of Confucian homilies regarding moral authority and civil order. The religious reform carried out under the watchful eyes of Confucian ministers in 31 B.C.E. removed the shrines to Houtu, Taiyi, and the Five Thearchs to remote sites and expunged nearly five hundred shrines from the official register of sacrifices. The religious reforms reoriented imperial worship toward exclusive veneration of Heaven (Tian) and Earth. In contrast to the ancient Zhou cult, though, the Han cult of Heaven rendered Tian into a moral abstraction devoid of personality. While still compelling allegiance, Tian no longer intimidated the mundane sovereign as the stern patriarch of Zhou religion had. Yet like the Han emperor, Heaven towered over the populace at large, dispensing justice in strict conformity to the letter of the law, deaf to all appeals for clemency. Among the people, calamities of flood and drought, the "tremblings of Heaven," represented not just portents of ritual or political mistakes, but severe punishments meted out by a cold, distant potentate. The trepidation with which Han Chinese beheld the gods was reinforced by newly arisen fears of the subjugation of the dead to punishment in the afterlife.

CHAPTER 2

The Han Cult of the Dead
and Salvific Religion

During the four centuries of Han rule, Chinese conceptions of death and the afterlife underwent a profound transformation brought about not only by new ideas about the divine, but also by changes in the relationship between the living and their ancestors. Han Chinese expressed deep anxieties about the fate of the dead. The spirits of the dead were believed to endure as vital beings in the tomb yet at the same time were subject to divine judgment and punishment. The emerging pantheon of celestial and terrestrial deities was complemented by a vision of a vast underworld bureaucracy conceived in the image of the Han imperial state and its organs of justice. The infernal gods meted out severe punishments to mortals who led a sinful life, penalties that might also bring harm to their descendants. Given the grim fate awaiting the dead in the afterlife, the spirits of the ancestors, always feared, now were pitied as well. No longer seen as gods with the power to confer or withhold blessings, the ancestors instead were regarded as abject ghouls wracked by deprivation and suffering. The purposes and forms of ancestor worship shifted accordingly. Dread of postmortem punishment also spawned numerous religious sects devoted to the expiation of sin through faith healing and austere living. Promise of salvation from mortal misery as well as infernal punishment kindled popular allegiance to these upstart sects and prepared the ground for the transplanting of Buddhism to Chinese soil in the centuries after the fall of the Han dynasty in 220 C.E.

Changes in ideas about death and afterlife are evident in the dramatic transformation of mortuary practices that occurred between the fifth and first centuries B.C.E. This transformation, far more profound than the transition between Shang and Zhou, is most readily visible in the construction and architecture of the tomb, the route of passage from the mortal world to the divine realm. Tombs of the early Zhou nobility, though lavishly furnished with bronzes and other grave goods, were simple vertical pits of modest dimension, barely sufficient to accommodate the coffin and its accompanying ritual paraphernalia.[1] Beginning in central China as early as the eighth century B.C.E., and most strikingly in the state of Chu in south-central China from the sixth century B.C.E., persons of noble descent were provided with more elaborate and better-protected tombs using stout, intricately joined wooden frames. From the late fifth century B.C.E. onward, vertical-shaft tombs were replaced by spacious chambers, often divided into two or more separate rooms laid out horizontally, with brick walls, arched doorways, and gabled ceilings. These multichambered brick tombs replicated the world of the living, their scale and amenities graded according to the deceased's rank in mortal society, which as time wore on was determined more by the individual's own achievements in public life than by the hereditary status of his or her family.[2] Living monarchs, starkly conscious of their mortality, began to provide for their own afterlife by building mausolea on a monumental scale, recreating within the tomb the sumptuous lifestyle to which they were accustomed. Even the modest catacomb tombs of those of more humble station reveal an effort to imitate domestic architecture in constructing a permanent resting place for the *po* of the deceased.[3]

An equally remarkable change in mortuary goods accompanied the transformation in tomb architecture. Zhou tombs, like those of Shang, were equipped with a ritual inventory that marked the occupant's rank and position within the lineage, present and past. In the Spring and Autumn era, tombs of the Zhou nobility were supplied with assemblages of bronze offering vessels (in quantities prescribed by ritual protocol), sets of bells and musical chimes, weapons and other accoutrements of warriors, and human sacrifices (subject to strong regional variation). Beginning in the seventh century B.C.E., the finely wrought bronze vessels used in rituals came to be replaced by cheaper or miniature replicas, known as *mingqi*, intended exclusively for entombment in the grave. The use of *mingqi* apparently originated in the northwest, where the Qin rulers were the first to build large, complex tombs.[4] During the Warring States period, the old bronze ritual vessel assemblages disappeared. Some new forms of bronze vessels appeared, and ritual regalia continued to exalt the nobility's supreme powers over life and death by featuring the "three great affairs of state"—warfare, hunting, and sacrifice—as the principal motifs of bronze decoration.[5] Yet the most striking features of Warring States mortuary goods were the novelties in tomb furnishings, including the introduction of lacquer utensils; domestic items like braziers, lamps, incense burners, mirrors, and ordinary cooking vessels; and wall murals illustrating the tomb occupant enjoying his postmortem existence within the tomb.[6] These changes in tomb construction and mortuary goods indicate that the tomb gradually became perceived as the postmortem abode of the dead, who maintained an ineffable yet material existence after burial.[7]

The new conception of the tomb as the perpetual abode of the po was also reflected in mortuary ritual. In Shang and Western Zhou religion, ancestral temples and tombs were integral elements in a cohesive regimen of sacrifice vital to the regeneration of the charismatic power upon which secular authority rested.[8] In the Spring and Autumn period, the temple still served as a sacred space for ritual renewal of lineage solidarity through communion between the living and the dead. By the Warring States period, though, the tomb began to supersede the ancestral temple as the focus of mortuary rites. The displacement of the temple by the tomb was loudly condemned by ritual experts of the Han dynasty, who blamed the notorious First Emperor of Qin for instigating this deviant practice. In fact the First Emperor's vast mausoleum, with its massive army of life-size terra-cotta guardians, merely represented the culmination of a trend that had been underway for several centuries. The displacement of the temple by the tomb as the primary site of ancestral sacrifices inherently changed the nature of the sacrifice itself. Whereas sacrifices made at the temple were offered to the ancestors as a collective body, rituals performed at the tomb were addressed to individual ancestors. It was this unseemly emphasis on the individual, and its potential for disrupting lineage solidarity, that most enraged Han scholars.

The spreading belief that the spirits of the departed continued to realize a sentient existence within the tomb provoked much anxiety about their welfare. Great mausolea like the one built by the First Emperor of Qin offer eloquent evidence of this unease. Apart from these magnificent royal monuments, though, most people provided for the material comfort of their ancestors in far more modest fashion by equipping tombs with utilitarian mingqi made in the likeness of granaries, livestock, stoves, wells, and other articles of domestic life believed to help sustain the spirit of the tomb occupant. Mingqi also represented people, places, and ob-

jects familiar to the individual, such as houses, servants, or musical instruments. Unlike the precious and finely made artifacts interred with
the Shang and early Zhou nobility, though, *mingqi* were typically crudely
rendered in plebeian materials, especially ceramics, on a miniature scale.
As offerings to the dead, *mingqi* enunciated the sharp disjuncture between
mundane existence and the afterlife.[9] *Mingqi* attested to an afterlife imagined not as a continuation of earthly splendor, but instead as its morbid
shade, a realm of vestigial vitality and darkness.

Confined to the tomb, the spirits of the dead remained woefully dependent on their descendants for sustenance. We see evidence of this concern in a set of tombs near Jining (Shandong) dating from the first century B.C.E., which contained ceramic jars filled with grain and wine
intended as victuals for the ancestor spirits. One jar bears an inscription
expressing the hope that the grain it contained would alleviate the ancestor's anxieties over provisions in the afterlife, and thus ward off any
curse the ancestor might visit upon his descendants.[10] Here again we
see that the living harbored lingering fears of ancestor spirits who might
take vengeance on their descendants for any lapse in piety. The living
provided minimal comforts to the dead, sufficient to encourage the latter to remain tranquil and content within the tomb, but remained ever
mindful of the need to keep a safe distance between themselves and the
departed.

The diffusion of the cult of the *xian* immortals among the aristocracy
in the Warring States and Han periods was registered in mortuary art by
representations of the *hun* soul rising to join the immortals in their paradise among the clouds. Perhaps the best example of this aspiration for
immortality is the funerary banner found at the Mawangdui tombs near
Changsha, within the Chu cultural sphere, which date from circa 168
B.C.E. The central tableau of the banner depicts emissaries of the immortals greeting an elderly woman, presumably the occupant of the tomb,
the Countess of Dai, who is escorted by several servants (figure 5). In the
lower tableau we see an assembly of ritual vessels representing the ancestral sacrifices offered by the living, while the top section displays a celestial paradise presided over by a female figure, most likely the Queen
Mother of the West.[11] The Queen Mother of the West assumed many different forms in Han mythology (see pp. 58–61), but in mortuary art she
was portrayed as a benevolent matriarch who welcomes the *hun* souls
of the dead into her heavenly paradise atop Mount Kunlun. While the
immortals beckoned the *hun* soul of the Countess of Dai to enter their
elysian paradise, the *po* soul, like the body itself, faced the grim prospect

of decay and putrefaction. A jade stopper had been placed in the count-ess's mouth, perhaps to prevent her *po* soul from escaping. The count-ess's family took elaborate care to embalm the corpse and encase it within multiple heavy-timbered coffins sealed in lacquer; in other cases, the body of the deceased was wrapped in suits of jade joined with gold filigree.[12] All of these exacting procedures were intended to forestall corruption of the body and dispersion of the *po*.

The sumptuous decoration and grave goods of elite tombs like those at Mawangdui clearly show that the occupants aspired to reach a heav-enly paradise via the tomb. By the first century B.C.E. the cult of *xian* immortality, once restricted to kings and nobles, had begun to attract a wider audience among the upper orders of Han society. But mortals of less exalted status viewed the passage to the afterlife and the prospect of infernal judgment with great unease.

Han tombs were outfitted with a variety of apotropaic talismans in-tended to protect the deceased from the forces of putrefaction and de-cay. Guardian figurines in the form of ferocious creatures—such as the hybrid beast from a Chu tomb whose imposing antlers, bulging eyes, and protruding tongue no doubt were intended to frighten off baleful un-derworld spirits (figure 6)—are found in tombs dating from the Warring States period.[13] This wooden figure is depicted in the act of devouring a snake—symbolizing the corruption of the body in the tomb—that it grasps in its hands. Similar motifs appear on the Mawangdui lacquered coffins, which are decorated with hybrid antelope-human figures engaged in combat with birds and snakes (figure 7). Late Han tombs often con-tain sculptures or stone reliefs of horned creatures placed at the entrance of the tomb as guardians.[14] It has already been noted that in Han times the tamed yet still fearsome Chiyou was invoked to protect tombs. Im-ages of the Queen Mother of the West were also placed at the entrances of tombs to repel evil spirits. Bronze mirrors, perhaps the most distinc-tive feature of the mortuary inventory of Han tombs, most likely were also intended to assist the deceased in their treacherous journey to the afterlife. These mirrors possibly served as a kind of cosmographic com-pass to guide the *hun* soul of the deceased to the world of the immor-tals.[15] By the fourth century C.E. the idea that mirrors revealed the true nature of a being, and thus could be used to expose disguised demons, had gained some currency, but it is not known whether this belief was present in the Han.[16] Recently it has been argued that the placement of bronze mirrors in Han tombs expressed aspirations for longevity (com-monly voiced in the inscriptions on the mirrors themselves) rather than

Figure 5. Funerary banner of Lady Dai. In this funerary banner from the tomb of Lady Dai (died ca. 168 B.C.E.), the noblewoman appears at the center being escorted to the celestial paradise in the upper portion of the banner. Between the sun and the moon at the top sits a hybrid female-serpent figure in repose. The identity of this figure is uncertain, but most likely it is a representation of the Queen Mother of the West. In the lower part of the banner an array of ritual vessels is displayed, while at the very bottom we see a pair of entwined carp, symbols of the netherworld, flanked by antelope-head figures representing guardian spirits that protect the encoffined body from decay. Mawangdui tomb no. 1, Changsha, Hunan. From Hunansheng bowuguan 1973, plate 38.

Figures 6 and 7. Tomb guardian figures. Figure 6 is made of wood and decorated with colored lacquer, excavated from a Chu tomb of the Warring States era in Xinyang (Henan); from *Wenwu* 1957.9, frontispiece. Figure 7 taken from painted lacquer coffin of Lady Dai (d. 168 B.C.E.), Mawangdui tomb no. 1, Changsha (Hunan); from Hunansheng bowuguan 1973, plate 17 (detail).

served an explicitly apotropaic or soteriological function.[17] Yet the unique placement of bronze mirrors in Han tombs near the head of the deceased suggests a functional use as an apotropaic device, or as a means of preserving the *po*.[18]

The changing forms and functions of tombs, grave goods, and mortuary ritual show that older conceptions of the ancestors as powerful and willful gods had become overshadowed by images of the dead as pathetic ghosts condemned to a bleak existence within the subterranean prisons of their tombs. This dramatic reversal was undoubtedly owed, in some degree, to the political disenfranchisement and marginalization of the nobility under the autocratic regimes of the Warring States kingdoms and the Qin and Han empires. As the aristocratic order of the early Zhou gave way to monarchic states founded on bureaucratic principles, the dead, too, were rendered subject to bureaucratic rule. Each individual, severed from the collective body of the lineage, faced his or her own personal fate in the afterlife.

Increasingly, Chinese viewed their mortal destiny as under the control of powerful (but, like the monarch, remote) gods. Astrologers proclaimed that human fortune was in the hands of imperious celestial bureaucrats residing in the far-off heavens. For example, the astral deity Siming (Sovereign of Life Destiny, associated with the constellation Ursa Major) was portrayed as a celestial minister invested with the authority to determine the life span of human beings.[19] Like a terrestrial magistrate, Siming also heard appeals on behalf of the wrongful dead who sought redress for their shortened life spans. One such petition appears in a recently excavated official document of the Qin state dated 269 B.C.E., which recounts the case of a man named Dan, who committed suicide in 297 B.C.E. after injuring another man in a sword fight. The governor of the region subsequently appealed to a subordinate of Siming, asking that Dan, whose fated life span had not yet been completed, be restored to life. Dan was indeed resurrected from the dead, but he still bore the scars of his sojourn in the netherworld: though eventually his senses revived and he could eat human food again, Dan never recovered the use of his arms and legs. Dan also was said to have instructed his familiars in the proper care of the dead. He emphasized that the dead gratefully welcomed even the most pedestrian offerings, but they were easily scared away and would only eat offerings that had been prepared in strict accordance with rules of ritual purity.[20] Dan's fate, and his beggarly plea for humble offerings, undoubtedly mirrored prevailing views of the dead as weak and powerless, enduring an abject and forlorn existence in the grave.

Around the end of the first century C.E., the cult of the dead began to assume increasingly elaborate forms. Elite mortuary ritual became fixated on ascension to the paradise of immortals presided over by the Queen Mother of the West. But in contrast to elite mythology, in which the dual *hun* and *po* souls implicitly aspired to ascend to paradise, plebeian religion evinced no separation of souls at death. Instead, the souls of the dead were believed to descend to the submontane netherworld to await infernal judgment. We find in Han religion a variety of gods who appear as supreme deities, controlling the fate of mortals in life and in death. As we have seen, contemporary mythology ascribed to Huangdi the power (not unlike that of Siming, the Sovereign of Life Destiny) to lengthen or shorten the life span of mortals in accordance with their good and evil actions. More commonly, the disposition of the dead was ascribed to the Lord of Mount Tai (Taishan fujun), the presiding deity of the sacred mountain of the east, chief among the Five Marchmounts (Wuyue). The Lord of Mount Tai ruled over an array of officials charged with recording all good and evil acts committed by individual mortals, as well as the appointed hour of their death, in voluminous registers of life and death. Those who ended their lives with a positive moral balance were welcomed into the royal paradise on the summit of Mount Tai; those whose crimes outweighed their virtues were sentenced to the "netherworld prisons" *(diyu)* beneath the mountain.

Although the Lord of Mount Tai prevailed over Huangdi as the supreme god of the underworld in later mythology, in Han texts the two deities seem to be virtually interchangeable. For example, a mortuary text dated 173 C.E. states that "the Yellow God [Huangshen; i.e., Huangdi] governs the Five Marchmounts, who are in charge of the registers of the dead and summon the *hun* and *po* souls."[21] This document suggests that the gods of each of the Five Marchmounts kept registers of life and death for the population within their jurisdiction, while Huangdi retained final control over the fate of the dead. Even more commonly, Han tomb documents refer to the supreme deity as the Celestial Thearch (Tiandi). The suzerainty of the Celestial Thearch over not only the dead but also the demonic spirits of the underworld is attested in a talisman recovered from a late Han tomb (figure 8). The top left corner of this wooden plaque bears the legend "talisman lord" *(fujun),* below which appears a dipper-shaped drawing of Ursa Major, seat of the celestial gods. The talisman, composed in esoteric script, is inscribed along the left edge of the plaque, while the legend at the lower right reads: "The name of the demon *[gui]* of those who die on the *yisi* day [one of the sixty days in the Chinese calendar] is Heavenly Light [Tianguang]. The spirit-master *[shenshi]* of the Celestial Thearch already knows your name; quickly remove yourself to a distance of three thousand leagues. If you fail to depart, Magistrate . . . [graphs illegible] of South Mountain will come to devour you. Promptly, in accordance with the statutes and ordinances."[22] Like other Han tomb documents (see below), this talisman invokes the awesome authority of the omniscient Celestial Thearch and his army of martial gods to protect the tomb occupant against the depredations of evil spirits, who dare not defy the imperial command.

The language of this talisman, which closes with the standard valediction used in Han imperial edicts, expresses the close correspondence between the operations of imperial and celestial government. The underworld magistrates before whom the dead were brought to be judged applied inquisitorial procedures that replicated the language and for-

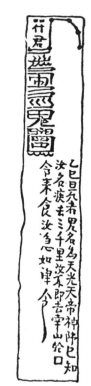

Figure 8. Apotropaic talisman from Han tomb no. 2 at Shaojiagou, Gaoyou (Jiangsu). The wooden talisman measures 28 cm × 3.8 cm, and the inscription is written in vermilion ink. First to second century C.E. From Jiangsusheng wenwu guanli weiyuanhui 1960: 21.

malities of the actual Han judicial system. The Celestial Thearch (or, alternatively, Huangdi or the Lord of Mount Tai) delegated authority over matters of life and death to subordinates who—like their counterparts in Han government, the local magistrates—determined guilt or innocence after meticulous review of the comprehensive documentary record of the individual's life. Although induction into the ranks of the immortals remained a theoretical possibility, the somber tone of Han grave documents suggests that most people anticipated a far bleaker end awaiting them in the afterlife.

The most intimate insight into popular beliefs regarding death and the afterlife can be gleaned from various kinds of mortuary documents recovered from Han tombs.[23] These texts, written on durable materials like lead or tile tablets or ceramic jars, sought to invoke the aid of the spirits of the grave site and the underworld on behalf of the soul of the departed. Among these documents are land-purchase contracts in which the survivors provide proof of their ownership of the tomb site and inventories of grave goods—typically ceramic figurines of slaves, chariots, horses, and the like—to be bestowed as gifts to the Lord Administrator of the Treasury, an officer of the underworld bureaucracy. From the end of the first century C.E. a new type of grave document appears in the form of lengthy petitions written on ceramic jars that perhaps contained food or elixirs intended to fortify the soul of the deceased during its sojourn in the netherworld. Composed in the style of legal plaints, these petitions were plainly modeled on the documents and judicial procedures employed by the Han government. The petitions were addressed to the Celestial Thearch or the Yellow God (that is, Huangdi). Early specimens of these documents, which Anna Seidel has called "celestial ordinances for the dead," beseech the magistrates of the underworld to make certain that the deceased was fated to die at this moment, and to protect the soul from hostile demons. They implore the magistrates of the underworld to be diligent in reviewing the registers of life and death, making sure that no errors have crept in that might have distorted the individual's record of conduct or wrongly altered the prescribed hour of death. The living supplicants also included prayers addressed to the local earth spirits upon whom the tombs of mortals intruded, seeking forgiveness for having disturbed their domicile.

Later petitions, dating from ca. 170–200 C.E., introduce a new concern, asking that the living descendants be exonerated from the crimes and misdeeds of the deceased and spared any punishment ordained by the tribunes of the underworld. The petitions essentially acknowledge the culpability of the deceased and at the same time try to minimize the gravity of their crimes. In exhorting the spirits of the underworld to take the souls of the dead under their care, the descendants also sought reassurance that the latter would not return to the world of the living as malignant ghosts. The following petition is typical of the genre (the ellipses in the translation signify effaced graphs on the original artifact):

> Third day, twelfth month, fourth year of Xiping [175 C.E.].
> The Celestial Thearch sealed up the tomb of the deceased Xu Wentai of Dingyi district and dispatched orders to the Tumulus Adjutant, the Lord of the Tomb, the Infernal "Two-Thousand-Bushel" Officers, the Spirits Above and Below the Tomb, the Guardian of the Center, the Spirits to the Left and Right of the Tomb, the Libationer of the *Hun*-Spirit Gate, and the Elders of Haoli Mountain,[24] stating:
> "The family of Xu Wentai, including his sons, grandsons, and all later generations, no longer have any connection with the deceased. Heaven above is clear and bright; the earth below is dark and obscure. The dead return to the world of *yin,* while the living belong to the world of *yang.* The living have their villages, while the dead have their own province. The

living owe fealty to Chang'an [the Han capital] in the west, while the dead
become subjects of Mount Tai in the East. Let neither, in their joy, yearn
for the other; nor in their sorrow shall they grieve for one another. When
the Lord of Mount Tai reviews the record of conduct of the dead, let the
ginseng serve. . . . If in the underworld Xu is found guilty of crimes, let
the wax figure substitute for him in performing convict labor.[25] Never again,
in a thousand autumns, in ten thousand years, shall [Xu] again make any
imposition on the living. Give aid to the living sons and grandsons of the
Xu family. May their fortune and fame wax ever more full, their property
and wealth multiply many thousandfold, let their progeny be fruitful and
multiply."

[The descendants speak:] "We humbly offer gold and silver . . . in gratitude to the Lord of the Tomb, that he keep the tomb firmly sealed until. . . .
The [ancestors within] three generations and five grades of mourning residing in the Xu family tombs, our august fathers and mothers, must not
compel those more recently interred to perform penal servitude in their
place once they depart from the tomb and tumulus . . . [to enter the paradise of the immortals?]. Let each rest peacefully in their proper abode. Once
the door of the tomb is closed, let not the deceased ever again disturb future generations. In all matters the order of the Celestial Thearch shall be
followed."[26]

This petition disavows any obligations between living and dead kin and
instead entrusts the welfare of the dead to the underworld bureaucracy.
It reiterates long-standing fears that disgruntled ghosts of ancestors may
return to haunt the living, and it implores the spirits of the grave site to
make sure that the tomb is firmly closed and sealed off from the mortal
world. The document also reveals that infernal punishment, like the
process of postmortem judgment itself, was conceived in terms of the actual dispensation of justice by the Han state. Those found guilty of
heinous crimes were believed to be sentenced to convict labor service. In
order to mitigate the sufferings of their ancestors, the survivors placed a
wax or lead effigy in the tomb in the hope that it could substitute for the
ancestor and perform penal labor in his or her stead.

Perhaps the most remarkable feature of this petition is the clash of interests among kinfolk, both living and dead. In addition to pleading that
the gods of the underworld keep the deceased in their custody and not
allow his ghost to return to the world of the living, the survivors also
ask the gods to prevent more senior ancestors from sloughing off some
portion of their sentence on the new arrival. In some cases the ordinances
ask that the punishment imposed on the ancestors instead be transferred
to innocent persons who happen to approach the grave site.[27] This au-

dacious request acknowledges a deep-seated aversion to graves and the dangers they posed to unwary passers-by.

The ordinances for the dead reiterated long-standing fears of the misfortunes that the dead can inflict on the living. But rather than reflecting fear of maverick vengeful ghosts characteristic of the Eastern Zhou era, the Han ordinances disclose new anxieties about the severe punishments meted out by a forbidding underworld bureaucracy acting in the name of the imperial sovereign. Fear of implication in the crimes of one's ancestors was rooted in actual Han jurisprudence, which mandated that individuals share in the culpability for crimes committed by any member of their family. The ordinances instead insisted that each individual is responsible for his or her own sins, and divine punishment must be restricted to the individual alone.

By late Han times, then, the afterlife loomed before mortals as a terrifying world of merciless judgment and harsh punishment. Wracked by the torments of penal servitude, the dead became a menace to their own family members, seeking to escape their ordeals by displacing the burden of guilt, or at least the pain of punishment, onto their living descendants. Illness and misfortune were commonly blamed on vexed ancestors who had filed with the underworld magistrates "writs of grievance from the grave" *(zhongsong)* requesting divine punishment for a panoply of personal grievances and ritual infractions.[28] However pathetic the dead might be, no matter how miserable their existence in the afterlife, they still posed a threat to the living, and especially to their own descendants.

In Han religion, death conferred power, both malevolent and benign. Once liberated from the confines of a mortal body, the spirits of the dead took on a new life. As in earlier times, the hierarchy of the divine reflected the social order of the mortal world. But the social order itself had changed. The imperial bureaucracy emerged as the model for the hierarchical order of the divine. Learned authors portrayed the gods not as transcendent beings, but as ethereal transmutations of dead humans whose exalted pedigree in the divine realm reflected their prodigious accomplishments during their mortal lifetimes. Still, the spirits of the dead did not fade away. Instead, two contrasting visions of the numinous realm existed side by side. In the newer conception, the divine was conceived as a simulacrum of temporal government, a hierarchical order of officialdom subject to the same constraints of law and administrative procedure imposed on imperial subjects. This bureaucratic model of the divine, which first emerged in the late Warring States period, enjoyed special currency among the educated elite, though it also found expression in popular religious movements as well. At the same time, cults devoted to spirits of the dead whose supernatural powers were fed by sacrificial offerings from the living, especially potent "blood sacrifices," continued to hold sway among all social ranks.

Certainly the deity who left the most marked imprint on Han myth and art was the Queen Mother of the West (Xiwangmu). The familiar iconography portraying the Queen Mother of the West as a regal figure presiding over a mountaintop kingdom of feathered immortals and fabulous creatures developed only in the last two centuries of the Han dynasty. In a separate, and earlier, mythological tradition preserved in the *Classic of the Mountains and Seas* she appears not as an imposing monarch (or, as a later tradition imagined her, a seductive temptress) but rather as a hideous ogre associated with ill-fated events and epidemics. In this form the Queen Mother of the West is described as a cave-dwelling hybrid creature having the tail of a leopard (or the body of a tiger) and tiger's teeth; she is skilled at whistling (used by demons to lure their prey into danger); and she commands spectral forces that spread misfortune and pestilence among mortals.[29] It is possible that these sharply contrasting portraits of the Queen Mother derived from distinct regional traditions; the regal and feminine image of the Queen Mother seems more akin to the *xian* mythology of Yan and Qi on the eastern seaboard than the putative "western" demonic representation. But the bestial image of the Queen Mother also resonates with older demonic images dating back to Shang times and perhaps earlier. The "tiger teeth" mentioned in the *Classic of the Mountains and the Seas* immediately remind one of the fanged "demon" faces found in jade iconography extending from Shang (and perhaps from as far back as the Liangzhu culture) to Han times. In the absence of any documents explaining the meaning of these "demonic" images it is impossible to link them to any specific mythical figures, but it seems likely that they represented an exorcist-priest wearing a mask or headdress in order to commune with the spirits.[30] The associations between the Queen Mother of the land of the setting sun, "who knows neither birth nor death," and the demonic imagery found in the *Classic of the Mountains and Seas* point toward a conception of her as a fearsome deity of death and perhaps, for a chosen few, immortal life.

In the late Han period, tomb murals typically depict the Queen Mother in regal pose flanked by her court (figure 9). By this time the older, demonic form of the Queen Mother had receded behind a refurbished image of her as a potent deity controlling the forces of nature. The idea that the Queen Mother was a divine counterpart of the earthly monarch who, in contrast to the severe gods of heaven and the netherworld, succored her mortal children permeated all levels of Han society. The pervasive belief in the benevolence of the Queen Mother was demonstrated most strikingly by the mass movement that erupted during the terrible drought of 3 B.C.E. Thousands of people thronged the roads to the capital bearing wands of straw and hemp representing the Queen Mother's "edict," presumably an order directing the emperor and his ministers to take action to bring relief to the people. Apart from her ubiquitous presence in mortuary cults, though, the Queen Mother was refracted into a variety of different forms at the regional and local level. Representations of the Queen Mother as a regal deity and avatar of cosmic *yin*—necessitating the invention of her binary opposite, the King Father of the East (Dongfangjun), as an icon of *yang* forces—were most prevalent in Shandong (figures 10 and 11). In the west, in Sichuan, the Queen Mother appeared as a more immediate and concretely maternal benefactress who granted boons to her mortal supplicants and protected them from harm.[31] Cast-bronze "money trees" depicting the Queen Mother and her immortal companions among branches full of glowing coins were a conspicuous feature of Han tombs in Sichuan. While the money trees derived primarily from the sun-tree lore associated with the paradise of immortals, the coins link this vision of paradise to the material bounty of the mundane world.[32] The Queen Mother was the first in a series of benevolent goddesses who attracted a great popular following, though in later times she was almost entirely eclipsed by the Buddhist goddess of mercy, Guanyin.

Figures like the Queen Mother of the West, the Lord of Mount Tai, and to some extent Huangdi were directly modeled on terrestrial monarchs, yet they remained transcendent gods. In contrast, most of the gods of Han religion were portrayed as once having been ordinary mortals. Because of their extraordinary accomplishments in life, or the circumstances of their death, these persons acquired numinous powers in the afterlife. In elite religion such deified mortals were incorporated into a bureaucracy of gods, each with its own proper sphere of jurisdiction. One such codification of the divine can be found in the *Treatises of Huainan* of the second century B.C.E.: "The Fiery Thearch [Yandi] invented the use of fire; upon his death, he became the God of the Hearth [Zao]. [The sage-king] Yu labored on behalf of humanity; upon his death, he became the God of the Soil [She]. Prince Millet [Hou Ji, mythical ancestor of the Zhou kings] taught humanity to sow and harvest grains; upon death he

Figure 9. Queen Mother of the West. In this stone carving from a late Han tomb, the Queen Mother of the West is shown in a regal pose wearing her H-shaped crown and surrounded by her retinue of immortals and fantastic creatures. On the left is the auspicious nine-tailed fox, an omen of good fortune; at the far right is the hare grinding with mortar and pestle the elixir of immortality that the Queen Mother bestows on fortunate mortals; and below the hare is a pair of dancing frogs associated with the moon and the female *yin* that the Queen Mother came to embody on a cosmic level. Below this celestial assembly is a pair of ritual vessels (containing offerings for the deceased), flanked by the living descendants in reverential pose. Daguocun tomb, Tengxian (Shandong). Second century c.e. From Zhongguo meishu quanji bianji weiyuanhui 1988a, plate 25.

became the God of Grains [Ji]. Archer Yi [Hou Yi] saved the world from peril; upon death he was worshiped as an astral spirit. This is how ghost-spirits *(guishen)* came into being."[33] Recent archaeological discoveries show that the origins of the belief that deceased mortals are assigned positions in the divine bureaucracy date back at least to the late fourth

Figures 10 and 11. Queen Mother of the West and King Father of the East. In these wall carvings the Queen Mother (fig. 10) and King Father (fig. 11), each wearing the Queen Mother's characteristic H-shaped crown, sit atop "mountains" in the shape of the Chinese graph for "mountain" (*shan*). They are also identified by their heraldic animals: the white tiger of the west and the blue dragon of the east. The Queen Mother is flanked by hares grinding the elixir of immortality, the King Father by winged immortals performing the same task. Yinan tomb, Shandong, 2nd–3rd century C.E. From Hayashi 1989, supplemental plate 2. Courtesy of Kyoto National Museum.

century B.C.E. The document describing the resurrection of the suicide
Dan identifies the Scribe of the Sovereign of Life Destiny by name, one
that corresponds to an actual historical figure of the fifth century B.C.E.[34]

In contrast to the *xian* immortals so avidly patronized by the monarchs of the Warring States, Qin, and Han, the gods accessible to ordinary mortals achieved divine status only by passing through death. Few
details are known about vernacular religious cults current in Han times,
but the limited evidence at our disposal suggests that most gods were believed to be the apotheosized spirits of dead mortals. Though worship
of the gods differed in substantial ways from the cult of ancestors, both
exemplified the centrality of the dead in the imagination of the living.
Worship of spirits of the dead other than one's own ancestors evoked
harsh criticism from officials and members of the Confucian-educated
elite, however. Such cults exceeded the bounds of ritual propriety and
perforce were branded as "profane" *(yinci)* and outlawed. But given the
limited means available to police popular piety, state sanctions generally
had negligible impact.

One of the most vibrant cults of the late Han centered on a prince of
the imperial house and grandson of the founder of the Han dynasty
named Liu Zhang, posthumously entitled Prince Jing of Chengyang
(Chengyang Jing wang). Liu earned fame for his forthright opposition
to the usurper Empress Lü and became a hero for his role in suppressing an attempted coup d'état by the Lü clan after the empress's death in
180 B.C.E. Two years later, while still in his twenties, Liu suddenly died.[35]
A shrine dedicated to Liu was erected at Chengyang (in modern Shandong) to commemorate his meritorious actions on behalf of the Han dynasty.[36] Though modest in scale, this shrine apparently galvanized fervent popular worship. According to Ying Shao, writing at the close of
the second century C.E., "from Langye and the six commanderies of Qingzhou to Bohai [an area encompassing all of modern Shandong], every
government seat, every township and canton, and every village raised
shrines in honor of Prince Jing."[37] Another contemporary claimed that
no fewer than six hundred shrines devoted to Prince Jing had proliferated
throughout this region. Popular festivals affirmed the god's dignity.
Merchants dressed images of the god in the official regalia of a "two-
thousand-bushel minister" (referring to Liu Zhang's stipend, which
placed him in the highest rank of Han officialdom). The images were then
paraded through the streets in five carriages to the accompaniment of
feasting, music, and theatrical performances lasting for days. Around the

end of the second century C.E., the governor of the region, the famous poet-general Cao Cao (155–220), ruthlessly suppressed the cult, but worship of Prince Jing apparently revived after Cao's departure.[38]

Another historical personage who became a popular cult figure after his death was Jiang Ziwen, bailiff of Moling (modern Nanjing), who died of wounds suffered while fighting bandits. In life Jiang was a venal and arrogant tyrant. Local legend records that after his death Jiang's spirit demanded that the people of Nanjing honor him as the tutelary deity *(tudi)* of the area. Rebuffed, Jiang punished the faithless populace with a plague to compel their allegiance. Sun Quan, who made Nanjing the capital of his Wu kingdom (222–80), likewise was bullied into erecting a shrine devoted to Jiang, who reportedly caused a great fire that destroyed much of Sun's palace. Sun conferred on Jiang the posthumous title of *hou,* or "sire," and his temple at Bell Mountain (Zhong Shan) outside Nanjing became one of the great pilgrimage sites of the age.[39] The founder of the Liu Song dynasty (420–79) singled out Jiang's temple as the chief target of his campaign to eradicate deviant popular cults, but a subsequent Song emperor rehabilitated Jiang and awarded him additional honors, including promotion within the official pantheon to the rank of king *(wang)*.[40] Among other historical figures widely revered as gods were Wu Zixu, a noble of the sixth century B.C.E. whose heroic efforts to avenge the deaths of his father and brother at the hands of the evil King of Chu transformed him into the supreme paragon of filial piety, and Xiang Yu, chief rival to the founder of the Han dynasty, who was widely celebrated in popular legend and song as a tragic hero.[41]

The common motif linking all of these popular gods was their stature as heroic warriors who met a premature, and usually violent, death. In this respect they resembled vengeful ghosts, whose life force, not yet exhausted, remained a palpable presence in the mortal world. Some of these spirits, like the ghost of Jiang Ziwen, were perceived as rapacious tyrants, while others were heralded as bulwarks of the established order, invested with rank and authority as supernatural arms of the bureaucratic state. Though the titles and honors showered upon such figures enhanced their dignity in the eyes of the people, it was not their bureaucratic office but the popular belief in the supernatural powers wielded by heroic victims of violence that made them into gods. Moreover, the cults of dead warriors proliferated among the populace without any sanction or control by state authorities, much to the consternation of the latter. Witness the contempt vented by Lu Xiujing (406–77),

a Daoist cleric waging a zealous campaign against the corruption of orthodox religion by popular beliefs, in his lurid description of popular
worship during the late Han period:

> The stale vapors of the Six Heavens[42] [Liutian Xieqi] took on official titles
> and appellations and brought together the hundred sprites and the demons
> of the five kinds of wounding [wubing zhi gui],[43] dead generals of defeated
> armies, and dead troops of scattered armies. The men called themselves
> "General" and the women called themselves "Lady." They led demon
> troops, marching as armies and camping as legions, roving over heaven
> and earth. They arrogated to themselves authority and the power to dis-
> pense blessings. They took over the people's temples and sought their
> sacrificial offerings, thus upsetting the people, who killed the three kinds
> of sacrificial animals [ox, sheep, and pig], used up all their prospects, cast
> away all their goods, and exhausted their produce. They were not blessed
> with good fortune, but rather received disaster. Those who died unjustly
> or early and violently could not be counted.[44]

Despite its fulsome invective, Lu's diatribe yields valuable insights into
conceptions of the divine in Han times and his own day. Vernacular religion was replete with violence and combat, demons and renegade gods,
the powerful and malefic spirits of dead mortals. Violence of course had
its place in the bureaucratic order of official religion, whose gods
unflinchingly applied corporal punishment to evildoers. Yet in official religion penal sanctions required imperial warrant; none dared take the
law into one's own hands, and the supreme deity—in the various personae of the Celestial Thearch, Huangdi, or the Lord of Mount Tai—
alone had the authority to sanction the use of violence. This image of the
righteous supreme deity also offered solace to the populace at large. The
Han ordinances for the dead disclose both a pervasive fear of renegade
ghosts and demons and also an abiding hope that the divine bureaucracy
will preserve order among the unruly legions of the dead.

Such, then, was the religious universe that gave birth to the Daoist religion in the second century C.E.[45] The Daoist religion traces its origins
to a sectarian movement that claimed a divine mandate from a supreme
deity, known as Lord Lao (Laojun), to found a community devoted to
the pure religion called the Way of the Celestial Masters (Tianshidao).[46]
When the Han dynasty, riven by factional conflict within and without
the palace, began to crumble in the late second century, the Celestial Masters created their own utopian "parishes" in rugged mountainous areas
of western China. The founders of the Daoist religion deplored popular
idolatry of "aberrant" gods, the ghosts and demons Lu Xiujing dubbed

"the stale vapors of the Six Heavens," but sympathized with the fears of death and the dead that permeated all levels of Han society. The early Daoist movements were also strongly tinged by the profound sense of sin and guilt manifested in the ordinances for the dead. In constructing their pure religion of Lord Lao, the Celestial Masters embraced the principles of bureaucratic authority that framed both Han social life and conceptions of the underworld. In contrast to the heterogeneous local cults of Han religion, though, the Celestial Masters established a formal, systematic pantheon of the divine. The Celestial Masters also undertook a determined effort to eradicate the countless "perverse" and "deviant" forms of contemporary religious worship. Members of the sect were prohibited from engaging in divination, consulting almanacs of taboo days and activities, or performing "blood sacrifices" (xueshi, that is, offerings of sacrificial animals to the gods). The sect also forbade any resort to the medical arts to cure illness. To protect their flock against such "superstitions," the Celestial Masters sought to sever themselves from the secular world by investing both sacred and temporal authority in their own hereditary priesthood.

Yet, in spite of its wholesale repudiation of much of current religious practice, the religion of the Celestial Masters incorporated many vernacular beliefs into its own distinct doctrinal, liturgical, and institutional framework.[47] The Celestial Masters did not deny the existence of the spirits of the dead; instead, they subjected them to heavenly authority. Celestial Masters' doctrine transformed the lawless ghosts and demons of profane religion into the subservient foot soldiers of celestial officers, without any diminution of their terrifying aspect. The Celestial Masters firmly proscribed worship of the dead, an injunction that implicitly encompassed virtually all vernacular gods. Daoist ritual codes, such as the one from which the above passage by Lu Xiujing is excerpted, delineated not only an official register of sacrifices, but also a hierarchy of cults, one that largely replicated the orthodoxy stipulated by Confucian ritual canons. Laypersons were permitted to worship only the soil and hearth gods, and to offer sacrifices to their ancestors five times a year.[48]

Although the Celestial Masters refused to condone prevailing forms of worship, they nonetheless addressed the main religious concerns besetting Chinese of the late Han period and after: the expiation of sin and protection against demonic attack. According to the Celestial Masters' doctrine, human conduct was under constant surveillance by a divine bureaucracy known as the Three Offices (Sanguan) of heaven, earth, and water, which maintained meticulous records of the sins committed by mortals. The priesthood of the Celestial Masters acted as the terrestrial ambassadors of this heavenly bureaucracy. Lay members of the sect could obtain absolution of their sins through confession mediated by a priest, who communicated with the celestial gods through written petitions (composed, like the ordinances for the dead, in formulaic language imitating the Han government's bureaucratic correspondence). In one penitential ritual, sinners demonstrated remorse by smearing their bodies with mud and charcoal and reciting their sins with their hands bound behind their back.[49] Although lay believers were required to submit a regular tithe to the priesthood (which gave rise to the sect's popular name, the "Five Pecks of Rice Teaching" [Wudoumi jiao]), sacrificial offerings to the gods were strictly forbidden. Deliverance from sin and infernal punishment depended on penance and contrition, not purchase of the gods' indulgence. It also seems likely that the Celestial Masters offered their adherents not only absolution from divine punishment but even the prospect of induction into the ranks of celestial officers, through postmortem appointment to the heavenly bureaucracy.[50]

The Celestial Masters also shared contemporary assumptions that ascribed illness and misfortune to demonic attack by the spirits of the dead. Ghosts, especially the shades of ancestors, were seen as the primary agents of demonic affliction. As we can see from the ordinances for the dead, spirits of the dead who harbored grievances against the living could appeal to the underworld bureaucracy for satisfaction. If the complaint was deemed valid, the culprit was subjected to appropriate punishment in the form of a curse. These "writs of grievance from the grave" (zhongsong) were typically directed against unfilial descendants. Also, ancestors condemned to infernal punishment might request that some portion of their sentence be transferred to their descendants (a possibility that, as the ordinances for the dead reveal, greatly worried the latter). Daoist priests often were sought out to protect the living against these "sepulchral suits." Armed with the necessary ritual paraphernalia to communicate with the divine (registers of the gods, petitions, and seals of office), the priest conducted an investigation to determine the source of the affliction and then enlisted the aid of the gods to dispel the curse. Sample petitions in Daoist liturgical texts contain lists of underworld officials that closely parallel the litanies of gods and spirits found in the ordinances for the dead, suggesting that in constructing their own models of the divine bureaucracy the Daoists borrowed heavily from their predecessors among Han spirit mediums.[51]

The total collapse of the Han dynasty at the turn of the third century ushered in a protracted period of political disunity and social turmoil. None of the contenders for the mantle of imperial rule succeeded in restoring a unified empire, nor could they mount an effective defense against the steppe nomads encroaching upon China's northern frontier. In 317, after north China was overrun by marauding nomad invaders, the reigning emperor of the Jin dynasty (280–420) reconstituted his court at a new capital in the lower Yangzi valley at the site of modern Nanjing. The Era of Disunion, during which China was sundered among weak Chinese dynasties in the south and a kaleidoscope of regimes set up by foreign conquerors in the north, lasted until the end of the sixth century. The channels of movement and communication opened between China and central and western Asia during this age accelerated the diffusion of the Buddhist religion throughout China. A vanguard of Buddhist evangelists had first reached China at the close of the first century C.E., but Buddhist beliefs and monastic institutions became entrenched on Chinese soil only after they gained the patronage of the aristocracies in both the north and south starting in the fourth century.

The complex history of the introduction and spread of Buddhism in China cannot be recounted here, but certainly the prime appeal of Buddhism to the Chinese lay in its doctrines of salvation.[52] In its pristine form Buddhism abjured the whole of the phenomenal world and sought to transcend the inevitable miseries incited by human desires through extinction of the self *(nirvāna),* attainable only through arduous regimens of austerity and self-discipline. But the Mahāyāna tradition of Buddhism that gained ascendancy in China promised salvation from the torment of continual rebirth in the world of suffering not just to a few, but to all. Mahāyāna Buddhism derided the clerical establishment's emphasis on the monastic vocation as the only path to salvation. Instead, Mahāyāna held out the possibility of salvation through the intercession of altruistic enlightened beings, known as bodhisattvas, and the eternal Buddha, who promise to come to the aid of devout believers. One of the chief innovations found in Mahāyāna doctrine is its pantheon of compassionate buddhas and bodhisattvas who preside over heavenly paradises and actively assist the faithful in their quest for salvation. Among these celestial saviors are Amitābha, buddha of the western ("Pure Land") paradise; Maitreya, the earliest cult bodhisattva and the future buddha of the Tuṣita Heaven, a land of inexhaustible bounty; Mañjuśrī, the bodhisattva of wisdom and eloquence; and Avalokiteśvara (best known by the Chinese name Guanyin), the omnipresent bodhisattva of compassion who responds to the heartfelt appeals of pious believers,

rescuing them from immediate peril and bestowing boons in answer to
their prayers.

Buddhist soteriology centered on the concept of karma, or the accumulated residue of human action and intention. Buddhists believed that
the moral balance of good and evil deeds generated through the operation of karma determined the nature of the individual's next rebirth
within the five classes of sentient beings *(pañca-gati)*: deity, human, beast,
"hungry ghost," and denizen of hell. The Buddhist adept sought to achieve
an enlightened state in which karma ceased to be produced, thereby free-
ing the self from the cycle of continual rebirth and enabling one to attain nirvana. Buddhist concepts of karma and infernal punishment thus
resonated with indigenous Chinese ideas about life and death. Although
karmic retribution was quickly grafted onto indigenous belief in postmortem punishment, in the process the doctrine of karma underwent substantial modification. In Buddhism, karmic destiny was determined
solely by the actions of the individual. In China, karmic destiny, and especially retribution for sin, was seen as shared by the family (living and
dead) as a whole. Fate was collective, not individual: the living inherited
the burden of the accumulated sins of the ancestors, while the wicked
deeds of the living were likewise projected onto dead ancestors. The doctrine of the transmigration of souls through cycles of rebirth of course
was wholly new to the Chinese. The Buddhist notion of reincarnation,
which simultaneously denied the continuity of the self/ego and insisted
that salvation was purely individual, never became fully reconciled with
the Chinese ancestral cult. Belief in rebirth did infuse Chinese religious
consciousness, but the Chinese tended to transfer karmic retribution to
the realm of the dead.

In Indian Buddhism, the laws of karma operate automatically, without mediation by any divine powers or gods. The individual's actions
spontaneously generated the causes and conditions that would "bear
fruit," to use a favorite Buddhist metaphor, in the person's future path
of rebirth. Yama, the Buddhist lord of the underworld, had been no more
than a passive instrument of the autonomous laws of karma, powerless
to alter an individual's fate. In Chinese religion, though, karmic merit
and sin were subsumed into the operations of the underworld bureaucracy and its vast apparatus of surveillance, record keeping, and judicial
review. Interposition of the many-layered Chinese pantheon of bureaucratic gods and their hordes of supernumeraries compromised the in-
eluctable workings of karma and opened up possibilities for manipulation of karmic destiny. The Indian notion of the underworld as a

sprawling charnel house of horrors replete with every imaginable form of physical torture had no precedent in Chinese religion. But whereas Buddhists viewed hell and its afflictions as one of the five karmic destinies *(pañca-gati)*, Chinese continued to see the underworld as a realm of death, not rebirth. The troubling prospect of parents and ancestors subjected to brutal, unremitting torture in the dungeons of death readily galvanized Chinese to undertake merit-earning actions on behalf of their deceased family members. Pursuit of salvation, like karmic destiny, was conceived as a collective enterprise rather than a solitary religious practice.

The soteriological goal of nirvana remained unfathomable to most Chinese, who were firmly wedded to materialist conceptions of the self. Nirvana was reconceived as deliverance from mortal cares; the vacuous annihilation of the self implied by the Indian term gave way to a quest for rebirth in a paradise of celestial splendor akin to the fantastic isles of the immortals. In Daoist religion, the ascent to paradise was depicted not as a reincarnation or transmigration of the soul but rather as the transmutation of the person's purified body to a realm beyond death.[53] Buddhist teachings never succeeded in dislodging Chinese belief in the essential unity of body and self. On the contrary, the reorientation of Chinese Buddhism away from the extinction of the self encapsulated by the doctrine of nirvana and toward rebirth in a heavenly paradise demonstrated the powerful pull Chinese religious concerns exerted on Buddhist doctrines. Similarly, the belief that individuals could earn merit on behalf of one's parents and ancestors, one of the many accommodations Buddhist monks made to Chinese values, repudiated fundamental Buddhist ideas of the self and karma (though it perhaps derived a tenuous theological justification from the Mahāyāna doctrine that the bodhisattvas could transfer some of their store of karmic merit to the unenlightened but pious faithful to help them attain salvation).

The interaction of Buddhism with Chinese culture was rendered even more complex by the emergence of new currents within native Chinese religion. Following the flight of the refugee Chinese court to the environs of modern Nanjing, two new Daoist traditions—inspired by the teachings of the Celestial Masters but also rooted in southern traditions of occult arts—emerged during the second half of the fourth century. The Shangqing (Supreme Purity), also known as Mao Shan, after the sect's mountain home outside Nanjing, and Lingbao (Miraculous Treasure) traditions both claimed the divine sanction of revelations transmitted to select lineages of adepts through the medium of sacred writings. In addition, both the Shangqing and Lingbao movements originated in the aristocratic circles that coalesced around the transplanted imperial court at Nanjing. In other respects, though, the two new Daoist traditions diverged sharply in doctrine and religious practice.

The Shangqing teachings revealed to a young visionary named Yang Xi between 364 and 370 instantly became the property of Yang's patrons, a powerful aristocratic family named Xu.[54] Yang Xi served as spiritual intercessor for the Xu family; he was one of a number of religious specialists engaged by the Xus who practiced a variety of occult arts originating both from southern local traditions and the Celestial Master priesthood.[55] After the Daoist parishes in western China disintegrated during the course of the civil wars of the third century, the priests of the Way of the Celestial Masters became unmoored from their sectarian communities and drifted among the ranks of secular society. Like the *fangshi* they once disdained, many priests began to offer their services as masters of mantic arts to private patrons. Thus, following the fall of the Han dynasty the priesthood of the Way of the Celestial Masters underwent a transformation, as Peter Nickerson aptly puts it, from leaders of a sect to members of a guild. No longer ordained priests ministering to a sectarian congregation, these "officers of the Way" *(daoshi)* were forced to compete with the gods and spirit mediums of "vulgar" religion for popular allegiance. Consequently, many priests added formerly proscribed practices like divination and spirit possession to their liturgical repertoire while still asserting their unique access to the true gods.[56] Priests of the Celestial Masters tradition did succeed in acquiring a clientele among the court aristocracy at Nanjing, including the Xu family, whose members were initiated into the sect. But Yang Xi claimed a higher spiritual authority than the gods of the Celestial Masters.

Shangqing religion centered on the goal of ascent to the paradise of the immortals without passage through death. Yang Xi spoke of a more exalted class of immortals known as the perfected *(zhenren)* who dwelled among the stars. The religious practice prescribed by Yang Xi chiefly focused on using techniques of meditation to purify the body and thereby escape the inevitable decay of mortal flesh. In contrast to the Celestial Masters sect, Shangqing religion remained a resolutely individual form of piety in which neither priests nor collective worship had any significant role. The Shangqing precepts and techniques of individual spiritual discipline transmitted through sacred scriptures were clearly intended for a select audience of aristocrats; no act was more harshly proscribed than divulging these scriptures to someone deemed unworthy to receive them.[57] The Shangqing adept sought to join the company of the perfected through a regimen of meditation and visualization of astral deities, but the gods themselves remained transcendent beings aloof from the mundane world. Though ritual purity was a fundamental requirement of Shangqing practice, the obsession with sin, demonic affliction, and exorcism that so strongly colored the religion of the Celestial Masters was wholly absent from Shangqing religion, at least in its formative stages.[58] Also, in contrast to the rival Lingbao movement, Shangqing Daoism borrowed little directly from Buddhism, even though the images of the demonic that appear in Shangqing teachings—embodiments of sensual vices who try to distract adepts and prevent them from achieving transcendence—display striking parallels with Buddhist ideas.

The Lingbao scriptures were compiled circa 397–402 by Ge Chaofu, a scion of the southern aristocracy, as a direct challenge to the religious authority claimed by the Xus, whose Shangqing religion had gained some currency among elite circles in the Nanjing area.[59] Lingbao religion borrowed heavily from Buddhist doctrines, and even more so from the evangelical methods of the Buddhist clergy. Ge adapted the literary tropes of Buddhist *sūtras,* sacred texts purported to be sermons spoken by the historical Buddha Śākyamuni, to produce a voluminous body of scriptures recording the preaching of the Primordial Celestial Worthy (Yuanshi tianzun), a new supreme deity cast in the likeness of the timeless and universal buddhas of Mahāyāna theology. In contrast to the esoteric religious practice of Shangqing, which was devoted to the salvation of the individual adept and his family, the Lingbao tradition fully embraced the Mahāyāna ideals of compassion and universal salvation. It spurned cultivation of the physical body through therapeutic regimens, alchemy, and meditation and instead propagated liturgies of collective salvation based on ritual performance, prayer, abstention from sinful acts, and above all recitation of holy scriptures (all of which betrayed Buddhist influence). The prime text of Lingbao Daoism, the *Scripture for Universal Salvation (Duren jing),* contained the secret language (rendered in psuedo-Sanskrit transcriptions) that could be used by the adept to invoke the aid of gods, demon-kings, and spirit warriors, as well as formulas for collective salvation borrowed from Buddhist writings.[60] Sacred texts like the *Scripture for Universal Salvation* also possessed miraculous powers that inhered in the book as a physical object. Recitation of the text not only summoned divine guardians, but it also enabled the blind to see, the lame to walk, and barren women to conceive.[61]

Like the Way of Celestial Masters—but in contrast to Shangqing religion—Lingbao Daoism interposed the priesthood as mediators between the sacred and mundane worlds. Priests and other initiates alone possessed the esoteric formulas necessary to invoke divine aid. Yet Lingbao rituals (such as the Yellow Register Retreats [Huanglu zhai] performed on behalf of the dead) provided ordinary laypersons a more accessible means of gaining deliverance from postmortem suffering than the austere religious discipline demanded by Shangqing Daoism and contemporary Buddhism. In addition, brief morality tales (clearly imitating parables of the life of the Buddha) were often inserted into Lingbao scriptures as concise and readily understandable illustrations of the workings of karmic retribution.[62] The accessibility of Lingbao teachings and liturgy earned them a prominent place in vernacular religious culture throughout later Chinese history.

The Daoist traditions also borrowed from Buddhism a new language of the demonic, though the Daoist concept of evil remained largely unaltered. Māra, the personification of evil in Buddhism, usually appeared in *sūtras* as the personification of ignorance, temptation, and death. Most commonly, Māra connoted the evil intent lurking in human hearts that obscures truth and hinders enlightenment. But in some cases Māra was portrayed anthropomorphically as lord of the Lower Six Heavens of Buddhist cosmology, the realms of sensual desire and the four lower paths of rebirth. The ready correspondence between the Lower Six Heavens of Buddhism and the decadent Six Heavens of Daoist lore facilitated adoption of Māra as the embodiment of selfish desire. Māra achieved particular renown in Chinese Buddhism as the satanic adversary of Śākyamuni, who ultimately foiled Māra's utmost efforts to thwart his entry into nirvana. It is in this guise, as a tempter who tests the spiritual resolve of the Daoist votary, that Māra appears in Shangqing and Lingbao scriptures. But Māra was also assimilated into the bureaucratic conception of the divine and cast as a fearsome deity who punishes sinful mortals. In this role Māra was depicted, like Chiyou in Han religion, as a vanquished demon who becomes a righteous avenger, marshaling the terrifying legions of justice against the forces of evil. In the Lingbao tradition, demons themselves became the objects of salvation. The "demon (Māra)-kings" *(mowang)* that appear in the *Scripture for Universal Salvation* resolved into two distinct types: stern judges who decide the fate of the dead and tempters who test the mettle of adepts seeking transcendence. Thus these demon-kings embodied both good and evil, or—in terms more recognizable to Chinese—order and chaos.[63]

The profound abhorrence of the grave and ghosts that pervaded Han religion continued unabated throughout the Era of Disunion and found new expression in the apocalyptic Daoist cults that arose in the fifth century. Fascination with ghosts was a basic trope of the "annals of the strange" *(zhiguai)* literature that proliferated during this period. Though written in a narrative mode often misconstrued as fiction, the "annals of the strange" claimed to be authentic accounts of interactions between human beings and the hidden world of darkness *(xuan)* beyond mortal ken.[64] Much of this literature consists of polemics intended as proofs of the validity of Confucian, Daoist, or Buddhist teachings, yet at the same time these stories are suffused by a common religious ethos reflecting conservative moral values. They depict the indissoluble correspondences linking the mortal world to the unseen realm and the logic of moral action that governs this relationship. As Robert Campany observes, the *zhiguai* literature sought to reconcile apparently anomalous disturbances of the order of nature with inexorable moral laws that govern both the phenomenal world of human perception and the unseen realm of spirits and the dead. Though this moral order was typically expressed in the Buddhist idiom of karma, the notions of reciprocity, cosmic resonance, and moral equilibrium that underlay its ethic of retribution can be traced to indigenous, Han-era sources.[65]

Among the most common figures in the "annals of the strange" genre are revenants, ghosts who return from the underworld to report on the terrors that await heedless mortals. Many stories feature ill-fated encounters with ghosts disguised as living persons. Often these ghosts are pathetic souls, caught in a liminal zone between the living and the dead, who seek the aid of mortals to make a successful transition to the afterlife, for example by providing the corpse of the deceased with a proper burial or sacrificial offerings.[66] The theme of these stories is abandonment, and the sites of these encounters often turn out to be disturbed tombs or neglected graves hidden by weeds. Another motif involves tomb guardian effigies that become animated by bodiless life forces and escape the grave, causing havoc among mortals.[67] Although many of these stories underscore the reciprocal bonds of sympathy that link the living and the dead, virtually all of them also mark the grave and ghosts as, at the very least, passively dangerous. Contact with the spirits of the dead, regardless of their intentions, posed a dire threat to the vitality of living human beings.

In contrast to the "annals of the strange," in which wandering ghosts are likely to seek out blameless mortals, Daoist religion placed the onus for demonic affliction squarely on the victim. In the fifth century, a va-

riety of Daoist (and also Buddhist) messianic movements sprang up that
portrayed the legions of malevolent beings abroad in the world as sinister omens of an approaching cataclysm. Once these demons cleanse the
world of evil, a messiah would appear to restore a paradise of plenty in
which the pious will abide in peace. The messianic movements attributed the calamities besetting China, especially the ravages of war and
epidemic, to the work of demon-kings (literally, "Māra-kings," *mowang*)
and their henchmen. According to the *Scripture of the Divine Incantations of the Grotto-Abyss,* a widely disseminated apocalyptic tract dating from this time, the demon-kings are spirits of dead sinners who proliferate uncontrollably in times of moral decay. In their ignorance and
confusion, the masses are led astray onto the path of perdition: they seek
solace by worshiping profane gods, and they compound their heresy by
making offerings of bloody sacrifices to them. The appearance of Messiah Li, an incarnation of Lord Lao of the Celestial Masters, will inau-
gurate a great cataclysm that will destroy these sinners, and only the devout faithful, the "elect" *(zhongmin),* will survive and enjoy the era of
Great Peace under the rule of the messiah.[68] (The term *zhongmin* literally means "the seed people," in reference to their role in repopulating
the earth after the apocalypse.)[69]

Although the *Scripture of Divine Incantations* unleashed a polemical
rant against the moral torpor resulting from the penetration of Buddhism
into Chinese culture, the text borrowed heavily from both the formal elements of Buddhist scriptures and the Buddhist eschatology of underworld torments and paths of reincarnation. The liturgical practices ad-
vocated in this work, including recitation of sacred books, charity,
communal retreats, and funerary rites, were also inspired by Buddhism.
Yet the theology of the *Scripture of Divine Incantations* ultimately derived from the Way of the Celestial Masters. Evil forces at work in the
world were ascribed to the proliferation of "demonic cults" *(guidao)* in
which charlatan spirit mediums extract from the naive masses offerings
of blood sacrifices for the spirits of the dead. Only through initiation into
the community of the elect could mortals escape the coming apocalypse.[70]

Like the Lingbao revelations, the *Scripture of Divine Incantations* describes a world overrun by hordes of "demon (Māra)–kings" who
spread pestilence and misery among humankind. In their mortal lives,
these demon-kings were renowned generals and warriors; in death, they
became (as the vernacular religion of the time fully attests) the objects
of profane cults. The first chapter of the text inveighs against "souls of
the dead" who "falsely claim to be great gods, receiving worship from

temple wardens at profane shrines hidden in the hills and forests. These dead generals of vanquished armies who have eluded registration among the dead and instead come to the aid of evil kings, spreading disease and affliction among mortals while refusing to comply with the Great Law, will be seized and beheaded by the executioner-spirits of the ten directions."[71] Yet the same text also describes the demon-kings as rehabilitated evil spirits who submitted to the authority of the Daoist priesthood and were appointed military officers in command of the legions of "petty demons" *(xiagui)*. Dread punishment awaited the demon-kings who fail to restrain their underlings and allow them to run amok, but those who heed commands, assist in the propagation of true religion, and bring relief to the people will be rewarded with promotion to high rank within the celestial pantheon.[72] Still, even these righteous demon-kings bring suffering and pain to humanity, for it is they who serve as the arms of vindictive justice, punishing evildoers by afflicting them with disease and misfortune.

Though the demon-kings and their minions portrayed in the *Scripture of Divine Incantations* and similar texts are tightly yoked to bureaucratic authority, their origins as spirits of the dead remain fully transparent. Like other Daoists (and some Buddhists), the leaders of these messianic movements sought to co-opt vernacular cults by converting their gods to true religion. The demon-kings of the *Scripture of Divine Incantations* in some cases were identified as actual historical persons, almost always heroic, martial figures who probably had become the objects of popular worship deemed heterodox by the Daoist priesthood.[73] Once profane spirits who extorted blood sacrifices from the people, they were now assimilated into the Daoist celestial hierarchy as the storm troopers of the gods. The *Declarations of the Perfected (Zhen gao)*, the corpus of Shangqing revelations assembled by the great Buddho-Daoist syncretist Tao Hongjing (456–536), likewise contains lengthy lists of minor divinities—spirits of those who suffered violent deaths—who had submitted to celestial authority and received appointments within the lower echelons of the supernatural bureaucracy.[74]

The Han cult of the dead played an important role in shaping Daoist and Buddhist ideas of the relationship between the living and the dead, yet at the same time indigenous conceptions of the afterlife themselves underwent profound change. The fear of the dead and their supernatural powers that so strongly marked Chinese religion of the Warring States and Han eras was increasingly supplanted by sympathy for one's deceased ancestors and the tribulations they endured in the afterlife. The deified ancestors of the Shang kings and nobles had long since faded away. Mighty warriors and men of rank retained in death the intimidating power they wielded in life, but the vast majority faced the grim prospect of penal sentences in the dungeons of the underworld. As fears of the "curse of the ancestors" abated, the concerns of the living shifted to rescuing the ancestors from their infernal torments, succoring them, and aiding their quest for transcendence and salvation. Moreover, in Buddhist soteriology, and in Lingbao Daoism as well, the sharp distinction between ancestors and ghosts (the immanent spirits of those with whom one has no kin relationship) became blurred. Both Buddhism and Lingbao Daoism championed an ethic of universal salvation, and their ritual practices were dedicated to the salvation of all beings regardless of kinship ties. Of course, we must not overstate the extent to which the ancestors dissolved into an undifferentiated mass of pathetic souls. Much of lay Buddhism centered on earning merit expressly for one's ancestors rather than the unshriven dead at large. Nonetheless, religious movements of the Era of Disunion tended to efface the boundary between the ancestors and the ghosts of strangers, instead demarcating between the pious faithful and abject sinners. This tendency was most apparent in the messianic cults, which divorced the spirits of the dead from their familial context as ancestors and instead merged them together as objects of sympathy and salvation.

Ancestors and ghosts, while retaining their distinctive features within each religious tradition, thus increasingly converged into a common image of pitiful sinners subject to postmortem judgment and punishment. Buddhist and Daoist concepts of godhood, however, remained starkly different. Chinese Buddhism was dominated by the cults of celestial divinities dedicated to the salvation of all sentient beings. The most popular deity of all was Guanyin, the ubiquitous bodhisattva of compassion, who assumed a wide array of human incarnations in order to propagate Buddhist teachings to those yearning for deliverance and salvation.[75] The celestial deities of Shangqing Daoism, in contrast, were remote, transcendent beings accessible only through possession of sacred books and performance of an austere religious regimen. The Daoist gods exemplified the normative moral order of the cosmos, which was governed by a simulacrum of the imperial bureaucracy. But within vernacular religion— the profane religion scorned by the elevated ranks of the Daoist clergy— fervent belief in the power of death to transform the souls of powerful mortals, especially those who live and die by violence, into gods and demon spirits remained undiminished. In the minds of the populace, the divine world did not divide neatly into the counterposed forces of good and evil. Instead, the divine and the demonic were bound together as inseparable aspects of supernatural power. Gods, like the human beings from whom they sprung, were capable of evil as well as good. The Janus-like gods brought both blessings and punishments, and mortals had to curry favor with them through propitiation and sacrifice. The gods of vernacular religion, like the ancestors, inspired reverence and fear in equal measure.

CHAPTER 3

Shanxiao

Mountain Goblins

Spirits of the dead figured as the primary agents of demonic affliction in the Chinese religious imagination. But other malefic forces were at work as well. Among them was a class of petty demons known as *shanxiao*, changeling spirits inhabiting the wild mountains and forests. As such, the *shanxiao* were akin to the goblins and fairies of pagan Europe, or the forest-dwelling *leshii* in Russian folklore.[1] But the *shanxiao* also betokened a greater divide in human affairs: the contested and shifting frontier between civilization and barbarism. Belief in *shanxiao* reflected fundamental human fears of the hidden dangers of the unknown wilderness. Chinese, like most peoples, envisioned strange lands beyond the pale of civilization rife with all types of bizarre and misshapen creatures. After the loss of northern China to foreign conquerors in 317, the Chinese rulers themselves were displaced to a new and unfamiliar landscape in the south. The humid monsoon climate, dense subtropical forests, and rugged mountain terrain of the Yangzi River valley and beyond contrasted sharply with the arid, flat plains of the temperate north. Moreover, the native peoples of the south, chiefly hill tribes alien to the culture of the Yellow River valley, appeared no less bestial and savage than the land they inhabited. Indeed, in Chinese eyes, the "barbaric" peoples of the south were kindred to the demonic spirits that lurked among them. Throughout the Era of Disunion, and even long after, the forested mountains of the south evoked images of demonic creatures like the *shanxiao*, ever ready to prey upon interlopers from the civilized world. In their earliest incarnation, the Wutong spirits were categorized as a species of *shanxiao*. Ultimately, the Wutong were rehabilitated and transformed into proper gods, but their sinister origins among the *shanxiao* goblins were never fully effaced.

Since at least the early Zhou period, Chinese perceived the world as an arena of relentless struggle between civilization and barbarism. The enlightened monarch, anointed by Heaven, used his authority to fashion a world of symmetry, regularity, and tranquility. But this ideal state was perpetually besieged by the entropic forces of disorder. Anomaly and deviation posed grave challenges to a civilization predicated on deference and hierarchy. Not surprisingly, then, the Zhou portrayed the sage-kings above all as civilizers triumphant over the wilderness landscape and its denizens. Political philosophers of the Warring States era viewed both barbarian lands and mountain wildernesses within the royal domain as *terra incognita,* and hence beyond the reach of the monarch's benign influence. At the same time they affirmed that the task of classifying and recording strange flora and fauna, mountains and rivers, and gods and peoples was an integral part of sage governance. Omniscience conferred power over not only the mortal domain, but also the unseen realm of gods, ghosts, and demons. By extension, writing served apotropaic purposes: the actualization of knowledge in the written word exposed the true nature of demonic entities and thereby rendered them impotent. This apotropaic function of writing was enhanced by the emergence of correlative cosmology, which assimilated all strange and uncanny phenomena to disruptions of the moral and political order.[2] From the perspective of correlative cosmology, nothing in the cosmos was truly abnormal. Yet anomalies foreshadowed fissures in the organic unity of heaven and earth.

The *yin/yang* and Five Phases cosmographies elaborated from the fourth century B.C.E. onward subsumed the vagaries and complexities of the immense natural world within regular and predictable patterns that the human mind could apprehend, and thus control. Alongside this burgeoning literature of cosmographic science we find a complementary body of anomaly lore that sought to explain the appearance of human, animal, and natural prodigies in terms of disturbances in cosmic matter and energy that produced deviant life forms. The metaphysicians and soothsayers known collectively as *fangshi,* or "masters of occult arts," assiduously courted ambitious monarchs, offering to place their profound knowledge of the world and its creatures at the ruler's disposal. In particular, the *fangshi* laid claim to knowledge of the distant past and remote territories beyond the mortal horizons of time and space, wisdom that would enable the ruler to cope with any untoward contingency or strange encounter.

The mythologies that coalesced around the figures of ancient sage-kings during the Warring States period depicted them as civilizers who tamed the hostile wilderness and its terrifying creatures. These myths accentuated the "panoptic gaze of the sage-ruler," to use Robert Campany's apt phrase: through tours of inspection and collection of tribute, the ruler acquired knowledge of the peoples and territories on the periphery of his realm and used it to fix them in their proper places within the orbit of imperial control.[3] Chief among these sage-kings was Yu the Great, reputedly the founder of the pseudohistorical Xia dynasty, whose Herculean labors in channeling and draining the waters of the primeval Great Flood made the earth fit for human habitation. An early tradition relates that after the founding of the Xia dynasty, the peoples of the "Nine Continents" formed by the rivers Yu dug sent missions to pay tribute to their benefactor. Each mission also submitted pictures of the unusual flora and fauna of its homeland. Yu ordered that nine bronze cauldrons be cast "bearing images of the hundred strange beings. In this way people could recognize all spirits and evil influences, so that when they traveled over rivers and marshes and through mountains and forests, they would encounter no adversity, and the specters of the mountains and waters[4] could not bother them."[5] In ancient China, bronze cauldrons were regalia used in rituals to propitiate the gods and ancestors, and thus embodied sovereign authority. Yu's act of casting the nine cauldrons affirmed his dominion over the entire world, including regions beyond his own ken, and all of its creatures. At the same time this passage also insinuates that foreign lands were populated by malevolent spirits who assumed bizarre physical forms: only through proper cognizance of these demons could visitors from the civilized world keep them at bay.

Other myths depict Yu measuring the length and breadth of the world (which early Chinese cosmography conceived as square in shape), recording the products of each of the Nine Continents, and compelling their inhabitants to submit tribute, a ritual gesture symbolizing their deference to his supreme authority. By the Warring States era, Yu's labors were also celebrated for enabling the free flow of wealth and communication, which was deemed integral to the imperial project of creating a unitary civilization.[6] Geographical knowledge thus had potent political uses. The importance of esoteric knowledge of distant lands is cogently revealed by the career of the fourth-century B.C.E. philosopher Zou Yan, who is credited with developing the Five Phases cosmology into a highly influential philosophy of history. In essence, Zou Yan and his legions of imitators offered contemporary rulers the hope of duplicating the heralded accomplishments of the great monarchs of the past. Knowledge of strange places and creatures inaccessible to ordinary mortals entailed mastery over them, enabling the ruler to expand his dominion to all corners of the world. Most importantly, the ability to penetrate the mystery enfolding aberrant phenomena and correctly deduce their portentous significance would guide the ruler in conforming his actions to the ever-changing norms of the cosmos. The historian Sima Qian's brief biography of Zou Yan describes Zou's political philosophy as grounded in claims to omniscience spanning both time and space:

> [Zou] plumbed the reciprocal successions of *yin* and *yang* and compiled records of astonishing and aberrant phenomena in a tract of more than one hundred thousand words entitled *A Complete History of the Succession of the Great Sages [Zhongshi dasheng]*. His theories, based on observation of petty phenomena from which he inferred universal principles, were extraordinary and unorthodox. Drawing upon the collective wisdom of learned men, Zou recapitulated the alternations of ages of prosperity and decadence from the present day back to the time of Huangdi. But then Zou proceeded to derive from this history laws of felicity and misfortune that he applied to the remote and unfathomable past as far back as the dim, dark ages before the birth of heaven and earth.
>
> Zou began by classifying the notable mountains and great rivers of China;[7] the birds and beasts of its manifold valleys; the abundance of its waters and soils; and its rare and precious products. But Zou went farther, extending his survey to lands beyond the seas and things men are unable to observe. He spoke of how the Five Powers [Wude, i.e., the Five Phases] have rotated in sequence since heaven and earth were first separated; how each epoch had its ruling power; and how auspicious omens corresponded to each epoch. In Zou's view, what orthodox scholars *[ru]* regarded as China occupied only one of the eighty-one divisions of the world. To China he gave the name Chixian Shenzhou [Divine Land of the Red Province], which encompassed nine regions, the so-called Nine Continents laid out by Yu the Great. In addition to China there were eight other territories equal to Chixian Shenzhou, which according to Zou are the true Nine Continents. These Nine Continents are surrounded by an ocean severing their inhabitants and creatures from the rest of the world. The Nine Continents thus form a separate division. There are nine of these great divisions, encircled by a vast ocean reaching to the point where heaven and earth are joined together.

Sima Qian's synopsis bespoke his strong antipathy to Zou's inductive method, which deduced patterns of historical change since earliest antiquity from events of the more recent past. Yet Sima also stressed that

Zou's philosophy ultimately rested on the conventional virtues of benevolence and righteousness, moderation and austerity, and the hierarchical principles defining ruler and subject, superior and inferior, and the six grades of kinship; "it was only in their premises that Zou's theories were preposterous," he concluded.[8] But, as Sima ruefully admitted, rulers of the Warring States era eagerly sought Zou's advice on how to transform themselves into supreme monarchs.

The concrete political rewards of geographical knowledge inspired prodigious efforts to map the world and its multitudinous creatures. One of the chief literary products of this quest was the encyclopedia of exotic places and their native flora and fauna known as the *Classic of the Mountains and Seas,* whose authorship was commonly ascribed to Yu the Great himself. This unusual work has survived through numerous mutations, notably the efforts of the prolific scholastic commentator Guo Pu (276–324) to impose order on the text by dividing it into concentric cosmogeographic realms extending outward beyond the "civilized world" of the Zhou realm.[9] The first five chapters of the *Classic of the Mountains and Seas,* the oldest portion of the extant text, identify the locations of more than four hundred mountains within the known world of Han China and detail the distinctive flora, fauna, and minerals of each. Later additions describe the "Realm Beyond the Seas" and the "Great Wastelands" lying beyond the Nine Continents surveyed and mapped by Yu. These remote and exotic lands were worlds of fantastic peoples and creatures, mutant life forms that defied belief. Regrettably, the illustrations that accompanied the original text of the *Classic of the Mountains and Seas* have long since been lost. But a second century C.E. tomb mural from Shandong depicts a parade of fantastic creatures, including numerous human-beast hybrids and bizarre morphological anomalies, highly reminiscent of those described in the *Classic of the Mountains and Seas* (figure 12).[10]

The *fangshi* also professed knowledge of mysterious worlds much closer at hand: the mountain wildernesses looming just beyond the cultivated fields and ordered settlements of the human habitat. Chinese regarded the mountains and forests as an eerie world of constant and surprising mutation detached from the regular symmetry of civilized life, inhabited by all manner of strange beasts no less exotic than the inhabitants of the most distant countries of the "Great Wastelands." The creatures of the forest perhaps bore some faint resemblance to the familiar fauna of the humanized landscape, but their grotesque forms belied vivid fears of the unknown and the unknowable.

Figure 12. Hybrid human-beast prodigies. Stone carving, Yinan tomb, Shandong. Second to third century C.E. From Hayashi 1989, supplemental plate 3. Courtesy of Kyoto National Museum.

Though located within the territorial compass of the Chinese empire, the wild mountains and forests remained intractably foreign terrain, beyond the reach of the emperor's authority. Geographies like the *Classic of the Mountains and Seas* and its successors were compiled with the intention of assisting the ruler to gain mastery over his realm. The bizarre creatures encountered in the pages of the *Classic of the Mountains and Seas* were not merely anomalous curiosities; they also were viewed as baleful omens. The older sections of the text, devoted to China proper, list numerous strange creatures whose appearances foretell impending disturbances of the natural and human orders (such as drought, flood, war, and epidemic).[11] Implicit in the worldview of these macrogeographies was the belief that nothing in the world is truly anomalous: the cognoscenti can discern the hidden patterns that underlie seemingly aberrant phenomena. Anomalies were inevitable by-products of a universe undergoing constant change, a universe in which natural phenomena responded organically to the vicissitudes of human affairs. At the same time anomalies were signs, the keys to a symbolic language that articulated the moments of rupture in the continuum of humanity and the cosmos.[12]

The *Classic of the Mountains and Seas* thus served not only as a storehouse of geographic knowledge, but also as a manual for warding off imminent disaster. In this respect it contains apotropaic elements similar to those found in exorcism texts such as the *Album of White Marsh,* which probably dates to the early Han dynasty. The "White Marsh" of the title refers to a mysterious creature who, according to a Tang dynasty version of the legend, taught Huangdi about all the dangerous and malevolent beings inhabiting the world:

> Huangdi went on a tour of inspection. In the east he reached the sea and ascended Mount Huan. At the seashore he encountered White Marsh, a divine beast who could speak in human language and had extensive knowledge of the natures of all creatures. Therefore Huangdi interrogated White Marsh about the spirits and demons of the world. He was told that from ancient times to the present there have been many numinous specters [*jingqi*] that assume corporeal form, and many wandering souls that undergo metamorphosis, a total of 11,520 kinds in all. Huangdi ordered his subordinates to record the names of the beings described by White Marsh together with illustrations of them so that they could be made known to the entire world.[13]

Today the *Album of White Marsh* exists only in fragments. A Qing scholar, Ma Guohan, assembled quotations from this work scattered throughout Han-Tang literature, some forty passages in all.[14] In addition, an illustrated manuscript entitled *Album of the Specters and Apparitions of White Marsh,* dating from the ninth or tenth century, was found among the cache of documents retrieved from the Dunhuang sanctuaries at the turn of the twentieth century.[15] The Dunhuang manuscript differs in content and form from the composite text recreated by Ma; perhaps it is a later recension, which would suggest that many variant texts circulated under this title. Whatever their textual differences, in their original forms the various versions of the *Album of White Marsh* contained illustrations as well as literary descriptions of the noxious demons (referred to as *jing,* "apparitions" or "specters") that might waylay unwary humans. In Ma Guohan's composite text, these spirits almost always are identified in terms of the places they inhabit. Some of these specters are associated generically with mountains and waterways; many others are specifically connected to ancient and decrepit objects and places routinely encountered in daily life: old gateways; abandoned graves; unused paths, ponds, and wells; discarded carts; and even defunct marketplaces. In some instances they are said to be creatures of great age, such as the hundred-year-old wolf or the thousand-year-old tree. In each case, calling the spirit by its true name, which the text supplies, ensures that it can inflict no harm.[16] Pictures included in the text provided visual keys for recognizing these spirits. The surviving illustrations from the Dunhuang manuscript, which displays greater concern with interpreting omens than expelling demons, do not feature hybrid creatures, however.

We now can trace back this tradition of demonological lore to at least the third century B.C.E. An exorcism text recently excavated from a Qin dynasty tomb dated to 217 B.C.E. contains many parallels to the demonology and exorcistic practices found in the *Album of White Marsh.* This text, entitled "Spellbinding," confirms that odious demons typically were believed to be aberrations of "vapors" *(qi).* Others were identified as the lost souls of dead children and infants, whose life force had not yet been exhausted. While demons of the former type were portrayed as consciously malevolent, those of the latter type, and indeed most of the remainder, appeared as pathetic, rootless ghosts seeking shelter and food.[17]

The word *jing,* translated here as "specter," also can mean "seed" or "germ" and often was used to denote the essential nature of a thing, a distillation of its vital force.[18] But we can infer from the *Album of White Marsh* that these specters are not innately present in certain creatures or objects; rather, they are transient beings who invade and lodge themselves in aged and decrepit things. The renowned collection of anomaly stories *Quest for the Divine,* composed ca. 335–49 by Gan Bao, offers corroboration of this conception of the demonic. In a speech put in the mouth of Confucius, who is called upon to explain strange phenomena and the nature of spirits, Gan wrote that "when things age, various and sundry specters *[jing]* lodge in them because they have become weak and vulnerable. Thus, when the six kinds of domestic animals, as well as tortoises, snakes, fish, turtles, grasses, and trees, become old, inevitably they are possessed by specters capable of causing baneful afflictions *[yaoguai].*"[19] Elsewhere in his book Gan Bao explains that demonic affliction results from possession by numinous specters *(jingqi):* "Disturbances of *qi* within are manifested by mutations in external form." These mutations, Gan declared, were produced by the ceaseless but imperfect transformations of the Five Phases.[20] Gan Bao also asserted that morphological difference reflected environment as much as the innate nature of beings: "Divergences in *qi* cause the nature of a being to vary; in different regions it will assume different physical forms."[21] The vital tie binding demonic spirits to their particular habitats is underscored in an anecdote recorded by Gan concerning a local official who while hunting in the mountains captured a strange creature that looked like a human infant. The official wished to bring his captive home, but when he emerged from the forest, it suddenly died. The official explained to his puzzled entourage that he recognized the creature from its description in the *Album of White Marsh,* which had predicted that if removed from its habitat it would perish.[22] Like entries in the *Album of White Marsh,* this anecdote reinforces the idea that baleful spirits are rooted to wild places beyond the horizons of civilization.

A similar point was made by Wei Zhao (ca. 200–273) in his commentary on the *Dialogues of the States,* a historical work of the late Warring States era. The *Dialogues* recounts an apocryphal episode featuring Confucius and a nobleman named Ji Huanzi from Confucius's home state of Lu. The *Analects,* which records Confucius's conversations with his disciples, depicts Confucius as an unwavering agnostic who refused to say anything on the subject of "spirits."[23] But the author of the anecdote in the *Dialogues of the States,* like Gan Bao and many others, invoked the authority of Confucius to make pronouncements about the logic of the supernatural world. In this story Ji Huanzi's men, while digging a well, unearth a clay jar containing a sheep. To test Confucius's knowledge of the spirit world, Ji reported to Confucius that he found a dog in the jar instead. Unfazed, Confucius replied, "From what I have heard, it was a sheep. Prodigies of trees and stones *[mushi zhi guai]* are known as *kui* and *wangliang*. Prodigies of water are known as *wangxiang*. Prodigies of earth are known as *fenyang* (literally, gelded sheep)."[24] Confucius's terse answer illustrated his conviction that even seemingly anomalous phenomena are readily comprehensible in rational terms: since "prodigies of earth" take the form of sheep, Ji should not be astonished at finding a sheep buried in the ground.[25] In his explication of this passage Wei Zhao observed that "trees and stones" should be read as a metaphor for mountain wildernesses. In other words, the import of Confucius's words was not that trees and stones were possessed by spirits, but rather that aberrant phenomena of this sort reflect the peculiar character of their natural environment.

The Chinese, like most cultures, associated lofty mountain peaks with powerful gods who commanded the elemental forces of nature. An older contemporary of Confucius reportedly warned his prince of the dangers of lapses in royal piety in the following words: "The gods of the mountains and rivers inflict calamities of flood, drought, and disease; therefore they must be propitiated with sacrifices; the gods of the sun, moon, stars, and planets cause unseasonable snow, frost, wind, and rain; therefore they must be propitiated with sacrifices."[26] Through proper worship and sacrifice the ruler could abate the wrath of the gods, but these mountain deities remained fearsome and unapproachable. The most powerful mountain gods, the marchmounts *(yue),* were believed to exercise sovereign power over their own vast domains. The Zhou kings also applied the name "marchmount" to ruling houses on the margins of the Zhou realm, signifying the independent authority they exercised within their own territories. By the Warring States period, the analogy between sovereignty and mountain gods was elaborated in the light of Five Phases cosmological correlations. The Chinese ecumene was believed to encompass Five Marchmounts, the sacred mountains of the five cardinal directions, each with its own corresponding deity.[27] The Zhou rulers associated themselves with the Central Marchmount, Mount Song, but by early Han times the Lord of Mount Tai, the Eastern Marchmount, emerged as the paramount mountain god, ruler of not only his Olympian paradise but also the subterranean prisons of the underworld.

Powerful gods of impeccable rectitude like the Lord of Mount Tai presided over the great mountains, but lesser places were infested with petty demons who preyed on vulnerable humans. These malevolent spirits posed a special hazard to *fangshi,* who often availed themselves of the solitude and telluric energy of the mountains to perfect their techniques. In his monumental treatise on occult arts, *The Master Who Embraces Simplicity,* the great philosopher-alchemist Ge Hong (283–343) observed that demonic forces ran rampant among the less exalted mountains: "Divine alchemy of the golden elixir cannot be performed in the numberless small mountains. None of the smaller mountains have a proper deity *[zhengshen]* ruling over them. Instead, in such places you will find many aberrations of trees and rocks; ancient, thousand-year-old beings; and blood-eating ghosts.[28] Spirits of this ilk are invariably demonic. They have no intention of benefiting mortals, but are fully capable of inflicting harm."[29] Venturing into the mountains, home to powerful gods and unruly demons, thus was fraught with hidden dangers. Ge Hong devoted an entire chapter of *The Master Who Embraces Simplicity* to strategies for ensuring one's safety while abroad in the mountains and forests. All mountains, no matter how small, have spirits, Ge wrote, and the unprepared voyager is vulnerable to illness, physical attack, and fright caused by these spirits. Ge enumerated the proper seasons and days for entering mountain regions, and provided detailed information on how to defend oneself against assault by changelings whose innocuous outward form disguised their true malefic nature. Like his younger contemporary and friend Gan Bao, Ge believed that "the specters *[jing]* of old things and creatures are capable of falsely assuming human form in order to confuse and deceive mortal eyes." Therefore the essential equipment for forays into the mountains included a mirror worn on the back to expose the true forms of demons, talismans for warding off evil spirits, and apotropaic books like the *Album of the True Forms of the Five Marchmounts (Wuyue zhenxing tu)* and the *Writs of the Three Sovereigns (Sanhuangwen).*[30]

Elsewhere in his treatise Ge Hong proclaimed that he valued the *Album of the True Forms of the Five Marchmounts* and the *Writs of the Three Sovereigns* as the two most important documents bequeathed to him by his teacher. From Ge's descriptions of these works, it's clear that he considered they had great value in protecting mortals from demonic affliction:

> Having a copy of the *Writs of the Three Sovereigns* in your home enables you to repel demonic and baleful ghosts and ethers of hot pestilence. It will forestall calamity and drive off affliction. In cases of serious illness where a person is on the brink of death, a devout believer of perfect sincerity who has this book in his possession certainly will not perish. . . . Having the *Album*

of the True Forms of the Five Marchmounts in your home enables you to
deflect violent assault and repulse those who wish to do you harm; they
themselves will suffer the calamity they seek to visit upon you.[31]

The *Album of the True Forms of the Five Marchmounts* consisted of talismanic images of the mountain gods that could be used to command
these deities to repel malevolent spirits.[32] The images essentially took the
form of esoteric mountain landscapes seen from a bird's-eye view. The
Writs of the Three Sovereigns no longer survives, but it probably consisted of esoteric incantations used to enlist the aid of divine powers. Ge
claimed that the book could be used to conjure celestial deities and visualize the spirits of the mountains, waterways, and temples in order to
make inquiries about the causes of demonic affliction and good and ill
fortune within their jurisdictions.[33]

The use of such formulas again demonstrates the conviction that
knowledge of a spirit's true identity and form enabled mortals to gain
mastery over gods and demons alike (recall, for example, the apotropaic
talisman from a Han tomb shown in figure 8). The prescriptions of the
Album of White Marsh and other early demonologies manifest an abiding faith in the power of esoteric knowledge to repel baleful spirits. Calling demons by their proper names—that is to say, exposing their true
identities—negated their supernatural powers and thwarted their evil designs. Ge Hong urged his disciples to consult books like the *Album of
White Marsh* and *Records of the Nine Cauldrons (Jiuding ji)* in order to
apprise themselves of the proper names of demons.[34] (The latter text,
otherwise unknown, undoubtedly contained the names and pictures of
the strange creatures purportedly recorded on the nine cauldrons of Yu.)
Also included in the vast corpus of esoteric writings Ge received from
his teacher was a three-scroll work entitled *Classic of Subduing Mountain Demons and Aged Goblins and Controlling Malevolent Specters
(Shou shangui laomi zhixiejing jing)*. Armed with such books, the adept
could travel freely throughout the wilderness without fear of the bogies
residing in it.[35]

Ge Hong mentioned numerous types of goblins and specters that might
waylay the unwary traveler. Several of these evil spirits are described in
nearly identical terms in the Dunhuang manuscript of the *Album of the
Specters and Apparitions of White Marsh.*[36] Among the predatory
"mountain specters" *(shanjing)* about which Ge warned his readers was
a creature known as *qi*[a], characterized by its small stature (it was the size
of a human child) and a single, inverted foot. This creature could harm

humans, but Ge assured his audience that calling the *qi*[a] by its proper name would drive it off. Ge Hong also mentions another mountain spirit, called *hui*, which was red in color, shaped like a drum, and had only a single leg.[37] Ge's description of the *hui* recalls that of a mountain spirit in the *Album of the White Marsh* called *kui*, which was "shaped like a drum and ran on one leg."[38] As noted above, the *Dialogues of the States* records that *kui* was one of the names given to "prodigies of trees and stones." The older sections of the *Classic of the Mountains and Seas* mention the *kui* only as a kind of large buffalo. But in a later chapter, the *kui* is described as a blue-skinned, one-legged, hornless bovine that utters a thunderous bellow. The *kui* provoked wind and rainstorms whenever it entered or left ponds and rivers, and legend had it that Huangdi fashioned from the skin of a *kui* a drum whose sound could be heard at a distance of five hundred leagues.[39] In the mythological literature of the Han dynasty the *kui* appears in anthropomorphic form as a musician whose melodies could make the hundred beasts dance (an instance, most likely, of reverse euhemerism). But even in this distorted and sanitized guise the musician Kui still shared with the bestial *kui* the distinctive trait of having only one leg.[40]

It seems probable that the image of the *hui/kui*, and of mountain spirits in general, derived from mountain-dwelling simian species of southern China. Wei Zhao asserted that the *kui* had a single leg and an ape's body, but otherwise was humanlike and capable of human speech.[41] An analogous beast known as the "mountain *hui*[a]" (*shanhui*) appears in the *Classic of the Mountains and Seas*. No mention is made of the *shanhui* having only a single leg like the *kui* and Ge Hong's (no doubt eponymous) *hui*; instead, it is described as a doglike creature with a human face that was fond of throwing objects and whistled or laughed upon seeing humans. The *shanhui* was said to run like the wind, and its appearance, like that of the *kui*, whipped up great windstorms.[42] Another creature resembling an ape or monkey was the *xiaoyang*, the name given to mountain spirits in the *Treatises of Huainan*, compiled in the second century B.C.E.[43] "Xiaoyang" appears in an early chapter of the *Classic of the Mountains and Seas* as the name of a country to the south of China whose inhabitants "have human faces and long arms, and black bodies covered with hair. Their feet are inverted. Upon seeing human beings they laugh."[44] In Han times the *xiaoyang* also was identified with a four-legged beast known as the *feifei*. A legend dating at least to the early Han relates that at the beginning of the Zhou dynasty one of the peripheral countries that swore allegiance to the Zhou submitted as tribute a beast called *feifei*[a] that was "human in form, but with inverted feet, given to spontaneous laughter. When it laughs its upper lip covers its eyes. It eats people."[45] The Han-era lexicon *Erya* records that the *feifei* was "similar to humans, but with long, unbound hair; it runs quickly and eats people." Guo Pu, in his gloss on this entry, identified the *feifei* with the *xiaoyang* described in the *Classic of the Mountains and Seas.*[46] It seems likely that the name *xiaoyang* originated as a specific local name for fearsome apes, and later became identified with demonic creatures of mountain landscapes known more generically as the *hui/kui.* The Tang collector of fantastic tales, Duan Chengshi (803–63), identified the *feifei* as a gibbon of prodigious strength capable of human speech (of a bird-song type). The *feifei* was clearly more than a rude beast, however, since it was also reported to have foreknowledge of matters of life and death, and drinking its blood enabled one to visualize demons.[47]

What made these "mountain specters" strikingly anomalous was their single leg (monopode) and/or inverted heels (antipode).[48] Monopodes and antipodes are typical of the zoomorphic oddities encountered in the pages of the *Classic of the Mountains and Seas.* The strange land of Xiaoyang, as we have already seen, was populated by antipodes, while the even more fantastic inhabitants of the country of Mouli were said to be both monopodes and antipodes. Closer to home, in the south of China, dwelt people known as the Gan giants who were described in the exact same words as the Xiaoyang race.[49] These motifs also appear as characteristic features of "mountain specters" in the zoological lore of the Era of Disunion.[50] The mythology of Vedic India also featured monopode demons known as *ekapada.* Greeks who traveled to India in the wake of Alexander's conquests, perhaps acquainted with these indigenous Indian myths, listed among the fabulous peoples of India the Monocoli, monopodes of great agility, and the antipodes of Mount Nulo, who had inverted, eight-toed feet.[51] Apart from the penchant for describing the inhabitants of remote and foreign lands in terms of morphological anomalies, it seems likely that this particular aspect of mountain-dwelling demons reflected actual observation of the elongated arms and prehensile hands and tails of arboreal primates.

It must be remembered that the northerners who fled with the court to south China following the sack of Chang'an in 311 had to acclimate themselves to a new and strange abode that, in their eyes, was no less exotic and eerie than the fantastic lands glimpsed in the pages of the *Classic of the Mountains and Seas.* The dismal subtropical environment and forbidding mountain forests of the south readily inspired visions of all

kinds of ogres and hobgoblins. Ge Hong, though himself a native of the
south, bluntly attributed the profusion of demons in the south to the region's fetid climate: "In the north, where the *qi* of the central plains is
pure and harmonious, there are none of the noxious fiends one finds in
the mountain valleys south of the Yangzi River. The wildernesses of Wu
and Chu [southeast and south-central China] are hot, wet, and unbear-
ably humid. Though proper deities like the Heng and Huo Marchmounts
reside there, still the south is infested with many kinds of poisonous vermin."[52] The rugged southern wilderness and its strange beasts proved
impervious to the civilizing efforts of not only human monarchs, but the
gods as well. It was in this inhospitable environment that the *shanxiao,*
a composite of savage beast and hostile foreigner, was conceived.

Shanxiao (also written as *shansao* or *shanzao*) was but one appellation for the specters and bogies of the mountain wilderness, who also
were known in demonological lore as *shandu* or *muke* (literally "tree
lodgers"). *Shandu,* according to Guo Pu, was the colloquial name for *xiaoyang* used throughout the mountain regions extending from southern
China to northern Vietnam.[53] The "annals of the strange" literature of
the Era of Disunion describes the *shandu* as short in stature but human
in form, covered with hair, and noteworthy for its distinctive whistling
and laughter, and also its habit of rapidly opening and shutting its eyes.[54]
A typical description, from the brush of Zu Chongzhi (429–500), acknowledges its ability to change form:

> In Nankang [the upper reaches of the Gan River valley, the backbone of
> modern Jiangxi province in south-central China] there is a spirit *[shen]*
> known as *shandu* that has a human body and stands slightly more than
> two feet high. It is black, with red eyes and yellow hair. It makes a nest
> in the shape of a bird's egg in the trees of remote mountains. . . . [The
> *shandu*] makes a double-layered skirt from bird feathers, with cock's feath-
> ers on top and hen's feathers underneath. It is capable of transformations
> and disguising its form, so it is rarely seen. The *shandu* belongs to the same
> category as the *muke* and *shanxiao.*[55]

According to the fifth-century *Gazette of Nankang,* the *muke/shanzao*
likewise resembled humans in form and speech, but instead of hands and
feet they had birdlike talons and nested in high trees.[56] The tree-dwelling
shandu and *muke* both seem to have some affinity with a changeling bird
known as *ye,* which nested in the high trees of the remote mountains of
southern China. The *ye* bird could change shape and take human form;
when humans violated its habitat, the *ye* bird commanded tigers to attack the trespassers. These creatures displayed a strong, defensive terri-

torial instinct, fiercely protecting their forest habitat from incursion by woodcutters and other human intruders.[57]

Yet the *muke* also figured in local legends as merchants who earnestly sold timber to Han settlers (the name *muke* could also mean "timber traders").[58] Descriptions of the silent trade between *muke* and their Han counterparts, which typically remarked upon the honesty and absence of greed among the former, are reminiscent of cross-cultural trade where linguistic barriers occasion resort to unspoken (and often unseen) forms of barter.[59] The description of the *muke* recorded by the geographer and historian Gu Yewang (519–81) betrays common Han Chinese perceptions of the inhabitants of the southern wilderness as semihuman aborigines:

> Shangluo Mountain in Ganzhou [southern Jiangxi] is full of *muke*, who are kindred to ghouls *[gui]*. In physical form, and also in speech, they resemble humans. From afar they can be seen distinctly, but when you approach them they retreat into hiding. They are skilled at felling timber of fir and sandalwood, which they pile up atop high ridges. When trading with humans, they exchange timber for knives and axes. The person making the trade sets down the goods to be exchanged beside the cut timber, then withdraws to a remote spot. The *muke* come forward to collect the trade items, leaving a quantity of timber proportional to the value of the goods they take. In conducting trade the *muke* are highly reliable and never cheat others. When a death occurs among them, they wail and mourn, and bury the departed in a coffin.[60]

Gu remarked approvingly upon the essential fairness of the *muke* in commercial transactions and their humanlike emotional attachments, which distinguished them from mere animals.[61] Nonetheless, Gu clearly discriminated between the cretinous *muke* and the human race to which he belonged. The poet Liu Yuxi (772–842), exiled to the recesses of the Nanling Mountains, described the region's aboriginal inhabitants, called Mak Yao by Tang Chinese, as blood relatives of the *muke,* with whom they shared common attributes and mysterious powers:

> The Mak Yao once born and grown,
> Take names and epithets, but lack tallies and registers,
> In market and trade they mingle with shark-dragon men,
> In wedding and marriage they intermix with the "tree lodgers."
> By the sites of stars they divine the eyes of springs,
> By sowing with fire they open up the spines of mountains,
> At night they cross gorges of a thousand fathoms,
> The sand mouthers have no power to spurt at them.[62]

Liu Yuxi's older contemporary and fellow exile Han Yu (768–824) likewise wrote that the aborigines of the Nanling "resembled langurs and macaques," the lanky, long-tailed monkeys prevalent in the forests of south China.[63]

Shanxiao also were viewed as baleful creatures capable of inflicting harm on humans. The *Classic of Spirits and Prodigies* (ca. 200 C.E.) describes the *shanzao/shansao* as a species of human being more than ten feet in height inhabiting the remote mountains of the west. The *shanzao,* which went about naked, fed on crustaceans and were said to seek fire from humans to cook their catch.[64] Wei Zhao recorded that *shansao* was the name the Viet peoples, the original inhabitants of the south China littoral, gave to the *kui* mountain spirits.[65] Similarly, Zu Chongzhi claimed that *shanzao* was a colloquial name in upland Zhejiang for one-legged anthropoid demons that preyed on humans.[66] A gazetteer of southern Zhejiang spoke of mountain-dwelling monopode demons who were fond of crabs and salt (which they stole from woodcutters); humans who crossed them invariably suffered harm.[67]

The attributes of creatures known as *shandu* or *shanxiao*—short stature, hairy body, humanlike face, whistling or laughing cries, speed in moving through the forest, and a predilection for eating crustaceans— all are reminiscent of primates, particularly the langurs and macaques indigenous to the region.[68] It seems likely that these demonic images derived from frightening encounters with denizens of the mountains, both human and ape. By Tang times the various strands of local legend and demon lore had been woven together into a common narrative of baleful mountain-dwelling demons known generically as *shanxiao.* Duan Chengshi collapsed all these creatures, including the *hui* of Ge Hong, the *shanzao* of the *Classic of Spirits and Prodigies,* and the *ye* bird, into the single category of *shanxiao,* which perhaps can best be rendered as "mountain goblins."[69]

Another archetypal image of the *shanxiao* appears in a ninth-century tale in which the *shanxiao* were said to be aged tree spirits that can assume a variety of human guises, both pathetic (beggars clutching infants) and seductive (beautiful women adorned in elegant dress). These *shanxiao* were poltergeists who caused all sorts of minor mischief, such as sitting on the eaves of a house and throwing roof tiles. Though usually not hostile to humans, they were capable of deadly violence if offended.[70] Interaction between Han Chinese and the *shanxiao* also took the form of seduction. *Shanxiao,* like restless wandering ghosts, might seek the comfort of human companionship. A twelfth-century tale recounts the story of a firewood gatherer in southern Fujian who one day returns with a one-legged bride. The strange woman failed to arise from her bed the next day, however, and when family members entered her chamber they found only a skeleton. Her trousseau chest was opened, but it contained nothing except tiles, stones, and paper money offerings for the dead. The family concluded that this woman was actually a *shanxiao.*[71] Though sexual encounters between humans and *shanxiao* do not appear in the folklore of Tang times and earlier, Song tales of *shanxiao* typically pivoted on the dangers of sexual predation posed by the one-legged mountain goblins. These themes of seduction and greed also pervaded the nascent cult of the Wutong spirits, who originated as a species of *shanxiao.*

Older myths concerning the *hui/kui* described them simply as denizens of the mountain wilderness, but the anomaly lore of the Era of Disunion and later times located the *shandu/shanxiao* specifically in the Wuyi and Nanling mountain ranges extending southward from the Yangzi River valley to Vietnam, the territories of the ancient Viet peoples. Belief in *shanxiao* was especially deeply rooted in the southern reaches of the Wuyi Mountains, in the prefectures of Ganzhou in southernmost Jiangxi and adjacent Tingzhou in western Fujian. A Tang etymologist defined the *shanxiao* simply as "one-legged demons of Tingzhou."[72] Another ninth-century author, recounting the advance of Han Chinese settlement in Tingzhou, observed that as settlers cleared the forests they encountered tree-dwelling *shandu* who appeared in a variety of forms: as humans, as pigs, and as birds (the last had human heads, though, and were capable of speech). The elusive *shandu* proved difficult to eradicate until an exorcist was employed who could immobilize these creatures and prevent them from transforming into another shape.[73] Ganzhou legends about the *muke/shandu* current in the early thirteenth century describe them as demons dwelling in the deep forests who ran about naked, whistling to each other; after storms pass, the hills filled with the sounds of drums and pipes as the *shandu* sang and danced. And yet these creatures, like the *muke* described by Gu Yewang long before, also consorted with humans through the common medium of commerce.[74]

Han Chinese colonists in Tingzhou built shrines in which they offered sacrifices to the mountain goblins. A local official stationed in Tingzhou in the mid-eighth century was sufficiently vexed by such pagan cults that he penned the essay "On the Nonexistence of Shades" for the edification of his constituents.[75] One of the most notorious of these mountain goblin cults was that of the Seven Sisters (Qiguzi), whose shrines and temples were found throughout Tingzhou and Ganzhou. The local inhabitants regarded the Seven Sisters as malicious spirits, yet nonetheless provided them with sacrificial offerings in hopes of warding off their afflictions.[76] Zhou Mi, the prolific late Song writer who generally expressed strong skepticism toward claims about the potency of spirits, nonetheless gave eyewitness testimony of the supernatural powers of the Seven Sisters. Zhou's father, upon his assignment as prefect of Tingzhou in 1255, intended to remove the Seven Sisters shrine he found within the prefectural examination hall. After a demonstration of the spirits' ability to work miracles, however, Zhou instead had the shrine renovated.[77] The Wutong likewise were widely venerated in Tingzhou as *shanxiao* spirits.

The *shanxiao* lore of Tang-Song times, although drawing on older images of mountain goblins, cast them in a new role as the hostile, barbaric forces resisting the relentless onslaught of Han Chinese expansion into the untamed southern wilderness. The following anecdote from Dai Fu's (fl. 738–94) *Wide World of Marvels*, although edged with sharp reminders of the dangers posed by the *shanxiao*, nonetheless underscores the symbiotic, if fragile, economy of mutual exchange that developed between the indigenous lords of the forest and the new colonists from the north:

> The *shanxiao* are found everywhere in the Nanling ranges. They are monopodes with inverted heels and three claws on their hands and feet. They make their nests in the hollows of great trees; these nests have wooden screens to shield them from the wind and are amply supplied with food. When southerners travel in the mountains they usually carry powder, rouge, cash, and other items with them. The male *shanxiao*, which are called *shangong* [sire of the mountain], invariably demand gold and coin; but if you encounter a female, known as *shangu* [lady of the mountain], she will demand powder and rouge instead. If you give them what they want, they will protect you.
>
> In the Tianbao period of the Tang dynasty (742–55) there was a stranger from the north traveling in the mountains of the Nanling. At nightfall, because of his great fear of tigers, he tried to climb a tree in order to pass the night there. Suddenly he encountered a female *shanxiao* among the branches. The traveler habitually carried money for expenses, so he climbed down from the tree, bowed deeply, and called out "Shangu!" From out of the tree a voice asked, "What goods do you have?" The traveler then presented her with powder and rouge, which pleased her immensely. "You may rest comfortably without any cause for fear," she told him. The man spent the night beneath the tree. In the middle of the night two tigers approached, but the *shanxiao* descended and stroked their heads, saying, "Striped ones, he is my guest. You'd best leave quickly." The two tigers then departed. The next morning, when the traveler took his leave, she thanked him graciously.
>
> What's difficult to fathom is that every year the *shanxiao* work in the fields together with humans. When humans come out to the fields to sow their grain, they find that the remaining fallow ground has been cultivated

by *shanxiao.* When the crops ripen, the *shanxiao* come forward to divide the harvest. By nature they are simple and honest. When dividing the harvest they never take more than their portion. Humans also dare not take more than their share; otherwise they will suffer heaven-sent illness and plague.[78]

In Dai Fu's telling, the *shanxiao* were feral creatures, kindred to tigers and other dangerous creatures of the forest. Yet at the same time the *shanxiao* displayed the all-too-human vices of vanity and greed. Though Dai Fu ridiculed their petty avarice, like other observers he also applauded their fairness and honesty in dealings with humans. The uneasy coexistence between humans and *shanxiao* depicted in Dai's anecdote undoubtedly testifies to the frictions, and potential for violent confrontation, between Han Chinese and the indigenous inhabitants of the mountain recesses of south China.[79]

Thus the *shanxiao* lore also reiterated the intensifying struggle between civilization and barbarism that accompanied the southward push of Han settlement. Old legends of mountain-dwelling goblins and fairies were revived in the dread image of the *shanxiao*, nimble poltergeists, denizens of the wilderness who stubbornly—if ineffectually—resisted the inexorable advance of Han civilization. Like the inveterate enemies of the northern frontier, the steppe nomads, the *shanxiao* oscillated between the roles of violent predators and benign trading partners in their relations with Han settlers.[80] But the Han could not discern, in the natives of the southern mountains no less than the misshapen, bestial *shanxiao,* any resemblance to members of the civilized races such as themselves. On the contrary, Han perceptions of the indigenous species of the southern forests, both human and animal, fused into the composite image of the *shanxiao,* one that inspired fear and loathing, and occasionally pity.

CHAPTER 4

Plague Demons
and Epidemic Gods

For noble and commoner alike, the scourge of illness was perhaps the most compelling evidence for the existence of demons. Chinese attributed illness, like misfortune in general, either to adventitious affliction by some malefic entity or to just punishment inflicted on the victim for his or her own moral transgressions. Thus the agents of sickness and plague were sometimes perceived as demons, and in other cases as the minions of divine justice. This ambiguity was also characteristic of the Wutong cult. Wutong was feared as an evil spirit that visited sickness and other miseries on luckless innocents, yet Wutong also appeared as a benevolent god who delivered the community from plague. In Wutong, the demonic and the divine were folded into a single entity. In the realm of illness and disease, as in Chinese religion in general, the emphasis shifted away from ancestors or malevolent ghosts toward gods and their underlings as the primary sources of supernatural affliction. From the Song dynasty onward a class of specialized gods emerged to whom communities would appeal for deliverance from the ravages of epidemic disease. Some of these gods were portrayed as stalwart champions of their mortal clients, but in other cases plague deities shaded toward the demonic, for they were perceived as both cause and cure.

An abiding concern with illness and its causes and remedies appears already in the Shang oracle bone divinations, which were principally devoted to securing the well-being of the Shang ruling class. The Shang attributed many physical infirmities to a common etiology: the curse of an ancestor. To the Shang, illness was not a discrete set of pathologies to be treated by specific therapies collectively categorized as "medicine." Instead, illness, like war and harvest failure, was an ominous symptom of a rupture in the reciprocal economy of exchange between deified ancestors and their mortal descendants. In the oracle bone inscriptions, the word "curse" (sui) generally signified illnesses inflicted by direct ancestors or other spirits of the dead. Treatment therefore centered on placating the offended spirit with offerings and reestablishing ritual harmony between the dead and the living. The Shang apparently also believed that some illnesses resulted from demonic affliction in the form of "evil wind." But there is no evidence that the Shang utilized drugs or any other kind of medication to cure illness, nor do we find a group of healers other than the diviners who interpreted oracles received from the dead.[1]

Belief in demonic causes of illness remained prominent in the Zhou and Han eras as well. Despite the efforts on the part of the Zhou to eradicate the ancestor cults of the Shang, the belief that the dead could harm the living persisted, spurring the invention of exorcistic therapies to combat demonic attack. Whereas the Shang concept of illness revolved around propitiation of dead kin and nurturing the symbiosis of ancestors and descendants, Zhou lore tended to emphasize the malevolence of the dead, particularly ghosts seeking revenge. A cogent example of Zhou belief in the demonic nature of illness appears in the *Chronicles of Zuo*'s account of the sudden death of the Marquis of Jin in 581 B.C.E. The marquis is reported to have had a dream in which he was visited by an ancestral spirit of the Zhao lineage, which the marquis had ruthlessly massacred two years before. The giant, menacing figure—readily recognizable as a demon by his "disheveled, unbound hair hanging to the ground"— gravely announced that he had petitioned the Celestial Thearch for permission to punish the marquis for his iniquity, and the supreme deity had granted his request. Sure enough, the marquis was struck by a sickness that neither spirit mediums nor physicians could cure, and he died soon after.[2] The belief that the ghosts of the wrongfully dead exacted revenge by inflicting illness on those responsible for their deaths endured in popular belief throughout Chinese history.

But demonic affliction did not necessarily spring from this kind of personal animus. Sudden outbreaks of disease or perturbations of the mind were often regarded as random events caused by malignant, though not necessarily evil, entities. The entries in the *Classic of the Mountains and Seas* suggest that the most common maladies travelers in strange lands were likely to suffer were derangement (huo) and malefic poisoning (gu).[3]

"Derangement" was a general term for infections of the mind that caused delusions, erratic behavior, and physical illness. Episodes of *huo* were typically blamed on demonic possession. *Gu,* already identified in the Shang oracle bones as a baneful affliction, appears to have been a general term for black magic, but *gu* also denoted a variety of debilitating illnesses.[4] One of the most systematic discussions of *gu* appears in a famous dialogue between a later Marquis of Jin and the renowned physician He recorded in the *Chronicles of Zuo.* In 541 B.C.E., the marquis fell ill and summoned He to cure him. Physician He diagnosed the marquis's ailment as a case of *gu,* which He described as a degenerative illness caused by sensual, especially sexual, indulgence. The learned doctor advised his patient that the most certain cure required that the marquis rein in his unbridled concupiscence.[5] The connection between *gu* and seduction by women insinuated in Physician He's admonitions also informed the widespread conviction that *gu* was a form of witchcraft. *Wugu,* or black magic practiced by sorcerers, figured in the most notorious witchcraft scandal of the Han dynasty, which occurred in 91 B.C.E., in the twilight years of the megalomaniac emperor Wu (r. 140–87 B.C.E.). This case, which was rife with sexual innuendo, centered on accusations that certain officials and even imperial princesses had used *gu* witchcraft in an attempt on the aged emperor's life. The hysteria whipped up by these charges, the investigations they prompted, and the recriminations launched by the targets of the accusers resulted in hundreds of deaths, including the executions of the most powerful civil official in the empire and two of Wu's daughters.[6] In this instance the sorcerers allegedly employed effigies and spells to curse their victims, but in later accounts *gu* witchcraft involved the use of poisons concocted from venomous reptiles and insects. Physician He identified *gu* with flying insects spawned by rotting grain, and later texts linked *gu* to maggots; such associations echoed the common belief that parasitic worms living in the human body could cause illness and death.[7]

The earliest surviving medical literature demonstrates that belief in the demonic origins of illness was deeply entrenched at the highest levels of Han society. The ancient medical treatise *Recipes for Fifty-Two Ailments,* recovered from the early Han tombs at Mawangdui (dated to 168 B.C.E.), prescribed a broad range of therapies for the alleviation of common ailments, both internal and external. What is striking about these remedies is their frequent recourse to spells and other exorcistic techniques such as ritual dances, magical weapons, and purgative drugs. From the evidence of this text, which probably drew on a medical tradition dating back to the Warring States period, we can conclude that physicians routinely engaged in exorcism, uttering maledictions against invasive demons and summoning spirits to drive them out of the victim's body. The use of these exorcistic incantations demonstrates once again the conviction that knowledge of a demon's identity endowed one with power over it.[8]

The rise of correlative cosmology in the Warring States and early Han periods profoundly altered Chinese conceptions of disease and medicine. Human anatomy and, even more importantly, the functions of the body were easily analogized to the organic processes of cyclical change, depletion, and renewal embedded in Five Phases and *yin/yang* cosmologies. These ideas crystallized into a sizable corpus of homeopathic medicine that linked the microcosmic functions of the body to the macrocosmic phenomena of the natural world. This emerging medical discourse postulated that human physiology was governed not only by the individual's own actions, but also by the movements of celestial bodies, the alternation of the seasons, and the constantly changing natural environment. The salience of any particular set of these ruling principles at a given time dictated the proper means of regulating the body through consumption of food and drink; schedules of movement and rest; choice of clothing, lodging, and all other appurtenances of daily life; and discipline of conduct and the emotions. The new medical tradition represented the correlations between the functions of the body and their governing macrocosmic forces in terms of *qi,* which in this context perhaps can be translated as "vital humors." Illness resulted from disruption of the normative rhythms of the body, which in turn was attributed not to evil demons but to "pathogenic humors" *(xieqi).* The therapies generated by this medical discourse spurned exorcistic practices in favor of regulation of the body and behavior in harmony with the macrocosmic environment.[9]

During the early Han dynasty, then, various theories of human physiology that disparaged demonic invasion as the principal cause of disease began to coalesce into what eventually became the classical tradition of Chinese medicine. Although antecedents of this new conception of the body can be glimpsed in the Mawangdui medical texts, it emerges clearly in the anthology of medical writings known as *The Inner Canon of Huangdi (Huangdi neijing),* compiled in the first century B.C.E.[10] The heterogeneous texts united in *The Inner Canon* did not constitute a single coherent tradition, but they established a core of basic ideas about the structure and function of the body. The body was conceived in terms of twelve functional vessels and the conduits connecting them, through which vital humors circulated. The physiology of circulation of vital humors through these vessels and conduits was based on analogy with internal organs of the body rather than anatomical evidence of the workings of specific organs, blood vessels, muscles, nerves, etc. The kidneys, for example, were classified as *yin* vessels in which the latent energetic forces of the body were concentrated, while on the psychic level the kidneys were associated with willpower and susceptibility to fear.[11] Medical therapy aimed at ensuring that vital humors circulated without obstruction through these conduits and vessels. This nascent canon of medical knowledge still admitted the importance of external influences on bodily functions, though. The application of analogical reasoning derived from correlative cosmology to the vessels of the body ramified into a complex system of correspondences between bodily functions and cosmological processes.

Essential to this new conception of the body was the idea that the individual assumed primary responsibility for his or her own health and well-being. Health and sickness were commonly expressed through political metaphors. Indeed, the transitive verb *zhi* was employed for both "cure" and "rule." The body came to be understood as a country headed by a ruler (the mind) in concert with his officials (organic processes identified with the five viscera) and populated by a coterie of spirits that animated the body and regulated its functions. As ruler of one's own body, each individual must conduct his or her life in such a way as to harmonize the vital humors within the body with the ever-changing macrocosmic *qi*.[12] Using the terms of Ge Hong's simile, the person who avoids dissipation and preserves the vitality of his body will prolong his life, just as the austere ruler who nurtures the welfare of his subjects thereby perpetuates his rule.[13]

By the second century C.E., the disparate strains of homeopathic medicine based on correlative cosmology became synthesized and codified into a "classical" canon of medical orthodoxy, one perhaps best described as "*qi* medicine."[14] Yet, while *qi* medicine triumphed as the dominant medical orthodoxy, it did not eradicate older beliefs in the demonic causes of illness and disease. Malign demons resurfaced in the subtly altered form of numinous influences, often given concrete expression as gods and spirits, emanating from celestial bodies and other phenomena of the natural world. One example is the baleful star known as Taisui, which shadowed the progress of Jupiter in its twelve-year rotation through the heavens. The "lodging" that Jupiter occupied in the firmament had its corresponding region on earth. As Jupiter moved through its celestial orbit, it brought blessings and good harvests to its terrestrial equivalent. But Taisui, moving in the reverse direction, sowed death and calamity in the regions that fell under its baleful influence. In popular belief, though, Jupiter and Taisui became conflated, and people sought to ward off the influence of Jupiter as well.[15] The two chapters of Wang Chong's book devoted to belief in baleful asterisms attest to the prevalence of the fears aroused by Jupiter/Taisui. Wang also bore witness to the frequent recourse to talismans and exorcisms to protect mortals from this chief of the spirits of pestilence.[16] The movements of another celestial spirit, Taiyi (who, as mentioned earlier, also figured as the supreme deity in official Han religion), were also linked to illness and death. The conjunction of the location of Taiyi and the direction of the wind was said to determine whether the wind would have malefic or auspicious effects. If the wind blew from the direction of Taiyi, blessings would ensue; but wind blowing in the opposite direction was an evil wind that caused sickness. The etiology of disease caused by Taisui or wind was couched in metaphors of war and combat. For example, Taisui, or alternatively wind, "launched offensives" *(chong)* against the victims of disease, who must mobilize their body's defenses ("camps" and "guards") to repel this demonic invasion.[17]

The demonic conception of disease also survived in the enduring belief that violent death left a residue of morbidity that could infect the living, a fear vividly expressed in the idea that victims of violent or premature death lingered in the mortal world as ghosts. (Indeed, another meaning of *gu* in Han times was demonic affliction caused by vengeful ghosts.) The malignant touch of these ghosts, much like the Shang curse of the ancestor, could result in potentially fatal illness. Exorcism was deemed the most effective remedy. "Ghosts of those who die violent deaths frequently inflict illness on mortals," wrote the commentator Gao You around the turn of the third century C.E., "but sorcerers are able to exterminate them by means of conjuration and inquest *(zhuhe)*."[18] The exorcist's use of spells to subject demons to summary investigation, judgment, and execution reflected his role as a magistrate of the world of shades. Just as the Lord of Mount Tai and his underlings conducted searching judicial inquiry into the mortal conduct of the dead, so too could the exorcist assume the mantle of bureaucratic authority in order to discipline and punish wayward demons.

As is true for most Chinese mythology, mythical accounts of the causes of plague appear fairly late in the written record, in texts of the

Warring States and early Han eras. One myth, evidently widespread in the Han, traced the origins of disease to the ill-fated progeny of the ancient sage-king Zhuanxu. Although Zhuanxu was celebrated in Zhou legends for siring eight talented sons who were boons to humanity, it was also said that Zhuanxu had three sons who died in childbirth and became plague demons: the fever demon *(nuegui)*, who dwelled in the Great River (presumably the Yangzi); the *wangliang* inhabiting the Ruo River[19] (elsewhere described as mountain goblins, in this instance the *wangliang* were associated with water, more properly the domain of the *wangxiang*); and a third who lurked in the dark, dank corners of human dwellings and frightened children.[20] The sons of Zhuanxu who died in childbirth clearly belonged to the category of the ghosts of those who suffered untimely deaths and continue to haunt the world of the living. According to Cai Yong (132–92), the Great Exorcism (Nuo), one of the most important rites of the Han court's ceremonial calendar, was performed primarily to drive these plague demons from the palace precincts.[21]

The Great Exorcism was a spectacular ritual conducted at the time of the midwinter La festival, when the cosmic powers of death and decay were at their height, to expel demonic influences prior to the inauguration of the New Year. The Great Exorcism is best known through descriptions of its performance in connection with the state cult, but similar rites were conducted by the populace at large.[22] The most detailed account of the Great Exorcism appears in the poet Zhang Heng's (78–139) "Ode to the Eastern Capital." In Zhang's description of the Great Exorcism, the chief exorcist, known as the *fangxiang,* donned an animal mask and led an assembly of officials through a series of purgations aimed at eradicating twelve classes of baleful demons. Palace attendants clad in fur, feathers, and horns masqueraded as the evil demons. The exorcist called upon specific deities to "devour" the demons, and with a great flourish of weapons the assembly dispatched each group in a specific manner of execution (e.g., mutilation, decapitation, or drowning).[23] Although little is known of the character of the plague-expelling deities invoked to repel the demons, it seems that they were associated with both the twelve months of the year and the twelve points of the compass, and thus represented guardian deities deployed across both space and time.[24]

The Great Exorcism thus was a rite of mortification and purification wherein exorcists impersonated spirits in order to stage a ritual combat against the specters of pestilence, drought, flood, and other calamities. The *Rituals of Zhou* described the *fangxiang* who presided over the Great Exorcism as "clad in a black tunic and crimson robe and having a bear (or tiger) skin with four golden eyes draped over his head, while grasping a lance and shield in his hands."[25] The bear headdress with four golden eyes suggests a totemic mask that endowed the wearer with supernatural powers, and many authors have concluded that the *fangxiang* was a type of shaman. William Boltz argues convincingly for seeing the *fangxiang* as a conjurer of visions, a phantasmagoricist who enables the troops of exorcists under his command to visualize and then put to death the multitude of specters that afflict humankind.[26] But the *fangxiang* was indeed a shaman in the sense that he was someone who impersonated the demonic spirits he sought to exterminate. The striking semantic resemblance between the names of the *fangxiang* and his chief adversary, the demonic *fangliang,* reinforces this sense of the *fangxiang* as a positive alter ego of the forces of disorder. Impersonation of spirits as a means of enabling mortals to communicate with them was a common feature of Chinese religious life. The *Odes* describes the use of mediums in ancestral rites to impersonate the dead and enable them to partake of the food offerings sacrificed to them, a practice that was still current in the Han dynasty.[27]

Although the Great Exorcism also aimed at eradicating demons representing calamities of fire and water, its main theme was the expulsion of pestilence *(zhuyi, zhuli).*[28] Individual households also performed rituals of expiation known as Nuo on the eve of the New Year as a means of protecting family members from sickness and pestilence.[29] One of these Nuo rites, recorded in a Han prognostication text but apparently plebeian in origin, involved tossing beans, sesame seeds, and locks of family members' hair into the household well while uttering a spell invoking the well spirit's protection against the "plague demons of the five directions" *(wufang yigui).*[30] In Tang times, Huangdi was credited with inventing the Nuo ritual as a means of expelling "evil specters" *(yaojing),* "fevers" *(zhen),* and "drifting, wandering, floating ghosts." Rather than annihilating these malign spirits, though, the ritual was supposed to banish them beyond the frontiers, at a safe remove from the community. This theme of expulsion of pestilential spirits outside the boundaries of the community later became a common motif of plague cults. We find no mention of the *fangxiang* exorcist in descriptions of the popular Nuo of Tang times. Instead, the ritual typically invoked the demonifuge spirit Zhong Kui to drive away malicious spirits, though in some cases the deities of the underworld such as Yama, the Lord of Mount Tai, or the General of the Five Paths of Rebirth (Wudao jiangjun) were summoned to reclaim the vagabond souls of the dead.[31]

Of the twelve classes of demons mentioned by Zhang Heng as targets of the Great Exorcism, the only ones specifically linked to plague and epidemic were mysterious specters known as the Wild Youths and Roving Lights (yezhong[32] youguang). Xue Zong (d. 243), in his gloss on Zhang's poem, identified the Wild Youths and Roving Lights as "evil spirits," adding that they were a group of eight brothers who often engaged in malice in the world of mortals.[33] The Dunhuang manuscript of the Album of the Specters and Apparitions of White Marsh also identified the Wild Youths and Roving Lights as a demon gang of eight brothers whose appearance foretells many deaths from plague throughout the empire.[34] The illustration accompanying this passage depicts a group of eight youths surrounding a fire-cart (figure 13). The fire-cart may reflect Buddhist influence; in the Treatise of the Perfection of Wisdom, one of the most influential Mahāyāna texts in Chinese Buddhism, sinners are transported to hell in a fire-cart, and later Buddhist depictions of the underworld include a "fire-cart hell."[35] But the fire-cart also symbolized an excess of yang humors, believed to be one of the chief causes of sickness. Already in Han times the Roving Lights plague spirits were associated with exorcisms conducted on Double Fifth (Duanwu, the fifth day of the fifth month), which immediately preceded the summer solstice, the apogee of fiery yang influence, as well as the midwinter Great Exorcism. The winter and summer solstices were deemed the most dangerous times of the year, because mortals were especially susceptible to demonic invasion at these times of extreme imbalances of yin (winter) and yang (summer) influences in the cosmos. Not surprisingly, then, the rituals performed both on Double Fifth and at the midwinter La festival, held around the time of the winter solstice, were principally devoted to exorcising baleful forces.

The association of disease with the hot, humid climate of the south, the direction of fiery yang, and the increased activity of insects and other loathsome vermin during the summer probably reinforced the notion that the fifth month was a time of great vulnerability to disease. Indeed, throughout the entire fifth lunar month Chinese scrupulously obeyed numerous taboos and took precautions to protect themselves from pestilence and other kinds of misfortune. As the Han ritual calendar, the Monthly Ordinances (Yueling), observed:

Figure 13. Wild Youths and Roving Lights, depicted pulling a fire-cart. The caption reads: "When abroad at night one might see the light of a fire, and underneath it several tens of youths who carry a fire-cart on their heads. These creatures constitute a single group, but they are given the names 'Roving Lights' and 'Wild Youths.' If you see them, the empire will be afflicted by epidemic and death. The youths are eight brothers." Dunhuang ms. of *Album of the Specters and Apparitions of White Marsh,* ninth to tenth century. From Pelliot no. 2682, rpt. in *Dunhuang baozang* 123: 287. Courtesy of the Bibliothèque nationale de France © BnF.

> In [the fifth] month the days attain their greatest length. Then *yin* again contends with *yang,* and death once again begins to overtake life. The su-perior man fasts and follows ritual taboos, remaining in retirement at home and avoiding violent activity. He puts a halt to music and spectacles, keeps his distance from women, curbs his intake of food, and avoids spicy flavors. He restrains his desires and soothes his spirit. The corps of officials cease judicial proceedings and inflict no corporal punishments. In these ways the transition to Ascending Yin can proceed in orderly fashion.[36]

The extremes of *yin* and *yang* were equally hazardous during this limi-nal period of cosmological transition. Ying Shao, writing in the late sec-ond century, mentioned the custom of "wearing the five colors to ward off the five weapons" (*wubing;* a metaphor for demonic attack) at the time of the summer solstice in connection with exorcising the Roving Lights demons. Ying reported that an epidemic that swept through the capital during the Yongjian reign period (126–31 C.E.) was blamed on plague demons known as the Wild Youths and Roving Lights. Afterward people ascribed outbreaks of epidemic to these same demons and wore five-colored silk cloths embroidered with the legend "Roving Lights" to render themselves immune. "Wearing the five colors," Ying explained, referred to attaching small pieces of green, red, white, black, and yellow silk to one's clothing as protective amulets.[37] Colored silk streamers also were tied to the entrance gates of homes to ward off plague. Plague exorcism rites grew increasingly elaborate during the Era of Disunion. A sixth-century work on annual festivals reports that in south China on Double Fifth people used mugwort (which, because of its red color and pungent aroma, was regarded as a powerful vermifuge) to bind up effigies (presumably representing the plague demons) and hang them from their gateways in order to dispel "pathogenic humors." They also wore colored silk ribbons attached to their sleeves, and silently intoned the name of the "demonic Roving Lights" to protect themselves against infection from virulent disease.[38]

The Great Exorcism and Double Fifth rituals both portray the expulsion of plague demons as a violent combat against heinous, terrifying creatures. In many remedies for demonic affliction preserved in the *Recipes for Fifty-Two Ailments,* the physician or the spirits he conjures subjugate the demon by violent means, using magical weapons such as a rammer, a thuja-wood pestle, or an iron hammer.[39] A relief carving from the Wu family shrine, constructed in the mid-second century C.E., very likely illustrates a conjurer engaged in just such an exorcism. The relief shows two figures, one wielding an axe and the other a hammer, coming to the rescue of the central figure, who is writhing in the clutches of a snake (the snake, of course, was a common metaphor for demonic affliction). Another figure, with fin-shaped legs, gesticulates in the background; this figure presumably is a spirit medium summoning the warrior spirits to kill or expel the demon.[40] Ying Shao's invocation of the five weapons as a metaphor for attack by plague demons undoubtedly alludes to Chiyou, the reputed creator of the five weapons. As noted in chapter 1, Chiyou was venerated in Han times as an apotropaic deity who uses his formidable arsenal to drive off evil spirits. Indeed, the *fangxiang* exorcist described in the *Rituals of Zhou* closely resembles descriptions of Chiyou, and it has been argued that the *fangxiang* assumes the alter ego of Chiyou to conduct the Great Exorcism.[41] A Han relief carving from a second-century C.E. tomb, which has been identified as an illustration of the Great Exorcism rite, portrays Chiyou as a demonifuge acting at the behest of the *fangxiang* exorcist (figure 14).[42] In this frieze, the figure at the far right, wearing a headdress with bearlike ears, is shown in the act of devouring a man, which recalls the metaphorical use of "devour" to connote demonic attack. The cannibal, undoubtedly a demon, is confronted by another fantastic bearlike creature flourishing five weapons, most notably a crossbow above his head. This figure, which appears repeatedly in Han mortuary art, can be firmly identified as Chiyou.[43] To Chiyou's right stands another figure, presumably the *fangxiang* exorcist, with a bear headdress and holding a shield and sword. Behind the *fangxiang* a series of figures run toward the demon carrying not conventional weapons but rather ladles, spades, and a flask. These demonifuge spirits battle demons by dousing them with some sort of purgative water or elixir. The efficacy of purgative waters for dispelling demonic invasion is well attested in other Han sources.[44] The mural's depiction of illness and cure as a mortal combat between violent demons and guardian warrior spirits again reminds us of the martial metaphors commonly used in Han medical texts.

In addition to rites of exorcistic combat tied to the ritual calendar, Chinese of the Han era employed a wide variety of charms and talismans to ward off sickness and plague. Recourse to such devices was at least as common as use of medicinal substances to cure illness. Among the flora and fauna mentioned in the older sections of the *Classic of the Mountains and Seas,* thirty-nine species are identified as having medicinal (primarily demonifugic) value and twenty-nine were worn on the body for protection against demons.[45] Wearing talismans and amulets prepared by sorcerers and priests was a common practice among all ranks of society. For example, a girdle ornament known as a *gangmao,* made of jade, ivory, metal, or peach wood and engraved with an apotropaic charm, was worn on the body as protection against illness (figure 15).[46] We have already encountered Ge Hong's claims that possession of sacred books like the *Writs of the Three Sovereigns* protected one's home from various malign influences, including "humors of illness and plague." Similarly, if travelers carried on their person the diagram of the True Image of the Southern Marchmount (south being the direction of fire and plague), "the five kinds of pestilence will not draw near."[47] The wood of peach and thuja trees was deemed especially baneful to demons. Many of the remedies included in the third-century B.C.E. "spellbinding" text involved making weapons such as arrows, hammers, swords, or staves out of jujube, mulberry, or peach wood.[48] Door guardians representing

Figure 14. Chiyou and exorcism. In this stone carving from a Han ancestral shrine, a demon at far right is about to swallow its miniature victim. Chiyou, brandishing his characteristic five weapons, leads a file of demonifuge spirits armed with shovels, ladles, and urns to exorcise the demon. Rear Chamber, Wu Family Shrines, Jiaxiang, Shandong. Ca. 150 C.E. From Hayashi 1989, supplemental plate 17.

Figure 15. Gangmao amulet. The inscription on the amulet on the right reads: "First month of the year, zenith of firm *mao* day. This divine wand is made foursquare; red, blue, white, yellow, the four colors inhere in it. The Thearch [Di] commands Zhurong [ruler of fire] to instruct the *kui* and dragons. Vile vermin and foul pestilence, none dare defy me." The left can be tentatively translated as: " Inauspicious day, harsh *mao*. The Thearch commands the changeling *kui*. Obedient, they surely yield, transforming this divine wand. So balanced, so square; so even, so straight. Vile vermin and foul pestilence, none dare defy me." From Tianjinshi yishu bowuguan 1993, plate 124. Courtesy of the Tianjin Municipal Museum of Art.

the demonifuge spirits Shenshu and Yulü also were typically carved from peach wood, reflecting a tradition said to have been initiated by Huangdi himself.[49]

The emerging canon of *qi* medicine explicitly condemned belief in demonic origins of illness and epidemic as vulgar superstitions. Wang Chong, diligently seeking rational explanations for mysterious phenomena, scoffed at his contemporaries' misguided belief in ghosts as agents of disease, which to his mind was rooted in terror of the unknown:

> Ghosts in this world are not apparitions of the spirits of the deceased; rather, they are spawned from the thoughts and ideas of men. Whence do these thoughts arise? Why, from illness. When men fall ill they become anxious and fearful, and in this state of mind they begin to see ghosts. None who are in good health entertain such anxieties and fears. Thus those confined to sickbeds live in terror of ghosts coming after them; once these anxieties are fixed in the mind, then the eye sees what does not exist.[50]

In Wang's view, human frailty, both of body and spirit, readily explained the tenacity of belief in ghosts and spirits. A fragment of a lost chapter of the *Zhuangzi* ridicules popular beliefs, too, but it also suggests that exorcism rituals actually had therapeutic value, even if the credulous masses failed to understand it:

> The Roaming Bird asked Xiong Huang, "Why is it that nowadays people strike drums and cry and shout to expel demons and ward off plague?"
> Xiong Huang replied: "The black-headed masses suffer from many illnesses. Thus, Huangdi dispatched Sorcerer Xian, who instructed the black-headed masses to perform ablutions and fasting in order to open up the Nine Apertures; to strike drums and ring bells in order to rouse their hearts; to exercise their bodies marching in processions in order to stimulate the *yin* and *yang* humors; to drink wine and consume vegetarian feasts in order to unblock the Five Viscera. As for striking drums and crying and shouting to expel demons and ward off plague, it is simply a matter of the black-headed masses, in their ignorance, believing that illness is caused by demonic curse."[51]

The author of this passage provided a rational basis, grounded in the precepts of *qi* medicine, for exorcism rituals. Although belief in demons could be dismissed as mere superstition, the physical activity of ritual performance had the beneficial effect of stimulating the circulation of vital humors throughout the body. But the strident tone of skeptics who derided belief in demonic affliction in itself bears witness to its tenacious hold on popular psychology.

Wang Chong, too, subscribed to the new medical orthodoxy based on *qi* humors. He attributed disease to somatic causes, especially inadequate hygiene and nutrition, that produced imbalances in the body's vital humors. Even more important in the spread of disease, though, was human ignorance of the real etiology of illness:

> Among the acute diseases afflicting humankind, rare are those that are not caused by wind and damp, or food and drink. After falling ill from exposure to wind or sleeping in the damp, the vulgar masses foolishly empty their purses and hire soothsayers to determine the cause of the curse they believe has been laid upon them. And after stuffing their bellies in gluttonous feasting, such people devote themselves to fasting and bathing to dispel the sickness that results. If the illness does not abate, it is said that the exorcism was not performed properly; if the patient dies, then the medium is blamed for committing some ritual error. . . .
> In cases where many people die in a brief span of time, with as many as ten coffins interred at once, people do not attribute the deaths to a contamination of *qi*, but rather to a baneful day of interment. Misfortune is blamed on some ritual transgression, rather than finding a cause in the physical

conditions of their existence: namely, the dilapidated, uninhabitable houses in which they live, infested with vermin and infected by putrifying corpses.[52] Crowded together in such hovels, these unfortunates pray to their ancestors to alleviate the calamities that have befallen them. In cases of acute illness they do not seek the counsel of physicians, but rather harbor dire fears of lapses in ritual piety.[53]

Elsewhere, Wang Chong's convictions about the environmental causes of disease led him to argue that the southern regions of the empire were unfit for human habitation. The toxic "fierce qi" of the hot, fetid south, the land of "Great Yang," infected not only the landscape and its creatures, but also the human beings who dwelled there. "The people of Chu and Yue are frenzied and febrile," Wang—himself a native of Yue (modern Zhejiang)—declaimed. "When southerners curse a tree, it dies; when they spit at a bird, it falls dead." It was precisely because of their birth "south of the Great River" that southern sorcerers possessed the power to cure the sick or curse the healthy by means of spells and incantations. By the same token, the myriad creatures of the south were exceedingly poisonous and injurious to humans. While the ignorant say that these creatures are "demons," in fact their morbidity is a result of the pathological excess of Great Yang characteristic of the southern regions.[54] Wang could thus comfortably reconcile the vaunted efficacy of the spells of southern sorcerers and the prevalence of disease in the south with his faith in the tenets of qi medicine.

But Wang Chong also delineated a moral etiology of plague, one that reaffirmed prevailing concepts of divine retribution. In his rebuttal against claims that the Great Exorcism was necessary to prevent epidemics, Wang argued that pestilence and other calamities act as barometers of the ruler's virtue. Thus the virtuous sage-kings of antiquity required no recourse to sorcerers and exorcists, but the reign of evil in the days of the tyrants Jie and Zhou unleashed rampant disease and devastation.[55] Wang shared with the learned men of his time the belief that a supreme deity governed human existence and expressed displeasure with or approval of the ruler's actions through "disasters and marvels."[56] In the new religious movements of the later Han dynasty, this notion of divine retribution became fused with an apocalyptic messianism, producing a radically different understanding of illness that rejected both the exorcistic practices of the *fangshi* and the homeopathic therapies of qi medicine.

The founders of the Celestial Masters and Great Peace sects in the second century C.E., Zhang Lu and Zhang Jue, first gained audiences as preachers and healers. Both sects rejected conventional medical arts and insisted that faith healing alone could cure the ills that tormented humanity. Although these religious teachers shared their contemporaries' beliefs in the demonic origin of illness, they also impressed on their followers the stern warning that illness was a punishment for moral transgressions. Invading demons were not simply malevolent parasites, but rather agents of moral authority acting in the name of divine judgment. Thus healing must begin with contrition and penance. Confession of sins was central to both the Celestial Masters and Great Peace sects. The Celestial Masters congregations practiced mass rituals of confession and penitence; in addition, they stipulated that victims of illness must write letters of repentance to the ruling gods of heaven, earth, and water (the Sanguan or Three Offices) seeking absolution for their sins. Similarly, the healing regimen propagated by Zhang Jue consisted of a threefold formula of repentance, absolution, and exorcism. Once the stricken person had demonstrated remorse and pledged to sin no more, the priest prepared a talisman that served as a warrant summoning spirit warriors to come to the aid of the victim. The talisman was then burned and immersed in consecrated water, which the victim drank. Finally, marshalling the spirit warriors through spells and ritual dance, the priest exorcised the disease and restored the victim to health.[57]

The idea that illness was punishment for moral and ritual transgressions of course dated back at least to the Shang dynasty. But the correlative cosmology that dominated Warring States and Han thought largely ignored the causes and conditions of individual existence and focused instead on the supreme role of the ruler in maintaining cosmic harmony. The "tremblings of heaven," omens of misfortune that would touch all of the empire's subjects, occupied the attention of rulers and their officials. The new religious movements of the Later Han, in contrast, shifted the site of divine retribution from the macrocosmic level of the empire to the microcosmic level of the individual person. The *Canon of Great Peace (Taipingjing)*, revered as revealed scripture by the Celestial Masters and Great Peace sects, condemned the evils of the present era while offering a vision of a reformed society in which each individual contributed to order and peace by fulfilling the duties of their calling. The *Canon* thus assigned to individuals a personal moral responsibility largely absent from the classical traditions of political philosophy. Once individuals assumed the burden of responsibility for their own actions, the ruler could attain the ideal of ruling by nonaction celebrated in the *Dao De Jing*.[58]

The moral order envisioned in the *Canon of Great Peace* rested on a bureaucratic infrastructure of gods and spirits engaged in constant surveillance of the individual's conduct. Every sin was duly reported to the divine authorities, who subtracted a corresponding number of days, months, or years from the miscreant's life span. Ge Hong, writing in the early fourth century, identified these watch-guard spirits as the Three Worms (Sanshi), which dwelled within the body and on every *gengshen* day (one of the sixty days of the Chinese calendrical cycle) reported the person's evil deeds to the Sovereign of Life Destiny (Siming), who adjusted the person's life span accordingly.[59] The Three Worms were believed to actively seek the death of their host, and so became objects of fear and loathing.[60] Yet in the eyes of the new religious movements, the agents of disease were not malevolent demons at all, but rather legitimate spirits duly deputized by the supreme gods to punish sinners. The plague demons of yore now became transfigured into deities acting as emissaries of divine justice.

The Daoist literature of the Era of Disunion spells out in detail the names, titles, and functions of these plague deities. Among the lengthy rosters of demons recorded in the *Demon Register of Nüqing,* a Celestial Masters text believed to date from the late fourth century, we find five "demon masters of the Five Directions" *(wufang guizhu)* dispatched by the supreme deities to punish the wicked and eradicate evil from the world of mortals. Each of the demon masters commands legions of plague demons who visit maladies on sinners (table 1).[61] Knowledge of the esoteric names of the demons and deities responsible for particular types of ailment or affliction that were recorded in the *Demon Register of Nüqing* enabled priests to heal the sick by summoning spirit warriors to repel the invading demons.[62] The origin of these five demon masters is obscure, but most probably they derived from a conflation of fears of wandering ghosts and popular god cults. Especially prominent in the demonology of the Celestial Masters are the "ghosts of the five tombs" *(wumu zhi gui),* who were associated with both vexed ancestral spirits and also victims of "fire, flood, calamity, bandits, and exposure." Whereas the former brought curses down upon their descendants by filing "sepulchral suits" with the gods of the underworld, the latter were vengeful ghosts condemned to remain in the mortal world because their corpses did not receive proper burial. Both were malignant specters whose touch caused sickness and death.[63]

Some of the demon masters, notably the martial spirit Zhao Gongming, apparently acquired a place in the popular pantheon. In one of

TABLE 1. PLAGUE DEITIES IN DAOIST TEXTS AND POPULAR LITERATURE

Text	Date	Collective Name	East	South	West	North	Center	
Nüqing guilü, 6.2a–b	3rd–4th c.	Wufang guizhu 五方鬼主	Liu Yuanda 劉元達	Zhang Yuanbo 張元伯	Zhao Gongming 趙公明	Zhong Shiji 鐘士季	Shi Wenye 史文業	Zhao Gongming
Taishang dongyuan shenzhou jing, 11.9b	Tang	Wufang guizhu 五方鬼主	Liu Yuanda	Zhang Yuanbo	Li Gongzhong 李公仲	Zhong Shiji	Shi Wenye	
Daoyao lingqi shengui pin jing, in Dunhuang baozang, 8: 119	Tang	Wufang guizhu 五方鬼主	Liu Yuanda	Zhang Yuanbo	Zhao Gongming	Zhong Shiji	Shi Wenye	
Shenxiao duanwen dafa, in DFHY, 219.10a–b	Song	Wuwen xing-bing baidu shizhe 五瘟行病百毒使者	Liu Yuanda	Zhang Yuanbo	Zhao Gongming	Zhong Shiji	Shi Wenye	
Zhengyi xuantan Zhao yuanshuai bifa, in DFHY, 232.3b	13th–14th c.	Wuda leishen 五大雷神	Liu Yuanda	Zhang Yuanbo	Zhong Shiji	Shi Wenye	Fan Juqing 范巨卿	

Source	Date									
SSGJ, xia.128, 125	Yuan	Wuwen shizhe 五瘟使者	Zhang Yuanbo	Liu Yuanda	Zhao Gongming	Zhong Shiji	Shi Wenye			
Taishang sanwu ban-jiu jiao wudi duanwen yi, 1a	Yuan/Ming	Tianxing yigui 天行疫鬼	Li Ziyao 李子邀	Zhang Yuanbo	Liu Yuanda	Wu Jiugui 烏九鬼				
Lishi zhenxian tidao tong-jian, 18.8b	Yuan	Babu guishuai 八部鬼帥	Liu Yuanda	Zhang Yuanbo	Zhao Gongming	Zhong Shiji	Shi Wenye	Fan Juqing	Yao Gongbo 姚公伯	Li Wenzhong 李文仲
Zhengyi wensi bidushen dengyi, 2a–5a	Yuan/Ming	Wufang xingwen shizhe 五方行瘟使者	Zhang	Tian	Zhao	Shi	Zhong			
Beifang Zhen-wu zushi xuantian shangdi chu-shen zhi-zhuan, 2.30b	1601		Liu Da 劉達	Zhang Yuanbo	Zhao Gongming	Zhong Shigui 鐘仕貴	Shi Wengong 史文恭	Fan Juqing	Li Bian 李便	Bai Qi 白起

Gan Bao's stories, the protagonist has a vision of Zhao Gongming and his ghostly horde while on his sickbed and dies shortly afterward. Gan's comment on this story mentions a "sorcerer's book" that depicts Zhao Gongming and Zhong Shiji as warriors dispatched by the Supreme Thearch to claim the souls of those about to die.[64] This brief reference makes no mention of plague, but it suggests that Zhao Gongming, in his role as the grim reaper, had already acquired some notoriety in lay society.

Tao Hongjing, the eminent scholar and conservator of the manuscripts of the Shangqing revelations, included in his *Declarations of the Perfected* what he believed to be a spurious document that identifies "Zhao Gongming and the others spirits of the Five Directions" as tomb spirits who cause harm to the living. In his notes on this document, Tao observed that Zhao Gongming was listed as a plague demon *(wengui)* in the *Protocols of the Twelve Hundred Officers (Qian erbai guanyi)*.[65] The actual text of the *Protocols* no longer exists, but it is believed to have been one of the original revealed texts of the Celestial Masters, containing the names and ranks of the entire celestial pantheon.[66] On the basis of this attribution it seems likely that the pentad of Zhao Gongming *et alia* was none other than the "plague demons of the Five Directions" *(wufang yigui)* that appeared as the objects of popular New Year's exorcisms in the Han dynasty. Support for this association comes from a much later source, a fourteenth-century hagiography of Zhang Daoling, revered by the Celestial Masters as the founder and patriarch of their religion. In this account, Zhao Gongming and the other demon masters, along with three other figures who are sometimes substituted for one or another of them, are identified as the Eight Demon Marshals. The demon marshals spread plague among mortals; each of the demon marshals was associated with a particular type of physical ailment, such as fevers, diarrhea, swellings, violent fevers and chills, headaches, and "red eye." They also haunted tombs, harassing filial children who came to pay respects to the dead and stealing offerings intended for their ancestors, and they invaded the fetuses of pregnant women. Zhang Daoling was said to have used magical powers to defeat and destroy the eight marshals and their demon hordes. In the end the vanquished demons make a pact with Zhang, vowing they will never again invade the world of mortals.[67] The close association of this particular group of demons with themes of death, disease, and tombs suggests that this late text perhaps does accurately reflect an early tradition in which malefic demons haunting tombs and cemeteries are vanquished by, and then enter the service of, righteous gods.

The demon masters of plague also appear in the Daoist apocalyptic literature of the Era of Disunion. The demon masters Liu Yuanda and Zhong Shiji are mentioned as the objects of heterodox "blood sacrifice" cults in the *Scripture of Divine Incantations,* which suggests that they originated as local deities.[68] A Tang dynasty supplement to the same text mentions not five but six demon masters. They are depicted as martial figures commanding legions of "demon-specters of the five wounds" *(wushang guijing)* who spread plague and disease among humankind.[69] As we saw in chapter 2, Lu Xiujing, the crusading reformer who sought to purge the Celestial Masters sect of popular superstitions, listed the "demons of the five wounds" among the profane cults that commanded the allegiance of his benighted contemporaries. Lu did not elaborate on the nature of these demons, but clearly he perceived them as false gods associated with violent death. In light of the passage in the *Scripture of Divine Incantations,* it seems likely that the "demons of the five wounds" were dead soldiers resurrected as demon warriors in the service of the plague deities. The "five wounds" also recall Chiyou and his five weapons, which reinforces the conclusion that the term is a metaphor for plague demons.

The depictions of the Five Demon Masters as plague deities in Daoist literature of the Era of Disunion illustrate the ambiguities attending the outbreak of plague and illness. The agents of disease were seen as both deities and demons or, more precisely, as terrifying demons meting out just punishments decreed by the celestial gods. Zhao Gongming and the other demon masters probably originated as demonic figures in popular worship, but Daoist lore portrayed them as defeated adversaries of the forces of order who are conscripted into the ranks of celestial legionnaires. Most likely, though, the nuances of this conversion of wanton demons into obedient subjects of the celestial gods were lost on the public, who saw disease strictly in terms of demonic affliction, however well deserved.

The *Enlarged Quest for the Divine,* a religious tract that gained wide currency in Yuan and Ming times, claimed that the demon masters (identified in this text as the Five Emissaries of Plague) were worshiped on Double Fifth already in the Sui and Tang dynasties.[70] The same book contains an account (probably apocryphal, since no contemporary sources corroborate it) of a dream experience of the Sui emperor Wendi (r. 581–604), in which the emperor was visited by five martial figures. After the emperor described his dream to his chief ministers, the court historian identified the apparitions as the Five Emissaries of Plague. The emperor subsequently awarded official titles to the five deities. Although we have no evidence of popular cults devoted to the Five Emissaries of

Plague in the Sui and Tang periods, worship of the five plague deities on Double Fifth during the Song dynasty is well attested, at least for Jiangxi and Hunan in central China. The inhabitants of Lizhou in western Hunan, for example, organized Assemblies of the Five Plagues (Wuwenshe) that held annual festivals to ward off epidemic disease. Each cult group (she) attending these assemblies built an elaborately decorated boat in which they placed lists of their members' names and birth dates, along with "Buddhist" religious paraphernalia. The boats were then set adrift on waterways to expel the plague deities.[71] Boat exorcisms later became central features of plague cults in the coastal regions of southeastern China, such as the Wen Qiong cult in Zhejiang, the Five Emperors (Wudi) cult in Fujian, and the Lords of Pestilence (Wangye) in modern Taiwan.[72] The boat exorcisms of these plague cults thus made explicit a theme foreshadowed in the *shanxiao* demonology: the need to define and enforce the boundaries of community and to expel marauding demons beyond the precincts of this unified community through the intercession of patron deities.

The Five Emissaries of Plague were also assimilated into the Thunder Magic rituals of the new Daoist movements of the Song dynasty such as Shenxiao (Divine Empyrean), Qingwei (Pure and Sublime), and Tianxin (Celestial Heart).[73] The Thunder Magic movements arose out of local ritual traditions during the tenth and eleventh centuries, but gained national exposure thanks to the zealous patronage of Emperor Huizong (r. 1100–25). Huizong sought to secure divine blessings for his rule by creating a Daoist theocracy that derived its inspiration and leadership from these local sects. Rooted in the liturgical traditions of Lingbao Daoism, the Thunder Magic sects featured the use of demonifugic powers not only in healing the sick, but also to remedy a wide range of social and political problems. The primacy of Thunder Magic in Song Daoism prompted a wholesale reorientation of Daoist religious practice toward healing by means of exorcisms that took the form of judicial inquisition.[74]

The Thunder Magic ritual traditions of the Song departed from the firm tenet of early Daoism that illness and disease were caused by the moral transgressions of the afflicted person (or his or her ancestors). Instead, the practitioners of Thunder rites shifted the blame for misfortune to aberrant demonic agency.[75] To combat demonic attack they employed an esoteric arsenal of incantations, talismans, and seals to summon, bind, interrogate, and expel the offending spirits. From the fifth century onward these techniques had been closely associated with the figure of Beidi, Thearch of the North, who appears in Daoist theology as both ruler of the underworld and a celestial divinity. Over the course of the Tang dynasty various exorcistic practices associated with Beidi coalesced into a set of personal therapies and communal liturgies, which then became integrated into the ritual complexes of the Tianxin and other Thunder Magic movements.[76] Practitioners of Thunder Magic, who included unlettered village healers as well as ordained Daoist priests and even government officials, invoked one of a number of fierce demonifuge warrior gods to exorcise malevolent demons. Chief among these divine intercessors were the Four Saints (Sisheng): Beidi (more commonly known in the Song and after by the imperially bestowed title Zhenwu, or True Warrior); Black Killer (Heisha); Heaven's Mugwort (Tianpeng), whose curious name of course alludes to the plant's demonifugic properties; and Heavenly Benefaction (Tianyou).[77] The Thunder Magic liturgies spawned a host of other demonifuge warrior-gods, one of the most important of whom was the transfigured chief of the erstwhile Five Demon Masters, Zhao Gongming.

The Five Demon Masters appear (sometimes with slight variations in personal names) in the Shenxiao and Qingwei exorcism liturgies under the titles Emissaries of the Five Thearchs (Wudi shizhe) or the Five Emissaries of Plague (Wuwen shizhe). Zhao Gongming was canonized as one of the cardinal deities of the Qingwei movement, and also ranked as one of the Four Grand Marshals (Yuanshuai), the demonifuge spirits featured in the liturgies promulgated by the thirteenth-century masters of the Shenxiao and Qingwei traditions. In this capacity Zhao no longer appeared exclusively as a plague deity; instead, he exercised broad dominion over the legions of demon warriors abroad in the world. Nonetheless, the Five Emissaries of Plague were key subordinates of Zhao (Zhao's place among the five was taken by a new figure; see table 1). At least one Daoist plague exorcism liturgy was exclusively devoted to Zhang Yuanbo.[78] Although these plague deities were heralded in the Thunder Magic scriptures as benefactors of humanity, in the theology of apocalyptic sects they reprised their older role as avenging messengers of doom.[79]

It was during the Song dynasty, too, that the Five Emissaries of Plague acquired definitive iconographic forms. The legend about the Sui emperor's dream preserved in the *Enlarged Quest for the Divine* describes each of the five deities as possessing a distinct type of weapon: 1) ladle and urn, 2) leather bag and sword, 3) fan, 4) hammer, and 5) fire gourd. These magic weapons, though clearly different from the five weapons of Chiyou portrayed in Han art, were reputed to be highly efficacious in combating plague demons; the ladle and urn and the hammer, as we have observed, appear in Han murals depicting exorcisms (figure 14).[80] *The Book of Transformations,* a hagiography of the divinity Zitong said to have been revealed to a medium in 1181, introduces the Five Emissaries of Plague bearing feathered insignia representing their "weapons of fire and water, and axe and chisel." This text also depicts the five emissaries as human-beast hybrids, each with a different animal head: tiger, cock, human, crow, and donkey.[81] A thirteenth-century Thunder Magic liturgy devoted to Zhao Gongming likewise describes the Five Emissaries as having animal forms, though the types of animals differ somewhat (tiger, cock, pig, horse, and "demonic visage" *[guixiang]*).[82] These iconographic motifs also are present in a section of a liturgical painting for the Buddhist Land-and-Water Mass believed to date from the second half of the fifteenth century. Here the plague deities, who are identified in the accompanying cartouche as the "Five Emissaries of Plague who rule the demon kings of illness," appear in the forms of: 1) a crow with a sword, 2) a horse holding a gourd (the horse is surrounded by flames, which suggests that the gourd is a fire-gourd), 3) a cock with mallet and awl, 4) a tiger with a fan, and 5) an anthropoid demon with a ladle and bucket (figure 16).[83] The weapons shown here are identical to those mentioned in the *Enlarged Quest for the Divine* and probably those alluded to in *The Book of Transformations* as well, while the animal heads essentially correspond to both texts. Although the iconography of the Five Emissaries of Plague was by no means exactly uniform, the generic consistencies suggest that a well-established iconographic repertoire had spread throughout both north and south China by the fifteenth century, and probably as early as the Song dynasty. This iconography shows that the erstwhile plague demons had become fully rehabilitated; they were no longer seen as scourges, but rather as benevolent spirits who exorcised the demons afflicting the sick.

Another spirit who defended mortals against demons of illness and epidemic was the demon queller Zhong Kui. The cult of Zhong Kui commonly is said to have begun with, or at least been popularized by, the Tang emperor Xuanzong (r. 712–55).[84] Bedridden from illness, Xuanzong had a dream encounter with the demon afflicting him in which a fearsome spirit suddenly appeared and seized the demon, gouged out the miscreant's eyes, and then devoured it. The emperor's rescuer identified himself as Zhong Kui and said that in his mortal life he had committed suicide after failing to earn high honors in the civil service examinations, but he was awarded posthumous honors by the second Tang emperor and thus pledged to devote himself to eradicating demons. Upon recovering from his illness shortly afterward, Xuanzong instructed the renowned artist Wu Daozi to paint an image of Zhong Kui based on the emperor's dream vision. The emperor was greatly pleased with Wu's rendering of Zhong Kui and subsequently had court painters produce copies that the emperor presented as New Year's gifts to favored courtiers.

There is compelling evidence that the demonifuge Zhong Kui antedated the Tang dynasty, however. In Ma Rong's lyric on the Great Exorcism of the Han court the troupe of exorcists flourishes hammers known as *zhongkui* in the ritual drama of expelling demons. Though written with different graphs, this *zhongkui* is a close homonym of the name Zhong Kui, and it is possible that the spirit's unusual name derived from these magical hammers (which, as exorcism texts of the Han era show, were believed to be efficacious weapons against plague demons). The sixth-century millenarian tract *Scripture of the Divine Incantations* invokes the spirit warrior Zhong Kui to exterminate the demon hordes besetting humanity, which suggests that the spirit may have already emerged as the object of a popular cult at that time.[85] But in the Tang and afterward Zhong Kui was invariably associated with the expulsion of demons on the eve of the New Year, in essence succeeding to the role of the *fangxiang* exorcist in the ancient Nuo rites. New Year's Eve spectacles in the Song period commonly featured a theatrical rite of exorcism known as the "Dance of Zhong Kui" that was performed before imperial as well as popular audiences.[86] In addition, beggars, perhaps mimicking these exorcistic rites, dressed themselves as Zhong Kui and his company of demons on New Year's Eve and marched through the streets of the capital striking drums and cymbals, stopping at each gate to extort payment before moving on to the next house.[87] The beggars' processions inverted the apotropaic rites of the New Year season. Instead of summoning Zhong Kui in his role as a demon tamer, the beggars masqueraded as Zhong Kui and other spirits associated with plague and death in order to wring bribes from the cowed populace.

Hanging a painted or printed illustration of Zhong Kui above the door gate on the eve of the New Year became virtually a universal custom in Song times.[88] Indeed, nearly all references to Zhong Kui in Tang-Song times pertain to these portraits.[89] Zhong Kui never became an independent deity, an object of sacrifice and prayer with his own shrines. Instead, Zhong Kui's demon-quelling powers were channeled through the talismans bearing his image. These mass-produced etchings and prints probably descended from Wu Daozi's famous painting of Zhong Kui, which

右第四十四主病鬼
王五鹿使者眾

Figure 16 (opposite). Five Emissaries of Plague. This scroll is one of 136 iconic paintings, probably dating from ca. 1460, preserved at the Baoningsi Monastery, Youyu county, Shanxi. The paintings depict the great assembly of divine beings invoked in the course of the Land-and-Water Mass. This scroll depicts the Five Emissaries of Plague, each equipped with demonifuge weapons. At front right stands a human figure carrying a bucket and ladle; at front left is a tiger-headed figure with a fan. Between and behind these two is a cock-headed figure holding a mallet in its right hand and an awl in the left. Behind the human figure is a horse-headed figure, its head wreathed in flame, holding a gourd. Finally, at the center rear is a crow-headed figure with a sword and an enormous gourd slung over its back. From Shanxisheng bowuguan 1985, plate 147. Courtesy of Shanxi Museum.

had been widely copied and disseminated. Although none of Wu Daozi's works, including his portrait of Zhong Kui, survive, a tenth-century author described Wu's painting as follows:

> In Wu Daozi's painting, Zhong Kui wears a blue robe and a leather boot on one foot. He has but one eye, with a tablet of official rank at his waist. His head is wrapped in a turban, his beard askew, and his hair hangs down unbound. He grasps a demon in his left hand, and with the second finger of his right hand he is gouging the eye of the demon.[90]

Zhong Kui was a popular motif in literati painting during the Song and subsequent dynasties, yet surviving literati paintings from this era bear no resemblance to this description. Instead, they typically depict Zhong Kui in scholar's robes escorted by a procession of grotesque demons (figure 17).[91] These paintings, which often evoke Zhong Kui as an alter ego of the neglected and despised scholar, probably were modeled after the New Year's Eve beggars' processions. A better likeness of Zhong Kui as Wu Daozi painted him can be found appended to Zhong Kui's hagiography in the Yuan dynasty religious primer *Enlarged Quest for the Divine* (figure 18). In this illustration a ferocious Zhong Kui is portrayed in the act of gouging out the eye of the demon, and this self-contained scene was surely more suitable for door-guardian images than the elaborate processions found in the hand scrolls composed by literati artists.[92]

The use of images of Zhong Kui as protective talismans to guard the home against demonic invasion recalls the legend that Huangdi had portraits made of his fearsome lieutenant Chiyou in order to intimidate criminals and instill a proper fear of the law. Both artistic and literary representations of Zhong Kui (again like the ancient Chiyou) emphasized his repellent ugliness, and his baleful visage no doubt is what endowed these talismans with apotropaic power. In addition to these echoes of the older

Figure 17. Zhong Kui procession. Zhong Kui sits on a crude palanquin borne by his company of demons. Detail of painting by Gong Kai (1222–ca. 1304). Courtesy of the Freer Gallery of Art, Smithsonian Institution, Washington, D.C.; Purchase, F 1938.4.

Figure 18. Zhong Kui vanquishes a demon. This illustration from the Yuan religious tract *Enlarged Quest for the Divine* shows Zhong Kui engaged in combat with a demon. Zhong Kui is gouging the demon's eye with his right hand, an iconographic detail said to have originated with the Tang painter Wu Daozi. From *SSGJ*, xia.123–24. Courtesy of Beijing Library.

Chiyou cult, the semantic similarity between Zhong Kui's name and the plague-exorcising magical hammer and Zhong Kui's habit of vanquishing demons by devouring them also resonate with motifs found in other plague cults. As his popularity grew Zhong Kui evolved into a generic demonifuge, but on the evidence of early accounts, most famously Emperor Xuanzong's dream, the Zhong Kui cult in its initial form was specifically dedicated to exorcising demons of plague and illness.

The Song dynasty also witnessed the development of specialized plague cults centered on local deities. One who achieved lasting fame as a protector against epidemic disease was Wen Qiong, whose cult originated in the eponymous town of Wenzhou, on the coast of southern Zhejiang province.[93] Wenzhou also was the birthplace of the Shenxiao movement, which became the foundation of Emperor Huizong's theocracy in the early twelfth century, and the Shenxiao priesthood seems to have played a prominent role in the propagation of Wen Qiong's cult. A Shenxiao hagiography of Wen Qiong written in 1274 portrays Wen as an ordinary mortal renowned for his martial prowess who upon his death was inducted into the ranks of officials in the underworld government of the Lord of Mount Tai. Although the apotheosized Wen Qiong was said to have refused temples dedicated to him personally, in Huizong's day local Daoist priests in Wenzhou repeatedly invoked Wen's aid to repel noxious demons afflicting the local community. The emphasis on Wen Qiong's humility and orthodox credentials (the author of the hagiography attributed the founding of Wen Qiong's cult to the contemporary patriarch of the Celestial Masters tradition, the official Daoist church) belies Wen Qiong's true origins as a popular deity who lacked the sanction of organized religion. In all of the Wen Qiong myths Wen dies young and by violent means, which of course conforms to the archetype of the vengeful ghost. The Wen Qiong mythology also bears traces of an older incarnation of Wen as a serpent deity, very possibly a demon who spread pestilence among the people. Paul Katz suggests that Wen Qiong, like other demonic figures, probably originated as a vengeful ghost turned into a plague demon, only to be rehabilitated and converted into a proper god by the priests of the Shenxiao sect.[94] Local lore in Wenzhou portrayed Wen Qiong as a heroic martyr who disobeyed a divine commandment to poison sinful mortals and instead swallowed the poison himself, causing him to metamorphose into a fierce demon figure. The supreme deity, moved by Wen's self-sacrifice, assigned him to the retinue of the great demon-quelling god Zhenwu, who employed Wen to root out and expel plague demons.

The development of the Wen Qiong cult thus sprang from the intersection of a local ritual tradition with the kind of popular god cult Daoists usually spurned as vulgar superstition. Katz argues that the case of Wen Qiong attests to a process of "reverberation" whereby a cult is created through reciprocal interaction between popular worship on one hand and appropriation and codification of such cults by religious specialists on the other.[95] The production of a corpus of ritual, myth, and iconography paved the way for inclusion of such popular cults in canonical religion, which in turn conferred legitimacy on the cult. Such was the power of canonization and bureaucratic rank, which erased the ambiguous identity of nefarious spirits and recuperated them into the phalanx of imperial order.[96] A similar process of incorporation and reverberation occurred in the transformation of Wutong from malicious demon to benevolent deity. In its earliest incarnation, Wutong became a tutelary deity who protected local communities from plague. Yet the ambivalence surrounding the god's true nature was never resolved. In many parts of south China during the late imperial period plague cults emerged that featured sets of five spirits, local variations on the archetype of the Five Emissaries of Plague. Several of these groups bore the distinct imprint of the Wutong legacy. Indeed, the Wutong spirits were cast in the opposing roles of both the agent of, and deliverer from, plague.

CHAPTER 5

The Song Transformation
of Chinese Religious Culture

The rise of the Song dynasty (960–1276) was accompanied by epochal changes in all aspects of Chinese society and culture, changes sufficiently great to mark the transition from Tang to Song as the turning point between China's early imperial and late imperial eras. The growing power of the imperial state eroded the aristocratic order of the early imperial era, giving rise to a more fluid hierarchy within the elite. Economic expansion generated abundant wealth, and possession of wealth endowed greater social distinction. Confucianism recaptured the intellectual allegiance of the ruling class, yet at the same time Buddhism became fully domesticated within Chinese society and culture. New social and cultural opportunities afforded by the growth of cities, burgeoning merchant and artisan classes, and the dissemination of printing gave birth to an intensely vital "commoner culture." All of these developments reshaped religious life.

Most profound of all of these changes was the shift in the center of gravity of Chinese civilization from the Yellow River valley in the north to the Yangzi valley in the south. Civil war and invasions of steppe nomads wracked north China from the onset of the An Lushan rebellion (755–63) to the turn of the eleventh century, provoking massive migrations to the Yangzi River basin and the southern coast. In 750, two-thirds of the population of the Chinese empire lived in the north, and only one-third in the south; by 1100, that ratio had reversed, and the south has remained more populous than the north to the present day. The primacy of the south reached its apogee following the conquest of north China, including the whole of the Yellow River valley, by Jurchen invaders in 1127. Remnants of the imperial family continued the Song dynasty after reestablishing their court at Hangzhou, at the southern terminus of the Grand Canal. During the Southern Song period (1127–1276), which ended with the even more humiliating conquest of all of China by the Mongols, the Chinese empire barely extended beyond the northern bank of the Yangzi River.

Intensive settlement and domestication of the southern frontier transformed the livelihood and material culture of the Chinese people. Rice replaced wheat and millet as the staple food; the abundant natural and man-made waterways of the south encouraged mobility and trade; and southern products like tea, sugar, porcelain, silk, and later cotton engendered new industries and new patterns of consumption. The unprecedented growth of cities and towns, which widened circulation of goods and enabled the acquisition of great fortunes through landowning and commerce, exerted a profound impact not only on social and economic life, but on religious culture as well.

Economic change also wrought a wholesale transformation of the social order. The aristocracy that had dominated Chinese society and government since the Han dynasty lost its political and economic privileges in the aftermath of the collapse of the Tang imperium. Most aristocratic families failed to adapt to the rising market economy, and the establishment of the civil service examinations as the primary instrument of official recruitment inhibited perpetuation of social station through hereditary rights to political office. The dissolution of the medieval aristocracy strengthened autocratic rule at the center and fostered the development of provincial elites whose social base remained rooted in local society, not the capital. Like the aristocracy of yore, these provincial elites derived their social status from landed wealth, investment in education, and endogamous marriage alliances. But henceforth the social and spatial dimensions of elite power were more spatially circumscribed, and often confined to the local level. Although these provincial elites exhibited remarkable durability and stability, the vicissitudes of examination success precluded the re-creation of aristocratic society, either at the national or at the local level.[1]

One consequence of the spatial transformation of the Chinese empire was the emergence of the Jiangnan region—the southern half of the Yangzi Delta, stretching from Nanjing on the bank of the Yangzi River southward to Ningbo on the seacoast—as its economic heartland (see map 2).[2]

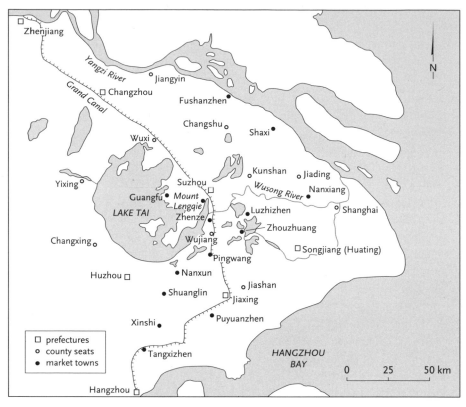

Map 2. Jiangnan

Although Nanjing had served as capital of the Chinese dynasties during the Era of Disunion, the delta's economic potential was not fully exploited until massive waves of immigrants from the north arrived in the late Tang and early Song periods. The infusion of human capital made possible reclamation of the delta's soil-rich marshes and development of a highly productive rice economy. The delta's dense network of canals, initially built to drain the marshes, also served as arteries of trade and transport. The ready availability of cheap water transport in the south, and especially in the Jiangnan region, facilitated rural-urban exchange and interregional trade, making south China the most dynamic economy in the world.[3]

The urban landscape was also transformed. The Northern Song capital at Kaifeng, and even more so the capital of the Southern Song, Hangzhou, departed drastically from the classical model of city planning and its symmetrical grid of streets and residential wards, strictly demarcated marketplaces, and distinct separation of city and country. Markets and residential quarters in Song cities no longer were encumbered by walled enclosures. Freedom of movement spawned a profusion of bazaars and craftsmen's alleys inside the city walls and out, as well as a suburban sprawl of wharves, warehouses, inns, taverns, and wholesalers' shops. In addition to the capital at Hangzhou, other great cities of the Southern Song—like Suzhou, Jiankang (modern Nanjing), Yangzhou, and Ningbo—continued to serve as important seats of government. Yet the lifeblood of these cities flowed through their commercial veins.

Commercial expansion also fostered the development of market towns with minimal or no official presence. These market towns sprang up along the Grand Canal between Yangzhou and Hangzhou and along other avenues of trade crisscrossing the delta. In addition, foreign trade and interregional domestic shipping stimulated the growth of seaports all along the coast from the Yangzi Delta southward to Canton. Market town development facilitated mobilization of rural produce destined for distant markets, and also provided villagers with a wide range of consumer goods. At the close of the Song dynasty, Fang Hui (1227–1307), a scholar-official from rugged upland country to the west, marveled at the prosperity of towns and villages in the plains of the Yangzi Delta, observing that villagers bringing rural produce to sell in the market town returned home laden with "incense, candles, paper offerings for the spirits *(zhima)*, cooking oil, salt, soy sauce, vinegar, flour, noodles, pepper, ginger, and medicines."[4] The striking presence of religious paraphernalia like incense, candles, and ritual offerings at the head of this list cogently reveals the importance of towns and commerce in the religious as well as economic life of the countryside.

Indeed, cities and towns dominated religious life as much as other spheres of social activity. Hangzhou, Suzhou, and Ningbo boasted magnificent temples both within the cities and in their surrounding hinterlands. Though Buddhist monasteries were often located in more tranquil settings in the hills, other temples, especially Daoist shrines and the temples of local tutelary deities, were almost always found within the precincts of towns. "Buddhism and Daoism flourish in Hangzhou more than anywhere else," wrote a local historian.[5] Urban temples thrived in concert with the burgeoning fortunes of smaller market towns, too. The seaport of Qinglong, located on the Wusong River, the main waterway connecting the inland cities of Suzhou and Songjiang with the ocean, enjoyed a remarkable growth spurt during the twelfth century, becoming home to so many "rich merchants and powerful lineages" that contemporaries described it as "Little Hangzhou." The town also became famous for its splendid architecture and the "three pavilions, seven pagodas, and thirteen Buddhist monasteries" that towered over "the hearths of ten thousand families." Magnificent religious edifices dominated the landscape and social life of towns like Qinglong, just as they did the cathedral towns of medieval Europe.[6]

The exuberance of the Song economy thus had a direct and pervasive impact on religious life. It has become commonplace for historians to conclude that the economic prosperity of the Song engendered a rising confidence in the power of mortals to manipulate the gods and thus shape their own destiny. Valerie Hansen has argued that the commercialization of the Song economy reshaped the religious landscape as merchants, through patronage of temples and dissemination of cults throughout trade networks, imprinted their own distinctive ethos on the character of the gods.[7] David Johnson likewise has suggested that the proliferation of *chenghuang* (commonly translated as "city god") temples from the late Tang onward resulted from merchant sponsorship.[8] Yet these hypotheses rest on slender pillars of evidence. The mere appearance of temples in centers of trade does not mean that merchants played a unique or dominant role in founding temples and propagating cults. Nor did the greater accessibility of these gods, made possible by the spread of simple and direct techniques of communication with the gods, necessarily reflect a positivist faith in human dominion over the divine. It would be just as plausible to assert that the proliferation of such techniques resulted from anxiety about the individual's fate that prompted a desperate resort to divine forces in the hope of finding security in an increasingly competitive and mobile society.

The vernacular religious universe on the eve of the convulsive transformations of the Song era can be most readily glimpsed through Glen Dudbridge's reconstruction of the folklore anthology *Wide World of Marvels* composed by Dai Fu (fl. ca. 734–81).[9] Virtually all of Dai Fu's anecdotes involve breaches of the margins between the seen and unseen realms, especially the boundary between life and death. A prominent theme coursing through Dai's stories is the notion that the institutions and practices created to regulate contact with the unseen worlds such as mortuary ritual, sacrifice, and acts of piety cannot wholly control irregular transgressions of these boundaries.[10] Ghosts, demons, and changelings abound in this world; the farther one ventures from the civilized domain of home and town, the greater the likelihood of chance encounters with them. The home itself is portrayed as a fortress defended against malign attack by an elaborate staff of household spirits arrayed across space (the well, stove, gate, commode) and time (different hours of the day and months of the year).[11] The supreme celestial gods are seen as remote figures; like the human emperor, they pay little heed to the petty tribulations of their subjects. Instead, ordinary people must arm themselves against these potentially deadly encounters with spirits by acquiring the weaponry of religious specialists like spells and talismans. Widely disseminated Buddhist tracts like the *Diamond Sūtra (Jin'gangjing)* and *Heart Sūtra (Xinjing)*, Tantric mantras, Daoist spells, and invocation of the Buddhist divinity Guanyin (on which see below) were deployed by laypersons as well as priests and monks to ward off demonic affliction. This vernacularization of ritual mechanisms, already underway in Dai Fu's day, becomes a defining feature of Song religious culture.

The pervasive fear of unseen powers that animated much of the popular religious imagination is most apparent in the growing concern with sin and punishment. Many of Dai Fu's tales dwell on the exercise of justice by the underworld bureaucracy. Penitence and the burden of karmic sin remained abiding features of Song religiosity, perhaps even more so than before. The cult of the dead had been central to Chinese religion from earliest times, but by the tenth century it had evolved into elaborate, indeed baroque, forms. The Daoist movements of the Era of Disunion had affirmed the Han vision of the underworld as a gigantic apparatus of civil and military control. In the *Declarations of the Perfected,* Tao Hongjing described an underworld divided into six great chambers, each supervised by its own complement of record keepers and inquisitors, all under the ultimate authority of Beidi, Thearch of the North (the direction of death and malign influence in Five Phases cosmology). Although Tao identified the six chambers with the fell Six Heavens, source of malefic emanations and bane to all mortals, he construed this infernal realm as a place of judgment, not corporal torment.[12] From around the seventh century Buddhist ideas fused with indigenous eschatology into a new concept of the afterlife centered on purgatorial punishment. Indian lore describing the gruesome tortures that befell the unfortunate dead *(preta)* became wedded to the terrifying prospect of official investigation, interrogation, and torture, producing a nightmarish vision of the afterlife in the form of the Courts of the Ten Infernal Kings.[13]

Drawn from both Buddhist and Chinese mythology, the Ten Kings were conceived as imperial officials presiding over law courts replete with scribes, bailiffs, and the "ox-head *yakṣa*" jailers of Indian myth. Souls of the dead appeared before each of the Ten Kings in turn and were subjected to rigorous examination of their mortal conduct. Retribution for sin was meted out through grisly corporal punishment. The "forest of swords," "fire wheels," and "bronze pillars" of Indian mythology were translated literally into instruments of torture: the infernal executioners pounded the bodies of sinners into paste with mortars and pestles; flung them into cauldrons of boiling oil; impaled adulterers on swords; and cut out the tongues of slanderers. The operation of karmic retribution, once a purely automatic process that determined the nature of the individual's subsequent rebirth, now became a purgatorial ordeal mediated by the underworld bureaucracy. Yet this image of the gods of the underworld as stern and upright officials was tinged with suspicion of government incompetence and malfeasance. The ample folklore concerning death and descent to the underworld, like the Han ordinances for the dead, was suffused with stark fears that death and infernal punishment might result from clerical errors and venal abuse of power rather than be meted out as just punishment for sin.

The intensification of this baroque cult of death stimulated the growth of salvific cults specifically focused on rescuing the souls of the dead from the torments of the underworld. In the *Scripture of the Ten Kings,* a noncanonical Buddhist tract that circulated widely beginning in the tenth century, the Ten Kings occupied positions subordinate to the bodhisattva Kṣitigarbha (Dizang), whose compassion for the inmates of purgatory could overturn the judgments of the underworld tribunes. In Daoist theology the role of Kṣitigarbha as bodhisattva of the underworld was assumed by the Supreme Heavenly Worthy Who Delivers Sinners from Suffering (Taiyi jiuku tianzun).[14] The cults of Kṣitigarbha and Jiuku tianzun offered solace by holding out the possibility of escaping the net of karma through contrition, repentance, and faith in the power of a compassionate savior.

This new concept of purgatory was propagated not only through texts like the *Scripture of the Ten Kings* (which circulated in many variant editions, often in pocket-sized breviary form), but also through visual imagery (figure 19). "Transformation images" *(bianxiang)*, didactic murals for religious contemplation and devotion painted on the walls of monasteries and shrines, often illustrated the "subterranean prisons" of the afterlife.[15] The painter Wu Daozi, who won great fame for his vivid portraiture, executed a series of *bianxiang* of the underworld at Chang'an's Zhao Jinggong Monastery in 736 that inspired universal imitation. Although Wu Daozi's murals do not survive, the remarkable statuary at the Southern Song rock temple at Baodingshan Grotto in Dazu, Sichuan

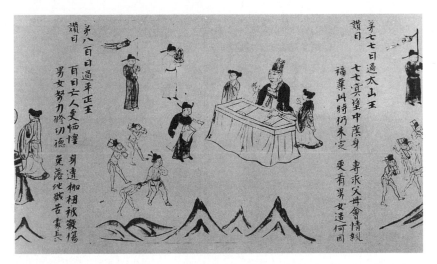

Figure 19. Judgment in the courts of the Ten Infernal Kings. One hundred days after death, the deceased are brought to the tribunal of the eighth of the ten kings, the Impartial King, depicted here in official robes sitting at a magistrate's bench. Two sinners in the foreground wear cangues around their necks; the third is being pulled by his hair. They are preceded by a petty official bearing the ledgers in which their mortal conduct has been recorded. At top two donors carry a banner and an image of the Buddha respectively. The hymn at left reads: "After one hundred days the dead feel ever more remorse and distress, / Their bodies bound by cangues and shackles, scarred by whips, / If sons and daughters make efforts to cultivate merit, / They will escape falling into the subterranean prisons, dens of eternal suffering." For the complete set of images from this illustrated manuscript, see Teiser 1994. Dunhuang manuscript of the *Scripture Spoken by the Buddha of the Prophecy Given King Yama Concerning the Sevens of Life to Be Cultivated in Preparation for Rebirth in the Pure Land (Foshuo yanluowang shouji sizhong yuxiu shengqi wangsheng jingtu jing)*. Tenth century. Pelliot no. 2003. Courtesy of Bibliothèque nationale de France © BnF.

province, powerfully evokes the sense of foreboding and terror ascribed to Wu's rendition of the torments of hell (figure 20). The Baodingshan Grotto, constructed by a wealthy lay postulant and his followers between 1177 and 1249, is comprised of thirty-one groups of colossal sculptures intended for the edification of the general public as well as initiates.[16] The sculptures reprise many familiar narratives drawn from contemporary Buddhist teachings, with particular emphasis on karmic destiny and the scourges of the underworld. The first monumental sculpture in this panorama is a looming figure of the satanic Māra, nearly eight meters high, clutching an enormous wheel illustrating the six paths of karmic destiny. One of Baodingshan's most striking elements is an enormous tableau (fourteen meters high and twenty meters wide) that depicts a huge figure of the bodhisattva Kṣitigarbha flanked by Buddhas of the Ten Directions and the Ten Infernal Kings. Below the ten kings, at eye level with viewers, are two tiers of scenes illustrating the eighteen hells of the netherworld. The predominant theme of this tableau is the punishment meted out for violating Buddhist prohibitions against speaking falsehoods and consuming wine and meat. The group of sculptures shown in figure 20, for example, features grisly scenes of the punishments that await those who, like the couple seated at the table, defy the taboo against eating meat (the servant to their right is butchering a lamb for their dinner).

Just as vivid imagery was used to convey the pain of torment in hell, deliverance from infernal punishment often depended on the miraculous powers inhering in physical images of the savior gods. Miracles evoked through veneration of paintings, statutes, and murals of Guanyin, Kṣitigarbha, and Jiuku tianzun were set down in books entitled *Anthologies of Verified Miracles (Lingyanji)*.[17] In one such tale, recorded in the *Record of Verified Miracles of the Daoist Teachings* by Du Guangting (850–933), a wayward Daoist cleric by the name of Zhang Renbiao dreams of a visit to an underworld in which he encounters hideous monsters "truly like those in paintings of the 'subterranean prisons' one sees in the mortal world." Terrified, Zhang repeatedly intones the name of Jiuku tianzun, but his captors laugh at this belated attempt to ward off divine retribution. When he is taken before the majestic Jiuku tianzun, Zhang prostrates himself, confesses his sins, and vows repentance. After delivering a stern rebuke, Jiuku tianzun forgives the priest's sins and restores him to life with the admonition to propagate images of the deity in order to convert others to right religion.[18]

Deepening fears of the charnel horrors of the underworld also were expressed through the elaboration of mortuary ritual. A major portion of both hieratic and lay rituals and observances was devoted to purgation of sin and absolution from (or at least alleviation of) suffering in the afterlife. By the sixth century Daoist priests had expanded funerary rites to include a series of ten memorial services (one for each of the first seven weeks after the passing of the deceased, and subsequently on the hundredth-day, first-year, and third-year anniversaries), which Buddhists also adopted. These memorial services, whose origins can be traced to both Daoist confessionals and Buddhist monastic practice, took the form of rituals of penitence and absolution in which priests invoked savior deities to help the deceased rid themselves of karmic sin and gain rebirth in (or ascension to) paradise. Daoist priests performed rituals like the

Figure 20. "Transformation Image" of infernal punishment. Clockwise from top left: 1) the Excrement Hell, in which three figures are submerged in a rectangular pool of filth, while a hideous warden wields a mallet to prevent their escape; 2) at center, in front of the couple seated at the table, the Halberd Hell, where a horse-headed warden impales a kneeling sinner bound to a pillar; 3) at front right, the Iron Wheel Hell, where a prostrate sinner is sawed with a large-toothed wheel; and 4) at right, the Boiling Cauldron Hell, where another horse-headed warden is about to throw a sinner into the cauldron (in this instance the sinner is being punished for evil and malicious speech rather violating the taboo against eating meat). Niche 20, Large Baodingshan Grotto, Dazu (Sichuan), twelfth to thirteenth century. From Chongqing Dazu shike yishu bowuguan 1991, plate 139. See also Howard 2001: 46–55. Courtesy of the Chongqing Museum of Dazu Sculpture and Art.

Yellow Register Rite (Huanglu zhai) and the Nine Shades Rite (Jiuyou zhai) in the course of these memorial services. The Land-and-Water Masses (Shuilu zhai), convened to perform acts of penance on behalf of untended souls condemned to purgatory, became one of the most important public Buddhist rites from the eleventh century onward.[19] Land-and-Water Masses also were held on behalf of private individuals.[20] The ubiquity of such rituals of redemption attests to the profound preoccupation with sin that suffused Song religion.

This deep concern with death and atonement also gave rise to the practice of establishing "grave chapels" *(fenan)*, Buddhist shrines at the grave site where resident monks would minister to the spiritual needs of the deceased as well as provide for the physical upkeep of the grave.[21] Elite families often established grave chapels, in some cases converting public monasteries to this private purpose. The endowments of land and funds attached to the grave chapels ensured the continuation of ancestral sacrifices in perpetuity, even if latter-day descendants should neglect them. In the Song period, sacrifices to the ancestors were commonly offered at the grave site rather than at the ancestral temple, despite the opprobrium of ritual specialists. Fang Hui observed that numerous icons of Buddhist and Daoist divinities—among which paintings of the bodhisattva Guanyin were the most prominent—were installed in these grave chapels.[22]

Tomb furnishings also underwent significant change during the Tang-Song transitional period. In the eighth century smaller, more intimate tombs that mimicked domestic architecture and furnishings began to eclipse the estates, palaces, and public gatherings depicted in the more grandiose brick-vaulted tombs prevalent in the Sui and the early Tang.[23] The sets of tomb guardians (either ferocious human-beast hybrid creatures or heavily armed human warriors) ubiquitous in tombs of the Era of Disunion and the Sui and early Tang periods disappeared by Song times. Song tombs were equipped with fine objects of daily use such as silver and porcelain vessels, gold and silver jewelry, and writing utensils, in contrast to the crude ceramic replicas that had predominated since the Han. One interpretation of this shift in mortuary practice suggests that fears of postmortem punishment were receding and that the upper classes of the Song, whose lives revolved around pursuit of success in the civil service examinations, had greater aspirations for attaining eminent station in the realm of the afterlife.[24] Indeed, there is literary evidence suggesting that Song literati and officials entertained expectations of receiving appointment and rank in the celestial pantheon commensurate with their achievements in their mortal lives.[25] Yet the baroque elaboration of the underworld and its torments clearly demonstrates that fear of retribution in the afterlife, far from abating, had intensified. The tomb itself was no longer the site of postmortem incarceration, however. Instead, the tomb served as a transitional space, a liminal junction on the journey to the infernal regions of the Ten Kings, rather than a permanent resting place for the soul of the deceased. The domestic motifs and architecture so notable in north China tombs during the Northern Song, Liao, Jin, and Yuan are virtually absent from Southern Song tombs.[26] Although the domestic comforts and familial intimacy represented in Northern Song tombs may have alluded to enduring ideals of conjugal, filial, and ancestral devotion, they hardly mitigated the prospect of divine retribution and punishment.

It was in the Song period, too, that Chinese began to quantify the burden of sin in an effort to alleviate punishment in the afterlife. The ledgers of merit and demerit that first appeared in the twelfth century assigned evil acts a specific moral value and prescribed good works to redeem one's sins.[27] An alternative approach involved measuring sin in monetary terms and purchasing redemption by burning spirit money (ritual offerings in the form of paper money), thus ensuring a positive karmic balance. Dai Fu's anecdotes attest to the widespread use of spirit money already in the Tang. Spirits of the underworld in Dai's stories inform mortals that transactions in the world of the dead, no less than among the living, require the accumulation and expenditure of money.[28] In Tang stories, offerings of spirit money were intended for souls of the dead, to enable them to purchase partial redemption for their sins and alleviation of infernal punishment. In Southern Song Daoist liturgy, spirit money was also employed to ward off affliction and death by making contributions to one's fund of "original destiny" *(benming)*. This practice derived from the idea that at birth each individual receives a sum of fortune (often expressed in monetary terms) that determines his or her destiny (life span, social station, and material well-being) in that lifetime. People can augment their stock of "original destiny" by making deposits in the form of spirit money offerings to their accounts in the celestial treasury. This type of ritual action also allowed individuals to build up a reserve of good fortune that could be used to allay punishment in the afterlife, lessening their dependence on offerings provided by descendants.[29]

From as early as the Warring States period folklore about death and the afterlife was often propagated in the form of return-from-the-grave tales in which a mortal, wrongly summoned to the world of the dead, returns to the realm of the living and delivers a first-hand report of all he or she witnessed.[30] Return-from-the-grave narratives became a standard literary genre from the sixth century onward. Although these stories tended to recapitulate generic, and hence literary or doctrinal, conventions (as we have seen in Du Guangting's anecdote about Zhang Renbiao), they also provide us with our most direct evidence of popular beliefs about the uncertain fate of the dead. An episode recorded in *Tales of the Listener* exemplifies beliefs about death and purgatory current in Song times.[31] The story concerns the visions of the twelve-year-old son of Madame Zhao, wife of a local prefect named Wei Liangchen who in 1155–56 would be appointed councilor of state, the highest office in the land. Madame Zhao died in 1151, and her family invited an eminent Daoist priest to perform the memorial services for her.[32] In the course of a Yellow Register Rite performed on the fifth of the seven-day memorial services, Madame Zhao's son has a vision of his mother in the ritual chamber and falls into a trance in which he sees celestial spirits arrive and receive the memorial sent up to the gods by the priest. That night the boy dreams that he is summoned to the palace of Jiuku tianzun to bear witness to the execution of justice. Awestruck, the boy watches as a host of sinners shackled in iron fetters is led into the court and then each is dispatched to the appropriate subterranean prison. The god instructs the boy on the procedures of the underworld bureaucracy: he learns the importance of solemnity and scrupulous adherence to detail in the performance of ritual; that sinners can be relieved of their suffering only through proper procedures spelled out in Daoist scriptures;[33] and that the officials of the underworld are to be called only by their bureaucratic titles, not by their former mortal names. As in all stories of this type, the boy is urged to report all he has seen when he returns to the world of the living, in order to enlighten others. During his tour of the underworld the boy discovers that a series of ritual errors have blunted the efficacy of the memorial services dedicated to his mother. Upon awakening he alerts his father to these discrepancies, including the placement of the altar too close to the kitchen; the presence of children at play; the employment of ritually tainted persons (in this instance, an old soldier with scabies) as attendants at the rite; and a miswritten word in the memorial dispatched by the priest to the gods. Once these problems are corrected, the rite is completed successfully. The boy's ability to identify these problems verifies the authenticity of his visions of the underworld. Though this trope was a long-standing literary convention, there is little doubt that such return-from-death experiences were commonplace and readily accepted as genuine. With each reenactment, belief in this vision of the underworld was freshly imprinted on the popular imagination.

The baroque elaboration of the tribulations of purgatory attested to abiding anxieties about not only one's own postmortem fate, but especially that of one's ancestors. Such concerns were most keenly expressed through the mythology and ritual practices centering on the figure of Mulian (Skt. Maudgalyayana), a disciple of the Buddha who became universally acclaimed in Chinese culture as the paragon of filial devotion to the salvation of ancestors. In Tang and Song times, Mulian was closely associated with the Avalambana Feast (popularly known as the Ghost Festival) held on the fifteenth day of the seventh lunar month to alleviate the suffering of sinners in purgatory. The myth of Mulian's epic struggle to rescue his mother from the most abysmal of the manifold Buddhist hells and ensure her rebirth in paradise was propagated through vernacular narratives known as "transformation scripts" *(bianwen)*, which—like *bianxiang* illustrations—were widely employed by Tang monks as evangelical tools. Although various aspects of Mulian's heroic quest appear in Buddhist scriptures and morality tales originating in India, the classic version of his story found in the "transformation script" narratives (and later in popular drama as well) was a product of the Chinese milieu. The *bianwen* tales feature Mulian's protracted journeys through the labyrinthine underworld in search of his mother and his encounters with various deities and groups of woeful sinners. Finally he discovers his mother in the most ghastly hell of all—the Avīci Hell, where she is impaled on a bed of nails in perpetuity for refusing to give alms to a mendicant monk. Though Mulian, as an advanced disciple of the Buddha, possesses formidable magical powers, he is unable to obtain her deliverance solely through his own efforts. Yet by combining his own ritual practice (magnified by his stature as a monk and a disciple of the Buddha), the merit-earning piety of the Buddhist faithful, and the saving power of the Buddha himself, Mulian ultimately wins his mother's release from hell and the lower paths of reincarnation and she is reborn in paradise.[34]

The Mulian story thus reconciled the perennial tension between Buddhist renunciation of the world and Chinese filial piety. Through faith, charity, and ritual effort the dutiful son and devout disciple of the Buddha succeeds in abrogating the laws of karma and expiating his mother's sins. The Mulian story also resolves another persistent tension in Chinese religion, the uneasy relationship between the ancestors and the legions of dead souls unrelated by kinship (i.e., ghosts). The Mulian *bianwen* and the Buddhist Avalambana Feast both champion the bodhisattva ideal of universal salvation, advocating devotion not only to one's own parents but also to all sinners. The *bianwen* pointedly teach that Chinese rites of ancestor worship are utterly ineffective, and only Buddhist piety can bring any comfort to sinners in purgatory. Nonetheless, the Mulian mythology often was separated from its original soteriological context and integrated into mortuary practices focused exclusively on the ancestors. Reenactment of the Mulian story through dramatic performance became an essential part of Chinese funeral rites.[35] Its universal popularity testified to the intense anxiety about the fate of the ancestors provoked by Buddhist eschatology.

As a catechetical device, the Mulian story was aimed primarily at an audience of pious laity rather than clergy. In its emphasis on the salvific power of the Buddha's compassion and its aspiration for rebirth in paradise the Mulian story resonated with the theology of the Pure Land (Jingtu) tradition in Buddhism. Although its roots lay in Indian scriptures, as a distinct movement Pure Land was a wholly Chinese product that emerged in the sixth century as a reaction against the proliferation of esoteric Buddhist schools patronized by the Chinese aristocracy. Pure Land expressed deep pessimism about the human condition and the ability of any believer, lay or clergy, to achieve deliverance from mortal suffering solely through one's own efforts. Abjuring the accumulation of karmic merit through performance of austerity, charity, and ritual, Pure Land Buddhism instead espoused faith and devotion to a savior, typically the Amitābha (Amituofo) Buddha or the bodhisattva Guanyin. Pure Land teachings stressed the performance of simple devotional acts, such as recitation of the savior's name *(nianfo)*, that did not require commitment to a monastic vocation, mastery of scripture and ritual, or even the mediation of the clergy. During the Song period Pure Land Buddhism became the substrate upon which much vernacular religious devotion and practice rested. Since Pure Land teachings did not comprise a distinct doctrinal "school" within the monastic orders, elements of them were adopted by all of the major ecclesiastic traditions of Chinese Buddhism. But it was the ecumenical turn taken by the Tiantai tradition in the eleventh century that was chiefly responsible for the diffusion of Pure Land Buddhism throughout all layers of Chinese society.

In the Sui and Tang dynasties the Tiantai school had enjoyed lavish patronage from the imperial court and the aristocracy. In the two centuries of turmoil after the An Lushan rebellion, however, Tiantai nearly sank into oblivion before being reborn in the Jiangnan region under the patronage of the rulers of the Wu-Yue kingdom in the tenth century. Initially, the Tiantai revival was centered at Ningbo, but by the Southern Song Hangzhou had eclipsed Ningbo as the leading center of Tiantai as both a lay and a monastic movement.[36] The revived Tiantai tradition embraced the devotional practices associated with Pure Land, and became particularly identified with penitential rituals and sponsorship of lay confraternities known as Lotus Assemblies (Lianshe).[37]

The liturgical foundations of Pure Land Buddhism in the Song were laid by the monk Ciyun Zunshi (964–1032), one of the leading figures of the Tiantai revival in Jiangnan. After earning widespread renown during his tenures as abbot at monasteries in Ningbo and Taizhou (Zhejiang), in 1015 Zunshi assumed the abbacy of the Lower Tianzhu Monastery

(Xia Tianzhusi) outside Hangzhou. During Zunshi's sixteen years at Lower Tianzhu the monastery began its ascent from a humble mountaintop retreat to one of the most illustrious centers of the Tiantai tradition, a formidable rival to the more senior Tiantai monasteries in Ningbo. Zunshi dedicated himself to the reform of popular religious practice and the eradication of its heinous "blood-eating" gods. In place of the popular ritual calendar of blood sacrifices offered to local deities, Zunshi proposed alternative liturgies intended to earn spiritual and material rewards for the supplicant as well as promote doctrines of universal salvation.[38]

Zunshi especially objected to contemporary mortuary practice, complaining that the Avalambana Feast had degenerated into little more than conventional mourning rites for the ancestors. Zunshi informs us that in his day most monasteries had separate Land-and-Water chapels *(shuilu'an)* where offerings were presented to "orphan souls," the dead who have no descendants to perform ancestral rites on their behalf. Zunshi condemned this exclusive focus on orphan souls (which implicitly acknowledged the primacy of ancestor worship) and insisted that the offerings should be provided for all of the dead.[39] He also decried contemporary fears of "hungry ghosts," emphasizing that the "gift of nourishment to hungry ghosts" *(shishi egui)* should be understood as an act of charity intended to provide spiritual as well as material sustenance to the unfortunate *preta*, rather than an exorcism of malicious demons.[40] Among the religious practices Zunshi promoted as alternatives to blood sacrifice were the Release of Living Beings (Fangsheng) and Golden Light Penance (Jinguangchan) rites. The Fangsheng ritual, which Zunshi initiated around 1020 on the anniversary of the Buddha's birth (the eighth day of the fourth lunar month) by releasing fish into Hangzhou's West Lake, pointedly repudiated the animal sacrifices offered to blood-eating deities. The Fangsheng liturgy also included rites of confession and repentance on behalf of the released creatures that would enable them to attain a better rebirth. In the performance of this ritual, as with the Avalambana Feast, Zunshi stressed the importance of aiding all sentient beings reborn into the lesser paths of reincarnation rather than focusing exclusively on one's ancestors. The Golden Light Penance was largely intended for monks, but its main components—confession of sins; profession of faith in the Buddha, his teachings, and the clergy; and eidetic offerings of incense and flowers— were also central to the practices Zunshi encouraged his lay audience to adopt.

Yet even Zunshi acknowledged that these rites brought blessings not only to less fortunate beings but also to those who performed them. The protocol for Land-and-Water Masses composed by Zunshi's disciple Lingjian focused not only on repentance and salvation, but also on mundane boons like wealth, progeny, long life, and harmony among kinfolk. The ritual invoked a massive assembly of divine beings encompassing not only buddhas and bodhisattvas but also the lords of the underworld and non-Buddhist spirits, including the various ranks of local tutelary gods and even "the demon-kings who spread sickness and calamity." All of these spirits were represented in iconic form, by either statues or paintings, in order to facilitate the postulant's concentration.[41] Murals and paintings depicting many hundreds of buddhas, gods, and divine beings became a standard feature of chapels dedicated to the Land-and-Water Masses in the Song and later periods.[42]

Tiantai monks fostered lay devotion by founding lay congregations (she) that met periodically to perform penance, recite scriptures, make eidetic offerings, and undertake charitable works. In 1009, Zhili (960–1028), abbot at Yanqingsi, Ningbo's chief Tiantai monastery, initiated annual mass assemblies for the purpose of offering alms to the clergy, conferring "bodhisattva precepts" on laity, and propagating the practice of nianfo recitation. Members of the assembly received almanacs to record the number of recitations they uttered each day. Such quotidian rituals of repentance and renewal of vows exhibit the Pure Land emphasis on the accumulation of merit through repeated actions and quantitative calculation of spiritual progress that also inspired the practice of keeping merit ledgers.[43] Zunshi also convened Lotus Assemblies, but with a more concentrated focus on the upper ranks of society. Subsequently these lay congregations—known by a wide variety of names, including Lotus Assemblies, Pure Land Assemblies (Jingtushe), Return-to-the-West Assemblies (Guixishe), and Assemblies to Gather Resources for Return to the West (Xizishe)—and Pure Land practices such as nianfo were fully embraced by the Tiantai ecclesiastic establishment. The popularity of Lotus Assemblies soon exceeded the bounds of the Tiantai monasteries. By the twelfth century, Lotus Assemblies began to proliferate throughout Jiangnan without the explicit sanction or tutelage of the Tiantai clergy. Though branded as spurious by the Tiantai clergy, these lay congregations attracted the devotion and financial support of wealthy landowners.[44] The People of the Way (Daomin), as they often called themselves, did not form a distinctive sectarian tradition, nor were they anticlerical. On the contrary, they sought to emulate monastic ideals within lay life. Acting more often as individuals than as groups, these lay Buddhists engaged in a wide array of altruistic activities to earn karmic merit, notably through donations not only to support the clergy and evangelical projects such as printing copies of Buddhist scriptures, but also for secular purposes like building bridges. Yet the more successful of these groups, such as the White Lotus Assembly (Bailianshe) founded by the preacher Mao Ziyuan (ca. 1086–1166) in the Suzhou-Jiaxing area, became targets of clerical jealousy and sporadic persecution. Mao spurned the performance of good works to gain karmic merit that was a cardinal feature of the monastic Lotus Assemblies, instead stressing the importance of contrition and simple devotional acts like *nianfo.* By the thirteenth century, the White Lotus Assemblies had become a broad-based religious movement throughout southeastern China, taking root in areas like Fujian and Jiangxi where competition with powerful monastic orders was less intense.[45]

The most importance lay practice championed by Zunshi and other Tiantai adherents to Pure Land teachings was a repentance ritual invoking the bodhisattva Guanyin (Skt. Avalokiteśvara). Guanyin was a protean salvific figure prominently featured in the *Lotus Sūtra,* the cardinal scripture of the Tiantai tradition and Mahayana Buddhism as a whole. In the *Lotus,* Guanyin is portrayed—as the literal meaning of the bodhisattva's name, "listening for sounds from the mortal world," implies—as a compassionate figure whom the devout faithful invoke to avert calamity and rescue them from life-threatening peril. Already in the Era of Disunion a large body of miracle tales featuring Guanyin circulated widely throughout China.[46] In the Tang period, Tantric elements were introduced into the cult that transformed Guanyin into the "Great Compassionate Bodhisattva Guanyin Who Delivers Us From Suffering" (Dabei jiuku Guanyin pusa), an awesome deity and ubiquitous guardian angel with "a thousand arms and a thousand eyes" (figure 21).[47] In this incarnation the bodhisattva vows to come to the aid of all in peril who with sincere heart intone the "invocation of the Great Compassionate Guanyin" *(Dabei Guanyin zhou).* Guanyin subsequently became the most important savior figure in Chinese vernacular religion.[48] Religious iconography commonly paired Guanyin with Kṣitigarbha, representing both as bodhisattvas who show special compassion for those suffering in the underworld.[49]

The cult of the Great Compassionate Guanyin combined simple acts of devotion like recitation of the Guanyin invocation with demonstrations of sincere repentance, most notably through physical mutilations. The Tiantai patriarchs Zhili and Zunshi also began to develop peniten-

Figure 21. Guanyin of a Thousand Arms and a Thousand Eyes. The towering figure (four meters high) of Guanyin is shown with forty-two arms bearing insignia symbolizing the bodhisattva's manifold epiphanies. In addition, Guanyin is encircled by an aureole of secondary arms with outstretched palms, in each of which an eye is depicted. The statue of Guanyin is flanked by relief sculptures of the bodhisattva's canonical twenty-eight sets of attendants. Niche 113, Mt. Zhonglong, Zizhong (Sichuan). Ca. 780–850. Courtesy of Angela F. Howard.

tial rituals centered on Guanyin.[50] Zunshi's disciple Biancai Yuanjing (1011–91) took the leading role in popularizing the Guanyin invocation as part of lay rites of contrition. In 1062, Yuanjing was appointed abbot of Hangzhou's Upper Tianzhu Monastery (Shang Tianzhusi), which housed a statue of Guanyin renowned for its curative powers. Yuanjing acquired considerable fame for his ability to cure illness and dispel malignant spirits using holy water consecrated through the Guanyin invocation rite.[51] In the course of his stewardship the Upper Tianzhu Monastery became the most important Guanyin shrine and, thanks to its famous statue of Guanyin, perhaps the single most important pilgrimage site of the Song period.[52]

The early Song period also witnessed the most significant development in the history of the Guanyin cult: the metamorphosis of the bodhisattva into a female deity. The potential for this transformation was inherent in the *Lotus Sūtra,* which listed thirty-three bodily forms, including seven

Figure 22. White-Robed Guanyin. This painting combines elements of the White-Robed Guanyin and Water-Moon Guanyin iconography. Guanyin is seated in the "royal ease" posture typical of Water-Moon Guanyin images, but wears a white robe and shawl partially covering the crowned head. The left hand holds an ambrosia vase and the right a willow-branch wand, implements that allude to the bodhisattva's healing powers. These elements had already become standard features in the Guanyin iconographic repertoire in Tang times. At right the donor-supplicant kneels in worship. Above the supplicant are two clouds, one of which bears an infant holding a small tray of offerings. The infant perhaps represents fulfillment of the supplicant's wish for a child, already a cardinal feature of the Guanyin cult in Tang times. Anonymous painting from Dunhuang. Tenth century. Courtesy of Palace Museum (Beijing).

female ones (nun, laywoman believer, wife of rich man, wife of a chief minister, wife of a Brahman, young girl, palace woman), that Guanyin assumed according to the needs and station of the supplicant. Nonetheless, down to the end of the Tang dynasty the iconography of Guanyin featured male, or in some cases androgynous, forms (figure 22). The earliest known examples of Guanyin iconography utilizing distinctly female forms come from the Dazu shrines in Sichuan and are dated to the Song period.[53] The White-Robed Guanyin (Baiyi Guanyin), which became a popular cult figure in the tenth century, acquired an unmistakably feminine form, perhaps because of indigenous scriptures that identified this figure as a goddess who granted children to worthy supplicants. The miracle-working statue of Guanyin at the Upper Tianzhu Monastery, which was identified as a White-Robed Guanyin, may have represented the bodhisattva in female form. The Water-Moon Guanyin (Shuiyue Guanyin), perhaps the most widely reproduced iconographic form of Guanyin in Song times, still appeared in androgynous form. In the Ming period, however, the Water-Moon Guanyin became indelibly identified with the shrine at Mount Putuo, on an island off the coast of Ningbo, where Guanyin was typically depicted in female form. Mount Putuo's status as the most important Guanyin pilgrimage site in the Ming-Qing period gave strong impetus to the conversion of Guanyin to a purely feminine image.[54]

Perhaps the image of Guanyin that contributed most to the popularization of the bodhisattva's female identity was that inspired by the cult of Miaoshan. The Miaoshan myth centers on a pious young woman of royal birth who spurns the enticements of marriage and a life of leisure to devote herself completely to Buddhist practices. Her impudent refusal to marry provokes the wrath of her father. The old king tries to dissuade his daughter by depriving her of the comforts of her station, eventually imprisoning her at a nunnery where she is compelled to perform arduous labor. Miaoshan's resolve remains unbroken, prompting her father to order that she be put to death. Miaoshan is miraculously spared, however, and she is transported to distant Fragrant Mountain, where she lives as an ascetic nun.

Years later, Miaoshan's father is stricken by a terrible illness that afflicts him with hideous sores. No doctor can cure the king, and indeed none can even look at him without being overcome by revulsion. Upon learning of her father's illness, Miaoshan comes to him disguised as a monk and proclaims that only a potion made from the eyes and hands of a person unbesmirched by anger and hatred could cure the disease. When the king objects that surely no such person exists, the monk replies that the ascetic of Fragrant Mountain is indeed such a person. The king then sends his envoys to Fragrant Mountain to make this audacious request, whereupon Miaoshan immediately gouges out her eyes and severs her arms. After taking the potion the king recovers and then embarks on a pilgrimage to offer thanks. When the royal party arrives at Fragrant Mountain the queen recognizes their benefactor as none other than their daughter. Overwhelmed by grief at his daughter's sacrifice, the king vows to devote himself completely to the Buddhist faith. Miaoshan then reveals herself to be an incarnation of Guanyin and transforms herself into the awesome form of the thousand-eye and thousand-hand bodhisattva.[55]

Though the origins of the Miaoshan myth are unknown, it seems likely that, like the Mulian myth, it was composed in China in an effort to reconcile Buddhist renunciation of the world with the supreme Chinese value of filial piety. The myth is first attested in China at the turn of the twelfth century, when a prefect at Hangzhou who had learned of Miaoshan's story during a previous assignment in central China had it inscribed on a stele. The stele was erected at the Upper Tianzhu Monastery, already renowned as a Guanyin shrine, in 1104.[56] The popularity of Upper Tianzhu as a pilgrimage site ensured that the Miaoshan story would soon spread throughout the empire. Miaoshan also became the subject of popular religious primers and later, in the Ming dynasty, full-length novels, and the dissemination of her story (often tailored for a variety of audiences) made her perhaps the most widely known incarnation of Guanyin.[57]

Like Mulian, Miaoshan is revealed to be a powerful thaumaturge who can overturn the laws of karma. Like Mulian, too, Miaoshan epitomizes a sublime form of filial piety that transcends mere submission to parental authority. But whereas Mulian symbolizes steadfast devotion to one's parents, creating a space for the monastic vocation within the larger culture of filial duty, repudiation of paternal authority lies at the heart of Miaoshan's story. Moreover, Miaoshan's self-mutilation takes selflessness to a much more extreme degree than anything encountered in the Mulian mythology. It is hard to imagine Miaoshan as a practical model for emulation. Instead, the Miaoshan cult connected private devotion to the awesome salvific powers of a great goddess. Miaoshan's sacrifice of her hands and eyes alludes to the fundamentally illusory nature of the world of flesh, while her epiphany in the form of the thousand-eye and thousand-hand bodhisattva manifests the true reality that can be perceived only through faith and devotion.

The female forms of Guanyin, together with the emergence of other goddess cults in the Song,[58] attest to a spreading phenomenon that perhaps can be called a "feminization" of compassion. In contrast to male gods cast in the role of upright monarchs and officials, stalwart defenders of social norms and the unbendable rule of moral law, female deities displayed deep empathy for the tribulations of mortal sinners. The emergence of these goddess cults and the feminization of compassion provide evidence for the growing importance of women in devotional cults.

Nonetheless, cults focused specifically on the lives and concerns of women did not emerge until after the Song period. For example, the image of Guanyin as "Deliverer of Children" (Songzi Guanyin) and patron of childbirth only appears during the period ca. 1400–1600, even though this attribute of Guanyin is specifically mentioned in the *Lotus Sūtra*. Likewise, the goddess *(niangniang)* cults of north China also seem to have first developed in the Ming dynasty.[59]

Obsession with sin and atonement, terrifying images of the afterlife, dissemination of the pragmatic Pure Land liturgies, and the feminization of compassion pervaded Song religion and society well beyond the confines of explicitly Buddhist doctrines and believers. Indeed, the most salient feature of Chinese religious culture in Song times is the emergence of a unified realm of the sacred that amalgamated religious beliefs and practices of disparate origins.[60] By "unified" I do not mean to imply that Chinese religion assumed a single, monolithic form. On the contrary, even the most basic features of this unified realm of the sacred were subject to constant reinterpretation and modification in the context of discrete social and historical experiences, and religious belief and practice displayed striking diversity across time, space, and social milieu. Nonetheless, we witness in the Song the crystallization of basic assumptions about the nature and structure of the divine and the laws governing interactions between mortals and spirits that informed vernacular religious consciousness throughout the late imperial era. The significance of these precepts can be grasped not through schematic models of the structure of Chinese religion, however, but only by studying their concrete historical instantiations.

Song religious culture evinced a growing awareness of the gods as part of human history; not the remote history of the ancient sage-kings, but the common history of communal memory, a history that took place in the past but is continually relived in the present through story and performance. The lore of the gods that accumulated in the storehouse of memory was brought to life through ritual gesture and community observance that reaffirmed the reciprocal relations—forged as much by history as by faith—binding the gods and their worshipers. The roles of memory, folklore, and ritual in shaping the religious traditions of family and community were by no means unprecedented. We can see them at work in the "annals of the strange" of the post-Han era, Buddhist miracle tales, and Dai Fu's anecdotes, all of which sought to reveal the workings of the divine through concrete and attestable historical events. What was novel in the Song and afterward was the vernacular framework of religious understanding.

The popular pantheon that emerged in the Song rendered the gods accessible and responsive to ordinary people. In Daoist theology, knowledge of the gods endowed power over them. Much of the scriptural and liturgical content of Daoism from the inception of the Celestial Masters movement in the Han dynasty centered on acquiring knowledge of the gods' names, powers, and places in the celestial hierarchy. Only through such knowledge could human beings harness supernatural powers and train them on worldly concerns. Thus, knowledge of the gods bestowed powers rivaling those of temporal suzerains. It was a closely guarded secret divulged only to worthy cognoscenti; ordinary mortals had no recourse except to seek priests to intercede with the gods on their behalf. In the Song period, laypersons began to exploit more direct avenues of contact and communication with the gods.[61] Simplified forms of divination like the casting of "moon-blocks" or choosing divination sticks could be performed without recourse to priests, texts, or ritual knowledge. Local communities also used their own increasing economic resources to create pantheons that reflected both the particular history of a place and the needs of its inhabitants. In the process, many of the gods invented in the Song bore a striking resemblance to their clients. In contrast to the astral abstractions of Daoist theology and the deified statesmen and generals of older "blood-sacrifice" cults, new local cults in the Song often featured commoners whose lives (or, more typically, deaths) imbued them with supernatural power. Local people could evoke empathetic response *(ganying)* from these gods precisely because of their shared membership in the local community.

Yet both Buddhist and Daoist clergy continued to occupy key positions in Song society. Though by no means as central to community life as the parish priests of medieval Europe, Buddhist and Daoist clergy were indispensable as celebrants at funerals and memorial rites, as well as at many communal festivals (though they were absent from births and marriages, which were purely domestic affairs). Neither Daoist priests nor Buddhist monks assumed leadership within village society, however. Instead, they served as temple wardens and religious specialists, ministering to the particular needs of individuals and families when called upon to do so. From the Tang period onward large numbers of clergy occupied such specialized niches within local society, and we can perhaps speak of their social roles in terms of a vernacularization of ritual. That is to say, the essentially generalized forms of ritual performed by clergy (e.g., communication with the gods by means of bureaucratic correspondence mediated by Daoist priests, or repentance and atonement of sin orchestrated by Buddhist monks) were situated not in a discrete theological and hieratic context, but rather within the framework of the secular life of lay postulants. As Kristofer Schipper has observed, Daoist liturgies like the Yellow Register Rite could be and were adapted to a wide variety of public uses.[62] The Daoist priest did not demand an explicit religious commitment from those who sought his services (though his Buddhist counterpart perhaps was more likely to). Instead, he provided a service to a client. Though the miracles wrought by priests and monks inspired belief and piety among the beneficiaries, the latter often withheld their devotion until the miracle occurred. It was common to approach the gods with a request accompanied by a promise to make offerings or perform acts of thanksgiving only after the supplicant's prayers had been answered.

In addition to Buddhist monks and Daoist priests, a heterogeneous class of "ritual masters" *(fashi)* emerged in the Song dynasty who specialized in one or another set of liturgical therapies for exorcising demons and restoring health to afflicted persons.[63] The term *fashi* encompassed every denomination of religious practitioner, both ordained and not, ranging from unlettered village mediums to learned masters of scripture. Their common denominator was the ability to invoke a specific patron deity by means of spirit possession and metamorphosis whereby the deity inheres in the body of the *fashi* and endows him with its supernatural power. *Fashi* were expert in techniques of spirit detection, often employing child-mediums to personify demons afflicting sick persons. Once identified, the offending spirit was forced from the body of the patient, subjected to judicial inquest, and banished. Ned Davis has suggested that Buddhist and Daoist *fashi* were imitating exorcistic practices that originated with the sundry local spirit mediums *(wu)*, while the latter adopted the patron deities and repertoires of liturgies and spells of ecclesiastic religion.[64] What seems to distinguish the two is the peripatetic nature of the *fashi,* who appear in Song accounts as highly mobile figures traveling widely in response to the summonses of clients. The *wu,* in contrast, remained rooted, as their patron deities were, to particular places. In any event, the *fashi* acted as the catalyst for the vernacularization and dissemination of ritual practices throughout Song society.

Temples, even modest ones (or indeed abandoned ones), were wreathed in an aura of sacred power. One of the most common tropes of folklore was the severe punishment meted out to impious visitors to temples who committed acts of desecration by toying with statues of gods and other sacred objects. Yet temples remained public places, open to any supplicant who approached the gods with private prayers. The use of merit ledgers and spirit money shows that laypersons increasingly pursued secular avenues of deliverance. Yet they were still engaged in a dialectic with the ideologies and institutions of established religion. Temple wardens had frequent contact with these supplicants and might perform services on their behalf. Communities of clergy, like the monastic orders of medieval Christianity, had far less direct involvement in the lives and religious practices of the great majority of the population. Nonetheless, the growing popularity of devotional cults like Pure Land Buddhism, and the Guanyin cult in particular, brought lay believers into more frequent contact with clerics. Priests and monks also officiated at community rituals on major feast days—including Guanyin feast days (especially on 2/19[65] and 6/19), the anniversary of the Buddha's entry into *nirvāṇa* (4/8), the Ghost Festival (7/15), and feast days of local gods—as well as at irregular community-wide events like the consecration of a new temple building and at rituals involving crises like prolonged drought. (At other times, though—including the New Year's season [1/1–1/15], the Qingming rites of sweeping the ancestors' graves [3/3], and the midsummer Duanwu festival [5/5], dedicated to the exorcism of demons—religious activities were largely confined to domestic rites that did not involve the participation of religious specialists.) As Jean DeBernardi has observed, the ritual calendar celebrated the totality of divine beings, even in the absence of doctrinal unity or congregational commitment.[66] The ritual calendar, and by extension the hierarchical order of the divine, varied from one local community to the next in keeping with their own local traditions and priorities. Sites of worship likewise were diffused, in space as well as time. The fluidity of this system of worship encouraged diversity and specialization of mediation with the divine, rather than a single, exclusive ecclesiastic order.

It is tempting to associate the vernacular religious culture of the Song and later Chinese history with local and essentially oral traditions, in contrast to the scriptural and hieratic traditions of organized religion. Daoist and Buddhist clergy themselves strictly demarcated between the pure theology and disciplined liturgy preserved in their respective canons and the motley variety of popular beliefs and practices. Yet there is no evidence to suggest that ordinary people conceived of religion in terms of such clearly segregated spheres. The encounter between the literate and oral realms took multifarious forms, and literacy was not a requirement for gaining access to scriptures. The precepts of scriptural traditions, no less than stories of miracles wrought by gods, circulated by word of mouth. As Hansen suggests, the tangible presence of gods in the forms of temples and statues provided important keys for ordinary people to learn about the gods, and a means of recognizing them when they appeared, as they often did, in dreams and visions. Yet temples also served as storehouses of scriptural knowledge. The iconography of temples and the repertory of services provided by the religious specialists they housed brought lay believers, however unwittingly, into the domain of scripture.

One example of the imbrication of scripture and lay religion is the *Scripture of Universal Salvation (Duren jing)*. This brief, one-chapter work was one of the primary revealed texts of the Lingbao liturgical corpus circa 400, and it was well known among educated men in Song times.[67] Lin Lingsu made the *Duren jing* the cornerstone of the Shenxiao revelations he presented to Emperor Huizong (r. 1100–25) in 1116, and this scripture, in a greatly amplified sixty-one-chapter version, became the foundation of Huizong's short lived Daocracy.[68] Recitation of the *Duren jing* was believed to ensure a place in paradise for both living postulants and their deceased ancestors, saving them from underworld torment. Reflecting Buddhist conceptions of the function and nature of sacred texts, the *Duren jing* departed from earlier Daoist works in expanding its soteriological concerns to embrace the salvation of all, not just the individual.[69] The text largely consists of the secret names of celestial deities, written in an esoteric language of Sanskrit transliterations. Well before Lin Lingsu, though, the text's fame had been embellished by priests such as the heralded oracle Xu Shouxin (1033–1108), who used its enigmatic language to tell fortunes. Xu responded to supplicants' questions by writing down a phrase, sometimes a single graph or two, seemingly taken at random from the *Duren jing* that proved unerringly accurate as prognostications. Greatly celebrated in his own day and patronized by three emperors (one of who built a monastery of five hundred bays in his honor), Xu nonetheless mostly catered to a clientele of ordinary laypersons. His popularity testified to the talismanic power of sacred texts, and the authority wielded by those who could manipulate such texts.[70]

Nor was Xu unique. Folktales from the Song confirm that the *Duren jing* often was used in fortune telling.[71] Intoning sacred scriptures also enabled believers to invoke their prophylactic and curative powers. Such practices seem to have been diffused among lay believers as well as clergy beginning in the Song period. Although tales of the miraculous benefits of reciting the *Duren jing*—to regain health, protect oneself from harm, or deliver one's ancestors from infernal punishment—are found in Du Guangting's *Record of Verified Miracles of the Daoist Teachings*, the protagonists in all of Du's anecdotes are Daoist priests, and the text itself is depicted as an esoteric scripture.[72] By contrast, a series of miracle stories appended to a Yuan commentary to the *Duren jing* features ordinary, and even illiterate, laypersons. In one story a blind man regains his sight through recitation of the text. In another, a lame man's infirmity is cured simply by hearing the *Duren jing* chanted during a religious festival devoted to collective recitation of the text.[73] Popular lore also attests to the talismanic powers of the *Duren jing*. Copies of the scripture, produced in mass quantities, could serve as currency in the afterlife, used to procure positions in the infernal bureaucracy or purchase escape from the dread hands of underworld judgment.[74]

The scriptural message of the *Duren jing* was also communicated to nonliterate audiences in pictorial form. For example, when Suzhou's main Daoist temple was renovated in 1146, its galleries were painted with "transformation images" *(bianxiang)* inspired by the *Duren jing*.[75] Grootaers's study of the iconography of Zhenwu temples in north China in the 1940s has shown that such temple murals played a crucial role in disseminating, and also in reworking, the lore of the gods. Through a comparison of legends concerning Zhenwu in two late Ming works, a popular religious tract[76] and a folk novel,[77] with murals preserved in twentieth-century rural temples, Grootaers discovered that the stories represented in these murals varied considerably from the literary sources. Some murals included episodes unknown in the literary records, perhaps derived from the theatrical repertory or devotional pamphlets. Grootaers also found that the mural captions contained numerous errors based on the form or sound of graphs, leading him to conclude that these legends had been transmitted chiefly by word of mouth.[78] The popularization of the conception of the underworld derived from the *Scripture of the Ten Kings* also underscores the importance of didactic illustrations in transmitting scriptural—albeit "uncanonical"—doctrines.[79]

In tandem with the growing tendency in the Song to make direct appeals to the gods, the bureaucratic metaphor used at least since Han times to express the relationship between the gods and mortals increasingly assumed concrete manifestation as a hierarchically ordered pantheon. The skeletal frame of the divine bureaucracy became fully fleshed out by ranks of officials headed by a supreme deity, himself a mirror image of the Chinese monarch. Like the Chinese emperor, the supreme deity was signified by his office rather than his person. The supreme deity was known by a variety of interchangeable titles, including the archaic Shangdi or Tiandi and titles that originated in Daoist theology, like the Jade Emperor (Yuhuang dadi) and the Primordial Celestial Worthy (Yuanshi tianzun).[80] The Song state promoted this idea of the divine realm as an extension of mundane government by seeking to integrate all religious cults into an imperially authorized canon of worship and sacrifice. Like earlier dynasties, the Song compiled registers of sacrifices *(sidian)* that defined the proper objects and forms of worship. The canon of Confucian ritual, itself a reflection of the aristocratic age of the Zhou dynasty, nominally restricted ordinary subjects to veneration of their ancestors and a limited number of household tutelary deities. All other forms of god worship were deemed "profane cults" *(yinci)* and strictly prohibited. By the Song period, the imperial state generally condoned communal observance of rites once restricted to the long-defunct aristocracy, such as offerings made to the spirits of sacred mountains and rivers. Over the course of the Song the registers of sacrifices swelled with the inclusion of hundreds of local deities who earned official recognition on the strength of the miracles they performed on behalf of both the dynastic house and the local community. Confucian critics of religious enthusiasm railed against magistrates and local dignitaries who succumbed to popular importunities and collaborated in the promotion of such cults, but to little avail. The Song government remained committed to the strategy of co-optation and regulation through official recognition, rather than outright suppression, as the most effective means of curbing the excesses of popular devotion. At the same time, religious iconography increasingly reflected the conception of the divine as a simulacrum of secular authority. Images of the gods were commonly dressed in the robes and regalia of rulers and officials (figure 23).[81]

The Song government's efforts to regulate and codify religious practice through official sanction of popular cults were hardly novel, but its attempt to create a standard and universal pantheon extending from the imperial cult down to local tutelary spirits constituted an unprecedented intrusion of imperial authority into religious life. From the outset of the Song dynasty, the central government subjected the Buddhist and Daoist monastic orders to tight regulatory discipline. Orthodox canons of sacred scriptures were compiled and printed at the state's behest, and the state also exercised substantial control over the ordination of clergy and appointment of abbots at the most important monasteries and shrines.

Figure 23. The Daoist celestial trinity. The Three Pure Ones, with Yuanshi tianzun (Primordial Celestial Worthy) at center, preside over the Daoist celestial pantheon. This niche is carved into a stone pillar at the center of a room whose walls are decorated with images of 360 gods arrayed in six tiers. Niche 5, Nanshan Grotto, Dazu (Sichuan). First half of the twelfth century. From Chongqing Dazu shike yishu bowuguan 1991, plate 203. Courtesy of the Chongqing Museum of Dazu Sculpture and Art.

The fervently Daoist Emperor Zhenzong (r. 997–1022) was especially energetic in granting titles and awards to Daoist gods, honoring the chief deities of Daoism with rank commensurate with his own imperial dignity.[82] The Lord of Mount Tai, the presiding deity of the underworld, was invested with the rank of "divine sovereign" *(dijun)* and granted the new title of Great Sage-Emperor of the Eastern Marchmount Coeval with Heaven (Dongyue qitian dasheng di). Zhenzong ordered that temples dedicated to Dongyue (as the god was now known) be raised in every administrative capital in the empire, and these majestic temples gave additional luster to the god's dignity. Zhenzong also accorded high honors to the Daoist divinity Beidi (rechristened Zhenwu, or True Warrior), who was further elevated to the rank of "divine sovereign" during the reign of Emperor Huizong in the early twelfth century. Zhenwu subsequently was installed as the chief deity of officially recognized Daoist shrines, known as Abbeys of the Munificent Saint (Youshengguan), in each locality.

Subsequently, particularly in the late eleventh and early twelfth centuries, the central government granted canonization to a large number of local deities and awarded them titles of nobility drawn from the archaic nomenclature of the Zhou aristocracy (e.g., king, lord, sire).[83] In addition, the state delegated to these local gods a specific territorial jurisdiction (making them divine counterparts to terrestrial magistrates), authorized the consecration of temples in their name, and designated an annual feast day for celebration of their cult. The process of canonization was not merely a matter left to the central government's discretion; devotees of popular cults competed with each other to win official recognition and honors for their own particular patrons. Powerful lineages claiming an ancestral tie to such figures vigorously lobbied to secure official honors for them. In other cases campaigns to seek canonization for a local deity mobilized a wide range of sponsors, including prominent local notables, clerics of all denominations, and local officials. Fierce struggles between rival claimants to miracles induced sponsors to employ all sorts of underhanded tactics, such as forging documents and stealing steles, to advance their causes. Official recognition (and subsequent promotion to higher rank) was granted on the basis of miracles performed by the god and authenticated through an elaborate process of official review not unlike the Roman Catholic Church's protocols for recognizing sainthood. By the end of the Song numerous local gods had been promoted to the second-tier rank of "king," but none apart from Dongyue and Zhenwu had attained the august mantle of "divine sovereign."[84]

One feature of the unified realm of the sacred, then, was the articulation of a hierarchy of gods and cults that structured religious time and space. Imperial sanction played a significant role in the formation of this hierarchy, but the pantheon was subjected to considerable alteration in accordance with the ebb and flow of popular devotion. For heuristic purposes, we can separate this hierarchy into four levels: 1) domestic cults; 2) local tutelary deities; 3) sovereign gods; and 4) regional cult centers. It should be emphasized immediately that these four tiers were not arrayed in strict relations of subordination (except, perhaps, in the subordination of local tutelary deities to sovereign gods). Nevertheless, the powers ascribed to the gods and the range of their authority roughly corresponded to this order of precedence. Moreover, all of the above cults impinged on the lives of the populace. Though each type of deity had its own distinctive characteristics, their roles were by no means exclusive, and the jurisdictions of gods overlapped in concentric circles extending outward from the sharply delimited sphere of household gods to the wide and potentially universal reach of regional cult centers. It is also worth noting that the gods inhabiting this pantheon varied substantially from one locality to the next, and the pantheon as a whole underwent constant metamorphosis, with new gods being created and old ones sometimes fading away. The gods at levels one (domestic cults) and three (sovereign gods) served in largely depersonalized bureaucratic roles, and thus tended to be highly stable, in contrast to the cults of the gods at levels two (local tutelary deities) and four (regional cult centers), whose survival and growth directly depended on the enthusiasm of their worshipers.

DOMESTIC CULTS

Chinese religious practice above all must be seen in the context of family worship and its history. The rubric of "domestic cults" should be understood as encompassing two distinct sets of deities: those whose jurisdiction was limited to the household, and those who were worshiped by family members within the confines of the home. From ancient times Chinese subscribed to a number of household cults centered on the protection of the family and the home from misfortune. The stove and door gods were generic deities who served in this capacity, and also (in the case of the stove god) conducted surveillance of the conduct of its members.[85] Every household had a family altar *(jiatang)* on which the tablets of the ancestral spirits would be arranged. In addition, icons representing sovereign and tutelary deities of local importance might also be placed on the family altar.[86]

Religious lore of the Song period indicates a growing orientation toward personal patron deities, rather than lowly bureaucratic supernumeraries like the stove god, for protection against both personal calamity and malign spirits. Guanyin's role as a personal savior of course had a long history owing to the popularity of the *Lotus Sūtra* and the abundant miracle tales portraying the bodhisattva as an omnipresent guardian angel. Devotion to Guanyin focused on portable images of the deity, usually small statuettes, and the so-called *Guanyin Sūtra (Guanyin jing;* actually the twenty-fifth chapter of the *Lotus Sūtra)*, which served as a personal breviary. The great Daoist demonifuge Zhenwu also enjoyed great esteem as a personal guardian. Although imperial patronage ensured that temples dedicated to Zhenwu were founded throughout the empire, popular worship of the god centered not on these Daoist shrines but on private devotional icons. Stories concerning Zhenwu in the *Tales of the Listener* primarily feature veneration of statues or painted images used as apotropaic devices or devotional icons that typically portrayed Zhenwu

Figure 24. Zhenwu, the True Warrior. Brandishing his sword, Zhenwu (foreground) stands at the head of a procession of Daoist divinities. Behind Zhenwu's right shoulder stands Tianpeng, another apotropaic Daoist warrior god. In keeping with the standard iconography of the deity developed during the eleventh century, Zhenwu is portrayed with disheveled hair, standing barefoot on the tortoise-and-snake heraldic creatures that signify the north in Five Phases cosmology. For a recent study of the mural and its iconography, see Jing 1994. *Procession of Daoist Divinities* (detail). Temple mural from Pingyang, Shanxi. Second half of the thirteenth century. Courtesy of the Royal Ontario Museum © ROM.

with unbound hair and armed with lance and sword (figure 24). Only three of the eleven stories concerning Zhenwu in the *Tales of the Listener* are set in temples (and in two of these cases it is the god's statue, rather than the temple, that is central to the narrative). By contrast, all eighteen Dongyue stories in Hong Mai's anthology feature temples dedicated to the god.[87] Festivals held in honor of Zhenwu on the god's feast day (3/3, coinciding with the Qingming grave-sweeping ceremony) were important communal events in some places,[88] but the god's primary role in Song religion was that of a guardian angel whose image served as protection from malign forces.

As we have already seen in Dai Fu's anthology, people saw themselves as susceptible to demonic attack even within their own homes. Perhaps the most common motif of supernatural stories in the *Tales of the Listener* involves family members or servants victimized by demonic attack or possession. Hong Mai recorded one episode of demonic possession that happened to his own family while his father was a minor local official in Jiaxing, and his account affords us a revealing glimpse of the Hong family's religious culture.[89] Hong reports that the office of public records in Jiaxing prefecture was haunted by the ghosts of peasants who had died of starvation following devastating floods the previous year. Even Hong's older brother, then nine years old, was an eyewitness to these apparitions. One of the ghosts possesses a family maid, but Hong's father subdues the ghost and demands a confession. Vexed by the ghost's ability to possess the young woman despite the manifold measures he took against demonic invasion, Hong's father interrogates the ghost to discover why his precautions failed:

> "Zhenwu, whom I worship, is an extraordinarily powerful god, and in addition our home houses Buddhist statues and images of *tudi* tutelary spirits and the stove god. How is it that you were able to enter?" The ghost replied, "The Buddha is a benevolent god who does not concern himself with frivolous matters. Each night Zhenwu, his hair unbound and brandishing his sword, flies above the rooftops, and I am exceedingly careful to avoid him. The *tudi* spirit behind the house is lax in his duties, although [the spirit of] the small shrine in the front of the house upbraids me whenever he sees me. When I entered the kitchen, the stove god asked where I was going, but I simply answered that I was taking a stroll. 'Don't cause any trouble,' he scolded, but I simply replied that I dare not, and thus I was able to arrive here." . . . Father said, "Every month on the first and fifteenth day I make offerings of spirit money to the *tudi* spirit; how dare he allow a stranger spirit to enter! You go and question him for me, and tomorrow I will destroy his altar!" The ghost retorted, "Is Your Excellency not aware? Although [the stove god] may have money for his expenses, of what use is

money to relieve an empty stomach? Whenever I enter someone's house I share whatever [food] I take with the household spirits, and so we countenance each other."

Hong Mai was a mere infant when this episode occurred, and his knowledge of it was surely shaped by the subsequent retelling of the event and its incorporation into family lore. Hong's father, though a government official steeped in Confucian skepticism, was clearly a pious man. His meticulous devotions to the household gods and Zhenwu as a personal guardian were typical of the great majority of the population.[90]

LOCAL TUTELARY GODS

Perhaps the most striking development of all in Song religion was the efflorescence of cults dedicated to deities rooted in the historical experience, real or imagined, of the local community. In contrast to the "dead generals of vanquished armies," as Lu Xiujing sneeringly described local deities of the early imperial era, many of the new local gods were portrayed as persons of common birth who performed heroic service on behalf of the community.[91] Yet, in most cases it was the circumstances of their death, rather than their achievements in life, that endowed these cult figures with an aura of supernatural power. Popular religious consciousness continued to see godhood as a transformation wrought by death, and commoner deities, like the "dead generals" of yore, were frequently distinguished by violent or premature death.[92] Indeed, it was precisely the enduring liminal presence of the spirit of the deceased at a specific site that defined a local god. The origin of local gods as actual human beings did not in itself distinguish them from other gods; hagiography supplied all gods with a mortal history. Instead, the chief attributes of local gods were ties to the locality and consequently their service as patrons of the living community, rather than their role as representatives of the distant celestial bureaucracy. Though occupying a lowly position in the divine hierarchies of Daoism and state religion, these local gods remained closest to the people, and thus were the gods most sympathetic to their plight and responsive to their needs.

Prior to the Song period, "*tudi* spirit" was a loose designation for spirits resident in a particular place, without reference to rank or status within a universal pantheon.[93] In Han times the term referred to spirits who literally inhabited the soil and must be appeased when breaking ground to raise buildings, cultivate fields, and dig graves. According to Wang Chong, on such occasions a clay effigy in macabre form *(guixing)* was made, which spirit mediums used to make entreaties, offering sacrifices as compensation for having disturbed the spirit's domicile.[94]

Han tomb ordinances typically entrust care of the deceased to the spirits of the grave site, and *tudi* also appear as petty spirits who escort the deceased to the world of the afterlife.[95] Such spirits were kindred to the "prodigies of trees and stones" *(mushi zhi guai)* and the *shanxiao;* in the Song period, they were worshiped at the ubiquitous rural shrines known as *congci* ("grove shrines"; see chapter 6). Yet *tudi* also came to refer to a class of tutelary gods who became the focal points of communal identity and welfare. Such spirits were almost always portrayed as deceased humans rather than nature spirits, though in some cases the dignity accorded to these tutelary gods was expressed by designating them as gods of mountains that dominated the local landscape. These new *tudi* cults, which emerged in the late Tang and proliferated during the Song, shed the violent, morally ambivalent character and grotesque forms of the older *tudi* spirits.[96] Kristofer Schipper has drawn attention to an assimilation of Daoist ritual and local cults, beginning probably in the Tang period, that invested local deities with the powers and majesty of Daoist divinities.[97] In addition, canonization by the Song state delegated responsibility for communal welfare to select local gods. Remolded to fit the prevailing norms of Confucian social ethics, these gods became paragons of justice, loyalty, and filial piety. Nonetheless, the new *tudi* cults of the Song period share with the older cults of "dead generals" a common origin in rituals for propitiation of the dead.[98]

This transformation of local deities into tutelary gods can be seen in the evolution of the cult of Filial Lord Zhou (Zhou Xiaogong), located in Yixing county (Changzhou), on the western shore of Lake Tai in the Yangzi Delta. In his mortal existence Filial Lord Zhou was Zhou Chu, a military hero and martyr of the third century. Legend relates that Zhou Chu was the wastrel son of a prefect stationed in Poyang (Jiangxi) whose wanton behavior became as much a scourge to the local inhabitants as the ferocious tiger and kraken that constantly preyed upon them. The haughty Zhou Chu took it upon himself to sally forth and battle the tiger and kraken; though he succeeded in slaying them, during the course of the struggle he was submerged in a lake for three days. The local populace celebrated the demise of Zhou Chu as much as their deliverance from the tiger and kraken. When Zhou Chu resurfaced he finally realized how much he was hated and vowed to reform himself. He traveled to Jiangnan and became a disciple to the celebrated scholars Lu Ji (261–303) and his brother Lu Yun, served the Wu kingdom and subsequently the Jin dynasty (265–420) as a military officer, and died heroically in battle in 299.[99]

Although a memorial stele celebrating Zhou's heroism was raised at his grave site after his death, there is no evidence of a cult dedicated to Zhou until the early tenth century. It is likely that local people had long venerated Zhou as one of the "dead generals of vanquished armies." His cult took on a new life in the twelfth century, after locals credited Zhou with protecting them from marauding armies during the Fang La rebellion of 1119–20 and Zhou was granted imperial recognition. Popular devotion to Zhou seems to have been inspired by miracles (copiously commemorated by local officials); protection of the community against drought, flood, plague, and bandits; and the god's potency as an oracle. An inscription of 1149 observes that the divination sticks (qian) at Zhou's temple had a well-established reputation for remarkable prescience, and people came "from one hundred leagues around" to use them. The divination oracles "encouraged virtue, warned against misdeeds, and promoted filial piety and loyalty," and perhaps they were the source of the epithet "Filial Lord."[100] A major expansion of the temple compound was undertaken in 1176 by a Changzhou prefect as a gesture of thanks for saving him and his family from drowning in a storm on Lake Tai, and numerous private donations provided the shrine with a permanent endowment. An inscription commemorating the 1176 renovation reports that the walls of the temple were decorated with murals depicting both Zhou's exploits of slaying the tiger and kraken and an "array of celestial beings."[101] This combination of individual heroic deeds and a pantheon of transcendent deities illustrates the assimilation of Daoist liturgy and ancient culture heroes described by Schipper.[102]

Another example of the new local tutelary cults of the Song period is the cult of Sire Li (Li Hou), which originated in Changxing county in Huzhou, adjacent to Yixing. While still a youth Li acquired a reputation as an uncanny seer. In 1121, at age eighteen, he suddenly announced his intention to serve his emperor by joining the campaign to suppress a rebellion then raging in Shandong, saying that he probably would not return for years. Thereupon Li sat down in a meditative posture and died. Li's fellow villagers built a temple to shelter his spirit until his return, and local spirit mediums came to rely on Li's spirit as an oracle. The shrine first gained imperial recognition in 1209, but the deity achieved renown in 1225, when Sire Li was said to have interceded to spare the people of Huzhou from imperial wrath after several Huzhou men tried to instigate the overthrow of the newly enthroned emperor, Lizong (r. 1225–64).[103]

The cult subsequently gained wider attention. In 1250, the celebrated Daoist priest Deng Daoshu, who had moved to Suzhou from Sichuan ten years before, consecrated a temple in Sire Li's honor in Changshu, one of the county seats of Suzhou prefecture.[104] Proclaiming Li's merits as a "defender of the faith," Deng placed the shrine in Changshu's main Daoist abbey. The preeminence of Sire Li in Changshu's local religious life was firmly established in the Yuan period, when Changshu served as the point of embarkation for the grain tribute fleets traveling the ocean route to the Yuan capital of Dadu (modern Beijing). Sailors prayed to the deity for protection, and the Yuan court formally recognized Li as the guardian deity of the tribute fleets. Thus in Changshu Sire Li became known as Sea God King Li (Haishen Li wang).[105] The close affinity between Sire Li and the local Daoist establishment persisted throughout the Ming, when the abbey was popularly known as the King Li Temple. While mariners worshiped Sire Li as a patron deity, the Changshu cult also developed its own rich mythology apart from the original cult in Changxing.[106]

The transplanting of Sire Li's cult from Changxing to Changshu confirms the growing mobility of cults in the Song period.[107] The spread of god cults beyond their place of origin exacerbated tensions between popular practice and official dogma, however. The ritual canons stipulated that the authority of tutelary spirits (typically imagined as the spirits of mountains and rivers), like that of the local officials who were their secular counterparts, was bounded by their territorial jurisdiction. Gods could be worshiped only within their officially recognized home territory. But the accelerated mobility of Song society facilitated the movement of cults into new territories. Still, tutelary deities like Sire Li generally remained fairly localized. Despite the "innumerable" temples dedicated to Sire Li within Changshu, according to a Ming gazetteer, the cult apparently did not spread (or at least did not endure) in neighboring areas.[108] The parochial qualities of such gods, tied to place and historical memory, hindered their movement much beyond their place of origin.[109] Evidence from Jiangnan and Fujian suggests that the diffusion of local tutelary deity cults like Filial Lord Zhou and Sire Li was gradual and finite; rarely did a local god win adherents in a catchment area larger than one or two prefectures.[110]

The most important occasions for worship of tutelary deities were the spring assemblies held at the gods' temples. In Jiangnan, where a settlement pattern of dispersed settlement and small hamlets prevailed, few villages had their own temples. Each hamlet or village organized a cult group *(she)*; the whole panoply of cult groups gathered together at the temple on the god's feast day for a communal celebration *(hui^b)*. Worship of the God of Saddleback Mountain (Ma'anshan; popularly known simply as the Mountain God [Shanshen]) in Kunshan county (Suzhou) seems to have been organized according to such principles. Each spring cult groups from many villages gathered in a grand assembly to pay homage:

> On the fifteenth day of the fourth month, the feast day of the Mountain God, the county greets the deity with Buddhist and Daoist ceremonies to pray for a bountiful harvest. The various *she* join together to form a common assembly *[bingshe weihui]*. From Mountain Canal to the county seat, each *she* raises a canopied rest house; the brilliant crimson and emerald tents fill the sky. Peddlers and merchants from other prefectures descend on the festival in droves, elbowing one another and stepping on each other's feet.[111]

The god's image was carried in a procession from its temple several kilometers outside the city to the prefectural yamen, stopping at each rest house to receive the villagers' oblations. Although this terse account does not indicate whether the *she* brought along images of their patron *tudi* as has been common in more recent times, it is clear that the God of Saddleback Mountain was regarded as Kunshan's paramount deity and thus enjoyed fealty of the whole population.

Evidence from later periods shows that *she* rituals in rural areas of Jiangnan fostered a sense of social identity based on common residence, and thus transected rather than paralleled kinship ties.[112] *She* membership, no less than kinship identity, was an ascriptive status: the sources repeatedly emphasize that no one could refuse to participate in, or provide financial support to, their *she*. While the *hui* festivals demarcated the range of the local tutelary god's jurisdiction through the procession of the god's image throughout the villages of its constituent *she*, the *hui* itself does not seem to have imparted a strong sense of collective identity. In urban areas, however, *hui* organized around the cults of the higher-order deities that I refer to as sovereign gods had a more powerful effect in strengthening communal identity and social solidarity.

The Song period witnessed a gradual (though not complete) elaboration of a hierarchy of cults in which *tudi* occupied a distinct niche in the celestial bureaucracy. By the end of the Song most *tudi* were understood to be subordinated to higher echelons of gods and ultimately to a supreme deity, even though in the eyes of the local community *tudi* remained the most visible and accessible gods. Already in the Song, but especially in Ming-Qing times, the designation *tudi* was applied to humble shrines with extremely circumscribed jurisdiction, extending no farther than a hamlet or neighborhood, or in some cases (as in the case of Hong Mai's home described above) a single family compound.

SOVEREIGN CULTS

The conception of the divine hierarchy as organized in accordance with the bureaucratic structure of the imperial state should be understood as an attribute of the Daoist religion, which assigned to the myriad gods discrete jurisdictions and specialized functional roles. The imperial state, in its effort to submit the gods to imperial control, adopted this model and applied it systematically to officially endorsed cults. But the distant supreme gods impinged on the lives of ordinary people far less than the local tutelary spirits. As ter Haar reminds us, the gods of local religion were typically anointed with titles like "lord," "king," or even "emperor"—in other words, titles that connoted not bureaucratic office but sovereign authority.[113] Local inhabitants regarded their *tudi* as sovereigns over their own territories. Yet at the same time these local cults were typically enmeshed in larger networks of affiliation and subordination centered on the sovereign cults of the towns.

In Ming-Qing times, the intermediate level between local tutelary gods and the celestial pantheon was occupied by a class of gods typically designated as *chenghuang. Chenghuang,* literally "god of moats and walls," commonly has been rendered in English as "city god," a translation that has been the cause of much confusion. Although *chenghuang* can be considered "city gods" insofar as cities were defined by walls (a definition that includes nearly all seats of government, but excludes most market towns), it is more appropriate to think of *chenghuang* as a bureaucratic rank equivalent to that of prefect in the imperial field administration. Many *chenghuang* were accorded official recognition on an ad hoc basis beginning in the tenth century, but the proliferation of *chenghuang* resulted more from popular initiative than imperial fiat.[114] *Chenghuang* first arose in the Tang period, perhaps as martial guardian figures conceived in the image of Buddhist monastic guardians *(qielanshen).*[115] But already in the Tang period the *chenghuang* had become closely associated with the administration of the underworld.[116] In popular folklore, the office of *chenghuang* typically was occupied by deceased local officials, who retained in death the authority they wielded in life.[117] The numerous stories in the *Tales of the Listener* that mention the *cheng-*

huang typically cast the god in the role of territorial governor, responsible for disciplining and punishing unruly spirits and demons within his jurisdiction—a role that conforms to that accorded to the *chenghuang* in Daoist theology.

As noted earlier, the proliferation of *chenghuang* cults simultaneous with the marked urban growth of the Song has led some scholars to attribute the popularity of the *chenghuang* to its role as an emblem of a nascent urban identity among merchants and other leading urban citizens.[118] Yet in the Song period *chenghuang* temples were invariably located in prefectural and county capitals, a distribution that conformed more to the political and administrative hierarchy than economic status. No *chenghuang* were found in market towns. The dissemination of *chenghuang* at the level of market towns was a late development, subsequent to the regularization of the *chenghuang* cult in religious reforms carried out by the first Ming emperor in the late fourteenth century (see chapter 6).

In the Song and Yuan dynasties, the most important sovereign god was Dongyue (figure 25). Zhenzong's edict mandating the worship of Dongyue throughout the empire violated the traditional ritual principle that the worship of gods must be confined to the actual place where the god was believed to reside, and thus gave imperial license to a proliferation of Dongyue temples under private as well as government auspices. The profusion of Dongyue temples even in towns that lacked imperial officials is particularly striking. In many market towns, citizens seeking to embellish their town's stature raised funds to build "detached palaces" (*xinggong,* signifying a secondary residence of the emperor) dedicated to Dongyue.[119] Indeed, the Dongyue temple became the hallmark of the dignity of market towns *(zhen)* that aspired to the official prestige of county and prefectural seats. The sovereign authority of Dongyue over local, rural *tudi* gods was demonstrated by the practice of sending images of local gods to attend the "court audience" of Dongyue *(chao Dongyue).* In the market town of Xinshi (Huzhou), for example, "each year at the time of the spring festival people come in droves from several hundred leagues around bearing gifts of money and silk which they present in audience *[chaoxian]* at the Dongyue temple."[120]

While the Dongyue temples served as crucibles for forging a distinctive town identity, the cult encompassed a wide range of meanings and believers. Inheriting the functional role of the Lord of Taishan as the arbiter of life and death, and also of poverty and wealth, Dongyue inspired awe and terror as well as reverence. The god's annual festival, at the close

Figure 25. Dongyue and the Celestial and Infernal Courts. Dongyue and his consort are seated at center. Around them, arrayed in five tiers, are seventy-five male figures dressed in the robes of civil officials, representing the various departments of the celestial bureaucracy. Beneath the thrones is another tier of eighteen officials representing the infernal bureaucracy. Niche 11, Shimenshan Grotto, Dazu (Sichuan). Twelfth century. From Chongqing Dazu shike bowuguan 1991, plate 221. Courtesy of the Chongqing Museum of Dezu Art and Sculpture.

of the third lunar month, brought together worshipers of diverse backgrounds and concerns, as the following description of Dongyue festivals in late Song Hangzhou indicates: "Some come solely to demonstrate their faith through offerings of incense; others prostrate themselves wearing shackles and cangues; shopkeepers of the various trades each present rare fruits and flowers, fine crafts, and delicacies; Buddhist monks and priests chant scriptures; while some simply approach the temple to offer homage."[121] Another thirteenth-century gazette of Hangzhou relates that the cult assemblies *(shemo)* devoted to Dongyue in the capital were so numerous that no single shrine could accommodate them all; thus on Dongyue's feast day the capital's *shemo* paid homage at five different Dongyue temples throughout the city and its suburbs.[122] Likewise, in Fuzhou (Fujian) local cult groups from throughout the prefecture "joined together to present oblations *[jieshe jianxian]*" at the city's Dongyue temple on the god's feast day, when "burnt spirit money swirled in the air like snow."[123] In Hangzhou, the *she* were generally organized along the lines of trade and occupation, but for the purpose of the Dongyue festivals special *she* assembled for the presentation of "money banners" *(qianfanshe)* and procession of penitents *(zhongqiu jiasuoshe)*.[124] By the seventeenth century, if not earlier, the penitents' acts of self-abasement included extreme gestures of mortification, such as turning themselves into "living flesh lamps" *(roushendeng)* by burning their flesh and piercing their arms and chests with hooks to hang lanterns.[125]

Penance and expiation of sin became a salient feature of the Dongyue and the *chenghuang* cults. Murals of the Ten Infernal Courts, complete with all of their grotesque tortures, often embellished these gods' temples. The ubiquity of rituals of redemption in the context of the Dongyue and *chenghuang* cults, as in other forms of piety, attests once again to a profound preoccupation with sin. Daoist clergy consciously strove to reappropriate the notion of purgatory by embellishing the mythology of the Ten Kings and reasserting the primacy of Dongyue as the overlord of the underworld. Dongyue temples often included individual shrines and icons for the entire panoply of seventy-odd departments of the supernatural subsumed under the god's spiritual domain.[126] Often the iconography depicted, in gruesome and frightening detail, the lackeys of the underworld inflicting punishment upon sinful mortals brought before the tribunals of the various departments. The author of an inscription written in 1284 to commemorate the rededication of Dongyue's base temple at Mount Tai observed with approbation that the temple's numerous and lurid statues "startled the eyes and sent shivers through one's heart," and thus instilled in the people's minds a proper sense of resolve to commit no evil.[127] The iconography of such temples in turn informed popular understanding of the soteriological message of established religion.

Popular mythology likewise depicted Dongyue as a stern and awesome judge. Stories concerning Dongyue in *Tales of the Listener* feature three distinct themes.[128] First, Dongyue is portrayed as presiding over the underworld, where he and his minions determine the fates of dead. By extension, ghosts—the spirits of the dead—also fall under Dongyue's authority. Second, Dongyue commands the legions of plague gods, which he periodically mobilizes to exact righteous punishment for sins of mortals. Third, the Dongyue temples serve as courts of appeal for mortals to obtain justice denied them by the terrestrial judicial system. All three themes are also characteristic of popular tales about the *chenghuang* gods, although there are differences of emphasis, too: Dongyue is much more prominent as ruler of the underworld, while punishment of wayward spirits and ghosts is more frequently mentioned in *chenghuang* lore. Despite these nuances, it is clear that Dongyue and the *chenghuang* occupied similar niches in the popular pantheon, that of sovereign gods who act as rulers over a given territory and all the gods, spirits, ghosts, and humans who reside in it.

The progressive elaboration of the divine hierarchy, a trend abetted by the state's patronage of local cults, produced an uneasy tension between the dual roles of local gods as patrons and protectors of the community on one hand and as humble agents of a supreme divine will on the other. This tension is exemplified by a case Hong Mai recounted in his *Tales of the Listener.* Set in Suzhou in 1195, the story centers on a resident of the city named Zhou, who fell victim to terrible fevers and sought relief by taking refuge in the city's *chenghuang* temple. Unbeknownst to the temple wardens, Zhou hides in the temple. At midnight he witnesses the marvelous spectacle of the statues of the *chenghuang* and his retinue of supernumeraries coming to life. The *chenghuang* addresses the assembly of *tudi* spirits, announcing that the supreme god, Shangdi, had issued a decree commanding the local gods to spread plague throughout the city. The *tudi* acknowledge their orders, but one of their number protests that the inhabitants of his district, the Xiaoyi ward, were good people who had committed no crimes. The *chenghuang* sternly reminds the dissenting *tudi* that he is a spirit of lowly station who must comply with the supreme god's directive. The *tudi* then asks that he be allowed to fill his quota of victims by afflicting children, a compromise to which the *chenghuang* assents. The next day Zhou reports all that he had seen and heard, only to be ridiculed for his mad delusions. A month later a terrible plague struck the city, yet in the Xiaoyi ward only children succumbed. The people of Suzhou then realized the truth of Zhou's story, and in gratitude to the *tudi* spirit built a great temple in his honor.[129] In Hong's tale, local deities cannot but accede to the will of the supreme gods (who appear as capricious, or at least inscrutable, since no explanation for visiting plague on the city's residents is given), just as a local magistrate must execute imperial orders without fail. At the same time it conveys the hope that local gods (and local magistrates, too) will be compassionate and merciful toward the people in their charge.

REGIONAL CULT CENTERS

The increased mobility of Song society was reflected in the wider circulation of gods beyond their original homelands. Imperial sanction for the proliferation of temples dedicated to gods like Dongyue and Zhenwu, protectors of the realm, led to the foundation of numerous branch temples *(xinggong)* throughout the empire. Buddhist deities had never been constrained by the tradition that worship of tutelary spirits be confined to a single locality, and the major Buddhist divinities, such as Guanyin, Maitreya, and Amitābha, had become ubiquitous even before the Song period. Local cults also spread to surrounding regions. A few were carried into the expanding networks of long-distance travel and trade, sinking roots in new host communities far removed from their place of origin.

Among the most mobile of cults were those dedicated to deities believed to render assistance to young men aspiring for success in the civil service examinations. Local gods like the King of Mount Yang (Yangshan wang) in Yichun (Jiangxi), the King of Broad Munificence (Guangyou wang) in Shaowu (Fujian), and Zitong in Zitong (Sichuan) earned reputations for the oracular pronouncements they delivered revealing the fate of examination candidates. Those who qualified to take the national examinations at the Song capital often stopped at the home temples of these gods seeking to discover their destiny. Consequently the cults of these gods also became transplanted to the capitals of Kaifeng and Hangzhou, though none of these examination cults became widespread until Zitong (rechristened as Wenchang) received official blessing as patron of examination candidates in 1316, when the Yuan dynasty reestablished the civil service examinations.[130]

Hansen has drawn attention to the phenomenon of local cults spreading well beyond their native locality in the Southern Song, which she attributes to the expanded horizons of merchant networks and the formation of regional consciousness during this period. She identifies four deities whose cults acquired a region-wide following throughout southeastern China in the Southern Song: Wuxian ("Five Manifestations"), Zitong, Consort Linghui (Linghui fei; "Consort of Miraculous Benediction"), and King Zhang (Zhang wang).[131] In Hansen's model, "regional cults" are transformations of local tutelary deities of commoner origin, and the chief agents of transmission are merchants and other local inhabitants who travel widely. She therefore omits from consideration deities such as Dongyue and Guanyin because of their institutional ties to ecclesiastic religion. Yet even these four cults display marked variation in character, origin, and range of distribution.

The cult of Consort Linghui—better known by the title Empress of Heaven (Tianhou), awarded to her by the Qing in 1737, or by her colloquial name Mazu—is the only one of these four cults to have received much scholarly attention prior to Hansen's study.[132] The origins of Mazu have been encrusted by many layers of myth, but most likely the cult coalesced around the figure of a preternaturally prescient young woman named Lin, renowned for her abilities as a fortune-teller, who died young and was subsequently revered as a goddess in her native Putian, on the Fujian seacoast. Like Sire Li, Lin was no ordinary commoner but a seer and medium whose premature death endowed her with a charismatic aura. After her death Lin was believed to come to the aid of seafarers endangered by storms. During the eleventh century her cult slowly spread along the Fujian coast, finally gaining imperial endorsement in 1123 after she was credited with rescuing imperial envoys sent to Korea. Yet not until the thirteenth century were Consort Linghui temples founded in areas outside Fujian, with the exception of a temple in the international trading entrepôt of Ningbo. The cult subsequently spread throughout coastal cities in the southeast, but it did not begin to penetrate the interior, even in the goddess's native Fujian, until the seventeenth century.

King Zhang probably is the least familiar figure among these four cults, but his cult achieved unparalleled prominence (measured in number of branch temples) among the regional cults of southeastern China in the Southern Song period. King Zhang's base temple in Guangde prefecture in modern Anhui province, like those of other regional cults, became a major pilgrimage site, attracting devotees from distant areas, and the site of an important temple fair as well. Hansen notes that the King Zhang cult also spawned a host of subcults. Not only did King Zhang's family and relatives receive official investiture as deities, but in addition numerous non-consanguineal deities were adopted into the family of cults sheltered under King Zhang's extensive patriarchy (including, for example, Sire Li).[133] King Zhang was said to have been a mortal of commoner origin who lived during the Han dynasty. But the mythology constructed around King Zhang recalls the civilizing exploits of the sage-king Yu, and his cult recapitulated features common to pre-Song cults dedicated to legendary settlers.

Zitong, as noted above, became a patron of scholars because of his reputation as an oracle who could predict one's fate in the civil service examinations. Zitong emerged as a local cult in northern Sichuan, a distant frontier in the truncated Southern Song empire. Zitong evolved from a primitive serpent cult dating back to at least the fourth century, though by the Tang the deity had been euhemerized as a more salutary human thaumaturge. A series of scriptures revealed at Zitong's base temple between 1168 and 1194 enhanced the god's popularity as a patron of the educated elite and stimulated the diffusion of the cult to southeastern China in the thirteenth century. In the southeast, Zitong temples were limited to major cities and patronized mostly by educated men. (Since Wuxian, an apotheosis of Wutong, will be discussed in detail in the following two chapters, I will only briefly observe here that the god was never identified with any historical figure, commoner or otherwise, and that there is no evidence of merchant sponsorship in the dissemination of this cult.)

The variations among these regional cults show that they do not conform to a single model. The most consistent feature of these cults is their association with a specific sacred site that becomes the cynosure of popular devotion, even as the cults themselves spread to other areas. It seems likely that cycles of festival and pilgrimage stimulated the diffusion of these cults. As Steven Sangren has recently pointed out, a reputation for miraculous power is not a sufficient explanation for the genesis and spread of cults; ultimately, the power of a cult derives from its potential for authenticating its devotees' social experience and sense of identity.[134] Sangren emphasizes that pilgrimage plays a vital role in spreading and sustaining cults by providing a sacred domain in space and time that unifies members of disparate communities and integrates their own discrete experiences through ritual and worship. Pilgrimage thus provides the means whereby a cult can cross the threshold of the territorially discrete community that nurtured it and serve to validate the spiritual life of outsiders as well. The Buddhist cults of relics, once translated to Chinese soil, provided an important inspiration for Chinese patterns of religious pilgrimage. Whereas older Chinese conceptions of the divine attributed the sacredness of a site to the potency of its resident deity, relics underscored the power of divine objects to endow a place with numinous power.[135] Annual festivals held at the base temples of renowned deities drew worshipers from throughout the realm. Pilgrims returned to their homes with tokens—such as images of the gods or ashes from the temples' censers—that provided the tangible link to the deity and the active yeast from which a branch cult and a new temple community would grow.[136] Although it is true that gods circulated with their believers, it seems that the agents of transmission more often were worshipers from the new host community rather than evangelists from the deity's place of origin. Nor should we underestimate the role of clergy in disseminating information about potent deities. As we have seen above, the Daoist priest Deng Daoshu played the crucial role in the transmission of the cult of Sire Li to its new home in Changshu, and the evidence from other regional cults also points to the important role of religious specialists in the propagation of such cults.[137]

Although Dongyue temples were initially linked to imperial patronage of Daoism, in the Southern Song the Dongyue cult spread in a fashion similar to other regional cults. Worship of Dongyue, as with other regional cults, was focused on a specific site that served as a national cult center. Of course, after the Jurchen conquest of north China in 1127 Mount Tai itself was no longer accessible to any but the most intrepid pilgrims. In its stead the Dongyue temple at Fushanzhen (Changshu), at the mouth of the Yangzi River, emerged as an alternate destination. The Fushan temple, first built on a mountain slope in the 1050s, was moved to a more convenient spot along the river in 1100, and then rebuilt on a more lavish scale in 1132. Local boosters, no doubt mindful of the supposedly temporary residence of the Song emperor at Hangzhou, dubbed Fushan's Dongyue temple the god's "detached palace."[138] It soon began to attract hordes of pilgrims.[139] From the capital of Hangzhou down to the region's scores of market towns, Dongyue's feast day was the crowning event in Jiangnan's annual cycle of religious festivals. Thus, the Dongyue cult cannot be labeled simply as a manifestation of institutionalized Daoism. The cult's identification with a specific sacred place, the proliferation of branch temples claiming affiliation with the base temple, the crucial role of popular support (notably in the forms of pilgrimage and festival) in sustaining the cult, its urban locus, and its diverse constituencies all suggest that the development of the Dongyue cult paralleled that of other regional cults.

The diffusion of the Guanyin cult proceeded in the same way. Of course, the Buddhist ecclesiastic establishment actively encouraged devotion to Guanyin. But the potency of particular shrines as sites of worship and miracles was typically rooted in tangible instruments of divine manifestation, above all in icons. As we have seen, the renowned statue of Guanyin at the Upper Tianzhu Monastery outside Hangzhou was the principal attraction for the throngs of pilgrims who made the monastery a famous shrine. The same pattern can be found in less exalted shrines, such as the Guanyin temple at the market town of Guangfu (Suzhou), on the eastern shore of Lake Tai. In 1040, in the midst of a drought, a local resident found a bronze statue of Guanyin in the mud near the town's eponymous Buddhist shrine (Guangfusi), which was deemed a propitious omen. The inhabitants prepared ritual regalia and prayed before the statue, whereupon rain immediately fell.[140] The fame of the statue's miraculous powers spread throughout Suzhou. Whenever the area suffered from drought or flood, it became common practice for the prefect at Suzhou to summon the goddess's aid by bringing the Guangfu statue to the city, where the civil officials conducted rites of propitiation.[141] In 1186 the statue was stolen, but it was recovered eleven years later. In 1275, as the Mongol armies approached, a monk took the statue and fled. The locals were forced to replace it with a wooden substitute, which over time was gilded and embellished with gold, jade, and silver ornaments.[142] As the author of a commemorative inscription for the Guanyin statue at Guangfu (writing ca. 1086–94) observed, epiphanies of Guanyin through miracle-working images were crucial to the creation of other major Guanyin shrines and pilgrimage sites at Upper Tianzhu, the Fenghuasi Monastery in Ningbo, and the Shuanglinsi Monastery in Wuzhou as well.[143]

Regional cult centers stood apart from the nested hierarchy of sovereign and tutelary deities. While the latter ruled distinct territories and thus required mandatory worship and sacrifice from the community defined by the god's jurisdiction, the regional cults were sustained by continual manifestations of the god's power (through miracle and revelation) and cycles of festival and pilgrimage that drew large numbers of worshipers to the god's temple. The communities of worship that gathered at pilgrimage sites were linked by common faith, in contrast to the ascriptive membership in the cult groups (she) of local gods. The shrines dedicated to these regional cults likewise stood apart from the territorially bounded temples of local gods. The regional cults prospered in proportion to the intensity of devotion they attracted from the populace at large. Yet these devotional cults—with the exception of Guanyin and her avatars—did not foster a sense of personal closeness between mortals and divine beings. Instead, they recapitulated the patterns of subordination of humble petitioners before powerful gods that we find in sovereign cults. This subordination is cogently expressed in the metaphorical language typically used to denote pilgrimage: "attending court at the mountain to present tribute of incense [chaoshan jinxiang]."[144] The gods of the regional cults were the most exalted beings within the ken of ordinary people, and thus inspired the kind of reverence and awe accorded to human monarchs.

The Song period thus witnessed momentous changes in religious culture. Preoccupation with death and atonement, increasingly baroque representations of postmortem punishment, and the sense of awe and terror that the gods evoked cast long shadows over popular piety. Yet the vernacularization of ritual and communication with the divine, in addition to the development of new liturgical practices for laity in both Buddhism and Daoism, gave ordinary people greater access to the gods. Elaborate hierarchies of gods and cults were constructed in response to changes in social life and religious needs, and these cults in turn transformed the religious landscape, redefining ritual time (festival) and space (temple). The diffusion of religious lore accelerated through the spread of the printed word and image, while the greater mobility of society was echoed by the expanded circulation of cults and worshipers. The state and ecclesiastic authorities sought to appropriate local cults for their own purposes, at the same time imposing their own definitions of orthodoxy and deviance, but popular devotion proved much too supple and creative to be governed by these interventions. The mutability of the gods testifies to the salient role of the popular imagination in creating them. The devout faithful, either as individuals or through collective action, tried to establish reciprocal, symbiotic relations with the gods, providing offerings and allegiance in return for protection and divine favor. The feminization of compassion in the forms of Guanyin and other goddesses is one reflection of this effort to establish a more personal relationship with the divine. Yet people never lost sight of their humble station before the sovereign might of the gods that controlled their destiny.

The unified realm of the sacred that coalesced during the Song period prevailed in Chinese vernacular religion throughout the late imperial period, and it remains the framework of Chinese religion today. Yet, although the structure of the religious universe has exhibited a basic stability, the divine realm remained an arena of constant conflict, negotiation, and change. Tensions within human society exerted pressure on the divine world as well. No aspect of Chinese religion exemplifies these tensions better than the Wutong spirits, to whom we now finally turn.

CHAPTER 6

Wutong: From Demon to Deity

The origins of the Wutong cult, like those of most popular deities, are obscured by time and myth. Many sources of Southern Song date or later place the beginnings of the cult in the Tang period. It is in the eleventh century, though, that the god first appears in the surviving literary record. From the outset Wutong possessed the diabolical attributes that so strongly colored his later incarnation as a god of wealth. Yet Wutong also figured as a benevolent deity who succored the sick. Although the Wutong cult gained the endorsement of both imperial authorities and the Daoist establishment in the Song period, its origins among the demonic *shanxiao* mountain goblins were never effaced. Indeed, in Ming-Qing times the complex and multifaceted god of the Song era became overshadowed, at least in Jiangnan, by the sinister character of the *shanxiao* from which it sprang.

As we saw in chapter 3, the *shanxiao* were particularly identified with the Wuyi mountain ranges dividing the Gan River valley (Jiangxi province) from the southeastern littoral of Zhejiang and Fujian. Hong Mai, who provides us with the most extensive discussion of contemporary beliefs about the *shanxiao*, traced Wutong to the *shanxiao* of this region.[1] The *shanxiao* of south China, Hong reported, were known by a variety of local names: in Jiangnan and Jiangdong (in Song times, Jiangdong encompassed northeastern Jiangxi, southern Anhui, and the westernmost part of Jiangsu, including Nanjing; see map 3) the *shanxiao* were known by the name "fifth lad" *(wulang)*; in the Gan River valley and Fujian

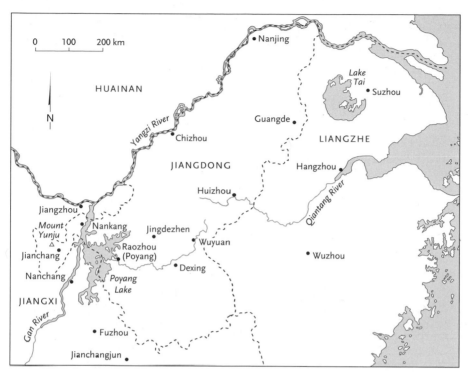

Map 3. Jiangdong in the Song Dynasty

they were called "third lad beneath the trees" *(muxia sanlang)* or "tree lodgers" *(muke)*; while the single-footed species was referred to as "one-legged Wutong" *(dujiao wutong)*. Despite the variations in nomenclature all of these noxious inhabitants of the mountains and forests were demonic poltergeists like the *kui, wangliang,* and *shanxiao* recorded in earlier literature. Hong also likened these changeling demons to the fox spirits of the northern regions. Furthermore, he identified the Wild Youths and Roving Eight Brothers (Yezhong you xiongdi baren), whom we have already encountered as plague demons, as another species within this common genus.

Hong Mai also linked the *muke,* as he calls them, to the two dominant motifs of Wutong lore: the god's roles as a capricious source of ill-gotten wealth and as a sexual predator. Small-minded people venerated them because they could bring sudden wealth to their clients, but even the slightest offense would cause the spirits to repossess whatever largesse they had granted.[2] At the height of summer the *muke* came down from the mountains to trade in timber. Because they seem to appear and disappear at will, inhabitants of this region treated the *muke* with the utmost circumspection, diligently laying out offerings to purchase their good graces. By nature wanton and lascivious, the *muke* often disguised themselves as handsome gentlemen to seduce unsuspecting and vulnerable women. In their true forms they resembled apes, dogs, or toads, but they were capable of mutating into different bodily forms and could move at great speed. Their touch was as cold as ice, and they were endowed with penises of impressive size.

Women despoiled by these creatures lost consciousness and endured painful fits and convulsions lasting for days, even weeks, which often brought them to the brink of death. Some of these women, upon regaining their wits, spoke of having been transported to splendid palaces where they enjoyed a life of sensuous pleasure. Once infected by the *muke/shanxiao* they acquired numinous powers, and many became spirit mediums. Others, however, descended into madness from which they never recovered. Hong Mai devoted particular attention to the monstrous births that resulted from sexual relations with such vile spirits. He related more than a dozen cases, apparently all from his native Jiangdong, in which intercourse with the *muke/shanxiao* resulted in macabre pregnancies, deformed newborns, and the madness and death of women (table 2). Song medical lore recognized the danger posed to pregnant women by malignant ghosts, especially the wandering spirits of dead infants.[3] Although precautions could be taken against demonic invasion, healers and sorcerers had no cure for the progeny of monstrous *shanxiao*.

Everywhere throughout the mountainous interior of south China people built small shrines dedicated to the *muke/shanxiao* called *congci*, or "grove shrines." *Congci*, typically small, crude structures, were usually placed at the foot of great trees or impressive cliffs believed to harbor these spirits, which suggests that they were located in the wilderness rather than within village compounds.[4] *Congci* performed an apotropaic function, keeping strange denizens of the forests at bay, but they also became sites at which local exorcists and spirit mediums practiced their trades. An official stationed in Zhenjiang in 1048 conducted a campaign to suppress *congci* precisely because they harbored bands of "sorcerers" *(wu)* who "extort money and goods from the local inhabitants to fashion statues in the likeness of *kui, sao* [i.e., *shanxiao*], *guimei, yiyang,* and *panghuang,* which they house together in their grove shrines *[congci]*."[5] This catalogue of *congci* deities is rife with literary allusions that betray the author's ignorance of the actual figures being represented, but all of

TABLE 2. MOTIFS OF *SHANXIAO* STORIES IN HONG MAI'S *TALES OF THE LISTENER*

Motif	Story Number													
	1	2	3	4	5	6	7	8	9	10	11	12	13	14
Possession of woman			•											
Intercourse with woman		•			•		•	•		•				•
Pregnancy				•	•	•	•		•	•	•	•	•	
Birth of monster-child				•	•	•	•		•	•		•	•	
Death of woman	•	•		•		•				•				•
Wanton mischief								•						

SOURCE: *YJZ*, dingzhi, 19.695–97.

these terms refer to aberrant and terrifying *shanxiao* and their kin.[6] A poem entitled "Old Temple" by Wang Ling (1032–59) vividly captures the dread and alarm that images of such baleful creatures could provoke. Touring a temple fallen into disrepair, Wang finds the glaring visage of the resident god (identified only as the "Divine Lord" *[shenjun]*) intimidating nonetheless. As he walks through a winding corridor in a side wing of the temple, he suddenly stops short:

> As the sun rises in the sky, a sight so grotesque to make me gasp appears,
> Horses, oxen, sheep, and sundry sorts of swine and fowl,
> Cretins with human heads, sprouting four limbs,
> Some among them have faces of men, yet bodies not human at all.[7]

The hybrid monsters Wang encountered on the walls of this temple immediately call to mind the morphological oddities of the ancient *Classic of the Mountains and Seas* and the parade of fantastic creatures shown in figure 12. Whether the Wutong spirits likewise were portrayed in such aberrant forms is uncertain, given the lack of surviving iconography. The statue shown in figure 26, which may indeed be a Song-era image of the one-legged Wutong, displays the exaggerated facial features characteristic of demon iconography but otherwise is human in form. In any event, worship of Wutong almost certainly originated in these *congci* shrines, and in domestic shrines fashioned in imitation of them.[8]

Ursula-Angelika Cedzich suggests that the name Wutong most likely was first applied to demonic beings like the *shanxiao* by Buddhist monks seeking to curb popular devotion to such deviant spirits. In Buddhist lore, *wutong* refers to five superhuman powers *(abhijñā)* attained through Buddhist meditative practice, although heretical sorcerers could also obtain

Figure 26. A one-legged Wutong? This statue, dating from the Southern Song period, has been identified as an image of the one-legged Wutong. However, the statue and its niche lack any inscriptions to confirm this identification, which is based on the assertions of an eighteenth-century visitor to the Dazu Grottoes (see Liu Changjiu et al., ed., 1985: 337, 340). This statue is grouped with a set of Daoist divinities, including the Jade Emperor and Dongyue (see figure 24), about twenty-two kilometers south of the more famous Buddhist rock carvings at Baodingshan (see figure 19). Whether or not the statue originally represented Wutong, it may convey some sense of how Chinese of a later era imagined the demon. Niche 7, Shimenshan Grotto, Dazu (Sichuan). Twelfth century? From Chongqing Dazu shike bowuguan 1991, plate 213. Courtesy of the Chongqing Museum of Dazu Art and Sculpture.

them by taking drugs and uttering magical formulas. Buddhist writings referred to those in possession of these powers as "Wutong transcendents" *(Wutong xianren)*. Aberrant spirits of this type that appear in Buddhist demonologies are akin to the indigenous *shanxiao*.[9] In his magnum opus synthesizing Chan and Pure Land doctrines, the renowned monk Yunming Yanshou (904–75) spoke of the fifth "power" *(tong)* as the "demonic power" *(yaotong)*, which he associated with fox spirits and the "changeling spirits of trees and rocks" that can assume human form. Yanshou observed that supernatural powers can be used for good or evil, and that only the accomplished adept can discern truth from falsehood. Thus most laypersons fall prey to the deceptions of demonic spirits.[10]

The earliest attestable reference to worship of Wutong appears in an essay entitled "Demolishing Idols," written in 1016 by the Tiantai monk

Zhiyuan (976–1022). Upon assuming the abbacy of the Ma'naoyuan Cloister in Hangzhou, Zhiyuan discovered that the monastery housed icons of the *tudi* and Wutong spirits. Zhiyuan immediately removed the Wutong idols, while redesignating the *tudi* as guardian spirits of the monastery grounds *(huqielan shen)*. He also observed that the inhabitants of Hangzhou commonly worshiped *tudi* and Wutong idols in their homes, a practice he found abhorrent. The name Wutong, Zhiyuan noted, derived from the Buddhist term *abhijñā*, but had been wantonly misused to disguise the true nature of "demonic goblins and sprites."[11] Zhiyuan's testimony reveals that worship of Wutong spirits was already prevalent in Jiangnan in the early eleventh century, but it tells us little of the nature of this cult apart from likening the Wutong to goblins and demons. A thirteenth-century magistrate, in a commemoration for a chapel devoted exclusively to the worship of Wutong founded by a Buddhist monk, stated that Wutong was widely venerated as a protector of the Buddhist faith. His testimony suggests that icons like those Zhiyuan discovered in his monastery represented the god as a fearsome temple guardian.[12]

The new Daoist sects of the Song period, largely devoted to exorcism and therapeutic liturgies, also took an active role in stamping Wutong spirits as malicious *shanxiao*. Daoist exorcism manuals dating from the early twelfth century and later grouped the Wutong together with the *shanxiao* mountain goblins.[13] The earliest extant ritual corpus of the Tianxin tradition, Yuan Miaozong's *Secret Essentials on Assembling the Perfected of the Most High for the Relief of the State and Deliverance of the People* (dated 1116), identified the *shanxiao* as emanations of anomalies in cosmic regeneration roaming the world of mortals; the *shanxiao* claim to be sages and worthies, debauch women, cause floods and fires, hurl bricks and stones, play tricks on farm animals, and engage in all manner of mischief.[14] Other exorcism manuals, probably dating from the Southern Song, described Wutong in similar fashion, and in particular stressed the deity's predilection for assuming the form of a handsome man who circulates among mortals and violates the sanctity of the marriage bed.[15] Hong Mai's stories are replete with accounts of ritual experts who use their skills as exorcists to expel demonic Wutong spirits; in one case the exorcist specifically employed the Tianxin Thunder Magic rituals.[16] Wutong also figured prominently in spirit medium cults. Mediums, usually females, invoked Wutong's assistance in communicating with the spirit world.[17] Corroboration of the prominence of *shanxiao*/Wutong in the mediumistic traditions of south China is furnished by another late-twelfth-century writer, Xiang Anshi (d. 1208). Quoting a local gazetteer from western Hunan, Xiang stated that "the Wutong spirits derive from Qu Yuan's 'Nine Songs.' Contemporary sorcerers of Lizhou refer to the father as 'Grand Unity' (Taiyi), and the sons as 'Cloud-Empyrean Fifth Lad' (Yunxiao wulang) or 'Mountain Goblin Fifth Lad' (Shanxiao wulang)."[18] A magistrate stationed in Hunan in the thirteenth century repeated this genealogy of the Wutong spirits, adding that these two brothers were one-legged *kui* goblins who contemporaries wrongly believed to be a group of five spirits.[19]

Buddhist theologians and Daoist sorcerers thus invariably associated the Wutong with diabolical *shanxiao*. In the popular mind, too, the Wutong, especially in the personae of Wulang and the "one-legged Wutong," were indeed identified with the *shanxiao*.[20] Popular images of Wutong reproduced all of the vices detailed in the exorcists' manuals, but they emphasized several features in particular. Above all, Wutong became closely associated with the acquisition and loss of wealth. In this respect the deity did not simply fill an existing niche in Chinese conceptions of supernatural agents, as was the case with its identification as a species of *shanxiao*. Instead, Wutong's emergence as a god of wealth betokened a burgeoning phenomenon in Song society: success or failure in a competitive money economy brought about abrupt changes in personal fortunes. It is not surprising that Chinese seeking to explain rapid oscillations in personal wealth would turn to the gods; what is noteworthy is that their attention focused on such a morally ambivalent figure.

The capricious behavior that Wutong exhibited in his guise as a *shanxiao* characterized his actions as a god of wealth. The Southern Song bibliophile and raconteur Wu Zeng recorded a story, set in Kaifeng in the mid-eleventh century, about a milliner who set up shop in one of the capital's most elegant neighborhoods. The milliner encounters a sportive and merry group of five young men, one of whom, after a long bout of convivial drinking, offers to invest a large sum of money in the milliner's business. Subsequently the milliner discovers the skeletons in his new partner's closets. Passing the night at his benefactor's home, he surreptitiously peers into the adjacent rooms. One he finds full of women and children nailed to the walls, while the other is packed with wailing prisoners in chains. The milliner, though greatly shaken, accepts his host's money and his business prospers. Wu Zeng offered no moral reading of this tale. He merely noted that people in Kaifeng say that the five men were the Wutong spirits.[21]

Tales of the Listener also contains a number of stories confirming that Wutong had acquired a reputation as a notorious god of wealth. In one story, a plebeian *(xiaomin)* receives from Wutong advance warning of every rise or fall in his fortunes.[22] In another, the sudden good fortune of a Mr. Wu, a former sandal maker who strikes it rich as a vegetable-oil dealer, raises the suspicions of his neighbors. When thieves loot the houses of several local notables, people accuse Wu of the crimes. Under torture Wu confesses that he had been visited by a one-legged spirit who offered him munificent rewards in exchange for sacrifices. After being released Wu renovates a defunct one-legged Wutong shrine, where he holds nocturnal rites involving extravagant "bloody sacrifices," during which his entire family sits, "heedless of rank," naked in the dark. Such indecency, according to local lore, enabled the Wutong spirit to have his pleasure with Wu's wife, who bore the deity's offspring. Many years later Wu's eldest son marries an official's daughter, but the well-bred wife refuses to participate in these rites. Denied this sexual conquest, the god angrily visits pestilence upon the Wu household. Only after Wu and his wife, along with the resolute daughter-in-law, fall ill and die, and their hoard of cash is scattered by violent winds, does the Wu family regret their blasphemous idolatry and halt their sacrifices to Wutong.[23]

Several elements of this story became hallmarks of the Wutong cult: a diabolical pact with a shady spirit; the seduction or rape of wives and daughters; and the culmination in tragedy and dissolution of the family's ill-gotten gains. Even unalloyed devotion to Wutong did not ensure benefaction. Another of Hong Mai's stories recounts the case of a wealthy landowner who was a zealous devotee of the Wutong cult. The deity, impressed by the man's piety, appears before him and requests additional offerings of bloody sacrifices. The landowner neglects his financial affairs and exhausts his fortune ministering to the god's increasingly insatiable needs. Several months later the hapless landowner's wife and daughter suddenly sicken and die. Finally the voracious demon is seized by the minions of celestial justice, but the landowner receives no satisfaction for his losses.[24] Here, as in most stories concerning Wutong, the god's favor entangles his mortal votaries in a skein of costly devotions and dire consequences.

In only one of Hong Mai's stories do the Wutong spirits appear to act as agents of moral justice, but even here the five deities bear little resemblance to either austere paragons of Confucian virtue or the vengeful warriors dispatched by Daoist celestials to exact divine retribution. Instead the deities are portrayed as Rabelaisian parodies of sensual appetite. In this account they descend upon the establishment of a Hangzhou brewer, who makes a handsome profit by supplying food and drink for their night-long revels. The wanton prodigality of his patrons excites the brewer's greed, and he makes an audacious request for additional gifts of silver and silk. The gods merrily consent, but they enjoy the last laugh: when the brewer returns home he discovers that the henchmen of the Wutong had in the meantime emptied his cupboards of every object of value.[25]

The popular image of Wutong, then, shared the diabolical features of the baleful demon appearing in exorcism manuals. At the same time Wutong captured the popular imagination by assuming the form of a god of wealth—not the avuncular benefactor common to modern Chinese mythology, but a caricature of caprice, latent misery masquerading as unexpected good fortune. Yet this was only one of the changeling god's many personae. In this same period Wutong achieved not only respectability but also the highest imperial honors, and he became an avatar of both Buddhist bodhisattvas and the demon-expelling divine agents (lingguan) of Daoist sorcerers.

In contrast to the cruel bogey who stalks the pages of Hong Mai's anthology, the Wutong spirit that became the focal deity of local cults was cast in a positive light. In the Southern Song period a number of places, all in the Poyang Lake basin, were identified as the original home of the Wutong cult. In these local traditions Wutong assumed the form of a tutelary deity and was often depicted as bringing relief from the scourge of plague. The earliest text depicting Wutong as beneficent is Li Gou's commemoration for a Wutong shrine outside his native town of Jianchangjun (Jiangxi). Li composed this text in gratitude for Wutong's aid in sparing the lives of his family and fellow townsmen during an outbreak of plague in 1034.[26] The relationship between these local cults and the demonic spirit of folklore is unclear. Certainly it is plausible that two separate cults existed, but I am inclined to speculate that the benevolent Wutong of the Poyang basin was a transfiguration of the noxious Wutong. Such transfigurations of demons into servants of the Buddha were standard features of Buddhist morality tales, and became part of the literary lore concerning the god's origins in later times.

It was perhaps the association with Buddhist wonder working that inspired the notion of Wutong as a queller of plagues. One of the texts claiming to identify the original home of the Wutong cult specifically linked it to Buddhism. In an inscription dated 1233, Zhang Dayou stated that the Biographies of Divinities (Shenzhuan) by Li Zeng (1119–93) traced the Wutong cult to the great Chan monastery at Mount Yunju in Jianchang county, in Jiangdong circuit.[27] Zhang traveled to the monastery to investigate further and was told by the elder monks that the cult originated in an encounter between the eighth-century monk Daorong and "five divinities" *(wushenren)*, who donated the land on which Daorong founded the Yunjusi Monastery. Subsequently Daorong honored the five spirits with the epithet Lords of Peace and Joy (Anlegong).[28] Hong Mai, in an anecdote set in the late eleventh century, reported that the Wutong spirits worshiped at the Yunjusi Monastery as the Lords of Peace and Joy were renowned for their miraculous powers.[29]

The inhabitants of Dexing, founded as a silver mining town in the early Tang dynasty, advanced an even earlier claim to the Wutong cult. Local lore in Dexing credited Wutong with having pointed out the location of the area's silver deposits to a local hunter in 651.[30] Dexing natives attributed their economic prosperity to Wutong's divine aid and eagerly sought official recognition of their claim to the Wutong cult. Interestingly enough, of Hong Mai's twenty-four Wutong stories, three of the four that cast the deity in a positive light are set in Dexing. In one account Wutong delivers medicine to the local population to relieve them from pestilence, a gesture of compassion that recalls Li Gou's benediction of 1034.[31]

The Song court, however, recognized not Dexing but the neighboring county of Wuyuan as the proper home of the Wutong cult. According to local tradition in Wuyuan, the Wutong cult originated in 886, when five divine beings were said to have descended from heaven and informed a local resident that they had been assigned to serve as patron deities of Wuyuan. The people of Wuyuan built a shrine for these gods, who won widespread renown for the miracles they performed on behalf of the residents.[32] In the 980s, the magistrate of Wuyuan had a dream in which the Wutong spirits instructed him on how to exorcise a plague then raging throughout the region. The dream occurred on the eighth day of the fourth month, coinciding with the feast day of Śākyamuni Buddha. Henceforth the people of Wuyuan held a liturgical festival *(zhaihui)* on this day to celebrate their deliverance from the plague.[33] In 1109, the Song emperor Huizong honored Wuyuan's Wutong shrine with a plaque bearing the legend "Potent and obedient" *(Lingshun)*. After the temple was destroyed during the Fang La rebellion a decade later, the same emperor sent another plaque, and invested Wuyuan's Wutong spirits with the title of "sire" *(hou)*.[34]

Between these two events, however, a curious event occurred in the capital. In the first month of 1111, Huizong issued an edict banning worship of Wutong and two other deities identified as the objects of profane cults *(yinci)*. At the same time the emperor ordered the closing of 1,038 shrines in Kaifeng and transferred the icons from those shrines to Buddhist, Daoist, or state-managed temples.[35] The intention of these edicts apparently was not to eradicate popular objects of worship, but rather to strengthen state control over them. Huizong had fervently embraced Daoism, and under the tutelage of the Shenxiao priest Lin Lingsu he inaugurated an unprecedented effort to centralize and systematize the certification of temples and cults. Huizong reversed his predecessors' policy of allowing local jurisdictions to compile their own registers of sacrifices *(sidian)*, and instead sought to establish a uniform national register. Above all, Huizong's policies aimed to curb the activities of spirit mediums and restrict the conduct of religious observances and stewardship of temples to ordained priests.[36] Though not specifically mentioned in Huizong's edicts, the *congci* shrines with their *shanxiao* goblins and attending spirit mediums surely would have been primary targets of persecution. Moreover, the injunction against worship of Wutong in Kaifeng was consistent with official ritual regulations stipulating that worship of gods must be confined to their native jurisdictions.

Most likely the proscription issued in 1111 was directed against the notorious Wutong of *shanxiao* lore rather than the officially recognized cult in Wuyuan. In any case, Huizong's efforts to assert central control over local religion failed. The outbreak of the Fang La rebellion in Zhejiang in 1119, which subsequently spread to Jiangdong as well, forced him to reverse course in the matter of canonization of local gods. Insurrection on such a large scale exposed the serious weaknesses of Huizong's government, and in its aftermath the court tried to repair its image by recognizing local gods believed to have rendered aid in the suppression of the rebellion. Seizing this opportunity, dozens of local communities throughout Jiangnan and Jiangdong successfully lobbied for canonization of their patron deities.[37] It seems likely that the official recognition accorded Wuyuan's Wutong shrine in 1123 was part of this wave of canonizations. The Wutong cult at Wuyuan continued to enjoy official favor throughout the Southern Song. In 1174, Wuyuan's patron deities were promoted to the status of "lord" *(gong)* and rechristened as Wuxian (Five Manifestations), and in 1202 they received a further promotion to the titular rank of "king" *(wang)*.

The two neighboring counties of Dexing and Wuyuan competed fiercely for proprietary rights to Wutong/Wuxian. The eminent Confucian scholar-official Zhen Dexiu mentioned that while serving as vice-minister of imperial sacrifices in 1213–15 he had came across the petitions requesting imperial honors for Wuxian from both Dexing and Wuyuan.[38] Both sets of petitioners identified Wuxian as a group of five brothers surnamed Xiao, thus providing them with a more seemly human ancestry untainted by any association with the demonic *shanxiao*. Hong Mai ascribed the origin of the cult to Dexing, and one of his stories revolves around the efforts of Dexing inhabitants to secure official recognition for its Wuxian deity.[39] But the court consistently upheld Wuyuan's claim.[40] The stakes were high, since localities granted exclusive rights to the worship of a deity often became centers of pilgrimage and attracted spendthrift devotees from distant parts of the empire. Wuyuan did become such a major pilgrimage site in the Southern Song period.[41] The peak dates of pilgrimage to Wuyuan's Wuxian temple were 4/8, the anniversary of the god's deliverance of the local community from plague in the 980s, and 9/28, said to be the date of the original epiphany of the Wutong spirits in Wuyuan in 886.[42]

Naturally, both Dexing and Wuyuan claimed to be the original home of the beneficent Wutong. Regardless of which assertion is closer to the truth, once Wuyuan's cult received imperial endorsement other communities throughout south China sought to associate their Wutong temples with the orthodox cult. Fragmentary records suggest that in addition to the *congci* shrines in the countryside and the domestic shrines mentioned by Zhiyuan, temples dedicated to Wutong existed in major cities as well by the tenth century.[43] A Wutong shrine adjacent to Yangzhou's famous Houtu temple was said to be the site where Wang Jie, erstwhile merchant and master of alchemical arts patronized by the Emperor Zhenzong in the first decade of the eleventh century, was said to have obtained crucial ingredients for his formulas.[44] There also is evidence for the existence of a Wutong temple in Fuzhou (Fujian) in the early eleventh century.[45] A local prefect in Jiangling (Hubei) is said to have desecrated a Wutong temple circa 1022.[46] The demonic form of the cult had reached the capital by the middle of the eleventh century, and the 1111 proscription of the Wutong cult in Kaifeng suggests that it achieved considerable popularity there. Hong Mai's anecdotes demonstrate that Wutong inspired fear and devotion throughout Jiangxi, Jiangsu, Anhui, Fujian, and Zhejiang in the twelfth century. But dramatic growth of the beneficent form of the cult seems to have followed the sanction accorded by the court's investiture of Wutong with an imperial title in 1123.

As Zhiyuan observed—and Hong Mai confirmed—small neighborhood or household shrines dedicated to the demonic form of Wutong were ubiquitous in south China. Imperial patronage encouraged the construction of public temples dedicated to Wutong, usually in the name of its now-official persona, Wuxian. In Suzhou, for instance, the first Wutong shrine within the city was built near the Zhili Bridge in 1127–30. The emperor's promotion of Wuxian to the rank of king prompted a spectacular spurt in temple building. In 1203, a Suzhou monk brought back to his retreat wooden images of the "five kings" carved in Wuyuan.[47] This shrine, located in the fashionable southwestern quarter of the city, apparently attracted a considerable following. The monk soon had sufficient funds to purchase adjacent property and renovate his retreat, and in 1225 a multistory galleried pavilion (ge) dedicated to another of Wutong's incarnations, the bodhisattava Huaguang, was added to the shrine.[48] In 1209, another set of carved Wutong icons arrived from Wuyuan and was installed at the Guangxiao Abbey, a Daoist temple.[49] In the late 1230s, the main hall of the older temple at Zhili Bridge was restored and subsequently complemented with two Huaguang pavilions. A third shrine, one that would become the centerpiece of the Wutong cult in Ming-Qing times, was established at a former Buddhist monastery on the crest of Mount Lengqie at Stone Lake, about ten kilometers southwest of the city, in 1265–74.[50]

During the thirteenth century Wuxian, enjoying full imperial favor as well as widespread popular homage, was honored with a great number of shrines. At the end of the Song dynasty, Hangzhou and its immediate suburbs contained at least nine Wutong/Wuxian shrines, six of which were found within the precincts of Buddhist monasteries (table 3 and map 4). Jiangzhou, the port city at the mouth of the Poyang Lake, where it flows into the Yangzi River, numbered five Wuxian temples, as did the city of Jiaxing.[51] Branch temples were also established in other parts of Jiangxi. The Wuxian temple in Fuzhou was identified as a branch of the Wuyuan temple.[52] Chen Chun, an inveterate critic of the excesses of popular religion, ruefully acknowledged the popularity of what he called "the heretical Wutong cult shrines venerated by the people of this age" in an essay composed in 1217.[53] According to a Ming source, the frequent promotions of Wuxian within the imperial pantheon in the first half of the thirteenth century encouraged a rapid proliferation of temples dedicated to the god: "the splendor of its incense and candles [i.e., votive offerings] was comparable to those of the Daoist and Buddhist divinities. Even in the most distant prefectures and inaccessible counties its name and titles were universally recognized."[54]

The chief architectural feature of many of these Wuxian temples, such as those in Suzhou and the one located on the grounds of the Rongguosi

TABLE 3. WUXIAN SHRINES
IN SOUTHERN SONG HANGZHOU

Location	Date of Founding	
1. Jiuqucheng, outside Qiantang Gate	Ca. 1130–66	Known as Wusheng temple; mural by renowned figure painter Su Hanchen (fl. 1120s–60s)
2. Pingchangwan, outside Houchao Gate	Mid to late 12th century	
3. Beigaofeng; in rear of Lingyansi Monastery	Before 1213	Rebuilt in 1213; said to "draw worshipers from near and far"
4. Pujisi Monastery, outside Houchao Gate	1213	Burned down in 1230; rebuilt in 1236
5. Baoshanyuan Cloister, Taihe Ward	1233	Founded as Wuxian shrine by prime minister Zheng Qingzhi. In Ming times this temple was known as the Huaguang Temple, and the facing street Huaguang Street
6. Linggansi Monastery, in Qiantang county	1235	
7. Nangaofeng; Wutong Hall of Rongguosi Monastery	Ca. 1237–46	Built to complement existing shrine at Beigaofeng; in 1270, Prefect Qian Yueyou added a Huaguang Pavilion
8. Yuantong chan'an Convent	1254	Founded as a Wuxian shrine
9. Xu Village, south of Liuhe Pagoda	Before 1275	

SOURCES: *Mengliang lu*, 14.252; *[Chunyou] Lin'an zhi jiyi* (1252), 1.9a; *[Xianchun] Lin'an zhi* (ca. 1265–74), 76.18a, 78.10a–b, 82.8b; *Wulin jiushi*, 413, 424, 436; Jujian, "Nangaofeng jian Wutongdian shu," *Beijian ji*, 8.38a.

NOTE: Shrines are shown on map 3, except for Linggansi Monastery and Yuantong chan'an Convent, whose locations are uncertain.

Monastery in Hangzhou, was a pavilion dedicated to the bodhisattva Huaguang (Flowery Light).[55] The relationship between Wuxian and Huaguang, a fairly minor figure in Buddhist doctrine, is shrouded in mystery. The name Huaguang (Padmaprabha) appears in the third chapter of the *Lotus Sūtra* as the name by which Śākyamuni's disciple Śāriputra will be known when he attains Buddhahood. Yet Śāriputra never appears in recognizable form in popular lore about Wuxian/Huaguang. The name Huaguang is also used to designate Aśvakarṇa, a Buddhist fire god. In

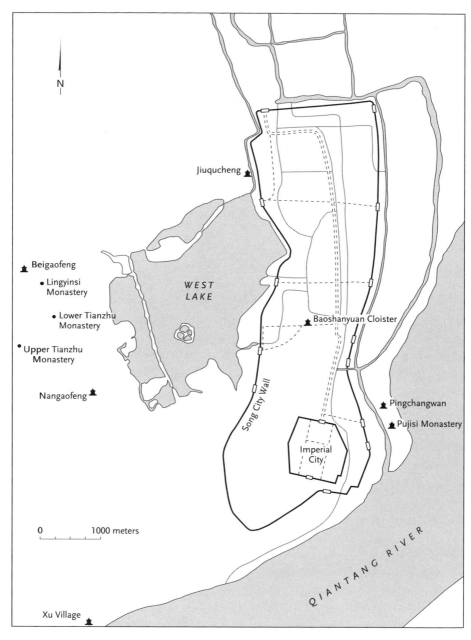

N

Jiuqucheng ▲

Beigaofeng ▲
• Lingyinsi
  Monastery

WEST
LAKE

• Lower Tianzhu
  Monastery

• Upper Tianzhu
  Monastery

Nangaofeng ▲

Baoshanyuan Cloister

Song City Wall

Pingchangwan ▲
Pujisi Monastery ▲

Imperial
City

0   1000 meters

QIANTANG RIVER

Xu Village ▲

Map 4. Wuxian shrines in Southern Song Hangzhou

Journey to the South, a sixteenth-century vernacular novel featuring Huaguang, Huaguang appears as an incarnation of celestial fire, and allusions to Aśvakarṇa abound; for example, Huaguang's divine father is identified as the King of Horse-Ear Mountain (Maer shanwang), an alternate name for Aśvakarṇa (see below). Yet Song texts are silent about the nature and origins of Huaguang and make no explicit connection between Huaguang and Aśvakarṇa.

The earliest association between Huaguang and the Wuxian cult, the building of Huaguang pavilions at the Wuxian temples in the thirteenth century, is iconic rather than literary. Lu Yinglong, writing in the 1240s or 1250s, specifically identified Wuxian as "the one whom the Buddhist writings refer to as Huaguang Tathāgata [Rulai]," an identification that is echoed in Ming and Qing texts.[56] Huaguang and Wutong are not linked in Hong Mai's tales, though in one place Hong does describe the fourth of the Wuxian figures as "by nature fond of the Way; abiding in ritual purity, he is solely devoted to distributing medicines and thereby accumulating hidden merit."[57] It is this fourth member of the quintet who is usually identified with Huaguang. Wuxian and Huaguang are more explicitly joined in the calendar of feast days. Both share the same feast day, the twenty-eighth day of the ninth lunar month,[58] and both are associated with the great communal liturgies held on the eighth day of the fourth month (4/8), in concert with the festival in honor of Śākyamuni Buddha.[59] The earliest testimony connecting Huaguang to the Wuxian cult center at Wuyuan is a poem dating from the turn of the fourteenth century that includes a line listing the "Temple of the Imperially Invested 'Potent and Obedient' King [i.e., Wuxian]; Tower of the Huaguang Buddha" among the notable sights in Wuyuan.[60] Huaguang is invariably associated with Wuxian rather than Wutong, which suggests that the emergence of Huaguang as a Buddhist alter ego for Wuxian originated with the Wuyuan cult.

At the home temple of Wuxian in Wuyuan, assemblies known as "great maigre feasts in celebration of the supreme goodness and all-pervasive mercy (Apratihata) of the Buddha" *(zhishan wuai dazhai)* were held on 4/8, attracting pilgrims from far away.[61] The Apratihata assemblies *(wuai-hui, wuzhehui)* had their origin in the mass convocations initiated by the pious Emperor Wu of the Liang dynasty (r. 502–49) to pray for relief from pestilence or express thanksgiving to the Buddha.[62] Unlike most "maigre feasts" *(zhai),* which were reserved for clerics alone, the Apratihata assemblies brought together laity and clergy in common worship to earn blessings for the multitude, both dead and living.[63] The relationship between the Apratihata liturgies and Huaguang/Wuxian can only be guessed at, but we should recall that the annual festivals at Wuyuan's Wuxian shrine originated as communal rites commemorating Wutong's intercession on this same date to save the community from pestilence.

Wuyuan's Wuxian festival achieved perhaps unparalleled popularity in the Southern Song period. One of Hong Mai's protagonists made a pilgrimage to Wuyuan's Wuxian temple in 1196 on 4/8 and worshiped there for eight days before returning to his home in Chizhou (Anhui).[64] A Wuyuan gazetteer boasted that the festival even attracted pilgrims from overseas.[65] In the late Song a judicial intendant for Jiangdong circuit, alarmed at the pilgrims who flocked to the Wuxian festival at Wuyuan, tried to ban the festival, to no avail.[66] In the 1280s, immediately following the Mongol conquest, Wuyuan's festival on 4/8 continued to draw devout followers of Wuxian from "the four points of the compass." The festival, described as a "Buddhist assembly" (fohui), gave a considerable boost to the local economy. The presence of great numbers of pilgrims made the Wuxian festival one of the great annual temple fairs of the Southern Song, and Wuyuan became "a hub for the merchants and tradesmen of the whole subcelestial realm."[67] The editor of a Yuan gazetteer of Kunshan county (Suzhou) noted with dismay the enthusiasm of Kunshan's inhabitants for undertaking pilgrimages to the Wuxian temple in Wuyuan.[68] In the late Song, a monk returning to Kunshan from a pilgrimage to Wuyuan had brought back incense ashes that were used to consecrate a branch temple in honor of Wuxian.[69]

In the thirteenth century, the custom of holding mass Wuxian festivals on 4/8 spread to Jiangnan as well. In the early 1240s, the two great Wuxian temples in Suzhou (both of which erected Huaguang pavilions) began to hold processions of Wuxian images around the city on the fourth and eighth days of the fourth month (the fourth was also associated with the Śākyamuni Buddha). The circumambulation of the city lasted past nightfall, and the great display of lanterns, carriages, lavishly decorated images, and ritual paraphernalia surpassed the city's renowned lantern festivals. Henceforth these processions, accompanied by theatrical performances, became annual events.[70] Cult groups (she) in Hangzhou held "Wuxian kings' assemblies to honor the Buddha" (wuxianwang qingfohui) on 4/8.[71] Presumably the Huaguang assemblies (Huaguang hui) held on this date during the Ming dynasty were a continuation of this practice. In the 1480s, the inhabitants of Hangzhou began to convene Huaguang assemblies on 9/28 at a temple at Beixinguan, one of the major commercial tax depots of the Ming empire and the site of a Wuxian temple in Song times. In 1494, the spectacle attracted such large crowds that the Beixin Bridge collapsed under their weight, causing more than thirty deaths.[72] This tragedy prompted local authorities to ban the event, though the assemblies lived on elsewhere. In the early sixteenth century Huaguang assemblies were held on 4/8 in Songjiang. By Qing times the custom seems to have died out.[73]

The most dramatic reversal of Wutong's unsavory image was, as Cedzich has observed, the god's transfiguration into one of the divine agents *(lingguan)* invoked by Daoist sorcerers to expel baleful spirits such as the *shanxiao* from which Wutong had descended. Tracing this remarkable rehabilitation is complicated by the difficulty of dating texts in the Daoist *Canon,* but it most likely occurred during the latter part of the thirteenth century. Two of the three texts in the Daoist *Canon* in which Wuxian appears as a demonifuge cannot be earlier than 1265, since the deities are identified by the titles given to them by the court in that year.[74] The third text, the *Wonderful Most High Dongxuan Lingbao Scripture of the Basic Deeds of Huaguang, Agent of Five Manifestations,* was not included in the recension of the Daoist *Canon* published in 1444–45; it appears only in the supplement added in 1607.[75] The Wuxian portrayed in this scripture represents a complete inversion of the noxious Wutong of yore. The Wuxian spirits assume the form of five Huaguang heavenly marshals who are dispatched by the supreme deity of the Lingbao liturgical tradition, Yuanshi tianzun, to protect the souls of sinful mortals against the depredations of evil demons. The Huaguang/Wuxian spirits, which descend to the human world in many forms, are Daoist bodhisattvas, charged with aiding mortals in their difficult journey to the afterlife. They command a vast array of supernumeraries, including thunder spirits and *chenghuang* and *tudi* gods. Ironically, their foes are none other than the *shanxiao!*

The preponderance of evidence suggests that Wuxian's transformation into a powerful demonifuge followed the god's elevation to the rank of divine "king" by imperial decree in 1202. In this instance Daoist hagiographers apparently took their cue from the court. The sanction of orthodoxy accorded Wuxian by imperial canonization conferred not merely legitimacy but also the aura of power. Practitioners of exorcism subsequently enlisted Wuxian into the ranks of divine agents, and in doing so they completely severed Wuxian from his erstwhile demonic form, Wutong.

Yet at least one Daoist text portrays the amalgam of Huaguang and

Wuxian as a malevolent spirit reminiscent of the demonic Wutong. A ha-
giographical account of the guardian deity Wen Qiong, written in 1274,
identified Huaguang as the resident deity of a Wuxian shrine in Chizhou.
The Huaguang spirit takes a liking to the concubine of the vice-prefect
and seizes her soul, causing her death. The vice-prefect's subordinates
persuade him to summon a local "man of the Dao" skilled in the esoteric rites used to invoke the aid of warrior spirits. This sorcerer conjures
up the Huaguang spirit (who identifies himself as "the fourth Huaguang
bodhisattva of the prefecture's Temple of the Five Kings") and demands
that he relinquish the woman's soul. The spirit refuses, forcing the exorcist to invoke the aid of Wen Qiong. Wen vanquishes the incarnation
of Huaguang and chops off his head. Although the temporal authorities
subsequently destroy the temple at Chizhou and its images, the unre-
pentant spirit scoffs at the power of the exorcist and proclaims that he
draws his power from all the sacred mountains and rivers; although no
longer able to draw sustenance from offerings at the Chizhou shrine, he
will continue to thrive elsewhere.[76]

In addition to the association with Huaguang, during the Southern
Song the Wuxian cult also began to appear under the alternate name
Wusheng (Five Saints). The sobriquet Wusheng first appears in connection with the Wuxian branch shrines in Hangzhou, but the close connection to the Wuxian shrines suggests a possible origin in Wuyuan.[77]
Indeed, the Wuyuan native Hu Sheng (fl. 1269), in an apologetic defense
of the legitimacy of Wuyuan's Wuxian cult, declared that "some people
equate the Wusheng [spirits] and the Wutong, but this view is wrong."[78]
The implication, of course, is that Wuyuan's imperially ordained Wusheng
(i.e., Wuxian) cult should not be confused with the demonic Wutong.
The name Wusheng appears only once in Hong Mai's anthology. In an
anecdote dated to 1177, an examination candidate from Fujian is said to
have prayed for success at a "Wusheng branch temple" outside Hangzhou's Qiantang Gate. In this instance the temple was said to be affiliated with the temple at Dexing rather than at Wuyuan.[79] Thirteenth-
century gazetteers of Hangzhou confirm that there was a Wusheng temple
at this location (see table 3, number 1) but make no mention of an affiliation with either Dexing or Wuyuan. In another anecdote from *Tales of
the Listener*, a *shanxiao* demon identifies himself as "Wutong jiusheng";
Hong Mai appends a note stating that Jiusheng, Wutong, and *shanxiao*
were all interchangeable names for the same class of demons.[80] Con-
ceivably the appellation Wusheng originated from a conflation of the
two terms Wutong and Jiusheng. But both Daoist writings and popular

Figure 27. Wusheng (Five Saints). This woodblock print
from the Yuan popular religious tract *Enlarged Quest
for the Divine* depicts Wusheng as five young men in
scholars' robes and caps. From *SSGJ*, xia.60. Courtesy
of Beijing Library.

hagiographies of the Yuan and Ming periods consistently identify Wusheng with Wuxian, not the demonic Wutong (figure 27).[81]

The transformation of Wutong into Wuxian/Wusheng did not entirely
eclipse the demonic form of the cult, however. Hong Mai noted that the
Wutong temple in Shaoxing (Zhejiang) ranked among the city's largest
shrines and enjoyed "the respect and awe of the people," even though it
was not regarded as an orthodox place of worship.[82] Many other Wu-

tong temples also did not undergo metamorphosis into Wuxian shrines. The association between Wutong and the *shanxiao* demons likewise endured in popular lore. A thirteenth-century sequel to *Tales of the Listener* composed by the Jin scholar Yuan Haowen (1190–1257) describes the sexual violation of a woman by a *shanxiao* whom her family members identify as Wulang. The spirit repays the family with riches, including an infant boy for the childless woman, although the child later died at age six.[83] A fourteenth-century catalogue of *zaju* drama even includes a piece entitled "The One-Legged Wulang."[84]

By the end of the Song dynasty Wuxian had become one of the most prevalent and widely celebrated cults across southern China. Scattered data on Song temple building culled from surviving gazetteers suggest that among popular cults, the number of Wuxian temples was exceeded only by those dedicated to King Zhang.[85] In the Yuan dynasty the orthodox Wuxian still enjoyed imperial favor. Although the cult's central shrine at Wuyuan was destroyed during the Mongol conquest, one of Wuyuan's wealthiest lineages, the Wang, rebuilt the temple and donated lands for a permanent endowment.[86] In 1314, the Wangs persuaded the court to issue an imperial plaque, bearing the legend "The five potent and obedient eternal bodhisattvas" *(Wanshou lingshun wu pusa)*, to mark yet another restoration of the Wuxian temple.[87] Renewal of imperial grace spurred similar rehabilitation projects elsewhere. In 1317, the branch temple at Suzhou's Zhili Bridge, which had received an endowment of rental property and built its second Huaguang pavilion two decades earlier, was renamed the Wanshou Lingshun Temple and supplemented with a treasure hall.[88] The imperially designated main shrine at Wuyuan apparently dwindled in significance by the end of the fourteenth century, however, while Hangzhou, with its many Wuxian temples, emerged as the center of the cult. At the end of the Yuan the common folk of Huating (the seat of Songjiang prefecture) formed cult assemblies *(huishe)* dedicated to Wuxian "in imitation of the custom in Hangzhou."[89] Ming sources uniformly assert that Wuxian originated in Wuyuan, yet at the same time they usually identify the people of Hangzhou as the cult's most enthusiastic adherents.

The establishment of the Ming dynasty in the second half of the fourteenth century resulted in a profound shock to popular religious life, in Jiangnan in particular. The Ming founder Zhu Yuanzhang (Emperor Taizu, r. 1368–98) took unprecedented measures to bring religious life under the heel of the state. At the very beginning of his reign, in 1370, Zhu enacted far-reaching religious reforms intended to abolish all "profane cults" *(yinci)* and impose a tightly regulated system of official sacrifices in their place. In contrast to the personalized, charismatic deities of popular religion, the state-mandated cults of the Ming dynasty were suffused with the stultifying hierarchy and anonymity that pervaded the secular state bureaucracy. The transformation of the *chenghuang* cult typified the new state religion of the Ming. Under the new system of official cults decreed by Zhu Yuanzhang, the *chenghuang* became the focal cults for each level of the administrative hierarchy, extending from the various branches of the central government at the capital down to the provinces, prefectures, and counties. Consequently, the distinctive personalities of the old *chenghuang* were erased. Simple wooden tablets bearing the deity's official title but no personal names replaced the anthropomorphic iconography of the old *chenghuang*. Worship at the *chenghuang* temples was restricted to the official spring and autumn ceremonies over which the chief local official presided.[90]

At the same time the government forbade private worship of any other gods, exempting only domestic rites dedicated to one's ancestors and the stove god. In an effort to inculcate proper moral temperament and community values, the Ming required its subjects to attend communal religious observances conducted twice a year, at the spring and autumn equinoxes. One of these ceremonies was intended to revive the ancient custom of offering prayers of thanksgiving to the soil and grain spirits *(sheji)*; the other, modeled on ancestral rites, entailed making offerings to the orphan souls of the unworshiped dead so that they, like the ancestors, may rest in peace for eternity.[91] Although evidence from local gazetteers indicates that local officials indeed set up altars to the soil and grain spirits and the unshriven dead, Zhu Yuanzhang's new religious order sank only shallow roots in the countryside, and after his death left little trace in the rural religious landscape.

The fist of official proscription fell much more heavily on cities and towns, however. Certainly the *chenghuang* cults, largely confined to walled towns, underwent radical transformation. The rash of imperial edicts prohibiting (among other religious activities) public liturgies, graven images of the gods, and communication with the gods through mediums, "petitions," and spirit writing must have muted public display of religious piety in towns and cities. Moreover, Zhu Yuanzhang went far beyond any of his predecessors in decreeing that Buddhism and Daoism, no less than the gods of the ignorant masses, were potentially profane forms of worship that must be strictly monitored and regulated. To curb the propagation of deviant teachings under the aegis of the Buddhist and Daoist orders, Zhu ordered a massive consolidation of Buddhist and Daoist temples. The two religions were permitted only a single monastery or abbey each within any given county. Though such a draconian reduction in shrines proved unfeasible, organized religion was more vulnerable to imperial whim than the refractory multitude of popular cults. In Wujiang county, for example, only twenty-one Buddhist temples and a single Daoist one survived the consolidation of shrines, and more than 110 were closed.[92] The edict consolidating Buddhist and Daoist shrines was relaxed by the Yongle emperor (r. 1402–20) in 1403, but many temples had suffered an irreparable loss of vitality and prestige.

The surge of lay piety galvanized by the White Lotus and similar movements during the Southern Song and Yuan periods was deemed especially pernicious by Zhu Yuanzhang, who once had close ties to a White Lotus group. Zhu branded the White Lotus a heterodox sect in 1370 and ruthlessly persecuted any suspected adherents. Elite families of the Yangzi Delta, already terrorized by Zhu's social and economic policies, sought to expunge the taint of religious heterodoxy by scrupulously avoiding any association with White Lotus groups or religious practices. Subsequently, "White Lotus" became an invidious label that might be applied to any group or activity that deviated from the Ming state's canon of religious conduct.[93]

Nonetheless, Wuxian occupied such an exalted place in the religious firmament that Zhu Yuanzhang included a Wuxian temple among the Ten Imperial Shrines raised in 1388 outside his new capital at Nanjing.[94] The official dedication noted that Wuxian had unfailingly heeded the prayers of the people of Wuyuan for deliverance from flood, drought, and pestilence. At the same time it described the Five Manifestations in the abstract terms of the cosmic principles of order that governed the natural world.[95] Wuxian thus became one of the few cults of distinctly popular origin to receive recognition as a national cult.[96] Active imperial sponsorship of the Wuxian cult did not survive the relocation of the Ming capital to Beijing in the 1420s, however. Although Ming officials continued to perform the semiannual sacrifices at the temple outside Nanjing, the Yongle emperor and his successors took no interest in Wuxian. Imperial patronage instead focused on figures such as Zhenwu, Guan Yu, and Mazu.

Over the course of the Ming, worship of Wutong/Wuxian gradually faded in many areas. In Jiangdong/Jiangxi, the birthplace of the Wuxian cult, popular devotion to Wuxian ebbed. Wuyuan no longer attracted large numbers of pilgrims, though Wuxian temples were still common in the region.[97] Interestingly, Huaguang became an important cult figure in the religious landscape of the rising porcelain manufacturing center of Jingdezhen, just downriver from Wuyuan. In the sixteenth century, Jingdezhen grew into a major city, swelled by the arrival of immigrants from neighboring areas like Wuyuan. A Huaguang temple was built adjacent to the imperial factory, which supplied the imperial capital's need for porcelain wares. Imperial officials on several occasions attempted to convert the temple for use as factory offices, only to be rebuffed by the city's potters, who claimed that the god rendered aid to ensure the successful firing of the kilns.[98]

In Fujian, the benevolent Wuxian/Huaguang cult flourished, but the diabolical Wutong largely vanished. In the mountainous interior of Fujian, long associated with *shanxiao* lore, worship of Wutong was gradually eclipsed by the Wuxian/Huaguang cult of Wuyuan. A prefect serving in Jianning in the mid-thirteenth century reported that it was the custom in Fujian to hold lavish festivals in the ninth month in honor of the birth of the "five kings," an unmistakable reference to the 9/28 feast day of Wuxian.[99] A 1258 gazetteer of Tingzhou lists three Wutong temples in the prefectural seat or its immediate environs; at least two of them dated to the twelfth century. In the first half of the thirteenth century four Wuxian branch temples were established in smaller towns throughout the prefecture; in one, built in the 1220s, a Huaguang pavilion was added in the 1250s.[100] A sixteenth-century gazetteer attests to diminished official sponsorship of the cult: only one of the Wutong temples still received mention and two of the Wuxian temples had been converted to other cults as part of the early Ming religious reforms, although four Wuxian temples had been raised in newly settled outlying areas.[101] Subsequently Huaguang prevailed as the centerpiece of this cult down to modern times. Although Huaguang continued to be identified with spirits called Wutong and Wuxian, no trace remained of the cult's demonic origins or its links to the *shanxiao* inhabiting the surrounding wilderness.[102]

The Wutong temple in Fuzhou, said to have been lavishly patronized by the great families of the region in Song times, suffered decline in the Ming.[103] The original temple fell into disuse at some unspecified date, but subsequently a Wuxian shrine was erected above the city's main gate. Another Wuxian shrine was founded in the provincial fiscal intendant's yamen in 1388, at the time of Wuxian's induction into the Ten Imperial Shrines.[104] By the late Ming, though, the city gate temple was largely defunct.[105] Yet the Wuxian/Huaguang cult continued to thrive in surrounding areas.[106] By the early seventeenth century, a group of plague deities known as the Five Emperors (Wudi) emerged as one of Fuzhou's most prominent popular cults. It is possible that the Five Emperors represent a metamorphosis of the Wuxian cult. Yet the mythology and liturgies constructed around the Five Emperors differ markedly from Wuxian, though they bear close resemblance to other plague deities, such as the Wen Qiong cult in adjacent southern Zhejiang.[107]

Although the cult of the demonic Wutong receded or was effaced in many parts of south China during the Ming, in Jiangnan it became deeply insinuated in popular mentality and religious life. The persistence of the demonic Wutong was reflected in nomenclature. Ming exegetes note that in Jiangnan the god was sometimes known as Wutong, or alternatively as Wulang, but perhaps most commonly as Wusheng, a name closely associated with the worship of Wuxian in the Hangzhou region.[108] The title Wuxian appears only rarely in the middle and late Ming, generally in the names of temples. By the mid-Ming period the beneficent figure of Wuxian derived from the ancestral cult of Wuyuan had become virtually defunct. Most late Ming and Qing sources indiscriminately lump Wuxian and Wusheng together with the pernicious Wutong. Major Wuxian shrines refurbished under government auspices during the Ming failed to attract lasting support from either lay devotees or the Daoist and Buddhist priests. In Suzhou, for example, the Wutong temple at Mount Lengqie, just outside the city, eclipsed the Wuxian shrines within the city as the center of cult activities.[109] Yet it was in the arena of domestic ritual life rather than great communal events that Wutong penetrated the lives of virtually every household, even the most exalted ones, in Ming Jiangnan.

Virtually all accounts of the Wutong cult from the early sixteenth century observed, with evident dismay, that a small yet magnificently embellished Wutong shrine could be found in nearly every Jiangnan courtyard, usually just inside the gate leading to the street.[110] These small shrines, a mere three or four feet high, gave rise to a curious legend claiming that the Ming founder created the Wutong cult. According to this account, after conquering his rivals, Zhu Yuanzhang had a dream in which tens of thousands of soldiers who had died in his service implored him to provide sacrifices for the benefit of their wandering souls. Upon awakening the emperor ordered that every household in Jiangnan set up a small altar and make offerings to the souls of the dead soldiers (who were assigned, in detachments of five, to the various domestic shrines).[111] This legend, preserved in a number of Qing sources, cannot be corroborated by the extant records of Zhu Yuanzhang's reign (or, as far as I can determine, by any Ming records).[112] It is highly unlikely that Zhu's patronage of Wuxian, mentioned above, extended to Wutong, and in any event the Wutong cult had far more ancient origins.[113] The story does testify, however, to the prevalence of the Wutong shrines. In addition, this undoubtedly spurious legend imbued the Wutong cult with an aura of legitimacy that helped to shield it from outright condemnation by tribunes of Confucian piety.

The earliest accounts that give a fairly full description of domestic ritual practices date from the turn of the sixteenth century.[114] Typically the ubiquitous domestic shrines included five figurines adorned with royal raiment, who represented the Wusheng or Five Saints, plus five consorts dressed as empresses. Shrines to Wutong also included images of the god's mother, known simply as the Grand Dowager (Taima), other generic cult figures (such as Guanyin, chenghuang, and tudi), and a host of divine supernumeraries who comprised Wutong's retinue.[115] Those too poor to afford such shrines but not wishing to be derelict in their devotions simply hung a print or drawing of the deity mounted on a wooden tablet. The reverence with which such icons were regarded is revealed in Huang Wei's (1490 jinshi) description of heads of households burning incense on their way to the artisan's workshop to fetch tablets and statues of Wutong for their domestic altars.[116]

The Wutong cult spawned, in addition to the Grand Dowager, a coterie of subordinate deities who became cult figures in their own right, with their own temples and devoted followings. Most prominent among these "lackey enforcers" was Lord Ma (Magong), reputed to be Wutong's uncle, though this figure undoubtedly derived from Wutong's incarnation as the Daoist Heavenly Marshal Ma (see pp. 213–20 below). Another "lackey enforcer," Premier Song (Songxiang) was portrayed as a fearsome figure associated, as an officer of the infernal Water Bureau (Shuifu), with death. In late Ming times the city of Suzhou contained at least three shrines dedicated to him. King Zhou Xuanling, whose cult originated in Dexing, likewise was considered one of Wutong's henchmen.[117] The god's image was inadvertently brought to a Buddhist monastery in Suzhou, where it acquired considerable notoriety and an impassioned following.[118]

The most prominent feature of the Wutong cult was the "tea séance" (chayan). During this night-long rite spirit mediums used esoteric language and song to conjure up the Wutong spirit and convey the wishes of their clients. Preeminent among the mediums who performed such rites were women who boasted of their expertise in the techniques of "dispelling fright" *(shoujing)* and "visualizing spirits," and who claimed knowledge of "occult teachings" *(yinjiao)* obtained through sexual intercourse with the god.[119] During the course of the ritual the host family presented munificent offerings of spirit money and bloody sacrifices to the god.[120] One observer reported that during the tea séance images of a number of other deities, including Huaguang, were worshiped.[121] Patrician and plebeian families alike resorted to the tea séance to seek the god's favor in all matters of dire concern.

The image of Wutong in Ming popular culture demonstrates that the sanctity bestowed on Wuxian by imperial and ecclesiastic authorities did little to alter the conception of Wutong as an actively maleficent, indeed demonic, figure who preyed on the weak and vulnerable. Diviners hired to determine the causes of illnesses often traced the affliction to Wutong, in which case patients were advised to forsake medical aid as futile and resign themselves to the inevitability of death. In some cases Wutong was perceived as little more than a prankster who harassed human beings by causing furniture to move or by breaking down doors; at other times people accused Wutong of stealing valuables or setting fire to their homes. Prayers and sacrifices were offered to Wutong less to ask for blessings than to ward off calamity.

From an analysis of a set of fifteen stories collected by Lu Can during the 1510s and published in his book *Gengsibian* two distinct profiles of the popular image of the god emerge.[122] In one set of stories (table 4, numbers 1–7) Wutong appears as a mischievous imp who is easily offended by human beings and causes unnatural events to occur. For example, one story begins with a literatus desecrating an image of Wutong by urinating on it. The incensed god thereupon begins to harass his family by battering doors and scattering excrement throughout the house. On one occasion the god snatches a bag of coins into the air. When the household servants curse the perpetrator of this magic the bag falls to the floor, spilling coins throughout the room; upon being picked up the coins are hot to the touch. Other episodes describe Wutong engaging in malicious mischief without apparent cause. Efforts to appease Wutong by making offerings seem to have little effect. In this group of stories the afflicted persons usually resort to exorcism or the destruction of the deity's temple before the vexations cease.

A second group of stories (numbers 9–15) reveals a far more sinister and diabolical portrait of Wutong. The central theme of these narratives is the god's possession of women through ecstatic trances or sexual liaisons. In some cases we are told of a woman who is suddenly possessed

TABLE 4. MOTIFS OF WUTONG STORIES
IN LU CAN'S *GENGSIBIAN* (CA. 1520)

Motif	Story Number														
	1	2	3	4	5	6	7	8	9	10	11	12	13	14	15
Appearance of deity															
Desecration of temple/icon			•			•									
Apparition	•	•		•	•		•								
Possession of woman									•	•	•		•		•
(at time of marriage)											•		•		•
Intercourse with woman									•	•		•	•	•	•
Supernatural manifestations															
Magic			•		•	•			•		•				
Affliction		•	•	•	•	•	•								
Exhaustion of wealth		•													
Palace of riches							•						•		
Bestows supernatural powers												•		•	
Bestows wealth	•											•			•
Calamitous consequences															
Insanity											•	•			
Premature death				•					•						
Unable to marry												•			
Denouement															
Destruction of temple						•									
Exorcism		•	•				•								
Propitiation (unsuccessful)		•							•						
Intervention of higher god		•												•	
Accepted by family									•			•	•	•	
God tires of woman and leaves												•		•	

SOURCE: *Gengsibian*, 4.40–41, 5.51–54, 5.65, 6.73, 9.101.

by the spirit and begins to behave in a lunatic manner, wildly dancing and singing, before she eventually succumbs to irremediable insanity.[123] In other stories Wutong appears as a handsome and radiantly attired youth who bedazzles susceptible young women just entering a liminal stage of life (puberty, betrothal, or marriage) and entices them into sexual intercourse. In return, the god offers riches to the woman and her family. The woman's husband or father does not necessarily regard the blatant violation of chastity and marital fidelity as a misfortune. On the contrary, they profit from the deity's largesse and encourage him to return.[124] The god's attentions and munificence are unpredictable, however, and in most cases they are ultimately withdrawn, as the following story illustrates.

> A rice merchant in Jiangyin had a daughter of comely appearance who, soon after beginning to wear hairpins [i.e., reaching the age of eligibility for marriage], was suddenly possessed by a spirit. A handsome and robust man seen entering the girl's bedchamber had sexual intercourse with her. The spirit called himself Wusheng. The woman's parents summoned a spirit medium to rid her of this affliction, but his efforts were to no avail. In the end the family had no choice but to accept the spirit's comings and goings. Whatever the young woman desired, regardless of whether it was out of season or from some distant land, she had but to lift her finger and it would appear. Sometimes the spirit would fill her room with gold, silver, pearls, and the like, but after letting her play with these a while he would snatch them away and refuse to give them back. The woman once saw several thousand ingots of gold piled in the corner of her room. But when she tried to pick them up, as soon as her hand touched them the gold turned into tiles and stones, or objects made of paper. Once she put them down they again transformed into gold.[125]

In the above story Wutong bestows riches that whet the impressionable young girl's appetites, but in the end they prove to be as evanescent as the god himself. The ephemeral nature of Wutong's gifts and the deity's underlying diabolical purposes are exposed more forcefully in the following tale, which combines the lure of material goods with perhaps the most treasured gift of all, sons.

> Madame Lü, wife of Mr. Shen and the daughter of an eminent family, surpassed all others in her domestic skills and physical beauty. At the age of nineteen she suddenly fell down dead; but after two days passed she began to revive, and she told the following tale: "I was summoned by the Divine Lord Wusheng to attend a feast. The deity displayed a chest of gold headgear and ornaments, and sixteen chests of fine clothes, which, though tiny in size, shone brilliantly and dazzled my eyes. The god told me, 'If you consent to live here, all of these treasures will be yours.' I cried and begged to return home, and his ladies-in-waiting repeatedly urged him to release me. Finally the god relented and gave me permission to come back, saying that he would grant me another ten years of life."
>   From this time forward the deity occasionally visited the Shen house, addressing Madame Lü as "wife" [niangzi]. At these times members of the

household were struck by a strange fragrance, whereupon they saw arrive a fair young man in fine clothes who would spend the night in Madame Lü's chamber. Ten years later Madame Lü again died, and once more she returned to life, saying that the god had told her that he would allow her yet one more year of life. In all Madame Lü bore five sons. Whenever she was about to give birth Madame Lü excreted a trickle of black liquid, but she did not bleed. Each of the sons was exceedingly beautiful, but after one full year passed the god would reappear and say, "I am now taking the child away." And sure enough, all five sons died prematurely. Finally Madame Lü gave birth to a daughter, but as soon as the infant emerged from her body the blood began to flow back into her womb and she died. Exactly a year had passed since the day she had come back to life.[126]

The import of Wutong's favors is clear: sexual indulgence brings transitory delights but leads all too quickly to tragedy.

In most of the stories in this second group women come to a bad end, suffering madness, death, or the living death of spinsterhood. Lu Can's depiction of Wutong as an incubus who lures young, vulnerable women into sexual relations by bestowing riches on them is confirmed by other contemporary anecdotes.[127] By the seventeenth century this facet of the god's character overshadowed malicious mischief as the dominant motif of Wutong lore. Thirteen of the nineteen Wutong tales related in Qian Xiyan's *Garden of Cunning* involve debauchery of wives or seduction of women; another deals with the sexual conquest of a young man (table 5). Although the *shanxiao* motif is still present in Qian's stories, it is decidedly secondary to transactions involving the exchange of women for wealth. In Qian's accounts, as in Lu's a century before, the woman's husband or family proves willing to give her up in exchange for the promise of riches. This feature of the Wutong cult is all the more remarkable considering that the sixteenth century also witnessed the growth of a cult of female chastity that honored the families of women who adhered to rigid standards of marital fidelity and sexual purity, and demanded that women expiate any stain on their virtue by taking their own lives.[128] Confucian savants like Lu Can usually expressed horror or pity rather than contempt toward women suffering from demonic possession. However, the costly sacrifices consecrated to Wutong elicited harsh condemnation, as did the female spirit mediums who beguiled the benighted common folk with fraudulent claims of occult powers. In the late fifteenth and early sixteenth centuries the popularity of the manifestly diabolical cult of Wutong provoked local magistrates to try to eradicate it.

In 1445, the newly appointed prefect of Suzhou, Li Congzhi, issued orders to destroy domestic shrines dedicated to Wutong. Shortly afterward,

TABLE 5. MOTIFS OF WULANG (WUTONG) STORIES IN QIAN XIYAN'S *GARDEN OF CUNNING* (1613)

Motif	1	2	3	4	5	6	7	8	9	10	11	12	13	14	15	16	17	18	19
Attributes of Wutong																			
Identified as *shanxiao*	●			●															●
Single leg				●	●														
Handsome youth or prince			●								●	●							●
Worship of Wutong																			
"Tea séance"							●						●						
Domestic altar							●										●	●	●
Worship by male youth																	●	●	
Manifestation of deity																			
Malicious mischief	●							●											
Affliction of woman (illness/mutilation)		●								●				●					
Possession of wife (debauchery)			●	●	●	●				●			●		●				
Seduction of (unmarried) woman										●	●		●	●	●				
Sexual liaison with male youth																			●
Woman given silks or riches					●	●	●						●	●					●
Husband or family exchanges woman for riches		●	●		●					●						●			
Consequences																			
Death of woman														●	●	●			
Death of person other than afflicted woman								●										●	●
Exorcism				●									●			●			
Depredations cease (after marriage/ remarriage)					●						●	●							

SOURCE: *Kuaiyuan*, 12.1a–16a.

though, Li fell ill and died in office. His death naturally was interpreted as a consequence of angering the potent and vengeful god, and the memory of this show of malevolent power reportedly deterred later municipal officials from taking such a brazenly hostile stance against the Wutong cult.[129] In 1488, the magistrate in the city of Changshu destroyed more than one hundred Wutong icons and converted the desecrated shrines into schools, storehouses, naval barracks, and other public facilities.[130] Several years later the prefect of Suzhou banned worship of Wutong and consigned images of the deity to fire, but as soon as the official was rotated out of office popular worship of Wutong resumed.[131] In 1520, around the time that Lu Can's work was completed, a prefectural judge in Songjiang destroyed the images of Wutong and his retinue in that city's major temple, which was subsequently converted into a shrine for the Tang dynasty official Lu Zhi, a more seemly exemplar of Confucian virtues.[132] Likewise, in 1496 the magistrate of Jiangyin converted his city's Wutong temple into a shrine dedicated to a Tang dynasty general.[133]

The furious campaigns of suppression mounted by local officials did little to deter popular devotion to the Wutong cult. After 1520, overt efforts to suppress the cult largely ceased, and the cult flourished throughout Jiangnan as never before. Local magistrates, perhaps weary of the futility of eradicating such an intractable foe, apparently gave up the struggle, and public display of cult activities revived.[134] Despite the desecration of Changshu's Wutong temple in 1488, at the beginning of the seventeenth century a temple for the Wutong of Good Merit (Fude Wutong) could be found in the watchtower over the city's main gate.[135] An exhaustive survey of Nanjing temples conducted in 1611 found fourteen Wuxian temples within the city, second only to Guanyin and far more than those dedicated to Zhenwu, Guandi, or Mazu (table 6).

The Jiangnan literati apparently resigned themselves to the obdurate tenacity of the Wutong cult as well. They continued to cavil at the bizarre and prurient tales of the demonic Wutong propagated in vernacular literature and storytelling, but condoned Wutong's incarnation as Wuxian as a legitimate object of worship sanctioned by the Ming founder.[136] Surprisingly, though, we find no evidence that the Ming tried to assimilate the Wutong cult into the officially prescribed pantheon, the usual strategy employed by the Song state to channel popular belief in spirits into acceptable modes of expression. The temple built by Zhu Yuanzhang outside Nanjing remained on the rolls of the Court of Imperial Sacrifices, but no Wuxian temples were constructed in Beijing after the relocation

TABLE 6. TEMPLES IN NANJING
AND BEIJING IN THE LATE MING

Nanjing Temples		Beijing Temples	
Guanyin	19	King Guan (Guandi)	20
Wuxian	14	Guanyin	10
Zhenwu	7	Tianxian (Bixia yuanjun)	8
King Guan (Guandi)	5	Zhenwu	8
Heavenly Consort	5	Dizang (Kṣitigarbha)	6
(Tianhou, i.e., Mazu)			
Dongyue	3		

SOURCES: For Nanjing: *Nanjing duchayuan zhi, juan* 21–22. For Beijing: *Wanshu zaji*, 19.232–33.
NOTE: Only temples within the city walls of Nanjing and Beijing are tabulated in these sources.

of the capital in 1421. State support for the maintenance of the Wuxian temples in Jiangnan dwindled as well. Wutong in his ubiquitous demonic incarnation remained an outlaw figure, receiving neither official titles nor sacrifices. Claims of Wutong's orthodoxy premised on Zhu Yuanzhang's patronage notwithstanding, Ming officials typically labeled Wutong, and even Wuxian, as a popular, local cult without official sanction *(turen sici)*.[137]

The erasure of Wuxian from popular worship also resulted from the separation of Huaguang as a cult figure from the Wuxian. Though nominally a Buddhist figure, Huaguang is represented in late Ming sources more as a Daoist demonifuge than as a Buddhist savior. Daoist liturgical and hagiographic works created a new avatar of Huaguang known as Marshal Ma (Ma Yuanshuai). The two divinities were subsequently merged together—and at the same time distanced from the nefarious Wutong—in late Ming fiction, drama, and edifying religious tracts. Huaguang thus became an independent cult figure.

A Daoist ritual code of the mid-fourteenth century, *The Statutes of the Black Code of the Infernal Regions,* tried to resolve the ambiguity of the Wutong spirits by dividing them into three ranks: the highest-order Wutong spirits were defined as sublime spirits, the refined condensations of the five elemental forces *(qi)* that constituted the physical universe; the middle rank consisted of spirits (including Huaguang) invested with official rank by the Jade Emperor; while the lowest sort, "stale breaths of weeds and trees," wrought havoc among mortals.[138] This text thus appropriated the figure of Huaguang and integrated it into the Daoist celestial pantheon. Other Daoist writings of the thirteenth and fourteenth centuries associated Huaguang with the Daoist demonifuge spirit Marshal Ma. Marshal Ma appears in the Thunder Magic exorcism rituals of Song Daoism as an awesome stellar deity of the southern sky, and thus a crystallization of the element of fire. Marshal Ma, said to have three eyes (a signal feature of Huaguang in later Ming texts), also possessed five supernatural powers *(wutong)* and wielded an array of weapons (a golden lance, a triangular brick, and various fiery weapons, including a fire wheel and a gourd filled with five hundred fire crows) to exterminate demons like the *shanxiao* and Wutong (figures 28, 29, and 30).[139] In effect, Marshal Ma is presented as a Daoist transfiguration of the noxious Wutong demons into a righteous warrior in the service of the celestial gods, and in this respect Marshal Ma essentially replicated the Buddhist Huaguang.[140]

The merging of the Buddhist bodhisattva Huaguang with the Daoist demonifuge Marshal Ma is more fully evidenced in fiction and drama of the Ming period. In the late Ming novella *Journey to the North*, Huaguang initially appears as a dissolute and irascible ruffian who flouts the dictates of the supreme gods of the Daoist pantheon until vanquished by Zhenwu. Huaguang hints at his origins in the diabolical Wutong cult by introducing himself as "Divine Agent Ma of Flowers and Wine" (Huajiu Ma lingguan), an allusion to his fondness for women and debauchery. Here Huaguang possesses all the attributes (three eyes, six arms, and his arsenal of golden lance, triangular brick, and fire weapons) assigned to Marshal Ma in Daoist liturgical works. After his defeat, Huaguang performs penance by serving as a lieutenant of the True Warrior in crusades against satanic forces. In the final chapter Huaguang is invested with the title "Sole and Orthodox Divine Agent Marshal Ma" (Zhengyi lingguan Ma yuanshuai).[141] The two figures are portrayed as alter egos in other popular literature of the Ming as well.[142] Although *Journey to the North* has been criticized for its supposedly vulgar rendition of Daoist doctrines, its portrayal of Huaguang as both scourge and savior deftly captures the ambiguous relationship between Huaguang/Wuxian and the forces of order found in the canonical literature.[143]

In a *zaju* drama version of "Journey to the West," dating probably from the early sixteenth century, "Heavenly King Huaguang" (Huaguang tianwang) appears as a guardian deity sent by the Jade Emperor to assist the Tang monk Xuanzang on his journey to India to obtain the genuine Buddhist scriptures. In an aria Huaguang introduces himself as a divinity of both the Buddhist and Daoist pantheons, a fire-wielding demon queller assigned to the southern regions. Huaguang also states that in Buddhist assemblies (a reference, perhaps, to the assemblies held in

Figures 28 and 29. Marshal Ma talismans. Figure 28: Instructions from a Daoist ritual text detailing how to make a paper talisman of one of Marshal Ma's characteristic weapons, a triangular gold brick imprinted with four "fire" graphs; from *Zhengyi hongshen lingguan huoxi daxian kaozhao bifa, DFHY,* 222.13b-14a. A talisman used in Daoist rituals to summon Marshal Ma, figure 29 shows a silhouette of the deity carrying his golden lance together with images of a dragon and one of his characteristic weapons, a fire wheel. From *Zhengyi hongshen lingguan huoxi daxian kaozhao bifa, DFHY,* 222.17b.

the name of Huaguang on 4/8) he is known as "Rightly Ordained Heavenly King Miaojixiang" (Zhengshou Miaojixiang tianwang). Miaojixiang appears in early Chinese Buddhist literature as a transliteration of the name of the bodhisattva Mañjuśrī, one of the Buddha's principal disciples, but nothing in the later Huaguang lore suggests any explicit reference to Mañjuśrī. The "Journey to the West" drama also depicts the "five plague spirits" *(wuwenshen)* and the "heroes of the five manifestations" *(wuxiansheng)* as minions of Huaguang.[144] Huaguang thus is linked here to the plague-quelling Wuxian cult of Wuyuan.

Huaguang figures most prominently in Ming literature as the protagonist of the novella *Journey to the South,* an eighteen-chapter work probably first published in the 1570s or 1580s.[145] In this novel Huaguang ap-

Figure 30. Marshal Ma talisman (incantation for summoning fire crows). This incantation for summoning the fire-breathing crows that attend Marshal Ma reads: "*Dingxinde*! All you thousand crows, hear my summons. Fly to the altar to receive my command. Make haste and quickly peck to death demons, bandits, and plague." From *Zhengyi hongshen lingguan huoxi daxian kaozhao bifa*, *DFHY*, 222.25a. (N.B.: *Dingxinde* is a purely onomatopoetic utterance.)

pears in the guise of an impudent troublemaker, entirely reminiscent of Wutong, whose wanton mischief prompts the Jade Emperor to banish him repeatedly to earthly exile (figures 31 and 32). But this Huaguang has a noble side as well. He rights wrongs, quells demons, and roots out deviant religious practices such as human sacrifice. Three times he is incarnated in the fetus of a pregnant woman and distinguishes himself as a paragon of filial piety devoted to his parents, both mortal and divine. Huaguang avenges the death of his divine father, the King of Mount Maer (Maer shanwang), and—in a retelling of the classic Mulian story—he embarks on an epic journey to rescue a human mother from the depths of the underworld. In his second human incarnation Huaguang makes his appearance as one of five quintuplet sons born (on the twenty-eighth day of the ninth month, of course) to the headman of a village in Wuyuan (the imperially endorsed home of the Wuxian cult). A demon possesses Huaguang's human mother and turns her into an insatiable cannibal. Her crimes come to the attention of a dragon king who casts her into the nether regions of hell. Earlier versions of the Mulian story largely focused on either the redemptive power of the Buddha or the horrors of the underworld. By contrast, *Journey to the South* dwells on Huaguang's adventures (and comic

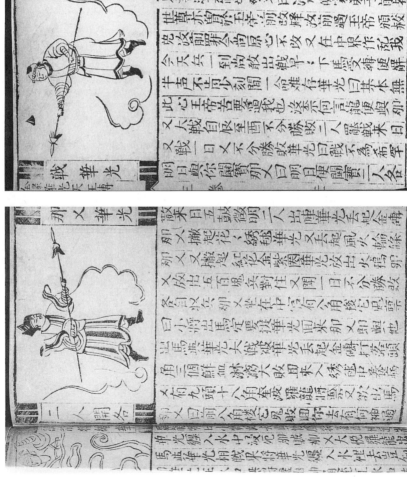

Figures 31 and 32. Huaguang battles Nezha. The novel *Journey to the South*, published in 1631, includes illustrations at the top of each page of text. In these two illustrations, Huaguang (figure 31) battles Nezha, the young warrior dispatched by the Jade Emperor to subdue the refractory Huaguang. Huaguang carries his golden lance, while above his head his triangular brick hurtles toward Nezha. Both of these weapons derive from the arsenal of Marshal Ma (see figures 28, 29). From *Huaguang tianwang nanyou zhizhuan*, 3.20a–b. By permission of the British Library.

misadventures), such as his impersonation of respected deities like Guanyin and the theft of the magic peaches that enable him to cure his mother's cannibalism and purchase her release from the tortures of hell.[146]

The image of Huaguang that appears in *Journey to the South* is compounded of many of the literary tropes current in Ming fiction and bears more than a little resemblance to the character of the irascible monkey-king Sun Wukong in the renowned one-hundred-chapter novel version of *Journey to the West* attributed to Wu Cheng'en. At the same time the god's roots in the Wutong cult are equally apparent, as can be seen in his incarnation as one of five sons of a Wuyuan village headman. There is even an allusion to the signal physical trait of the ancient Wutong: at the end of the novella Huaguang is tricked into chopping off one of his legs. The mythology of Huaguang that appears in *Journey to the South* is also alluded to in the one-hundred-chapter version of *Journey to the West*. At the very end of the novel, the monk Xuanzang and his fellow pilgrims pass by a "branch temple of Huaguang." The author explains that "the bodhisattva Huaguang was a disciple of the Flaming Five Lights Buddha. Because of his campaign of extermination against the Demon King of Poisonous Fire he was demoted in official rank and transformed into the divine agent Wuxian."[147] This parenthetical observation is unmistakably derived from *Journey to the South* or its antecedents, which identifies Huaguang in exactly the same terms.

The association between Huaguang and Marshal Ma is further underscored in a popular religious handbook dating from the end of the sixteenth century bearing the title *Great Compendium of Unseen Spirits and the Traces of Their Origins in the Three Teachings*.[148] In this text, Wusheng (i.e., Wuxian) and Marshal Ma are given separate entries. Yet the hagiography of Marshal Ma identifies him as a "avatar" *(huashen; nirmāṇakāya)* of the Supreme Miaojixiang Tathāgata (Zhi Miaojixiang Rulai), who at the outset is punished for an act of desecration by being born into human form (figure 33). The remainder of the entry briefly recapitulates the plot of *Journey to the South;* the two texts clearly derive from the same source. This spare account concludes by stating that Marshal Ma, like Huaguang in *Journey to the North,* was rewarded for his meritorious actions with an appointment as a lieutenant of Zhenwu (though in this case stationed in the western regions, not the south).

The amalgam of Wuxian and Huaguang that appears in *Journey to the South* was also disseminated through theatrical performance. A late Ming critic of vernacular literature, Shen Defu (1578–1642), in a diatribe against the "ludicrously bizarre exaggerations" found in popular

Figure 33. Marshal Ma. In this illustration from the late
Ming popular religious tract *Great Compendium of
Unseen Spirits and the Traces of their Origins in the Three
Teachings,* Marshal Ma is dressed in official robes and
carries his trademark golden lance. Above his head fly
two fire-breathing crows. From *Sanjiao yuanliu soushen
daquan,* 5.215. Courtesy of the National Archives of
Japan.

dramas, specifically cited a work entitled "Huaguang Manifests His Holiness" *(Huaguang xiansheng).* Shen deplored the ravenous appetite for
such entertainments as sad testimony to the ignorance and credulity of
the public.[149] Although we know nothing about the content of "Huaguang Manifests His Holiness," the text of which has not survived, a
Qing dynasty drama in twenty-seven acts entitled "Blessed with a Thou-

sand Autumns" *(Xiang Qianqiu)* essentially reiterated the plot and mood of the Huaguang story as told in *Journey to the South*.[150] Whatever their literary merit, these works attest to the vigor and complexity of the Wutong cult in its manifold forms.

Daoist scriptures and works of vernacular fiction such as *Journey to the South* show that the demonifuge Huaguang/Wuxian endured in hieratic religion. The existence of cults centered on the merged Huaguang/Wuxian deity can be glimpsed through both literary and historical sources. The two gods became indistinguishable in the cult at the Huaguang Temple in the Baoshansi Monastery in Hangzhou, the setting for a Feng Menglong tale, "Imposter Spirits Wreak Havoc at the Huaguang Temple." In this story the divine agent Wuxian is summoned to expose and expel a pair of demons, posing as the Daoist transcendents Lü Dongbin and He Xiangu, who used the lure of examination success to inveigle a young student into wanton sexual (including homosexual) liaisons. The narrator of the story took pains to emphasize that the popular identification of Wuxian with Wutong was plainly false (but made no mention of the similarity between Wutong's proclivities and those of the impostor spirits).[151] The claim that Wuxian/Huaguang is wrongly accused of wanton behavior, especially sexual predation, is also an important theme of *Journey to the South*. In both works the god is eventually exonerated of the kind of crime typically blamed on demons like the Wutong spirits. Indeed, works like *Journey to the South* can be read as apologia intended to dispel the "mistaken" association between Huaguang and the demonic Wutong, and in so doing recuperate Huaguang as a force for good. Interestingly, though Huaguang clearly was a Buddhist figure in the Song period, Daoist elements predominate in depictions of the deity in late Ming literature. When the Huaguang of *Journey to the South* reprises Mulian's rescue of his mother from the underworld, he does so by assuming the form of the Daoist divinity Taiyi jiuku tianzun. The contests between demonic adversaries that constitute the main content of *Journey to the South* can also be seen as literary elaborations of Daoist liturgies in which ritual experts summon the god to vanquish demonic entities, including the *shanxiao*.[152]

Literary sources also provide evidence that Huaguang endured as an independent cult figure in late Ming times. The author of *Journey to the South* notes in closing that Huaguang was worshiped by people seeking children, merchants (who expect that divine aid will earn them a tenfold return on their capital), and students aspiring to examination success.[153] Similarly, the Marshal Ma entry in *Traces of Origins in the Three Teach-*

ings states that Marshal Ma responds to appeals for wealth, "emolument" (*lu;* in this case, probably referring to longevity), wives, and sons; but he can also be invoked by spirit mediums seeking the god's aid in righting injustices or answering their clients' prayers.[154] Works like *Journey to the South* served to popularize knowledge of the deity's powers and to advertise the efficacy of appealing to the god for aid.

Efforts on the part of ritual practitioners to distinguish the righteous Huaguang/Wuxian from the original Wutong cult do not seem to have been wholly effective, however. *Journey to the South* refers to Huaguang as the "Bodhisattva Miaojixiang" (Miaojixiang pusa), once again invoking a name employed in the "Journey to the West" *zaju* drama and *Traces of Origins in the Three Teachings* to distinguish Huaguang from the Wutong cult. But some records concerning Wutong temples specifically identify their resident deities by the name Miaojixiang Huaguang. Sixteenth- and seventeenth-century gazetteers from Tingzhou report that local legends identified Wutong as "an avatar of the Flower Light Treasure King Bodhisattva Miaojixiang" (Huaguang zangwang miaojixiang pusa) and note that Huaguang, like Mulian, was revered for his heroic rescue of his mother from the underworld. Here the Wuxian were depicted as a group of five gods separate from Huaguang.[155] Clearly local votaries of Huaguang/Wuxian were aware of the Huaguang story as narrated in *Journey to the South,* although some continued to worship the god under the name Wutong. We also find a reference to the inclusion of icons of Huaguang in tea séances dedicated to Wutong in a late Ming gazetteer of Hangzhou that likewise refers to Huaguang as Miaojixiang.[156] However much Daoist ritual experts sought to sever Huaguang from Wutong, the two remained linked in the popular imagination.

The early history of the Wutong cult thus vividly demonstrates the complexity of the interplay between popular cults, state-sanctioned religious activities, and the Daoist scriptural tradition. Far from being merely a debased relic of classical religion, vernacular religious culture actively influenced the construction of official and ecclesiastic canons. Of course, the Wutong/Wuxian cults did have their champions. The local communities in Jiangdong that competed for imperial endorsement of "their" patron Wuxian deity understandably chose to present the god as beneficent. Merchants probably had some hand in the spread of the cult throughout Jiangnan, though there is no evidence to confirm that merchants as a group patronized the cult in any distinctive way.[157] Above all, the induction of Wutong into the official pantheon resulted from the pervasiveness of popular faith in the god's powers, a faith in no way diminished—and perhaps strengthened—by Wutong's demonic proclivities. The transformation of Wutong in Daoist literature from odious fiend to loyal servant of the supreme Daoist deities reflected, and probably resulted from, the god's elevation within the hierarchy of official cults. Yet both imperial and doctrinal sanction indirectly acknowledged the preeminence of popular belief. We would be mistaken to interpret the popular conception of Wutong as a vulgarization of a sublime theology. On the contrary, the orthodox Wuxian represented a truncated caricature of a multivalent popular deity.

CHAPTER 7

The Enchantment of Wealth

Money has an ancient history in China, but perhaps at no time did money have greater symbolic import than in the late Ming period, when domestic economic growth and the infusion of foreign silver engendered a rapid expansion in its use. The irruption of money in manifold forms into the daily lives of virtually every household in Jiangnan, the most commercialized region in China, resulted not only in a new set of exchange relationships, but also in an elaboration of the ways in which money was conceived as a symbol of the profound changes wrought by the money economy. To many, the proliferation of money unleashed the hordes of Mammon and ruptured the delicate bonds of reciprocity binding a solidary moral economy. "Gold's decrees rule heaven, while the god Money looms over the earth," proclaimed a gazetteer of Huizhou, whose merchants and moneylenders epitomized the irresistible power of wealth.[1] Even champions of Confucian ethics seeking to shore up conventional moral standards succumbed to the compelling metaphorical qualities of money. Authors of practical handbooks for moral guidance adopted accounting systems that enabled readers to calculate the sum of their moral behavior and to augment merit-earning actions to ensure a positive balance.[2] New forms of religious piety invoked the language of the marketplace—"accumulation," "savings," "debt," "management"— to illustrate moral teachings centered on accruing and preserving "moral" capital.[3]

The popular imagination also invested money with cultural meaning. Most conspicuous among the symbolic representations of money in late Ming Jiangnan was the "god of wealth" *(caishen)*. In modern times the god of wealth has been a ubiquitous feature of domestic ritual life and a fixture of the New Year's celebrations. The modern cult of the god of wealth actually encompasses a number of distinct supernatural figures, each representing different facets of wealth: He He Erxian, the twin genii of concord, symbolize the resolution of conflicts among business partners essential to commercial success; the cherubic Liu Hai represents abundance and generosity; the powerful warrior god Guandi personifies the qualities of loyalty and trust upon which business transactions depend.[4] Despite the pervasive presence of these figures in family altars and public temples, though, the roots of the god-of-wealth cult in popular religious life have remained hidden. In Jiangnan, since the eighteenth century the cult of the god of wealth has focused on a group of five deities known as the Gods of the Five Paths to Wealth (Wulu caishen). These deities comprise the chief officials of the Ministry of Wealth, a branch of the vast celestial bureaucracy presided over by Daoist divinities. The Wulu caishen are not ancient gods; rather, they are derived, in greatly altered form, from the cult of Wutong.

It was in the late Ming period that Wutong as a god governing the dispensation of wealth emerged as the dominant cult figure in Jiangnan. The notion of a god of wealth was by no means entirely new. The Immortal Official of Profitable Markets (Lishi xianguan), a minor figure in Daoist liturgies, dated back at least to the Song period, and early Ming iconography portrayed generic gods of wealth in forms closely corresponding to their modern representations.[5] It was the image of Wutong, however, that dominated the popular imagination in late Ming Jiangnan. The most remarkable feature of the Wutong cult was its diabolical character. Wutong was perceived not as a culture hero or reification of noble human qualities, but rather as an embodiment of humanity's basest vices, greed and lust. As an actively maleficent demon that preyed on the weak and vulnerable, Wutong was very much the antithesis of the modern gods of wealth.

Over the course of the Ming dynasty, the Wutong cult in Jiangnan underwent considerable evolution. Wutong infiltrated all levels of religious worship, in both domestic worship and public cults. Despite the Southern Song–Yuan rehabilitation of the demonic Wutong in the forms of the positive images of Wuxian and Huaguang, though, the Wutong cult in late Ming Jiangnan retained distinctively demonic forms. Confusion about the god's "true" identity perplexed the guardians of public morality, as Wang Zhijian's (1576–1633) essay entitled "An Exegesis of the Wutong Kings" reveals:

> Previous [Suzhou] gazetteers separated Wutong and Wuxian and regarded them as two distinct deities. But in customary usage in Wu [Suzhou], the two names are frequently used interchangeably. Although investigation shows that Wuxian is a local god of Wuyuan, Our Eminent Founding Emperor [Zhu Yuanzhang] established a temple dedicated to Wuxian at the southern capital [Nanjing]. There can be no doubt that Wuxian is a proper

deity. The wicked and uncanny events and the specious and exaggerated stories recorded in works of fiction and propagated by vulgar custom sometimes identify the god by the name Wusheng, or in other cases as Wulang, and in yet other instances the god is worshiped by a different title. The truth cannot be discerned. It is also said that the god has brothers surnamed Xiao and a mother called Grand Dowager [Taimu], but such absurd babble spread by vulgar custom is utterly unreliable.[6]

It is true that the names of the god were often used interchangeably. Yet the particular names applied to Wutong also reveal distinctive local identities.

The imperial title of Wuxian, despite the sanction it enjoyed thanks to its recognition by Zhu Yuanzhang, occurs infrequently in late Ming records, and chiefly as the name of long-established temples. Within Jiangnan, the name Wuxian was most prevalent in the Hangzhou region, a relic of Hangzhou's preeminence as a cult center during the thirteenth century. As noted earlier, in Ming times Jiangnan people commonly referred to Wutong by the name Wusheng, a usage that also traces back to Southern Song Hangzhou. In the Ming period the name Wusheng was especially common in the silk-producing region around Hangzhou, encompassing in addition to Hangzhou prefecture the adjoining prefectures of Jiaxing and Huzhou, a subregion known as Hang-Jia-Hu. The names Wutong and Wulang were more common in the rice- and cotton-farming regions just to the north, in the prefectures of Suzhou and Songjiang. Inhabitants of Suzhou-Songjiang were also noted for their devotion to a plague god, Wufang xiansheng (Worthy Saints of the Five Directions), which became closely associated with the Wutong cult.

The thirteenth and fourteenth centuries witnessed the consolidation of local tutelary cults in Jiangnan into forms that endured down to modern times. Most of the tutelary deities of Jiangnan were first granted recognition during the Yuan dynasty, which issued patents to local cults that awarded them the title "commandant" *(zongguan)*. *"Zongguan"* was a common title during the Yuan, applied to those holding a wide variety of appointments, but it was especially important as a designation for local prefects. The Yuan state expanded on the Song practice of conferring honorary noble titles on local tutelary deities by also assigning them a specific jurisdiction as "commandant" of their native region. In subsequent dynasties inhabitants of the region used the title *zongguan* as a generic designation for tutelary deities, who were invariably identified with local historical figures.[7] Among the most prominent *zongguan* cults of Jiangnan was that of Commandant Jin (Jin Zongguan), which appears to have originated as a cult dedicated to members of a prominent family surnamed Jin from the market town of Zhouzhuang, in Kunshan county of Suzhou prefecture.[8] Two members of the family, Jin Yuanqi and Jin Chang, were said to have received the title of "commandant" from the Yuan imperial government for their service in protecting the tribute fleets making the ocean voyage from the delta to the capital at Beijing. After their deaths local inhabitants worshiped "Commandant Jin" (either separately or together) as tutelary spirits. By the seventeenth century Commandant Jin had become the most common deity in local territorial cults throughout Jiangnan.[9]

Another deity whose cult became widely diffused in Ming-Qing Jiangnan was Fierce General Liu (Liu Mengjiang). This cult dates back perhaps to the late Song, but layers of later myth have rendered its original form wholly opaque.[10] The "canonical" version of the god's history, ratified through award of an imperial patent in 1724, identified Liu as a Yuan martyr who committed suicide when the Yuan was overthrown by Zhu Yuanzhang. The Qing honored Liu as a tutelary deity who protected the region from the scourge of locusts, though this feature of the cult itself—not mentioned in any pre-Qing sources—appears to have been a recent invention. The cult first appeared in the northern counties of Suzhou prefecture, but official recognition by the Qing court accelerated its diffusion throughout the Yangzi River delta. In rural areas Fierce General Liu was closely linked to the agricultural cycle. Villagers held festivals in honor of the god both in the spring (either during the New Year season or at Qingming, the third day of the third month) and in the fall, after the gathering of the rice harvest in the eighth month. The autumn harvest festivals (locally known as *qingmiaoshe*) featured processions during which images of the Fierce General were paraded through the precincts of the temple's territory.

Since relatively few Jiangnan villages had their own temples, small shrines were erected in villages, along roads, and in the fields where local people could readily present modest offerings or recite prayers to these tutelary gods. Although Wutong, unlike Commandant Jin or Fierce General Liu, did not become a focal deity of territorial cults, small shrines dedicated to Wutong were ubiquitous throughout the region. Qian Xiyan observed that "among the people of Suzhou and Hangzhou it is common practice to erect a small shrine, no more capacious than a *dou* measure [approximately two liters], beneath large trees. The Wulang spirits—including the mother, her several sons, and their wives—are painted on a square board. Incense and candles are laid out, and from time to time offerings are presented without fail. These deities are known as 'Wusheng-Beneath-the-Trees' [Shutou Wusheng]."[11] Wusheng was also worshiped at domestic altars within the home.[12] In these respects the Wutong/Wusheng gods were an even more immediate presence in quotidian life than the local tutelary gods.

The Wusheng cult was equally pervasive in the Hang-Jia-Hu sericulture region, whose fortunes were closely tied to the violent oscillations of the commercial economy. The principal annual festival in the silk trade center of Tangxizhen, in Hangzhou prefecture, was the Wuxian festival held at Qingming, which marked the advent of the silk production season. This festival had already attained prominence in the sixteenth century, when Lü Xu (1514–93), a local poet of some distinction, composed a verse mentioning its connection to the fortunes of the silk industry.[13] Local historians in Huzhou recorded that every village possessed Wusheng shrines (tangzi), which were simple makeshift structures, approximately one meter high, that were placed at the entrance to the village and housed a statue or painted image of the god.[14] Peasants hung images of Wusheng in many places—in the home, in the still, and in the pens where cattle, pigs, and chickens were kept—to ward off ghosts and demons.[15] Such practices were common in Suzhou and Songjiang, too.[16] In Jiangnan the name Wusheng itself (like the Buddhist term pusa or "bodhisattva") came to mean "deity" in a generic sense, and numerous gods had "Wusheng" incorporated into their names. One prominent example was a sericulture deity known as Canhua Wusheng.[17]

The ancient association between Wutong/Wuxian and deliverance from pestilence also endured in Jiangnan, most conspicuously in the form of a deity known as Wufang xiansheng. The exact relationship between Wufang xiansheng and Wutong remains unclear, although the two were closely associated in the eyes of early Qing officials who tried to stamp out both cults. The Wufang xiansheng cult cannot be traced back earlier than the second quarter of the sixteenth century. Gazetteers for the town of Luzhizhen in Suzhou prefecture report that early in the reign of the Jiajing emperor (1522–66) the townspeople founded the Five Plagues Temple (Wuwenmiao) devoted to Wufang xiansheng.[18] As we saw in chapter 4, by Song times the most common designation for plague gods was "Five Emissaries of Plague." Wufang xiansheng seems to have been a local variation on this generic title. A Five Transcendents Temple (Wuxianmiao) in nearby Changshu was explicitly identified with the Five Emissaries of Plague; here, "Five Transcendents" was apparently used as shorthand for "Worthy Saints of the Five Directions," and thus this temple too was part of the Wufang xiansheng cult.[19]

A brief essay by the Suzhou scholar Wang Zhideng (1539–1612) details the extravagant festivals held in honor of Wufang xiansheng in Suzhou at the turn of the seventeenth century.[20] Wang was unable to identify Wufang xiansheng with any certainty, but he noted that popular belief held that the god governed sickness and disease. Consequently, festivals dedicated to Wufang xiansheng, like other rituals intended to purge plague demons, were held in the fifth month. Wang also observed that during times of drought and other calamities the local people staged festivals for gods like King Guan (Guandi), Guanyin, and Fierce General Liu, but in his day Suzhou's Wufang xiansheng festival surpassed all others. In Luzhizhen, too, the Wufang xiansheng feast on 5/18 was one of the town's four principal annual religious festivals.[21] Yet Wang Zhideng makes no reference to Wutong in connection with Wufang xiansheng. The most suggestive evidence for a tie between the two is found in a contemporary collection of folklore, in which we read that "by local custom many people in the Nanjing area fear a one-footed *shanxiao* demon known as 'Wutong xiansheng.'"[22] Despite the similarity between the names Wutong xiansheng and Wufang xiansheng, though, this Wutong xiansheng spirit is depicted as the familiar incubus of Wutong lore rather than a plague demon.

The Wufang xiansheng seem to be a local variation of the Great Spirits of the Five Paths (Wulu dashen), who figure in Daoist exorcism rituals as demonifuge warrior spirits summoned by priests to dispel plague. These Spirits of the Five Paths are none other than the Five Emissaries of Plague, and are identified as such in the fourteenth-century ritual compendium *Daofa huiyuan*.[23] In their capacity as plague quellers the Great Spirits of the Five Paths play a central role in the boat exorcisms that were the centerpieces of festivals dedicated to plague deities like Marshal Wen and the Five Emperors.[24] In Daoist ritual, and especially in vernacular accounts of Daoist ritual, these spirits are referred to as the Five Fierce Demons (Wuchanggui).[25] The Five Fierce Demons, possessing the same Janus-faced character as the Five Emissaries of Plague, were cast in the roles of both evil demons and demon-quelling warriors. For example, the Five Fierce Demons were invoked in the course of the purification rituals enacted as part of "tranquility operas" *(ping'an xi)*, dramas typically on the theme of Mulian's rescue of his mother from hell that were staged at the temples of local tutelary gods during the baleful

fifth month.[26] Actors costumed as demons cavorted about the stage, terrifying the audience, until driven off by the god. In his account of the
lurid spectacles staged in these Mulian operas, Zhang Dai (1597–ca.
1684) commented that audiences were especially terrified of a suite
known as "Summoning the Evil Ghosts of the Five Directions" *(Zhao
Wufang egui).*[27] In both of these cases the Five Fierce Demons appeared
as evil spirits requiring exorcism. But in other ritual operas the Five Fierce
Demons themselves perform the roles of demon slayers. The Wulu spirits shared this ambivalent nature, too, as the following passage in a
gazetteer of Jiading county reveals:

> In the *jiazi* year of the Kangxi reign [1684], rumors of an epidemic inflicted
> by the Wulu spirits suddenly abounded. Whenever anyone walked along
> a road they might hear someone calling their name from behind. If you re-
> sponded, you were immediately stricken with incurable illness. It was said
> that if you carried with you a bronze coin of the Kangxi era bearing the
> legend "fortune" *[fu]* you would be spared.[28] Experience demonstrated
> that these talismans were effective, and people placed great trust in them.
> Coins with the "fortune" legend thus became very valuable for a time, until
> the epidemic passed.[29]

On balance, then, it seems likely that Wufang xiansheng derived from
the venerable folklore that entwined the Five Emissaries of Plague and
their alter egos, the Spirits of the Five Paths and the Five Fierce Gods. As
we shall see, the Spirits of the Five Paths merged with Wutong as a god of
wealth during the seventeenth century, and in the Qing period the cult
of the Wufang xiansheng became closely identified with the demonic form
of Wutong.

Song and Ming folklore, as we have seen, reveals a strong connection
between Wutong and wealth: the deity bestowed riches on mortals but
in turn demanded a heavy price, nothing less than the sexual conquest
of women. Fathers and husbands are shown as willing to accept this bargain. In the second half of the sixteenth century Wutong began to emerge
more specifically as a god of wealth. Yet the character of the deity changed
little. Far from becoming an industrious husbandman or frugal business
manager, Wutong retained his sinister bent.

The earliest explicit statement of Wutong's power to "convey" *(yun,*
which I interpret to mean both give and take away) wealth appeared in
the mid-sixteenth century and was later incorporated into the definitive
description of Wusheng published in a 1609 gazetteer of Hangzhou:
"Hangzhou folk place the utmost faith in Wusheng. The origins and par-
ticulars of the cult cannot be traced, but . . . it is said that the deity is ca-

pable of conveying wealth, defiling women, and visiting both fortune and misfortune upon mortals."[30] Around this same time worship of Wutong as a god of wealth was incorporated into the schedule of New Year's rituals. According to a Changzhou gazetteer of 1598, the city's inhabitants offered lavish sacrifices to Wutong at the close of the year, a time for settling accounts and winning the favor of those deities charged with reporting on the family's behavior over the past year.[31] Since at least Song times the townsfolk of Jiangnan had offered sacrifices and prayers to spirits at New Year's in hopes of conjuring a "profitable market" *(lishi)*.[32] By the late seventeenth century, peasants and city dwellers alike dedicated such sacrifices (known as *shao lishi*) specifically to Wutong.[33] In the argot of the late Ming, the phrase *shaoge lishi,* which denoted burning spirit money as an act of propitiation, acquired the meaning "making a killing," in the sense of a windfall profit.[34] In this context worship of Wutong implied not simply a desire for general prosperity, but rather a desire to strike it rich.

Around this same time, too, the God of the Five Paths to Wealth (Wulu caishen) emerged as a surrogate of Wutong. The first reference to worship of Wulu caishen on the fifth day of the New Year appears in an early seventeenth-century gazetteer from Changshu.[35] Another contemporary source states that "on the fifth day of the first month it is the custom in Suzhou for every family and every household to hold a ceremony and make offerings to the Great Spirits of the Five Paths [Wulu dashen]; this practice is called *shao lishi.* Only after eating a 'profitable market' meal *[lishi fan]* do people leave their homes and begin to conduct business."[36] Henceforth the practice of worshiping Wulu caishen on the fifth day of the first month, when shops reopened after the New Year's holiday, spread throughout Jiangnan. The Changzhou prefectural gazetteer of 1694 specifically states that Wulu caishen was worshiped at New Year's in order to invoke the god's aid in gaining wealth.[37] In Hangzhou, Wutong was worshiped outright as a god of wealth without the mask of the God of the Five Paths. Hangzhou shopkeepers offered sacrifices to Wutong not just at New Year's, but on the fifth day of every month.[38] Pilgrimages to major Wutong shrines peaked at New Year's, when shrines were besieged by those of all classes of society, from members of the wealthiest households to itinerant peddlers, seeking the god's aid in resolving the weighty problems of business and marriage.[39]

The cult of Wutong as a god of wealth coalesced around a new central shrine, one conveniently located on the outskirts of Suzhou, at Mount Lengqie, ten kilometers southwest of the city. Mount Lengqie is a ridge running along the western flank of Stone Lake (Shihu), a scenic spot long favored by men of culture and leisure such as Fan Chengda (1120–93), the renowned Song poet who took "Stone Lake" as his literary sobriquet. Mount Lengqie was named after a Buddhist monastery built at this site in the early seventh century. The Lengqiesi Monastery was one of a number of Buddhist shrines raised on this ridge, but the striking profile of its seven-story pagoda at the crest of the mountain attracted particular attention (figure 34). Rebuilt in the late tenth century and substantially renovated in the 1630s, the pagoda still stands today.[40] A Wutong temple was founded within the monastery's precincts in the final years of the Song dynasty, but this temple does not seem to have attracted special attention before the late Ming, when it suddenly emerged as one of the region's principal pilgrimage centers.

By late Ming times, Mount Lengqie had become better known among Suzhou folk as Mount Shangfang, a name that became inextricably linked with its Wutong shrine. A native of the town of Hengtang, a few kilometers to the north of Mount Shangfang, within sight of the pagoda, left a brief description of the temple as it existed in late Ming times: "Entering the monastery's 'mountain gate' [i.e., the main gate], there are two main halls, one above the other on the slope of the hill. The hall in front is dedicated to Guanyin, that in the rear to Wutong. Along both wings of the temple are located subsidiary shrines and altars. During festival seasons the god's votaries ceaselessly make offerings and perform processions."[41] Qian Xiyan confirmed that at Mount Shangfang's Wutong temple "music of pipes and strings fills the air; wine and blood of meat drench the ground. Each year countless numbers of animals are slaughtered for sacrificial offerings to the god."[42] Donations from worshipers enabled the resident monks to undertake renovation of the pagoda in 1636. The dedication for the rebuilt pagoda professes ignorance of when the monastery became associated with "Wuxian," but boasts that from the hilltop one could see an unbroken chain of worshipers approaching the temple from as far away as Hengtang. The pagoda itself became a focal object of worship, referred to as the "Wuxian penitential service pagoda" (Wuxian chanye ta).[43] Other sources confirm that pilgrims ascending Mount Shangfang mounted great processions, complete with painted floats and music of flutes and drums, that filled the roadways and flowed, day and night, in endless streams.[44]

Thanks to Wutong's reputation as a god of wealth, Mount Shangfang and Stone Lake acquired the sobriquet "Mountain of Meat, Sea of Wine."[45] Especially prominent among the worshipers who flocked to

Figure 34. The Lengqiesi pagoda at Stone Lake. In this realistic panorama of the countryside around Suzhou, painted to commemorate a visit by the Qianlong Emperor in 1755, the pagoda of Lengqiesi (top left) looms over the pleasure grounds of Stone Lake below. The Wutong temple at Lengqiesi became the main shrine of the Wutong cult from the sixteenth century onward. Xu Yang, "Gusu xihua tu" (1757). From Liaoningsheng bowuguan 1988. Courtesy of the Liaoning Provincial Museum.

Mount Shangfang were merchants who attributed their success in business to having borrowed capital from Wutong, a loan that must be returned, with interest, in the form of lavish sacrifices. Money borrowed from Wutong, once employed in trade, was reputed to return a multifold profit. In addition, whenever merchants borrowed or lent money they felt compelled to present offerings to Wutong to guarantee that the debt would be paid in full. Qian Xiyan described the process by which wealth circulated between Wutong and his votaries:

> At the beginning of each year shopkeepers and merchants in Suzhou draw up a contract to seek a loan from Wutong. First they purchase a large quantity of spirit money, which they present to the god at this temple. Then they bring the spirit money back to their home and suspend it over their domestic altar. Throughout the year they are exceedingly circumspect in making offerings. At the end of the year they take the spirit money—adding some "interest" to the original amount—to Mount Lengqie, where it is burned to "redeem the debt" [nazhai].[46]

According to more recent testimony concerning "borrowing a covert loan" (jie yinzhai) from Wutong, female mediums acted as intermediaries in this transaction. Supplicants presented offerings of incense and candles, "tribute of coin and grain" (sheaves of spirit money bound together with straw), and a variety of forms of spirit money representing gold, silver, paper money, and bronze coins. The medium, who had entered a trance and was possessed by the Wutong spirit, recited the terms of the loan, which the borrower would acknowledge. Then the borrower took four paper yuanbao ingots from the altar, and upon returning home placed them on the family's domestic altar.[47] If after several days the paper ingots retained their original shape, the god was said to have approved the loan; if the paper had shriveled, then the request was denied. Subsequently offerings were made as part of domestic worship on days after the full and new moons, and after the passage of a year the borrower would return to the Mount Shangfang temple to "settle accounts" by making offerings that included "interest" owed on the loan.[48]

Belief in karmic debt, and specifically debts that must be requited through a type of monetary exchange (spirit money), had been widespread at least since Song times. Hou Ching-lang has shown that one of the most prevalent functions of offerings of spirit money was to replenish one's personal account in the celestial treasury by repaying loans of good fortune, or for life (more precisely, a specified life span) itself. According to a Daoist scripture dating probably from the thirteenth century, each person at birth receives an "emolument" (lu) from the celestial treasury consisting of a physical body and a "covert loan" *(yinzhai)* that determines the degree of wealth the individual will attain in that life-time.[49] Enjoyment of prosperity threatened to deplete one's "emolument," however, and necessitated "replenishing one's fate" *(buyun)* through de-posits of spirit money. Ritual action thus enabled one to redeem the debt of life and secure one's fortune.

Ming vernacular literature, deeply tinged by ideas of moral equilib-rium, frequently underscored the futility of material gain by offering didactic lessons illustrating the impossibility of securing riches in perpe-tuity. Augmentation of fortune at one point in time inevitably entailed a corresponding diminution in the future. Those who accumulated money and goods were commonly denied male offspring, a telling testament of the essential fungibility of different forms of "wealth," including fecun-dity and longevity as well as material possessions. Excessive profit, es-pecially from commerce, augured future ruin, often in the form of wastrel sons who dissipated their father's hard-earned gains. All debts are even-tually repaid according to precise rules of exchange. The injustice suf-fered by an innocent is eventually recompensed, if not in this lifetime, then by future generations. Only through renunciation of material wealth can one secure less tangible—but ultimately more valuable—fortune in the form of male heirs to carry on the family line.[50]

Yet this Buddhist ethic of renunciation proved too extreme. The Con-fucian elite of the late Ming largely repudiated religious action (whether Buddhist asceticism or Daoist rituals) to improve one's stock of fortune in favor of a positivist ethic of determining one's own fate *(liming)* through moral action. The so-called "morality books" *(shanshu)* of the late Ming, especially the "ledgers of merits and sins" *(gongguoge)*, ad-vocated judicious investment in good actions as the reliable means of en-suring personal and family welfare. Accumulation of merit through vir-tuous action—defined in secular rather than religious terms—engendered tangible rewards, measured not in terms of mere lucre, but in even more valuable commodities: examination success, an abundance of sons, and more diffused benefits enjoyed by society as a whole.[51] Such ideas in-spired increased interest in philanthropy among Confucian patricians of the late Ming.[52] These men likewise embraced a social ethic of temper-ance, a life purged of the four evils of drink, lust, greed, and wrath yet premised on moderation and restraint rather than self-denial.[53] This ethic, sheathing its utilitarian goals with moral armor, endorsed the accumu-lation and conservation of wealth. Above all, the "tempered self" who embodied this ethic gained mastery of his own destiny and no longer had to resign himself to the inexorable workings of a supernatural system of retribution.

Ideas of wealth and fortune were intimately bound up with beliefs concerning life and destiny on the popular level, too. Yet the conception of destiny expressed in transactions whereby votaries "borrowed a covert loan" from Wutong conformed neither to the Buddhist notion of moral equilibrium nor the Confucian reaffirmation of positive moral action. Indeed, the moral character of the supplicant is never examined. Wutong's blessings were evoked through punctilious performance of sacrifice and abject surrender to the god's will, not moral practice and self-discipline. Once beholden to the god's benefaction, however, the supplicant becomes ensnared in a web of thickening obligations and subject to the whims of a capricious deity. We have here, I would suggest, a notion of debt that is fundamentally incompatible with the capitalist ethic of ever-increasing aggrandizement. As the Daoist concept of "replenishing one's fate" suggests, each person lived in a state of perpetual indebtedness. Good fortune did not conjure visions of a prosperous future; rather, it kindled fears that one's allotment of life, wealth, and fortune might soon be exhausted and therefore needed to be renewed through recourse to a powerful supernatural patron. This type of exchange with the *yin* realm of the divine, cogently exemplified by the solicitation of a "covert loan" from an amoral deity like Wutong, was not a capitalist transaction.[54] Instead, monetary exchange with the gods illustrated the powerlessness and vulnerability felt by those caught in the throes of the money economy.

Wutong's transformation into the preeminent god of wealth in Jiangnan did not diminish his diabolical character. On the contrary, the motif of exchanging women for wealth remained central to the popular construction of the cult. Witness the Wutong depicted in a mid-seventeenth-century anecdote recorded by a native of the town of Shaxizhen, an important center of the cotton trade in Suzhou's Changshu county:

> The Wutong deities . . . were five brothers who controlled good and evil fortune, and also roamed the world and played sport with mortals. The gods selected boys and girls to whom they took a fancy and had illicit sexual relations with them. Those who submitted to their will were rewarded with gold and silver; whatever they desired and prayed for would instantly appear. In many instances the youths' families suddenly became fabulously wealthy.
>
> Now in our town there was a certain gentleman from an eminent lineage who had four or five wives and concubines. His daughter, upon reaching the age of sexual awakening, was suddenly visited by a spirit who inveigled her with tenderness and soothing words. This spirit, who was of

handsome and youthful mien, attired in embroidered gowns, and clever of tongue, was none other than Wutong. Each time he visited he rode in a carriage accompanied by servants on horseback, as resplendent as any prince, yet no one else could see him. The daughter thus secretly took him into her bed. Although she laughed and talked as before, gradually her spirit subtly merged with the shades. From time to time she accompanied the spirit to his home, a paradise within the Grotto Heavens, entirely apart from the mortal world. . . .

This went on for several months. The woman's father had a concubine of unblemished beauty who was also visited by a spirit pretending to be the city god of the district. This impostor spirit seized the concubine and would not allow her to have carnal relations with the old gentleman. Whenever the latter came to the concubine's boudoir the spirit would fling the woman to the floor and cause her to writhe in agony. The old gentleman, unable to cope with the situation himself, summoned a talented wizard steeped in the lore of charms and talismans to mount an altar and perform rites to expel the spirit. The spirit, speaking through a medium, hurled imprecations at the exorcist. The Wutong spirit was summoned to act as a mediator, and ultimately fashioned a compromise whereby the impostor spirit and the old gentleman would spend alternate nights with the much-prized concubine.

Prior to all this the young daughter, having already reached the age of wearing hairpins, had been promised in marriage. The nuptial arrangements had been concluded, but when her future spouse's family caught wind of these events they annulled the betrothal and sought another wife for their son. The old man, a miserly sort, had heard that the Wutong spirit possessed the power to bestow wealth. The spirit promised that within a fortnight the old man would reap a fortune of tens of thousands of taels of silver in exchange for his daughter. The old man immediately consented to select an auspicious time for a wedding and exchanged betrothal gifts, just as if it were a marriage between mortals. In the end, though, the spirit did not live up to his promise, and the old man lost hope of profiting from the match. Hearing of an expert in the arts of talismans and holy water in Changshu, the old man brought him to his home to perform an exorcism. A heavenly host descended to drive off the Wutong spirit, whose apparition could be dimly seen—it looked roughly like a tortoise or a hog or the like—and then it disappeared for good.[55]

Many similar tales circulated in the seventeenth century. One told of a man in Jiaxing who in 1669 bought a house containing a Wutong altar in the library. His daughter, upon reaching the age of marriage, was visited in her bedroom by a stranger who promised to reward her family with riches in return for her sexual favors, and threatened dire consequences if she refused. The stranger came to the young girl's room every night; she, however, became thinner and more haggard by the day. The family, suspecting that the Wutong shrine was the source of their daughter's affliction, sold the house and moved away, but the daughter died shortly afterward.[56] Pu Songling included in his renowned *Strange Stories from the Studio of Leisure,* published in 1679, two Wutong stories involving the daughters of wealthy Suzhou merchants. In both cases the sinister Wutong (identified here as the fourth of the five spirits) forcibly imposes himself on the women, raping one and demanding the other in marriage in exchange for one hundred taels of silver. Finally the Wutong spirit is driven off by a heroic demon slayer who cuts off one of his legs, leaving the spirit to hobble off encumbered by his trademark handicap.[57]

The connection between acquisition of wealth and possession of women, already present in the Song conception of Wutong, achieved particular prominence in the late Ming period. Propitiation of Wutong involved drawing on the dark powers of *yin* forces, associated with death, disorder, and the dangerous potency of women. The desire for wealth itself was a disruptive force. Its satisfaction required altering, if not overturning, the prevailing distribution of wealth, and by extension the normative order. As modern ethnographers have noted, those seeking the aid of gods for self-interested favors usually turn to female deities, who are perceived as susceptible to personal pleas. In this respect female deities embody amoral supernatural powers that can be manipulated for personal ends.[58] Wutong, more akin to malevolent ghosts and denizens of the underworld than the exalted celestial gods, occupied a similar niche in the realm of the supernatural. Women, who as embodiments of *yin* are at once vulnerable and powerful, served as the bridge to this dark side of the divine. Yet this path to riches was a treacherous one, rutted with many pitfalls. The caprice of Wutong, like that of women, threatened to consume even the god's devotees. The popular conception of wealth thus bore a striking resemblance to the conventional portrait of women as alluring but inconstant, pregnant with destructive power.

Though worship of Wutong surely constituted a "profane cult," ultimately the Ming state took no decisive action against it. Neither did the Ming imitate the Song practice of co-optation by incorporating local cults into the orthodox pantheon. By contrast, the Qing government, once its attention turned from conquest to ruling, moved swiftly to uproot deviant religious practices. Despite repeated efforts to eradicate the Wutong cult, it persevered in private, domestic devotions, if rarely in public worship, down to the twentieth century. Nonetheless, as attitudes toward wealth changed, Wutong's primacy among Jiangnan's gods of wealth eroded.

In 1685, the newly appointed governor of the Jiangnan region, Tang

Bin (1627–87), launched an intensive campaign against the Wutong cult.[59] Apparently Tang learned about the Wutong cult from a complaint filed by a local man who believed that his daughter, on the eve of her marriage, had been possessed and defiled by the god. The distraught father made repeated offerings to secure her deliverance, but to no avail; the woman died, prompting the father to seek redress from local officials. Tang Bin's initial target was the cult's preeminent shrine, the temple at Mount Shangfang outside Suzhou. Appalled by the profligate sacrifices offered by worshipers at Mount Shangfang (variously estimated as costing "more than a hundred silver taels per day" or "enough to impoverish ten families of middling means"), Tang Bin ordered his deputies to seal the gates to the temple. The faithful, fearing the god's wrath more than the governor's writ, continued to gather outside the temple compound, where they milled about and importuned the guards to allow them to enter. Tang himself went to Mount Shangfang to supervise the destruction of the Wutong icons. First the statues were stripped of their official robes and bound with chains; then each image was punished with forty strokes of a bamboo cane. Finally, wooden statues of the deity were burned, while clay images were cast into the waters of Stone Lake. In their stead Tang placed an image of Guandi, the paragon of deference to authority.[60]

Tang Bin then began a campaign to uproot deviant religious practices throughout the province. He explicitly identified the "gods who go by the names Wutong, Wuxian, Fierce General Liu, and Wufang xiansheng" as "spurious fakes without any canonical authority" utilized by charlatan soothsayers to swindle simple-minded folk.[61] Tang also took the unusual step of seeking an imperial ordinance banning worship of Wutong so that his successors would be bound by edict to bar any renewal of popular devotion.[62] In the spring of 1686 the court granted Tang's request. The subsequent national campaign of suppression extended even to the original home of the Wuxian cult in Wuyuan, where the gods' images were destroyed and the temple was converted into a Guandi shrine.[63]

In his memorial to the emperor Tang specifically singled out the penchant of shopkeepers and merchants, some of whom came from distant parts of the empire, for seeking "loans" from the god and beliefs concerning the susceptibility of women to demonic possession as the two most pernicious features of the Wutong cult.[64] Popular lore attributed sudden grave illness in young women to Wutong's penchant for seizing the souls of nubile women; those who suffered from fevers and fainting spells often claimed that they had been betrothed to Wutong. According to Tang's testimony, local officials in Jiangnan every year reported several dozen cases of women who around the time of marriage experienced delusions, claimed to have sexual relations with the god, gradually became weak and emaciated, and died. Unscrupulous female mediums, upon hearing of illness afflicting a local woman, would proclaim to the family that Wutong had possessed her, desiring her as either a maidservant or a concubine. Family members would then feel compelled to make offerings to the god to win the woman's release.[65] Most reprehensible of all, Tang complained, the families of these women did not consider the death of their daughter a misfortune. On the contrary, they believed that the god would amply compensate them for their loss.[66]

Tang Bin's indictment thus recapitulated the salient features of Wutong—god of wealth and debaucher of women—present in the popular tradition. Both motifs can be found in Song popular folklore, but they were partially erased by the efforts to transform Wutong into more salubrious deities like Wuxian and Huaguang. Song and early Ming sources typically report that the benighted masses prayed to Wutong, much as they would to a local tutelary god, for relief from the common misfortunes of drought, flood, and pestilence. In late Ming Jiangnan, by contrast, Wutong is depicted as wielding influence over the more circumscribed spheres of business and marriage. Indeed, to the extent that marriage was conceived principally as an economic exchange, Wutong can be seen as a specialist in the acquisition of wealth.

At the same time, the cultural topos of Wutong as an incubus could be employed as a strategy by desperate young women wanting to free themselves from their conjugal duties. It does not take much imagination to recognize that betrothal or marriage to an utter stranger could easily incite depression, mania, and a host of other psychological ills. No doubt many young women, faced with an unknown fate and undergoing the psychic and physical tensions of sexual maturation, did indeed fall ill, and in extreme cases died.[67] Once the idea of demonic possession by Wutong was joined in the popular mind with psychosomatic disorders, it then became available as a culturally accepted explanation for aberrant female behavior. The same cultural construct also offered women an avenue of escape from the conjugal duties imposed on them. Lu Can stated that husbands of women possessed by Wutong dared not sleep with their wives; "even those who were determined to lay by their wives found themselves thrown to the floor by the demon."[68] The god's insistence on exclusive dominion over the sexual favors of the women he possessed is also a motif of the anonymous seventeenth-century story from Shaxizhen recounted above. Women could turn this characteristic of Wutong to their advantage, cloaking their amorous adventures with woeful tales of violation and victimization. Feng Menglong recounted a case in which a young woman attempted to cover up her sexual indiscretion by claiming to have been debauched by Wutong's henchman King Zhou Xuanling.[69] It seems that many gods of dubious moral standing engaged in such behavior.

The peculiar role of the Wutong cult in sexual politics is fully illustrated in a Qing anecdote purportedly dating from the time of Tang Bin's suppression of the cult.[70] This story is set against the background of Suzhou's religious processions and pageantry, which surpassed all others in ostentatious display and attracted immense crowds of onlookers. Such pageants provided a rare chance for women, normally sequestered in the recesses of their homes, to venture out onto a balcony to watch the passing spectacle, and thus gave young men an equally rare opportunity to catch a glimpse of potential brides. In Suzhou, large groups of young men accompanied the processions through the streets with an eye on the balconies above, comparing and judging the women on their beauty. Afterward the youths gathered and deliberated, often for days, to determine which woman should be chosen as *zhuangyuan,* or "optimus" (the term also used for the candidate who took first place in the triennial palace civil service examinations). The family of the optimus could expect to be besieged by flocks of suitors coveting their daughter's hand in marriage.

The anecdote relates the star-crossed fortunes of a clerk at the city mint named Zhao Wuguan, who fell into a terrible fit of anxiety upon discovering that the woman chosen as optimus on one of these occasions was none other than his own fiancée. Given his humble station in life and a paltry income of only ten-odd strings of cash per year—barely enough to support himself and his mother—Zhao could not afford to marry, and thus stood to lose his promised bride to one of his now numerous rivals. Zhao learned from his mother that his deceased father had once contributed to a lending society from which members could borrow a hundred strings of cash or more. The right to draw on the society's funds, however, was determined by casting dice. Zhao decided to seek the assistance of Wutong. He visited the god's temple and vowed that if he was successful in the competition to obtain a loan he and his future bride would return together and thank the god for his aid. Zhao succeeded in throwing a perfect score and was able to borrow the money needed to complete his marriage arrangements.

At the betrothal ceremony Zhao was elated to discover that his bride's beauty fully warranted her selection as optimus; his bride, however, was repulsed by Zhao's ugly countenance. Following the marriage ceremony and the couple's visit to pay their respects at the Wutong temple, Zhao entered his wife's bedchamber to consummate the marriage. He was puzzled to find her still fully dressed in her wedding clothes. The bride rebuffed Zhao's advances, saying that she had been married not to Zhao but to Wutong, who was about to arrive and claim her as his bride. She finally drove Zhao out of the room with the threat that the god would punish him if he dared to lay a hand on her. Zhao then rushed off to find a doctor to treat his apparently deranged wife. Upon returning home, though, he found her dead, her room pervaded by an eerie odor.

The notion that women who died young had been taken as consorts by gods was common in Chinese popular religious culture.[71] Despite Tang Bin's vigorous campaign of suppression, throughout the eighteenth century illnesses and deaths of young women were commonly attributed to Wutong, according to the eyewitness testimony of the historian Zhao Yi. Popular medical lore categorized these afflictions as "communion with the gods" *(shenhebing)*.[72] Women, by virtue of their *yin* qualities, were especially vulnerable to demonic possession, but their access to the divine world could also be a source of power. In her determination to yield only to her supernatural consort, Zhao Wuguan's bride resembles the spirit mediums described in *Gengsibian* as having gained their supernatural powers through sexual union with Wutong. Sexual liaisons with potent spirits like Wutong, though tinged with morbidity, at least offered women release from the male-dominated institutions that defined and delimited their social existence.[73]

Tang Bin's campaign against the Wutong cult was more successful than most state efforts to restrain popular religion. Major temples were destroyed or converted to other purposes, and for some time even domestic shrines to Wutong disappeared. In keeping with Tang Bin's decree, Wufang xiansheng temples also became targets for suppression.[74] A local gazetteer from Changshu noted that in addition to Wutong temples, shrines dedicated to the god's alter egos such as the Grand Dowager (Taima) and Five Transcendents (Wuxian[a]; an alternative name for Wufang xiansheng here) were also converted to other public uses.[75] Yet the late seventeenth- and early eighteenth-century accounts that credited Tang with having fully uprooted popular worship of Wutong proved to be premature.[76] By the mid-eighteenth century, Confucian custodians of public morals ruefully conceded that the cult continued to thrive in new guises.[77] Tang Bin had intended to convert the desecrated Wutong temples into public schools.[78] More often than not, though, they were simply dedicated to other popular deities with equally suspect credentials. The Wutong temple in the town of Puyuanzhen in Jiaxing, which had eclipsed the adjoining Dongyue temple in the Ming period, reverted to service as a Dongyue shrine.[79] The temple at Mount Shangfang, though initially rededicated to Guandi, later emerged as a shrine to Commandant Jin and eventually reverted to a Wutong shrine.[80] The Wuxian temple outside Nanjing's main gate had also been converted to a Guandi temple, but the Wutong cult continued to thrive at a separate shrine located within the same temple compound.[81]

In 1732, another governor-general of Jiangsu, Yin Jishan, launched a new campaign of suppression aimed at eradicating the Wutong and Wufang xiansheng cults.[82] This effort, too, had only a transient effect. A few years later, the Suzhou counties of Wujiang and Zhenze reported that the custom of holding tea séances had revived. The central position among the array of deities placed on an altar during the séances was occupied by an anonymous ruler of the district *(junzhu)*, understood to be none other than the mother of Wutong; a painted image of Wutong usually hung by her side.[83] A local historian in nearby Zhouzhuang dated the revival of spirit medium cults focused on Wutong to the late eighteenth century.[84]

Worship of Wutong (usually under the name Wusheng) also continued to flourish in the Hang-Jia-Hu sericulture region. In Huzhou, Wusheng and the tutelary deity Commandant Jin were paired as twin gods of wealth: "In the eyes of the townsfolk Commandant Jin and Wusheng are regarded as gods of wealth and honored with temples and sacrifices. On the second and sixteenth days of each month the inhabitants provide offerings of three kinds of meat to both gods. This rite is known as 'propitiation for a profitable market' *(bai lishi)*."[85] On the eve of the Qingming festival, people "from one hundred *li* around" flocked to the Wuxian temple outside the town of Tangxizhen in Hangzhou prefecture to seek the god's blessings during the upcoming silkworm-raising season.[86] By the beginning of the nineteenth century, the Wusheng cult had fully revived in the Huzhou silk manufacture center of Shuanglinzhen: "Rural families pray equally to gods of agriculture and sericulture. They worship Fierce General Liu and make offerings to the Horse-Head Maiden (Matouniang, a local sericultural deity), and shrines to Commandant Jin are found everywhere. Belief in demons is an abiding custom in Huzhou, and the Wusheng shrines are most numerous of all."

Shuanglinzhen's inhabitants worshiped Wusheng at the close of the year, at the Qingming festival in the spring, and at the summer Duanwu festival, when offerings were made to the gods of pestilence.[87]

Despite official persecution, the Wutong cult remained widespread in Jiangnan, even though it was far less visible than before.[88] In order to evade the prohibition against worship of Wutong, people frequently turned to surrogates such as the Grand Dowager (i.e., Wutong's mother) or Lord Ma (i.e., Marshal Ma).[89] In the Jiangnan countryside—especially in the Hang-Jia-Hu region, but also in Suzhou and Songjiang—the cult of Wutong persisted throughout the nineteenth and early twentieth centuries.[90] The god's terrifying aspect endured as well. The image of Wuxian seen in a Nanjing temple in the 1840s was described as a fierce, evil-looking statue cast in a pose of throttling and trampling upon small children.[91] Wutong's reputation as a debaucher of women remained a commonplace of nineteenth-century elite lore about the god, in which Wutong's role as a god of wealth was largely rendered invisible.[92] The Wufang xiansheng cult also flourished in some localities in the nineteenth century. In the Suzhou countryside, village worship societies celebrated the spring festivals (usually dedicated to tutelary spirits) in honor of Wufang xiansheng, while they devoted the autumn harvest festivals to Fierce General Liu and other local gods.[93]

Interestingly enough, the memory of Tang Bin's campaign of suppression was perpetuated not only by elite critics of vernacular religion, but also through the apotheosis of Tang into a demonifuge spirit who does battle against demonic attack. In 1823, Tang Bin received posthumous imperial honors and was inducted into the pantheon of Confucian worthies. Wooden plaques bearing his name were installed in the Confucian temples of public schools. Subsequently those who believed themselves to be suffering from affliction caused by Wutong would take Tang Bin's plaque from a school temple and place it on their domestic altar in the hope that Tang's spirit would exorcise the demon.[94] Yet this resort to Tang Bin's spiritual aid merely underscores the tenacity of popular belief in Wutong's interference in people's lives. The influence that Wutong was believed to exercise over ordinary people despite campaigns of suppression by the likes of Tang Bin is the theme of a story related by the poet and raconteur Yuan Mei (1716–98) in his collection *Things of Which the Master Did Not Speak*. In this anecdote a local man, disgusted by the fact that a statue of Wutong in a Buddhist monastery in Nanjing stood in a position superior to that of Guandi, took the liberty of moving the statues to reverse their hierarchical order. That night the man was vis-

ited by an enraged spirit who identified himself as the "Great King Wutong." The spirit said that although he was powerless against exalted and
righteous officials like Tang Bin and Yin Jishan, he would not forgive this
"petty town dweller" *(shijing xiaoren)* for his insolent act of desecration.
The man collapsed, raving, and despite the efforts of his family members
to appease the god with sacrifices he died shortly afterward.[95]

In 1835, the Manchu governor of Jiangnan, Yuqian (Boluoqian), reported that disreputable monks and spirit mediums were once again ply-
ing their trade at Mount Shangfang, exacting considerable fees in exchange for invoking Wutong's intercession on behalf of their clients.
Yuqian also complained that merchants and shopkeepers, just as in Tang
Bin's day, spoke of becoming rich by borrowing from the god's stock of
supernatural capital. The merchants did not use Wutong's name; instead
they appealed to Lord Ma or the Grand Dowager to assist them with a
"covert loan."[96] Yuqian directed local officials to take forceful measures
to halt such practices, arrested the monks at the Mount Shangfang temple, and ordered the destruction of all shrines dedicated to Wutong, Wuxian, or Wufang xiansheng. Four years later, though, he conceded that
his campaign had made little headway against entrenched superstition.[97]

In addition to condemning the practice of "borrowing covert loans"
(jie yinzhai), Yuqian fulminated against the activities of female spirit mediums *(shiniang)* who claimed to act as intercessors with Wutong.[98] The
mediums preyed upon sick women, whose illnesses they diagnosed as
afflictions caused by the god. Credulous family members would follow
the medium's instruction to take the women to one of the god's shrines,
where a healing ritual known as "invoking joy" *(jiaoxi)* would be performed.[99] These mediums also performed another healing ritual known
as "the Grand Dowager's penance" (Taimu chan), which, because it was
an esoteric rite unknown to Buddhist or Daoist priests, was far more
costly than other types of ritual healing. Mediums also continued to perform tea séances (in this instance referred to as "attending séance"
[daiyan]) in the homes of their clients to succor the ill and bless marriages. Yuqian discovered that although the monks at Mount Shangfang
dared not openly worship Wutong, an empty alcove covered by a cur-
tain but containing no icon was set aside for those who wished to seek
the god's blessings. The monks also purveyed a variety of icons—small
portable shrines; paper images of Wutong, the Grand Dowager, and Lord
Ma; and wooden seals carved with the legend "Pursue fortune and blessings will descend" *(Quji jiangfu)*—to the public at hefty prices. Many
families discreetly placed a Wutong altar in their bedchambers or toilets,

well hidden from public view; others, unwilling to harbor images of Wutong anywhere in their home, paid mediums to make offerings to Wutong in their stead.[100]

In Beijing, where the cult elicited little attention from the authorities, the imperially endorsed Wuxian continued to be worshiped as a god of wealth throughout the Qing period. Indeed, the major temple dedicated to a god of wealth in eighteenth-century Beijing was the Wuxian God-of-Wealth Temple outside the capital's Guang'an Gate.[101] In the late eighteenth century, a Five Brothers Temple (Wugemiao) outside Beijing's Zhangyi Gate was said to be a shrine for "the Wutong of the southern region." At this temple, according to Yu Jiao, a native of Shaoxing and observer of Beijing mores, mountainous stacks of gold and silver spirit money were piled up before the statues (depicted in martial poses) of the five gods in this temple. "Seekers of wealth" first performed rites of purification and ablution before approaching the altar, where they would "borrow" the amount they required. Several months later the borrowers would return to present meat offerings and return twice the amount of spirit money they had taken. Yu intercepted one such votary and asked him whether he had obtained the money he sought. The man replied "No," but added that by returning spirit money to the god despite not having received anything he was demonstrating his sincerity and could expect the god's favor in the future. A diminution in his offerings, on the other hand, would surely preclude any chance of becoming rich.[102]

Just as Wutong's penchant for debauchery persisted as an explanation for illness and premature death among young women, Wutong continued to be worshiped as a god of wealth. Yet over the course of the eighteenth century the conception of the god of wealth itself underwent a fundamental change. In large part this transformation resulted from the appropriation of the god of wealth by urban shopkeepers and wealthy merchants, groups who began to develop a bourgeois ethic of collective entrepreneurship and solidarity. The first stirrings of this bourgeois consciousness can be found in didactic popular literature of the late Ming, which promoted a synthetic ethic of moral integrity, wise investment of money, and philanthropy as superior to the straitlaced parsimony of both the sanctimonious Confucian and the abstemious miser. In contrast to the devotional emphasis of organized religion, this ethic of moral temperance stressed the practical piety of good deeds and magnanimity toward others as the wellsprings of fortune, for oneself and one's descendants. While embracing self-reliance, hard work, and individual entrepreneurship, it also encouraged moral self-reflection, positive acts of charity, and commitment to the welfare of society. This ethic thus offered a middle path between ostentatious self-indulgence and ascetic frugality that had particular appeal for the urban middle class of self-made shopkeepers, petty merchants, and artisans.[103]

The ethic of moral temperance was abetted by the greater accommodation of merchants and mercantile wealth within elite Confucian discourse in the late Ming and Qing periods.[104] More significantly, the ideology of moral temperance became a hallmark of merchant corporations—trade guilds, native place associations, philanthropic institutions, and worshiping societies—that proliferated rapidly from the seventeenth century onward.[105] All of these groups sought to cement their bonds of solidarity and to promote collective prosperity through religious ritual, with a particular focus on patron saints and tutelary deities. Not surprisingly, guilds and other merchant groups defined collective prosperity in terms of material wealth and gain. Thus many patron saints became gods of wealth in their own right. Merchants and bankers from Shanxi and Shaanxi provinces, whose far-flung network of partnerships and business contacts comprised the most powerful commercial institution in eighteenth-century China, routinely attributed their commercial success to the omnipotence of their own patron saint, Guandi. Gradually Guandi came to be venerated specifically as a god of wealth, and his cult spread throughout China.[106]

In Jiangnan, the Wutong cult's unsavory qualities and the shadow of official proscription rendered it unsuitable as a vehicle of bourgeois aspirations. Urban shopkeepers instead paid homage to the god of wealth, under the title of the God of the Five Paths to Wealth (Wulu caishen), as an entity separate from Wutong. Gu Sizhang, in a work published in 1799, wrote that "the God of the Five Paths was formerly known as Wusheng"; after the Wutong cult's suppression by Tang Bin "[the deity's] name was changed to Wulu, also known as 'the god of wealth.'"[107] Wulu caishen gradually superseded Wutong as the focal deity of the god-of-wealth rituals performed on the fifth day of the New Year. Qing sources refer to the principal ceremonies on this day and the preceding evening as Greeting the Pathfinder (Jie lutou). This event, essentially a shopkeeper's festival, is described in an early twentieth-century gazetteer for the silk-weaving town of Shuanglinzhen:

> On the night of the fourth day of the New Year, at the fourth or fifth watch, sacrifices are prepared for the god of wealth. This ceremony is known as Greeting the Pathfinder. The sound of exploding firecrackers lasts all night without cease, even exceeding the commotion made on New Year's Eve. A

statue of the God of the Five Paths to Wealth rests in the Taiping Bridge
Temple. The city's merchants join together in worshiping societies, which
meet on the evening of the fourth to entertain the god with music and
fanfare. At midnight they assemble and carry the god's image and regalia
in processions throughout the four precincts of the city.[108]

The practice of seeking loans from the god of wealth, central to Wutong's
role as the god of wealth, endured in the Wulu caishen cult. On the fifth
day of the New Year merchants would enact the ritual of "borrowing inaugural treasure" (jie yuanbao) from wealth gods. This loan is taken in
the form of spirit money, in return for which the borrower makes
sacrificial offerings to the god during the course of the year, and then repays double or ten times the amount borrowed the following year.[109] Another ritual commonly performed as part of Greeting the Pathfinder was
hanging from the rafters a pair of live carp to which paper imitations of
the yuanbao ingots were attached. The frantic jumping of these "living
yuanbao" was taken as an auspicious omen of the household's future
success in overcoming obstacles to obtaining wealth.[110]

    Wulu caishen's votaries were unabashedly devoted to the pursuit of
material gain, but they devised a variety of theories concerning the god's
origins to sanitize the cult and efface its sinister past. Gu Lu, chronicler
of early nineteenth-century Suzhou customs, accepted the theory that
Wulu caishen originally referred to the five sons of Gu Yewang, a Suzhou
native and eminent official of the sixth century. He thus provided Wulu
caishen with a legitimate origin as a cult dedicated to the emulation of
an exemplar of Confucian virtues. But Gu also admitted that in the Ming
period the cult had grown into the excessive and deviant forms that Tang
Bin sought to extirpate.[111]

    The effort to cloak the cult in the robes of orthodoxy largely succeeded.
Temples dedicated specifically to the god of wealth, omitting any mention of Wutong, proliferated throughout Jiangnan in the eighteenth century, apparently with the full approval of local officials.[112] In 1773, for
example, the prefect of Suzhou, in concert with local notables, raised
funds to purchase land and construct a magnificent temple to Wulu
caishen.[113] Additional god-of-wealth temples were built in Suzhou in
1796, 1807, and 1818, and by the early twentieth century numerous god-
of-wealth shrines existed throughout the Suzhou countryside.[114] The god
of wealth also figured as the principal icon in some merchant guildhalls,
though guilds, particularly those organized along the lines of native place
associations, tended to use patron saints rather than a generic god of
wealth as their focal cult.[115]

At the same time ordinary townsfolk throughout Jiangnan constructed, on a far more modest scale, shrines to Wulu caishen, known as
halls of the Five Paths *(wulutang)*. These small temples were especially
prominent in the region's textile manufacturing and marketing towns,
including Nanxun, Shuanglin, Zhenze, Pingwang, Nanxiang, Luzhi,
Shaxi, and Huangjing. The local histories of these towns, in contrast to
Suzhou, where Wulu caishen had been stripped of any association with
Wutong, do not hesitate to identify Wulu caishen with Wutong. A late
eighteenth-century gazetteer from Huangjing, for instance, states that "on
the fifth day of the New Year the townsfolk worship Wutong, colloquially known as Wulu caishen."[116]

Alongside Wulu caishen another figure, the hoary plague god Zhao
Gongming, also emerged as a staunchly virtuous god of wealth. This
deity, grouped with Wuxian's alter ego Marshal Ma as one of the four
great heavenly marshals, had an ancient pedigree in the Thunder Rites
exorcism literature.[117] Cryptic passages in a fourteenth-century ritual
compendium associate Zhao and his twin lieutenants He He Erxian with
good fortune in trade and imply that Zhao, in his capacity as a celestial bureaucrat, ensures that prosperity and amity prevail in the world
of commerce.[118] This account of Zhao's origins, powers, and role as a
god of wealth is reprinted almost verbatim in a popular religious tract
of the Ming period.[119] Whereas the scriptural tradition claims that Zhao
was a Daoist adept who withdrew from the secular world in the dark
days of the Qin dynasty, the sixteenth-century novel *Investiture of the
Gods* portrays Zhao as a potent generalissimo in the employ of the vile
King Zhou of Shang who is subdued by the supernatural legions of King
Wu of Zhou. At the close of the novel, though, Zhao is reconciled with
the forces of good. The supreme deity, Yuanshi tianzun, awards him the
title Perfected Lord of the Dark Altar (Xuantan zhenjun) and charges
him with bestowing blessings on the good and bringing the wicked to
justice. To aid him in these tasks Zhao is assigned four assistants, whose
titles clearly indicate their function as wealth gods: the Celestial Venerable Who Discovers Treasures (Zhaobao tianzun), the Celestial Venerable Who Dispenses Rarities (Nazhen tianzun), the Messenger Who
Brings Wealth (Zhaocai shizhe), and the Immortal Official of Profitable
Markets (Lishi xianguan).[120] Yet, although Zhao Gongming was widely
worshiped as a god of wealth in modern times, especially in southern
China, observers of popular customs and ritual life made scant reference to him before the nineteenth century.[121] In the latter part of the
Qing period Zhao, dubbed the Martial God of Wealth (Wu caishen),

財　進　路　五

Figure 35. Zhao Gongming and the Five Paths to Wealth. At the center of this New Year's commemorative print is the Bowl That Gathers Treasure (Jubaopen), from which sprouts a money tree. To the left of the table, holding an iron staff, is Zhao Gongming in his role as the Martial God of Wealth. To the right of the table is the Civil God of Wealth, holding a *ruyi* ("as you wish") scepter. In front of the table are He He Erxian, twin genii of wealth, one carrying a string of coins, the other a partially opened spherical container. The legend at top reads: "Wealth Enters by Five Paths." Modern recutting of Qing dynasty woodblock print. Wuqiang county, Hebei. From Po and Johnson 1992, plate 58.

and his four assistants merged into the cult of the Gods of the Five Paths to Wealth (figure 35).[122]

Thus Wutong did not disappear; in many cases the deity was simply submerged in the cults of its surrogates. Yet as the god of wealth was shorn of his malevolent features and recast as a bulwark of conventional virtues, Wutong receded from view. This change occurred not as a direct consequence of the state's suppression of the Wutong cult, but rather because merchants and shopkeepers increasingly abandoned the older conception of wealth as a diabolical force in favor of the new bourgeois ethic. Consequently, the cult of the god of wealth came to serve a different purpose. Rather than disrupting the existing order, the god of wealth confirmed it, and thereby legitimated the prosperity enjoyed by the merchants who patronized his cult.

Consider, for example, the image of Wulu caishen presented in a popular religious tract, *The Precious Scroll of the God of Wealth,* in common circulation by the middle of the nineteenth century.[123] In this version of the god-of-wealth legend, set in high antiquity, a wealthy but childless elderly couple decides to disburse their fortune through charity in hopes of being rewarded with a child. Their virtuous conduct is brought to the attention of the Jade Emperor, who bestows on them five sons, each born on the fifth day of the first month.[124] When the sons reach the age of sixteen each wishes to make his way in the world as an official, a soldier, a shopkeeper, an overseas merchant, or a pawnbroker. Their father dissuades them, arguing that farming is the noblest occupation of all. Henceforth the five sons enrich the family through their keen instincts for managing the family farm and keeping sharp eyes on the markets for their goods. On one occasion they purchase charcoal at a low price from the town merchants and reap a great profit when heavy, unseasonable snows fall the following autumn. On another occasion the brothers buy up a peddler's inventory of fans after the summer heat had already passed, and then sell them off at a handsome profit when midwinter weather turns freakishly hot. The brothers also perform pious acts, such as releasing a carp bought from a fishmonger. The carp turns out to be the son of the Dragon King, whose father is eternally grateful to the five brothers for their act of compassion. At the close of the story the Jade Emperor appoints the five brothers as celestial bureaucrats entitled Great Generals of the Five Paths (Wulu da jiangjun), who are charged with overseeing the distribution of wealth among mortals.[125]

The Precious Scroll of the God of Wealth is suffused with conventional social values, such as the commonplace axiom that farming is a morally superior calling. Its secular bent—the brothers neither seek nor receive divine aid in their ventures—and the abiding insinuation that gaining wealth is linked to personal morality and the performance of good works underscore the vast distance between Wutong and the emerging modern cult of the god of wealth. At the outset, the narrative reiterates the notion, already prevalent in didactic literature of the late Ming, that accumulating an abundance of material wealth invariably entails diminution of other forms of wealth (lack of male progeny).[126] Yet the sons' exploits ultimately reaffirm the acquisitive ethic of moral capital celebrated in late Ming and Qing merit ledgers.

The cult of Wulu caishen, unlike its progenitor, emphasized typical business virtues: hard work, modesty, thrift, and integrity—in short, making money by using one's own wits and talents rather than depending on a diabolic bargain with a malevolent spirit. No longer was

Figure 36. Civil and Martial Gods of Wealth. In the center foreground rests
the Bowl That Gathers Treasure, filled with giant coins, silver ingots, and
trees of coral. To the left of the treasure bowl one of the He He Erxian twins
holds a partially opened box (the other stands outside the frame of this detail),
while to the right Liu Hai'er, bearing a string of coins, dances atop his toad.
On either side of the table in the background sit the Civil and Martial Gods of
Wealth. Detail of colored woodblock print. Nineteenth century. From Rudova
1988, plate 94. Courtesy of St. Petersburg Museum of the History of Religions.

the acquisition of wealth predicated on recourse to dark, occult *yin* powers and overturning the status quo. Instead, wealth was conceived as a *yang* virtue and associated with powerful gods of incorruptible rectitude such as Guandi and Zhao Gongming. New Year's prints of the nineteenth and twentieth centuries unabashedly celebrate the multitude of riches—rank, money, and above all a happily united family—that the rich and powerful enjoy (figure 36). In the face of this "yangification" of wealth the fiendish Wutong and his coterie of surrogates like the Grand Dowager eventually faded away.[127]

The pronounced contrast between the character of the modern gods of wealth and that of Wutong raises the question of why the modern version emerged from such tainted origins. Never does anyone suggest that Wutong possesses any redeeming virtues worthy of emulation. Wutong at best is mischievous; more commonly he is seen as actively malevolent, violating women, disrupting family life, and causing madness and death. The riches and good fortune Wutong brings are often illusory or temporary; sometimes the god appears as a thief or causes people to lose what wealth they possess. Merchants who had appealed to Wutong saw themselves as living on borrowed money that must be repaid with substantial interest. In short, the development of the Wutong cult suggests a pervasive sense of anxiety about money: how to get it, and, especially, how to keep it. In the popular mind, wealth was not produced by living virtuously, or through prudent investment and planning. Instead, money was believed to be under the control of malicious and notoriously unreliable supernatural forces. This conception of money reflects, I think, the profound economic insecurities generated by the rise of the money economy in the sixteenth century. By contrast, the stability of the market economy in the eighteenth century fostered a more positive image of money and wealth.

The ubiquity of the Wutong cult throughout Jiangnan attests to the marked psychological impact of money and the market on the individual and the household economy. The economy of Jiangnan in the late Ming period was robust, but also highly volatile. Only slowly did social and economic institutions adjust to the rise of the money economy. A telling illustration of this lag can be seen in the inability of either the state or the market to stabilize the currency system. Imports of bullion from the New World and Japan in the final decades of the sixteenth century fed commercial expansion and inaugurated a long-term cycle of growth. At the same time the flood of silver wreaked havoc with a domestic currency system predicated on maintaining the fragile balance in the exchange ratio between bronze currency and uncoined silver.[128] Actually, the scarcity of bronze specie had led to the de facto establishment of silver as the dominant standard of monetary value long before the influx of foreign silver. Already at the beginning of the sixteenth century the Ming state frantically tried to reassert control over the money supply by increasing the output of its mints. Yet throughout the century China suffered from an acute dearth of coin. Outside the two capitals and the economically advanced areas along the Grand Canal corridor bronze coins virtually disappeared from circulation. The demand for coin encouraged counterfeiting, which in turn frustrated the state's efforts to sustain the nominal value of its coins and eventually caused a severe depreciation of legal tender. Silver, its quantity dramatically increased by imports, usurped most functions of bronze coins both in the marketplace and in state finances in the last half of the sixteenth century. But uncoined silver remained a primitive, indeed regressive, form of money. Its worth was determined solely by its intrinsic value, which could be ascertained only through cumbersome measurement of its weight and purity. Proliferating use of silver stimulated commercial growth, but it also injected new insecurities into economic exchange.

Bronze coins endured in the urban sector of the economy, whose daily petty transactions required a more convenient means of payment. Yet virtually all of these coins, as government officials woefully admitted, were counterfeit. Throughout the last century of the Ming dynasty fiscal planners careened back and forth between restrictive and expansionary policies. Every state initiative to control the money supply prompted merchants, money changers, and the urban populace in general to devise countervailing strategies to protect their incomes. Throughout the first half of the seventeenth century rampant counterfeiting of coins drove the state to debase its own issues, triggering depreciation and inflation. Erratic state monetary policy also incited repeated violence and rioting in Jiangnan cities. In the eyes of many plebeians, money in its physical forms, whether silver or bronze coins, exhibited the diabolical capriciousness attributed to the fickle god of wealth upon whom fortune depended.

Thus, the new forms of economic exchange tended to generate fear and unease rather than optimism and rising expectations. The rapid growth of the money economy fostered urbanization without producing social institutions that might help to integrate immigrants from the countryside into the unfamiliar urban environment or to shield them from the fluctuations of the money economy. Guilds were in their infancy; none of the corporate institutions that William Rowe sees as promoting the development of civic consciousness in nineteenth-century Hankou played a significant role in late Ming cities. Not surprisingly, then, the initial expansion of the money economy gave rise to a conception of wealth as a dispensation from inconstant and demonic forces.

From the eighteenth century onward the image of the god of wealth in his various permutations evolved in the direction of a more standard god, one that human beings could easily manipulate. The god of wealth became a euhemeristic embodiment of domestic and public virtues. Such a conception of wealth was obviously congenial to the state and prosperous merchants, yet popular acceptance undoubtedly could not be won simply through ideological appeals. Instead, the transformation of Wutong into Wulu caishen in the eighteenth century should be seen in the context of a more stable commercial economy (especially in terms of monetary stability) and urban social milieu. The stability of the economy in the eighteenth century stood in marked contrast to the rapid oscillations between boom and bust that plagued the late Ming. Once exploitation of Yunnan's copper mines began on a massive scale in the 1730s, the Qing state was able to produce bronze coins in sufficient quantities to establish a sound currency. The predictability of the exchange values of currency and widespread confidence in both forms of money spurred a sharp increase in the use of coin. Bronze coins once again prevailed as the predominant means of exchange.[129] The reliability of currency and stability of prices that characterized most of the eighteenth century coincided with the growth of corporate bodies, notably native place associations, trade guilds, and social welfare institutions, that provided refuges from the rigors of the marketplace and city life.[130] Thus both the money economy and urban society evoked a sense of stability and security wholly absent in the sixteenth century. Correspondingly, given the lack of institutions to control prices or cushion town dwellers against economic shocks in the late Ming period, we can readily understand why the money economy initially inspired a conception of the god of wealth as a malevolent rather than benign force.

Yet even the combination of imperial repression and displacement by the temperate piety of the growing urban middle classes did not uproot the Wutong cult from the religious landscape of Jiangnan. Though largely eliminated from urban religious life, especially in towns with a substantial official presence, worship of Wutong remained central to rural religious life. In the early twentieth century, the small, makeshift shrines housing a statue or painted image of the god that had been hallmarks of the Wutong cult since the sixteenth century were still commonly found at the entrance to villages and homesteads. These shrines could even be as rudimentary as three bricks, two standing on end and one laid on top of the others, on which a label bearing the god's name was pasted.[131] A survey conducted in Jiashan county (Jiaxing) in the 1940s revealed that 289 of its 580 shrines (excepting Buddhist and Daoist ones) were dedicated to Wusheng. The same survey reported that the county's 783 shrines (including Buddhist and Daoist ones) contained 1,455 Wusheng icons, far more than any other deity.[132] As in the Qing period, devotion to Wusheng was most fervent in the Hang-Jia-Hu sericulture region. Canhua Wusheng, depicted in popular iconography as a male figure with three eyes and six arms holding various equipment used in raising silkworms and manufacturing silk, was venerated at each stage of the silk manufacture process.[133] In addition to Canhua Wusheng, one also found cults dedicated to Kelong Wusheng (Cocoon Wusheng), Chetou Wusheng (Silk Reel Wusheng), and Jishen Wusheng (Loom God Wusheng). Although our sources do not specify whether this set of deities was regarded as benevolent or baleful, the capricious trickster Wusheng certainly would have served as a fitting symbol of the economic insecurity that plagued Jiangnan's peasant silk producers in the first half of the twentieth century.[134]

In rural religion, then, the Wutong cult and the god's explicit association with wealth and fortune survived and even flourished.[135] Wuxian, Wusheng, and Canhua Wusheng continued to hold positions of honor among the gods of wealth in the grand assembly of gods convened by spirit mediums who performed the "purchase of divine blessings" *(tanfo)* ritual on behalf of their clients. Although Zhao Gongming was included among the gods of wealth in these rites, Guandi was not.[136] A woodblock print from the early twentieth century shows that Mount Shangfang and its reigning deities remained prominent in popular lore about the vicissitudes of wealth and fortune (figure 37). The maxims illustrated in this print fully acknowledge that wealth confers power, but warn that greed and underhanded means of gaining wealth will inevitably bring ruin. Still, we find here express affirmation of the belief that "wealth can communicate with the gods." Piety augments, but by no means displaces, invocation of divine aid by means of eudaemonistic offerings.

The cult center at Mount Shangfang has remained a popular pilgrimage site, despite periodic persecution that has continued into the Republican and Communist periods. Today Wutong's mother, the Grand Dowager (now generally known as Taimu), has displaced Wutong as the focal deity of the Mount Shangfang temple, and the major feast day now

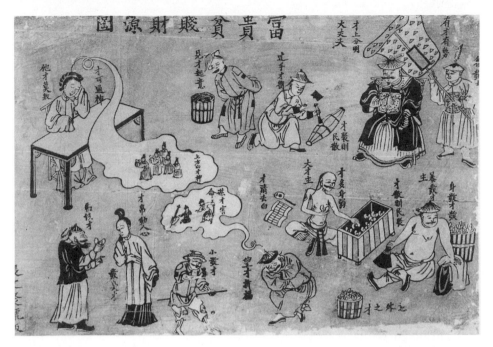

Figure 37. "Sources of Wealth for Rich and Poor, Base and Mean." This early twentieth-century woodblock print from Suzhou depicts rich and poor figures, each identified with several maxims about gaining and losing wealth. The woman seated at the table at the upper left is shown having a dream about the "Five Gods of Wealth of Mount Shang-fang," who are depicted in the dream nimbus as five figures in official dress making a hand salute. The epigrams on either side of the woman's head read: "Wealth can communicate with the gods," and "Do not covet the wealth of others." From Bijutsu kenkyūjo 1932, plate 33.

falls immediately after the Mid-Autumn Festival, on 8/18. Yet worshipers still come to the temple primarily to "borrow a covert loan" *(jie yinzhai)*.[137] The ability of the cult to accommodate shifting tides of ideological control is epitomized by the pair of hanging scrolls flanking the temple's main altar, which celebrate Tang Bin, the cult's most celebrated nemesis, as a paragon of "correctness" *(zheng)*.[138] Here once again we see the symbols and instruments of state power expropriated by ordinary subjects to sanctify their own gods, just as the regalia of imperial ritual are appropriated in service to local deities throughout China.

The evolution of the Wutong cult belies the common assumption that vernacular religion is conservative, inherently resistant to change. Nor should we see this vernacular religious culture as diffusely spread across boundaries of class and community, and thus acting as a kind of cultural integument that reduces social frictions and binds society together. The divergent paths of the Wutong cult in eighteenth-century Jiangnan reveal the inability of vernacular religion to contain and sublimate contrasting values and identities within local society. The emerging middlebrow culture of the towns, with its bourgeois ethic of self-improvement and conventional Confucian ethics, clashed with the egotistical pursuit of wealth by mantic means upon which worship of Wutong as god of wealth was premised. Consequently worship of Wutong atrophied within the urban milieu. Yet at the same time devotion to Wutong, understood precisely as a capricious god of wealth, intensified in the countryside, most notably in the sericulture region of Hang-Jia-Hu, where peasants were most vulnerable to the vicissitudes of the market economy. Rather than unifying urban and rural religious cultures, the Wutong cult of the recent past increasingly marked the disparity between them.

Conclusion

The shape-changing Wutong, lurid caricature of polymorphous sexuality, seems out of place in the urbane Song world, from which radiated waves of Confucian learning that brought rational reflection and sober faith in human perfection to the farthest reaches of the empire. Or at most the Wutong spirits might appear to be a vestige of an earlier era of benighted custom and rustic ignorance. Yet the Wutong cult was very much a part of its age, giving expression to the lures of wealth, ambition, and desire that epitomized the convulsive changes in social mores taking place during the Song and afterward.

Song religious culture was charged with ostentatious emotion and lurid spectacle: witness the grisly tortures meted out by the Courts of the Ten Infernal Kings, the penitents in Dongyue processions who turned themselves into "living flesh lamps" by hanging flaming braziers from hooks impaled in their arms and chests, Miaoshan's sacrifice of her eyes and arms to heal her father's horrible affliction, and the swarms of beggars dressed as the ghostly lackeys of Zhong Kui who materialized on every household's threshold on the eve of the New Year. This riot of sensation, real or imagined, bespoke a profound elaboration of the preoccupation with sin, death, and atonement that had emerged in the Han period. The baroque cult of death fixated on the torments of infernal punishment gave force and immediacy to the notion of a cosmos predicated on moral equilibrium. Yet astringent Confucian homilies did little to relieve eschatological anxieties. Growing despair over the burden of sins accumulated over many lifetimes clashed with Confucian faith in human improvement. The Confucians' stoic belief in chance destiny likewise provided thin gruel for souls hungry for a less impoverished life, either in the mortal world or beyond.

Transformations wrought by death had been central to Chinese religion since earliest times. Exalted rulers of the Shang and early Zhou eras, supreme over mortal men, lived in thrall to intemperate ancestors and their ravening appetite for sacrifices. From the Han onward, as the dead themselves became subject to divine judgment and punishment, deceased ancestors evoked more pity than fear. The ancestors still compelled reverence, but no longer inspired awe. The charismatic majesty that had once captivated their living descendants faded before the terrifying prospect of summonses from the stern underworld tribunes delivered by the ox-headed and horse-headed minions who did their bidding. As in the past, though, the local cults of Song vernacular religion coalesced around human figures transfigured by death. Most gods, especially those honored as local tutelary deities, were initially envisioned as ghosts, spirits of dead humans whose unspent life force lingered in the mortal world. In death these spirits retained the charismatic power they manifested in their mortal lives—as officials and warriors, but also as mediums and seers. Miraculous demonstrations of these powers *(lingyan)* prompted human beings to worship them, not simply out of reverence, but perhaps most importantly to appease these troubled spirits. Gods deemed responsive *(linggan)* to the entreaties of mortals (entreaties that were invariably mediated by sacrifice and pledge) achieved recognition as patrons of local communities. Yet just as the Song imperial state displaced military force with civil authority, the "dead generals" of earlier local cults became subordinated to a new pantheon composed of civil officials invested with bureaucratic authority, ruling not through brute will but rather in accordance with a strict canon of laws. Power and station in mortal life translated into exalted position in death. Civil magistrates were believed to maintain their dignity in the afterlife by virtue of appointment to the infernal government or as local *chenghuang* (the two most bureaucratized parts of the divine world, we might note). Yet charismatic individuals of humble station might also ascend to the ranks of the gods, serving their communities as *tudi* spirits.

Chinese of the early imperial era looked out upon an enchanted world populated by august mountain gods, fiendish fairies and goblins, ancient stones and trees that might suddenly come to life, ghosts of the unshriven dead lurking around grave sites, and resident spirits inhabiting every patch of ground. Mortals could carve out their own domains only by appeasing the multitude of spirits upon whom their farms and homes trespassed with timely sacrifices and prudent reverence. The progress of settlement in south China during the Song gave birth to a new class of territorial cults with tightly circumscribed sovereignty, each extending no farther than a cluster of villages or a township, and many confined to a few hamlets or an urban neighborhood. Unlike spirits who inhered in the landscape, these *tudi* gods were bound to the community through bonds of affinity and sentiment *(ganqing)* that originated in their mortal lives as members of the community. The *tudi* spirits shared a common history with the communities they served. Some *tudi* had been virtuous and illustrious notables, others uncanny seers and practitioners of occult arts, and still others ancient heroes whose deeds remained alive in memory and folklore. Graves rooted these spirits to particular sites, though temples allowed them a certain mobility, enabling them to reside in more distant places as well. The *tudi* stood in ambiguous relation to the heavenly pantheon. They did not simply serve as terrestrial supernumeraries of the recondite celestial gods, carrying out the decrees of their superiors; the *tudi* were also patrons and shepherds of their communities. Through a continuous stream of miraculous interventions—relieving drought, quelling floods, subduing epidemics, and fending off roving bandits and marauding armies—the *tudi* renewed their bond to the community and secured its devotion. Though the *tudi* occupied the lowest rank of the divine pantheon, each was sovereign within his own domain. Hence their mortal clients invariably hailed them as "kings," with or without the endorsement of the imperial state.

The creation of these *tudi* cults was facilitated by the vernacularization of ritual and the means of communication with the gods. Daoist rites of petition and propitiation required the mediation of priests, but the rising tide of Pure Land Buddhism fostered a lay piety grounded in direct appeal to divine saviors. The proliferation of cults devoted to deities like Guanyin and Zhenwu abetted the vernacularization of ritual practice and enabled ordinary people to approach the gods through simple and direct channels of prayer and supplication. Both Daoism and Buddhism flourished not as ecclesiastic churches centrally governed by canon law, but as countless local parishes nested in the communities that nurtured them. Masters of ritual *(fashi)*, whether ordained or not, adapted theology and ritual therapy to practical purposes, to win blessings, avert calamity, and exorcise the omnipresent demons. Many of these therapeutic regimes were subsumed into ecclesiastic religion, but institutionalized Buddhism and Daoism themselves remained congeries of local traditions. Some modern scholars have suggested that the essential unity of Chinese religion is to be found in a "shamanic substrate" underlying its disparate traditions.[1] Ned Davis has modified this proposition by asserting that spirit possession mediated by *fashi* within the context of exorcistic and therapeutic rituals was the common basis of Chinese religious practice.[2] Through the *fashi* the vast ritual arsenals of both Daoism and Buddhism were placed at the disposal of ordinary people, widening access to divine power and blessings. In many cases the *fashi* merged with the local spirit mediums *(wu)*. But the *wu* remained rooted in the locality and its resident spirits, while the *fashi* circulated widely, as did the ritual practices they brought with them.

The close identification of *wu* with their patron gods may have played an important role in the emergence of *tudi* cults. Hamashima Atsutoshi has proposed that not only did the *wu* foster the *zongguan* tutelary cults of Jiangnan, but the *zongguan* deities themselves were the apotheosized ancestors of the *wu*, who were members of a hereditary profession that laid proprietary claims to particular territories.[3] The actual genealogical connection between the *wu* and their patron deities remains unclear; it was common for mediums to take the names of their patrons as a sign of a spiritual bond.[4] It is worth noting, though, that Jiangnan's *zongguan* cults originated in the thirteenth to fifteenth centuries, a period in which clerics held high status and unusual authority within local society. In the competition for popular allegiance, alliances of patrician leaders, local wealth (landed or mercantile), and charismatic clergy no doubt carried considerable weight in determining which gods should represent the interests of the community as a whole.

Daoist and Buddhist clergy as well as the imperial state sought to appropriate these local gods and subordinate them to established authorities within both the divine and temporal realms. Ecclesiastic leaders and imperial officials each sought to impress their own particular brands of orthodoxy in recruiting proper candidates for inclusion in their respective pantheons. Yet political exigency, particularly in the Southern Song, when the refugee government at Hangzhou desperately needed to shore up popular support, often prompted concession to local interests. Nor could the clergy, possessing only modest economic resources of their own, easily defy popular will and entrenched belief. The procedures for incorporation in the official registers of sacrifices, despite the apparent rigor of multiple independent confirmations of a god's miraculous deeds, served to broaden rather than narrow the domain of orthodox worship. Hieratic and imperial canonization generated elaborate pantheons that were arrayed in hierarchical order but still elastic enough for periodic expansion and local modification. The proliferation of cults resulted not in uniformity, but rather in continual adaptation to local contexts. Definitions of ritual space and time, given concrete expression through temples and festivals, displayed remarkable heterogeneity across the empire.

The mobility of Song society, accelerated by the shift from overland to water-borne transport, encouraged the circulation of religious beliefs, and the gods that inspired them. The advent of printing and greater ease of pilgrimage brought tales and images of the gods to far-flung audiences. Through some combination of popular devotion, hieratic patronage, and imperial canonization local gods could gain new constituencies, transcending their original cults and entering the mainstream of religious culture. In a very few cases (Guandi and Tianhou being the most notable examples), a cult figure that originated as a local tutelary spirit could rise to the most exalted ranks of the imperial pantheon and achieve universal recognition. Yet even in these cases, in which imperial honors were wrapped in dense layers of official propaganda dictating the manner and meaning of worship, the hierarchs of orthodoxy failed to impose uniformity on Chinese religion. Prasenjit Duara has drawn attention to the ways in which myth and cultural symbols (to which we can also add liturgical action) are simultaneously continuous and discontinuous. Different groups, from village communities to the imperial state, inscribe their own interpretations on cultural symbols and practices, widening their "interpretive arena" and redefining their meaning. Duara describes the layering of interpretation that accumulates over time as a process of "superscription." In Duara's view, superscription creates not a hegemonic discourse, but rather the means by which different groups can draw upon a common cultural vocabulary to articulate their own distinctive worldviews without necessarily challenging or undermining the validity of other interpretations.[5] Paul Katz has modified Duara's analysis by suggesting as an alternative to superscription "cogeneration," which emphasizes not the layering of myth and interpretation over time but the dynamic process by which meanings are simultaneously created at different levels of a cult and instantiated in worship and liturgy.[6] The diversity of symbolic meanings attached to Wutong in all of the deity's manifestations—in state religion, hieratic myth and liturgy, and popular devotion—is a signal example of this dynamic aspect of cult, and the range of meanings attached to deities and their cults.

The complex history of the Wutong cult illustrates the flexibility of vernacular interpretations of the divine realm within Chinese religious culture. Particularly striking is the moral ambiguity of divine beings. Blessings and misfortune issue from common sources, and the powers wielded by divine beings can be used for both good and evil. Many preeminent gods of impeccable virtue originated as demons who were forcibly converted to the side of good. Conversion of demons was an abiding theme of Buddhist mythology (typified perhaps most dramatically by the legend of Hariti, the prolific mother who ate her young), but it also became a central theme of Daoist theology, as the apotheosis of Zhenwu, as well as that of Wuxian, attests. This process of conversion can likewise be seen in the transformation of Zhao Gongming from plague demon to righteous demonifuge, and his later transfigurations into chief of the Five Emissaries of Plague, who inflict epidemics upon mortals as punishment for their sins, and into the Martial God of Wealth. Not all demons and ghosts are tamed and transformed, however. The *shanxiao* goblins, for example, remained resolutely alien, denizens of the margins of civilization who wrought havoc and mischief in their interactions with human beings.

The diabolical character of Wutong was rooted in the *shanxiao* lore already widely diffused throughout southeastern China by the beginning of the Song dynasty. In contrast to other cults established in this age, the Wutong cult originated not in veneration of the dead nor in ecclesiastic theology, but rather in fears and anxieties about the dimly perceived yet palpably sinister worlds of foreign lands, wilderness forests, and nocturnal commotion. The transformation of Wutong into a Buddhist saint who delivered the inhabitants of Wuyuan county from epidemic in the tenth century was a crucial episode in the metamorphosis of this malicious imp into an honored god. In Wuyuan and elsewhere in Jiangdong, where local communities fought bitterly to lay claim to this benevolent Wutong as their own, the god was embraced as a *tudi* deity despite the lack of any personal or historical connection to these constituencies. Imperial validation of Wuyuan's Wutong cult no doubt whetted popular faith in the god's miraculous powers, and Wuyuan's emergence as one of the major pilgrimage destinations of Southern Song China ensured that its reputation would filter down to distant provinces. Buddhist and Daoist clergy were quick to take measure of the god's popularity and incorporate worship of Wutong into their own religious practice, at the same time refashioning the god into avatars of Buddhist grace and Daoist virtue.

Yet despite manifold efforts on the part of the state and the clergy to convert Wutong into a more salubrious deity, the demonic aspects of Wutong endured. Indeed, with the emergence of Wutong as the reigning god of wealth in Jiangnan in the late Ming, the demonic qualities of the god, his insatiable lust and greed, became more prominent than ever. In addition to the regal and magnanimous Wuxian enshrined in great temples in Hangzhou, Suzhou, and other cities, the unregenerate Wutong persisted in the ubiquitous small shrines scattered throughout the narrow lanes of the towns and across the rural landscape, and indeed in the alcoves of innumerable homes. This Wutong was the province of the *wu* spirit mediums. Especially prominent among these mediums were women who had fallen prey to Wutong in the guise of an irresistible incubus, and thus obtained the privileged access conferred by sexual intimacy. Like the *fashi,* these mediums served private clients, not the community as a whole. Yet the *wu* mediums did not presume the superior authority of *fashi* conducting judicial inquests to expunge wayward demons. Instead they approached the god as humble supplicants, surrendering to his suzerainty while seeking to curry his favor.

The diabolical character of Wutong illustrates the fear and trepidation ordinary people felt before the gods. The notion of divine retribution for mortal sin thoroughly permeated religious culture of the imperial era, and religious practice above all was devoted to the expiation of sin and relief from postmortem punishment, for oneself and for one's ancestors. In addition, the mundane world was populated by countless evil spirits, and the gods themselves employed legions of demon-soldiers to carry out the punishments they ordained. Popular healers and mediums offered a multitude of mantic therapies for exorcising demonic forces, appeasing disgruntled ancestors, and gaining the succor and support of the gods. Yet transactions with the divine realm remained fraught with uncertainty. The Wutong cult arose as much from fear of the god's wrath and malice as from the hope of securing its aid.

The Wutong cult also demonstrates the primacy of the eudaemonistic regime of sacrifice and exorcism in Chinese vernacular religion. Cultic lore repeatedly emphasized that obtaining the god's aid depended not on personal moral behavior, but rather on diligent devotion in the forms of sacrifice and ritual offerings. Despite encouragement by the state, the patrician Confucian elite, and the higher levels of the ecclesiastic establishment, notions of a cosmic moral equilibrium governed by righteous celestial gods did not alter the fundamentally eudaemonistic character of humane relations with the divine realm. By the late Ming, the moral equilibrium orientation had achieved dominance in the urban print culture of Jiangnan. This orientation thoroughly permeated vernacular literature of the late Ming and Qing, most strikingly in literary masterpieces like the novels *Journey to the West* and *Golden Lotus* and Feng Menglong's fiction, but also in "morality books," didactic religious literature such as the "precious scrolls," and sundry literature produced by commercial publishers for entertainment as well as edification, of which *Journey to the South* and its tale of Huaguang's exploits is wholly representative. Not until the eighteenth century do these ideas of moral equilibrium and retribution become ascendant in the middlebrow religious culture of the cities, however. In rural religious life, the eudaemonistic orientation continued to prevail down to 1949.

Yet the "ideologized" (in Weller's sense of the word) transfigurations of Wutong like Wuxian, Marshal Ma, and Huaguang, stamped with the seals of official and ecclesiastic orthodoxy, still exerted significant influence on vernacular religion. The ideologized versions of Wutong, like the god's demonic images, were propagated and reproduced through the dissemination of temples, icons, ritual texts, and folklore. Indeed, the Wutong cult and its many personae ramified into a multiplicity of local cults, each with its own distinct history and culture. Fiendish rogue, powerful demonifuge, merciful bodhisattva, trickster god of wealth: the roles performed by Wutong fully demonstrate the multivalence of divine power in Chinese religious culture, and the inadequacy of apprehending this religious culture through any neat taxonomy of the divine beings who ruled it. The meaning of the Wutong cult, and the devotion it elicited, can only be grasped by examining the local social and cultural contexts it inhabited. Needless to say, the same holds true for other cults, perhaps even more so for those, like Guandi and Guanyin, that were carried to every corner of the empire.

China's religious culture thus did not simply mirror the social order and its essential values. Yet religious beliefs and practices were integral to the consolidation, reproduction, and transformation of social relationships. Certain structures of Chinese religion exhibit considerable stability over long periods of time. For example, the conception of the divine pantheon and its hierarchical order and the repertoire of rituals used in communicating with the gods that emerged during the Song transformation of Chinese religion endured down to the twentieth century. Yet the stability of such structures—what we might conceive as the "interpretive arena" (to use Duara's language) of Chinese religion—masks significant change in actual religious practice, and constant mutation of meaning as social and economic relations evolved.

The conception of the divine realm in Chinese vernacular religion was very much a product of active effort by ordinary people to make sense of, and gain control over, their lives. The gods meant many things to many people. An array of forces, including the state and ecclesiastic authorities, impinged on vernacular religious culture, but conformity to ideologized standards of religious belief and practice remained superficial. The gods of vernacular religion were in most instances multivalent, exhibiting both providential and demonic aspects. It is precisely this mutability of the gods that testifies to the salient role of the popular imagination in creating them. Conversely, by examining the ever-changing world of vernacular religion we can catch a glimpse of how the lives and thoughts of ordinary Chinese were conditioned by the times they lived in.

Abbreviations

The following abbreviations are used in the Notes and Bibliography:

BJXS   *Biji xiaoshuo daguan* 筆記小說大觀 collectanea. Taibei: Xinxing shuju, 1973–.

BPZ   *Baopuzi neipian jiaoshi* 抱朴子内篇校釋.

CSJC   *Congshu jicheng* 叢書集成 collectanea. Shanghai: Shangwu yin-shuguan, 1935-39.

DFHY   *Daofa huiyuan* 道法會元.

HNZ   *Huainan honglie jishi* 淮南鴻烈集釋.

HY   *Daozang zimu yinde* 道藏子自引德. Weng Dujian 翁獨建, comp. Harvard-Yenching Institute Sinological Index Series, no. 25, 1935. Rpt. Taibei: Chinese Materials and Research Aids Center, 1966.

LH   *Lunheng jijie* 論衡集解.

SBCK   *Sibu congkan* 四部叢刊. Shanghai: Shangwu yinshuguan, 1919–37.

SHJ   *Shanhaijing jiaozhu* 山海經校注.

SJ   *Shi ji* 史記.

SKQS   *Wenyuange Siku quanshu* 文淵閣四庫全書 collectanea. Taibei: Tai-wan shangwu yinshuguan, 1983.

SSGJ   *Xinbian lianxiang soushen guangji* 新編連相搜神廣記.

SSJ   *[Xinjiao] Soushen ji* [新校] 搜神記.

SYDFZ   *Song Yuan difangzhi congshu* 宋元地方志叢書. Taibei: Dahua shuju, 1970.

T	*Taishō Shinshū Daizōkyō* 大正新滲大蔬經. Tokyo: Taishō issaikyo kankōkai, 1922–33.
TPGJ	*Taiping guangji* 太平廣記.
TPYL	*Taiping yulan* 太平御覽.
YJZ	*Yijian zhi* 夷堅志.
ZZ	*Chunqiu zuozhuan zhengyi* 春秋左塼正義.

Notes

INTRODUCTION

1. *Yijian zhi*, zhijia, 1.717–18.

2. *Zuodao* literally means "the way of the left." Just as the Latin word *sinister* (the left) connoted perversity and malign influence, *zuodao* too associated the left with deviance.

3. *Liji zhengyi*, 13.1344a. Unless otherwise noted, all translations are mine.

4. Although the received recension of the *Canon of Ritual* probably did not attain definitive form until the late first century C.E., the frequent use of the charge of "resort to sinister doctrines" in writs of censure in the first century B.C.E. indicates that the passage cited above already had become codified into law. See, for example, *Han shu*, 75.3193, 82.3374, 83.3408, 85.3464. On impiety *(budao)* as a category of especially heinous criminal behavior in Han law, see Hulsewé 1955: 156–204.

5. For examples, see *Han shu*, 25B.1260, 75.3193.

6. The most famous case occurred in 91 B.C.E. (see chapter 4, p. 100, below). On "spells and curses" in the Han and afterward, see Sawada 1984: 174–212.

7. *Han shu*, 93.3731; see also ibid., 97B.3982–83.

8. Zheng Xuan (127–200), in his commentary on the passage from the *Canon of Ritual* quoted above, glossed *zuodao* as "sorcery *[wugu]* and other vulgar and proscribed practices." See *Liji zhengyi*, 13.1344a.

9. *Sanguo zhi*, 2.84.

10. Legal codification of the crime of "resort to sinister doctrines" can be found in the Tang Code. See *Tanglü shuyi jianjie*, 18.1299–1303, 1311–18.

11. As can be seen in the Song legal casebook *Minggong shupan qingming ji*, 14.547–49.

12. *Song huiyao jigao,* li, 20.10b–12b. For further discussion of Xia's campaign against spirit mediums, see Nakamura Jihei 1978: 67–70.

13. For a catalogue of official proscriptions against religious heresy during the Song dynasty, see Shen 1995.

14. Maspero's (1928) encyclopedic catalogue of divinities in modern Chinese religion makes no mention of demons, nor does C. K. Yang (1961) in his sociology of modern religion. Anthropologists (notably Weller 1987, Feuchtwang 1992) have recognized the importance of the demonic in the construction of Chinese religious culture. For a brief typology of demonic spirits based on fieldwork in modern Taiwan, see Schipper 1971. Some substantial work has been done on plague demons; see Schipper 1985a; Katz 1995; and chapter 4. The ambiguous nature of the gods is studied in the essays in Shahar and Weller 1996. Among the important historical studies of deities and their cults, see Seidel 1969; Johnson 1985; Hansen 1990; Schipper 1990; ter Haar 1990; Dean 1993; Kleeman 1994a; Katz 1995, 1999; and the essays in Shahar and Weller 1996.

15. Poo 1998: 69–85.

16. On the problem of stereotypes in Chinese historical records of religious groups and activities, see ter Haar 1992, esp. 11–15, 44–63.

17. Wolf 1974.

18. Ahern 1981; Feuchtwang 1992.

19. For critiques and modifications of the Wolf model, see Sangren 1987; Weller 1987; and the essays included in Shahar and Weller 1996.

20. The term "popular religion" itself has fallen into disrepute, however, because even when shorn of the implication that "popular religion" is tantamount to vulgar superstition, it nonetheless tends to replicate the artificial dichotomization of "elite" and "popular."

21. Yang 1961: 20–21.

22. Hansen 1990.

23. Ebrey and Gregory 1993; Zürcher 1980: 146; see also Shahar and Weller 1996: 1–2.

24. Shahar and Weller 1996: 1–2.

25. See the cogent review and critique of this debate in Bell 1989.

26. Yang 1961; Freedman 1974.

27. Watson 1976, 1985.

28. Sangren 1987.

29. Weller 1987.

30. The most vigorous exponent of this thesis is James Watson. See Watson 1988.

31. Weller 1987: 172.

32. Yang 1961: 294–300.

33. Weller 1987: 142–43, 168–71.

34. Ahern 1981: 92–108.

35. Watson 1988.

36. Paper 1995: 26.

37. Sangren 1987: 55.

38. See Rawski 1988 for a critique of Watson's dismissal of belief. Not all anthropologists dismiss belief as a crucial component of Chinese religious cul-

ture, of course; for a dissenting view, see Feuchtwang 1992: 9. A balance between the relative emphases on ritual and belief is struck in the essays contained in Johnson, ed., 1989 and Johnson, ed., 1995.

39. Schipper 1985b, 1985c.

40. Schipper 1985c: 47.

41. I define "eudaemonism" as a system of values that is centered on enhancing human welfare, either individual or collective, rather than imposing a transcendent ethical code. My use of this somewhat archaic term is not meant to suggest a direct connection to the religious ideas of Plato and other Greek philosophers.

42. Poo 1998: 3–4.

43. Ibid., 58.

44. Campany 1996b: 343–62. According to Campany's taxonomy of Chinese thought, this "doctrine of Heaven and Humanity" is a distinct tradition apart from Buddhism, Daoism, and Confucianism. I would modify this conceptualization of the "doctrine of Heaven and Humanity" and suggest that it was not a separate tradition but rather a fundamental orientation that informed the worldview of all of the Three Teachings.

45. Ibid., 356.

46. Sangren 1987: 211.

47. Burkert 1985: 179–81.

48. Ibid., 332.

49. See the comments in Yang 1961: 79; Weber 1951: 240–42. Recent ethnographic research has shown that the tendency of Judeo-Christian discourse to reify money into moral absolutes—either as the root of temptation and sin, or as an instrument of liberation and freedom—may be unique. Most cultures portray the moral ambiguities of money in far less dichotomized fashion. See the essays in Parry and Bloch 1989.

50. On this problem see Ginzburg 1980: xiv–xxii, 154–55.

51. Bakhtin 1968.

52. Sabean 1984: 3.

53. Rawski 1985: 32.

CHAPTER 1. ANCESTORS, GHOSTS, AND GODS IN ANCIENT CHINA

1. Extant inscribed oracle bones pertain only to the last phase of the Shang kingdom, when the capital was located at Anyang (ca. 1250–1050 B.C.E.). See Keightley 1978b. Ritually used but uninscribed oracle bones have been found at residential sites of the nobility, but the surviving inscribed bones thus far discovered pertain only to the Shang kings and the rival lords of Zhou. For a selection of translated oracle bone inscriptions, see Eno 1996.

2. The following discussion of Shang religion draws principally on Keightley 1976, 1978a, 1991, 1999, 2001; K. C. Chang 1980, 1983, 1990; Childs-Johnson 1998.

3. Weber 1978, 1: 399–401. For a discussion of the charismatic nature of Shang kingship, see Levenson and Schurmann 1969: 19–22.

4. The Shang also addressed the royal ancestors as Di, but most scholars distinguish between Di as a supreme deity and the ancestor spirits. This conception of Di has been challenged by Eno (1990b), but Eno's interpretation of Di as a designation that exclusively denoted the corporate body of lineage ancestors has not been widely accepted. Early Zhou texts refer to their supreme deity as Shangdi (Supreme Thearch) or Tian (Heaven), but the term Shangdi appears rarely, if at all, in surviving Shang inscriptions.

5. Poo (1998: 28) emphasizes the morally neutral character of this exchange, which he describes as a *do ut des* ("I give so that I may receive") relationship with the divine.

6. Chang 1980: 236.

7. ZZ, 20.356a (Lord Wen, 18th year). The name *taotie* appears in Zhou literature as a metaphor for voracious gluttony; the earliest text to use the word *taotie* to describe the mask on early bronzes dates from the third century B.C.E. See *Lüshi chunqiu jiaoshi* 16.947.

8. For arguments in favor of interpreting the *taotie* and other fantastic creatures in Shang art iconographically as tutelary animal spirits who assist the living in communicating with the dead, see Chang 1983; Allan 1991, 1993. Art historians generally reject any iconographic interpretation of the *taotie,* preferring to study it strictly in formal terms. See, for example, Bagley 1987, 1993. Kesner 1991 tries to reconcile the two positions, rejecting iconographic interpretation while emphasizing the religious significance of the *taotie* motif. But Kesner's claim that the *taotie* served as a generic expression of the social and political dominance of the Shang ruling class is too vague to do justice to the unique qualities of this motif. Moreover, Kesner's acknowledgment that the meaning of Shang bronzes inhered not in their symbolic value as markers of status (as was the case in the late Zhou) but rather in their actual use in sacrifices would seem to undercut his argument about the purely symbolic dimension of Shang iconography and instead favor a literal (i.e., iconic) interpretation of bronze decoration. A compelling argument in favor of an iconic interpretation of the *taotie* has recently been advanced by Elizabeth Childs-Johnson (1998). Childs-Johnson argues that Shang *taotie* iconography is derived from four principal species of wild animals (tigers, buffalo, deer, and bighorn sheep) that were objects of both royal hunts and sacrificial offerings. Furthermore, she proposes that the *taotie* served as a signifier of metamorphosis, symbolizing the power wielded by human priests (the Shang king above all) to invoke the ancestral spirits by donning animal masks during the performance of sacrifice.

9. Akatsuka 1977. For a critical review of Akatsuka's methodology that nonetheless endorses his general characterization of the Shang polity, see Keightley 1982; see also Keightley 1983: 551–54.

10. Keightley 1976: 19; 1978b: 177.

11. The last two Shang kings added the word *di* (thearch) to their titles. The charter myth of the succeeding dynasty, Zhou, justified the Zhou usurpation of Shang rule precisely on the grounds of the Shang kings' blasphemous claims of godhood.

12. On this point see Schwartz 1985: 22–25.

13. On the origins of cities as ceremonial centers, see Wheatley 1971.

14. Chang 1990; Hayashi 1990; Li Xueqin 1993. For illustrations, see also Yang Xiaoneng 1999: 117–35.

15. Chang 1990: 14. Chinese scholars have tended to see more or less continuity between Liangzhu and Shang iconographic styles. See Li Xueqin 1993; Wu Hung 1995: 28–44. But Kesner (1991: 49–50) observes that the stylistic idiom of the Liangzhu jades had been lost by the time of the earliest Shang bronze vessels, which in any case display imagery far cruder than that of the Liangzhu jades. He argues that even if Shang bronzes reflect stylistic echoes of the older Liangzhu culture, the religious import of the Liangzhu iconography would have ceased to have any meaning for the Shang. Childs-Johnson (1998: 19–20), in contrast, argues that the animal-mask headdress iconography of Liangzhu and Longshan jade carvings and the *taotie* motif in Shang bronzes indicate continuity not only in representation but also in religious belief. Keightley (1998: 786–88, 796–97) notes that in contrast to Liangzhu mortuary practice jades occupied only a modest place among Shang grave goods, but this shift may not be too significant given the radical change in ritual technologies that accompanied the emergence of bronze metalworking.

16. Chang 1980: 33–34, 192–93.

17. Chang 1983: 54. Other nobles also performed the *bin* ritual to convene with their departed ancestors. Chang likens the *bin* ceremony to a form of shamanic transport, in which the king enters a trance and visits the ancestral realm. Keightley (1998), who denies that the Shang kings engaged in any form of "shamanic" ecstasy or spirit journeys, argues that the *bin* ritual did not entail a spirit journey on the part of the king; instead, the king "hosted" his ancestors, who came to him. Whichever interpretation is correct, it is clear that the king (or lineage head) personally performed the ritual, and that his presence was indispensable to it.

18. The exact date of the Zhou conquest of Shang has long been debated. The date of 1045 B.C.E. adduced here follows the painstaking analysis of Shaughnessy 1991: 217–35. In any event, most scholars now favor a mid-eleventh-century date over the traditional date of 1127 B.C.E.

19. Von Falkenhausen 1993: 152–61; Rawson 1999a: 364–68.

20. Of course, the Shang oracle bones and the inscriptions on Shang and Zhou bronzes are the most ancient literary records of Chinese civilization, but the oracle bones were unknown to later Chinese until the advent of modern archaeology, and the bronze inscriptions were never accorded recognition as literary works. Confucius's (551–479 B.C.E.) reverence for the *Odes* and *Documents* attests to their sacred stature among the Zhou nobility.

21. On the role of Tian in the ideological consolidation of the Zhou political order, see Eno 1990a: 19–27; Creel 1970: 93–100.

22. It has long been thought that the moral character of Tian in contrast to the amorality of Di—best exemplified by the early sections of the foundational text of the Zhou, the *Shang shu (Documents)*—was already manifest at the time of the Zhou conquest of Shang. Recent research instead suggests that the religious culture of predynastic and early dynastic Zhou differed little from that of Shang, and that the new conception of Tian described here emerged only a century or so after the establishment of the Zhou dynasty, at a time when royal au-

thority was subjected to challenge. See Eno 1990a; Shaughnessy 1991: 185; Poo 1998: 30. More recently, Shaughnessy has argued that the idea that the Zhou succeeded to the Mandate of Heaven was already present in debates about the constitution of royal authority that took place immediately after the founding of Zhou. See Shaughnessy 1999: 310–17.

23. On these themes of world ordering, see Bodde 1961; Birrell 1993; Loewe 1982; Lewis 1990: 165.

24. Creel (1970: 370–72) expressed doubts about whether the *She* ceremony was integrated into the Western Zhou investiture ceremony. But Kominami (1987) argues that the Soil Altar and the *She* ceremony performed a crucial role in link-ing the Zhou vassals to the sovereign heritage of the Zhou royal house. In his view, the *She* ritual of Zhou grew out of the earlier totemic religion of tribal cul-tures in which the altar (in the form of a stone, a tree, or a raised earthen plat-form) represented the union of heaven and earth and by extension the divine sanc-tion accorded to Zhou suzerainty. As the Zhou kingdom expanded beyond the confines of its original territory, the Soil Altar provided the material link between the reigning king and the homeland of his ancestors. The clod of earth placed at the Soil Altars of the Zhou vassals thus expressed the subordination of the vas-sal to the Zhou king while reinforcing the ties binding the vassals to Heaven's Mandate.

25. ZZ, 10.179a (Lord Zhuang, 28th year). See Wheatley 1971: 174.

26. Von Falkenhausen 1994: 1–5. For the ritual context of Zhou bronzes, see also von Falkenhausen 1993: 146–52.

27. The crisis in royal authority precipitated by military defeats at the hands of foreign invaders is believed to have begun during the reign of King Mu (r. 956–918 B.C.E.). In response, King Mu instituted a more centralized and bu-reaucratic form of government in an effort to buttress royal power, but his re-forms apparently did not check the continuing erosion of the Zhou's command over even its own vassals. See Shaughnessy 1999: 323–31.

28. The archaeological record attests to a dramatic change in ritual regalia, especially bronze ritual vessels, in the early ninth century B.C.E. that marked a complete rupture from the ritual traditions inherited from the Shang. See Raw-son 1999a; von Falkenhausen 1999. Shaughnessy (1999: 331–32) connects this "Ritual Revolution" to the political reforms of King Mu, though Rawson (1999a: 360, 434) places the Ritual Revolution somewhat later, in the first half of the ninth century B.C.E. The precise religious significance of the ritual reforms has yet to be spelled out. The changes in ritual regalia attest to greater stan-dardization, an emphasis on formal hierarchy of rank, and codification of ritual practice. Ironically, then, even as Zhou royal authority suffered serious decline, ritual uniformity and homogenization of elite culture, suggesting a common set of political and religious values, seems to have proliferated within the Zhou ec-umene. See von Falkenhausen 1999: 543–44.

29. On the prominence of blood sacrifice in Zhou ritual, see Kleeman 1994c.

30. Lewis 1990: 17–28.

31. Von Falkenhausen 1994: 3–5.

32. Eno 1990a: 24–27; Poo 1998: 38.

33. Lewis 1990: 28–52.

34. Creel 1970: 348–49.

35. ZZ, 17.288a–b (Lord Xi, 31st year).

36. ZZ, 44.763a–764b (Lord Zhao, 7th year).

37. Ibid.

38. This passage from the *Chronicles of Zuo* (fourth century B.C.E.) is the earliest mention of a dualistic conception of the body divided into *po* and *hun* "souls." The word *po* appears in earlier texts; *hun* was apparently a later addition. By the early Han period the idea that the *hun* is made up of refined, ethereal *qi,* whereas the *po* contains the grosser, corporeal *qi,* was well established in elite culture, though not necessarily among the populace at large. See Loewe 1979: 9–10; Yü Ying-shih 1987a: 369–78; Seidel 1987a: 226–27; Brashier 1996; Poo 1998: 62–67.

39. For Confucius's statement, see *Analects* 6.22.

40. The most extensive treatment of the theory and technology of attaining immortality through physical, liturgical, and therapeutic techniques is Needham 1974: 71–154.

41. See chapter 2, pp. 58–60. The literature on the subject of the Queen Mother of the West is enormous. For recent studies, see Loewe 1979: 86–126; Fracasso 1988; Wu Hung 1989: 108–41; Cahill 1993; and James 1995.

42. For more extensive synopses of correlative cosmology, see Schwartz 1985: 350–82; Graham 1989: 313–82; Lewis 1999; Harper 1999.

43. Schwartz 1985: 180.

44. *SJ*, 28.1355.

45. Kleeman 1994b: 227–28. See also Mori 1970: 123–47.

46. *SJ*, 28.1358. This passage is translated in Kleeman 1994b: 228–29.

47. Although Shaohao disappeared from the standard roster of the Five Thearchs in the Han and after (compare, for example, *SJ*, 1), he was included among the Five Thearchs in some historical schemes current during the Warring States and early Han periods. See, for example, ZZ, 48.835a–838a (Lord Zhao, 17th year); *HNZ*, 3.88–89.

48. *SJ*, 28.1364. On Huangdi's defeat of the Fiery Thearch, see *SJ*, 1.3, and Lewis 1990: 179–83.

49. On official Qin cults during the reign of the First Emperor, see Poo 1998: 104–6. The Qin state expressly forbade "anomalous sacrifices" *(qisi)* and the establishment of "demon cult-sites" *(guiwei).* See Harper 2000.

50. Kominami 1994: 52.

51. Chinese words with identical romanized spellings are distinguished by superscript letters throughout this book. See the Glossary.

52. Le Blanc 1985–86: 45n1.

53. The following synopsis of the Huangdi mythology is derived from Lewis 1990: 165–212. See also Mori 1970: 149–74; Le Blanc 1985–86.

54. This version of the Huangdi myth first appears in the third-century *Book of Lord Shang (Shangjun shu)* and later served as the basis of Sima Qian's authoritative "biography" of Huangdi in *SJ*, 1.1–9 (translated in full in Lewis 1990: 174–76).

55. Most scholars regard stories about Huangdi as a divine figure associated with rain and storms as vestiges of an older oral mythology. Puett (1998) has

challenged this view, instead arguing that the deified Huangdi was a later transfiguration of a figure originally portrayed as a mortal sage-king who symbolized the necessity of the monarch's resort to legitimate force to create a civil society. Puett rightly disparages the notion that there is a single, coherent mythology of Huangdi, and he is probably correct in asserting that the image of Huangdi as the archetypal civilizing ruler is a product of the political discourse of the late Warring States era and not derived from any putative older oral traditions. Yet Sima Qian's claim that the Qin rulers already in the fifth century B.C.E. worshiped Huangdi and the Fiery Thearch, presumably as paired gods of rain and sun, should not be dismissed out of hand. As in the case of the Queen Mother of the West, it is probable that there were regional variations in the myths related to Huangdi.

56. For surveys of the mythological lore regarding Chiyou, see Lewis 1990: 183–212; Puett 1998; Bodde 1975: 120–27.

57. Lewis (1990: 183–85) describes Chiyou as an alter ego of Huangdi, associated (like Huangdi) with dragons and storms, an interpretation that finds support from the research of Mori 1970. But Allan (1991: 67) instead identifies Chiyou with the Fiery Thearch, and thus the antithesis of the Huangdi.

58. Puett 1998: 437–38, 463–67.

59. *Longyu hetu* (a now lost work), cited in a Tang commentary to *SJ*. See *SJ*, 1.4. On the *Longyu hetu*, see Chen Pan 1991: 414–23. The same general depiction of Chiyou also can be found in *SHJ*, 17.286. Another early legend claims that Chiyou was a traitorous subordinate of the Fiery Thearch who sought to depose his lord; the latter ordered Huangdi to put an end to Chiyou's depredations. See *Yi Zhou shu*, 56, "Changmai jie."

60. *Longyu hetu*, cited in *SJ*, 1.4n3.

61. *Shuyi ji* (Ren Fang), shang.2a.

62. *Hanfeizi jishi*, 10.172; translation modified from Lewis 1990: 181.

63. In at least one version of the Huangdi myth the Wind Lord and Rain Master were originally allies of Chiyou in his battle against Huangdi; they shared in Chiyou's fate, and like Chiyou were later incorporated into Huangdi's retinue. See *SHJ*, 17.286. Both the Wind Lord and the Rain Master were common motifs in Han funerary art. See Hayashi 1988: 162–65.

64. *HNZ*, 3.94, translated in Major 1993: 71. See also Seidel 1987b: 29.

65. *HNZ*, 17.561.

66. Henri Maspero applied the term euhemerization to Chinese religion in the opposite sense, denoting the transformation of gods into historical human figures. See Maspero 1924: 1–2. Most scholars have followed Maspero's lead; certainly this "reverse euhemerism," to use William Boltz's more accurate phrase, was a pervasive feature of Chinese mythology in Warring States and Han times. As Boltz (1981: 142) puts it, "if the Greeks can be said to have mythologized their history, the Chinese historicized their mythology." See also Bodde 1961: 372–76.

67. Recently, some scholars have argued that already by the third century B.C.E. Taiyi was revered as a powerful deity who protected and conferred boons on mortals. See Li Ling 1995–96; Harper 2000.

68. On the imperial cults of Han, see Loewe 1971, 1982: 127–43.

CHAPTER 2. THE HAN CULT
OF THE DEAD AND SALVIFIC RELIGION

1. To date, no royal Zhou tombs have been discovered, and we cannot determine whether the mortuary practices of the Zhou kings differed from those of their vassals, or from their Shang predecessors.

2. Thote forthcoming; see also Thorp 1991; Rawson 1999b.

3. On the growing architectural scale of royal tombs of the Warring States era and the ways in which the tombs replicated the actual palaces of living kings, see Wu Hung 1988: 90–96, 1995: 110–21; von Falkenhausen 1994: 6–7; Kominami 1994.

4. Von Falkenhausen forthcoming.

5. For illustrations of these motifs, see Weber 1968.

6. Rawson 1999b, 2000.

7. Rawson (1999b) emphasizes that these changes in tomb architecture and mortuary goods were often initiated on the periphery of the Zhou ecumene, notably in the southern state of Chu, but after the Qin-Han unification they spread throughout the empire, fully displacing the mortuary traditions of the Zhou heartland.

8. Although Wu Hung (1988, 1995: 110–12) emphasizes the functional disjuncture (as well as the physical distance) between the tomb and the ancestral temple in Shang and Western Zhou religion, von Falkenhausen (1994: 3–4) argues that there is no appreciable difference in the inventories of bronze ritual vessels found at tombs and temples, suggesting that sacrifices may well have been offered at tombs as well as at temples. Kominami (1994: 11–17) believes that sacrifices at tombs in Shang times were limited to quelling the spirits of powerful (and thus potentially dangerous) persons of high social rank; these rituals thus were more in the nature of exorcisms than sacrifices. But the distinction drawn by Kominami between sacrifice and exorcism seems to be an artificial one, given the ambivalent standing of the deified ancestors as bearers of both blessings and curses.

9. Von Falkenhausen 1994, forthcoming.

10. Kominami 1994: 6–7.

11. The most thorough studies of the banner are Loewe 1979: 17–59; James 1996: 5–33. On the place of Mawangdui in Han funerary art, see Powers 1991: 50–58.

12. The practice of enclosing the body of the deceased in fitted jade suits, which apparently began in the first century B.C.E. and continued into the late Han, seems to have been reserved to members of the imperial clan. See Thorp 1991: 35–36. For illustrations, see Yang Xiaoneng 1999: 390–93. The practice of placing a profusion of jade discs and plaques in tombs as apotropaic talismans was already widespread by the third century B.C.E. See Rawson 1999b: 49–50.

13. Tomb guardian figures, such as this example, first developed in the Chu cultural sphere. See Fong 1991b; Thote forthcoming.

14. Fong 1991b: 86–89.

15. This theory is expounded in Loewe 1979.

16. *BPZ*, 17.300.

17. Brashier 1995.

18. The use of bronze mirrors as mortuary objects may have complemented the use of jade, most spectacularly in the instance of the jade burial suits of the Han prince Liu Sheng and his wife, to preserve the body and its *po* spirit. See Thorp 1991.

19. Mention of Siming as a recipient of sacrifices offered in the course of funerary rites dates back to the sixth century B.C.E. See Inahata 1979: 3. See also Poo 1998: 142–43.

20. Harper 1994.

21. Cited in Wu Rongzeng 1981: 59; translation modified from Seidel 1987a: 705. See also Seidel 1987b: 28–29. Little is known about this Yellow God, or the underworld under his dominion, but it is assumed that "Yellow God" was simply another name for Huangdi. The association of the lord of the underworld with the color yellow most likely derived from the Yellow Springs, the most commonly used metaphor for the final resting place for the dead, and the correspondence between yellow and earth established by correlative cosmology.

22. Adjacent to this talisman archaeologists also discovered a clay seal bearing the legend "envoy of the Celestial Thearch" *(Tiandi shizhe)*. Jiangsusheng wenwu guanli weiyuanhui 1960: 20.

23. Seidel 1987a, 1987b; Kominami 1994; Poo 1998: 169–76.

24. Haoli Mountain was a lower summit below the peak of Mount Tai.

25. Another inscription, dated 173 C.E., mentions that ginseng placed in the tomb was intended to "substitute for the living," while lead (rather than wax) figurines were intended to "substitute for the dead." Lead figurines have been recovered from a number of Han tombs. One text describes the lead man as a versatile worker who can grind grain, cook, drive carriages, and write letters. See Kominami 1994: 42; Poo 1998: 171–73. Presumably the ginseng was meant as a gift to spare the living from sharing in any punishment meted out to their dead ancestors. The use of ginseng for this purpose probably owed to the resemblance of ginseng root to a human body (hence its Chinese name of *renshen*) and its vaunted efficacy in prolonging life.

26. Cited in Kominami 1994: 31. This particular jar was not scientifically excavated, so its provenance is unknown.

27. Kominami 1994: 33.

28. Kominami 1994: 56–57; Maruyama 1986.

29. These depictions appear in the oldest portions (dating from the fourth and third centuries B.C.E.) of the *Classic of the Mountains and Seas*. See *SHJ*, 2.31, 16.272; Fracasso 1988: 8–13.

30. Dohrenwend 1975.

31. Wu Hung 1989: 108–41; James 1995, 1996: 70–91.

32. Erickson 1994: 37.

33. *HNZ*, 13.460–61; cf. Larre et al. 1993: 192.

34. Harper 1994: 14.

35. *Han shu*, 38.1991–96.

36. The date of the shrine's founding was not recorded, but it was in existence by the first decade of the first century C.E. At that time Prince Jing was

greatly favored by the infamous spirit mediums of Qi, a region long renowned for its shamanic cults. See *Hou Han shu,* 11.479–80, 42.1451.

37. *Fengsu tongyi jiaoshi,* 9.333–34.

38. Ibid.; *Sanguo zhi,* 1.4. See also Stein 1979: 80.

39. *SSJ,* 5.35, no. 92. For other contemporary legends about Jiang's cult and his temple at Bell Mountain, see items no. 93–96 in ibid., 5.35–37.

40. *Song shu,* 17.488. See also Stein 1979: 79–80.

41. On the myth and cult of Wu Zixu, see Johnson 1980. For the cult of Xiang Yu, see Miyakawa 1964: 386–414.

42. According to Daoist doctrine, prior to the founding of the Celestial Masters sect in the late second century C.E. Han religion was dominated by worship of what they called the Six Heavens, the rulers of the dead. The "stale vapors of the Six Heavens" denoted loathsome ghouls greedy for blood sacrifices and other putrid offerings. In Daoist lore, the Six Heavens became a metaphor for the powers of evil, in contrast to the good Three Heavens. On the origins of these terms, see Kobayashi Masayoshi 1991: 498–503.

43. "Demons of the five kinds of wounding" most likely is an allusion to Chiyou and his five types of weapons. Chiyou of course became the object of his own cult (see chapter 1, pp. 39–41).

44. *Lu xiansheng daomen kelüe,* 1a; translation from Nickerson 1996: 352.

45. Throughout this book "Daoism" refers exclusively to the religious traditions descended from the Way of the Celestial Masters of the second century C.E. To Western audiences, Daoism almost invariably evokes the mystical philosophy associated with Eastern Zhou works like the *Dao De Jing* and the *Zhuangzi.* This mystical tradition, what scholars often have designated as "philosophic Daoism," actually developed fairly late, subsequent to the fall of the Han dynasty in the early third century C.E.; it will not concern us here.

46. For a general overview of the Way of the Celestial Masters and the early history of Daoism, see Robinet 1997: 53–77; for detailed studies, see Fukui 1952; Ōfuchi 1991; Kleeman 1998. On the deification of Laozi, putative author of the *Dao De Jing,* and his transformation into the messiah Lord Lao, see Seidel 1969.

47. Cedzich 1993: 27; Nickerson 2000.

48. *Santian neijie jing,* shang.6a. See also Stein 1979: 68–71.

49. Robinet 1997: 60.

50. Cedzich 1993: 32.

51. Maruyama 1986; see also Strickmann 1981: 144–59; Nickerson 1994: 52–55. Some scholars of Daoism (for example, Lagerwey 1987) sharply distinguish between ordained Daoist priests *(daoshi)* and spirit mediums *(wu),* reserving the latter term for untrained (and often illiterate) mediums who are possessed by spirits. In this book I use spirit mediums in a more general sense to refer to any religious specialist who acted as intermediary between the gods and their human supplicants. See Nickerson 2000; Davis 2001.

52. The outstanding study of the early history of Buddhism in China is Zürcher 1959.

53. Bokenkamp 1989.

54. For the early history of the Shangqing movement, see Strickmann 1977, 1981; Robinet 1997: 114–48.

55. Strickmann 1977: 6–9; Robinet 1984, 1: 64.
56. Nickerson 1994: 63–66.
57. Strickmann 1977: 15–30; Robinet 1997: 127–28.
58. Robinet 1984, 1: 59–70.
59. On the early history of the Lingbao sect, see Bokenkamp 1983; Robinet 1997: 149–83.
60. *Lingbao wuliang duren shangpin miaojing.* On the composition of this text, see Bokenkamp 1983. For a translation, see Bokenkamp 1997: 373–438.
61. Robinet 1997: 164.
62. Zürcher 1980: 102.
63. Kamitsuka 1996: 44–50.
64. On the historical rather than fictional nature of *zhiguai* literature, see Campany 1996b: 161–201.
65. Campany 1996b: 343–62.
66. Campany 1991.
67. For citations of stories dating from the Era of Disunion, see Campany 1996b: 247. The trope of tomb guardian effigies coming to life is also common in the ghost-story literature of the Tang dynasty. See Kobayashi Taiichiro 1947: 192–93. During the Era of Disunion the tomb guardian figurines of horned creatures typical of the Warring States and Han periods (see figure 6) were replaced with hybrid creatures with human faces, and, beginning in the sixth century, fully human warrior figures. See Fong 1991b.
68. *Taishang dongyuan shenzhou jing,* on which see Mollier 1991; Strickmann 2002: 89–97. These apocalyptic movements were distinct from the three dominant Daoist scriptural traditions of the Era of Disunion (Celestial Masters, Lingbao, and Shangqing), which channeled millenarian aspirations into quests for heavenly rather than earthly rewards. For parallel trends among "heretical" Buddhist sects, see Zürcher 1982.
69. On the concept of "seed people," see Kobayashi Masayoshi 1991: 336–41; Bokenkamp 1997: 157.
70. Mollier 1991: 47–52, 72–77.
71. *Taishang dongyuan shenzhou jing,* 1.9a.
72. Shinohara 1977: 232–34; Mollier 1991: 104, 114.
73. Shinohara 1977: 235–36; Mollier 1991: 37–38, 75.
74. Stein 1979: 59.
75. On the early development of the Guanyin cult in China, see Campany 1996a; Yü 2001.

CHAPTER 3. *SHANXIAO*

1. Thomas 1971: 606–14; Ivanits 1989: 64–70.
2. Campany 1996b: 122.
3. Ibid., 106.
4. Two types of spirits are mentioned here: the *chimei* and the *wangliang.* The Han scholar Fu Qian (125–ca. 195) glossed *chimei* as a four-footed beast with a human face "born of the aberrant *qi* of the mountains and forests." See *ZZ,* 20.356a (Lord Wen, 18th year). According to the commentary of Du Yu

(222–84) on this passage, the *chimei* were mountain spirits, and the *wangliang* were "aberrations" *(guai)*. Other lexicographers of this era identified the *wangliang* as "mountain spirits" and *wangxiang* as "water spirits." See Kiang 1937: 72–99. It is likely, as William Boltz observes, that *wangliang, wangxiang,* and other similar names for demonic spirits (e.g., *fangliang, fangxiang,* and *fenyang)* are all cognates of a common word rendered in ancient Chinese as "BLjang-BZjang." See William Boltz 1979: 432–33.

5. ZZ, 21.368a–b (Lord Xuan, 3rd year). On this and other myths featuring Yu the Great, see Birrell 1993: 146–59. For further discussion of Yu's nine cauldrons, see Kiang 1937: 130–47.

6. Schaberg 1999.

7. *Zhongguo,* translated here as "China" (which is the modern meaning of the word), at that time more properly would have been understood as "the Central States," the polities that swore allegiance to the Zhou kings.

8. *SHJ,* 74.2344.

9. This organizing principle, expressed most cogently in the *Dialogues of the States (Guoyu,* "Zhouyu shang") and the "Tribute of Yu" ("Yugong") chapter of the *Documents,* was also applied in works like the *Classic of Spirits and Prodigies (Shenyijing),* probably dating from the late second century C.E., and the *Records of the Ten Continents (Shizhouji;* ca. 300). See Campany 1996b: 43–45, 53–54, 102–26.

10. Although such human-beast hybrids had a long history in China, dating back to the myths and iconography of Shang-Zhou religion, by Han times their meaning had changed. In contrast to the totemic figures of Shang, which enabled human rulers to communicate with the gods through divination and oracle, in later times hybrid creatures were typically seen as malefic beings that menaced humans. On the growing antagonism between the human and animal realms in Zhou culture, see Loewe 1978.

11. Fracasso 1983: 670–71; Nagahiro 1969: 107–12. According to Nagahiro, of the hundreds of creatures mentioned in the *Classic of the Mountains and Seas,* only four were deemed auspicious.

12. Campany 1996b: 293–94.

13. *Xuanyuan benji,* in *Yunji qiqian,* 100.19a–b. This legend dates at least to the early fourth century, when Ge Hong wrote that Huangdi had recorded the words of White Marsh in order to attain an exhaustive knowledge of spirits and demons. See *BPZ,* 13.219.

14. *Baize tu.* A Tang bibliography states that the text originally contained 320 items. See Chen Pan 1991: 280. Anna Seidel (1983: 321) identifies the *Baize tu* as a product of the prognostication literature of the Later Han dynasty.

15. *Baize jingguai tu.* Two fragmentary manuscripts are preserved in the Dunhuang collections, one at the British Museum (Stein no. 6261) and another at the Bibliothèque Nationale (Pelliot no. 2682). Gao Guofan argues persuasively that these two manuscripts were originally part of a single scroll. For studies, see Gao Guofan 1989: 342–68; Rao Zongyi 1969; Chen Pan 1991: 273–92.

16. *Baize tu,* passim.

17. The "Spellbinding" text is translated in its entirety in Harper 1996. For studies, see Harper 1985; Liu Lexian 1993.

18. Kleeman (1994c: 231n35) observes that *jing* originally referred to the energy imparted by food to the body. The compound term *jingqi,* rendered here as "numinous specters," refers to formless vitalities that can inhere in concrete objects. The meaning of *jingqi* in demonology is entirely different than in the homeopathic medical canon that crystallized over the course of the Han dynasty. In a medical context *jingqi* denoted sublime distillations of particular qualities. For example, the sun (pure *yang*) constituted the *jingqi* of fire, and the moon (pure *yin*) constituted the *jingqi* of water. See Unschuld 1985: 110.

19. *SSJ,* 19.148 (no. 445). The prevalence of this belief is attested by the Han dynasty skeptical philosopher Wang Chong (27–ca. 100 C.E.): "There are those who say that demons are the spirits of aged things and that these spirits can assume human form. It is also said that there are creatures who by nature can spontaneously metamorphose without growing old and assume humanlike form." See *LH,* 22B.450.

20. *SSJ,* 6.41 (no. 102).

21. *SSJ,* 12.93 (no. 309).

22. *SSJ,* 12.91 (no. 303), reprinted in *Baize tu,* 1a.

23. See *Analects,* VII.21: "The topics of which the Master did not speak were prodigies *[guai],* feats of strength, disorders, and spirits *[shen].*"

24. *Guoyu,* "Luyu xia," 5.68–69. A slightly different taxonomy of anomalies appears in the second-century B.C.E. *Treatises of Huainan,* in a passage ridiculing the popular belief that such unfamiliar creatures are manifestations of demonic spirits: "Mountains produce *xiaoyang;* waters produce *wangxiang;* wells produce *fenyang*[a] (literally, 'grave mound sheep'). People who regard them as aberrations have limited experience and shallow knowledge of things." See *HNZ,* 13.458. The association made between wells and the *fenyang*[a] in this passage undoubtedly stems from the anecdote about Confucius in the *Dialogues of the States.* (On the identification of *xiaoyang,* see below, pp. 90–91.) The *Zhuangzi* confirms at least some of these identifications, in a speech by Guan Zhong to his prince, Lord Huan of Qi: "In the waters dwell *wangxiang;* in the hills, *shen*[a]; in the mountains, *kui;* in the wildernesses, *panghuang;* and in the marshes, *weishe.*" See *Zhuangzi jiaoquan,* 19, "Dasheng," 2.694.

25. Most later renditions of this passage, and paraphrases like the passage from the *Treatises of Huainan* cited in the previous note, use a different graph for *fen* that means "grave mound" (*fenyang*[a]), thus reinforcing the rationality of Confucius's explanation for the presence of an entombed sheep. See *HNZ,* 13.458; *Bowu zhi,* 1.3a.

26. *ZZ,* 41.706b (Lord Zhao, 1st year).

27. Kleeman 1994c: 226–31.

28. "Blood-eating ghosts" referred to spirits who must be propitiated with "blood" (i.e., meat) sacrifices. It was believed that "proper deities" partook only of vegetarian offerings, and "bloody sacrifice" became a metaphor for deviant spirits and heterodox worship. On the practice of "blood sacrifice" and prohibitions against it, see Kleeman 1994b.

29. *BPZ,* 4.76.

30. *BPZ,* 17.273–82. For more details on Ge Hong's apotropaic measures, see Kleeman 1994c: 230–31.

31. *BPZ*, 19.308–9.

32. For a detailed study of the complex textual history of the *Album of the True Forms of the Five Marchmounts*, see Inoue 1926. Inoue argues persuasively that the text entitled *Dongxuan lingbao wuyue guben zhenxing tu* preserved in the Daoist *Canon* is the oldest extant version. Inscriptions and pictorial representations from Mount Tai dating from the fourteenth century onward bearing the title *Album of the True Forms of the Five Marchmounts* have been studied in Chavannes 1910: 415–26. But as Inoue shows, these depictions, which differ markedly from those in *Dongxuan lingbao wuyue guben zhenxing tu*, derive from a later, post-Tang development of the cult. According to the apocryphal preface of the Daoist *Canon* text, attributed to the Han thaumaturge Dongfang Shuo (fl. 130), Huangdi personally drew the images of the mountains transmitted to later generations as the *Album of the True Forms of the Five Marchmounts*. See *Dongxuan lingbao wuyue guben zhenxing tu*, 2a. A virtually identical account of the origins of the text is contained in *Xuanyuan benji*, a hagiography of Huangdi. See *Yunji qiqian*, 100.22b.

33. *BPZ*, 19.309. In another place Ge Hong referred to "the techniques of the *Writs of the Three Sovereigns* for summoning celestial deities and telluric spirits." See *BPZ*, 4.61. Inoue (1926: 80–81) speculates that the *Writs of the Three Sovereigns* and the *Album of the True Forms of the Five Marchmounts* were originally a single text, the latter consisting simply of illustrations appended to the former. For the most authoritative study of the *Writs of the Three Sovereigns*, see Ōfuchi 1964.

34. *BPZ*, 17.282.

35. *BPZ*, 19.306.

36. See Gao Guofan 1989: 361–66. Gao discounts the idea that the Dunhuang manuscript *(Baize jingguai tu)* might be identical to the *Baize tu* text in Ge Hong's possession; instead, he thinks that the Dunhuang manuscript was derived from older demon lore found in texts like Ge's *The Master Who Embraces Simplicity*. Gao also notes that the passage on the nightmare demon Boqi in the *Album of the Strange Specters of White Marsh* is nearly identical to the description of Boqi in the third-century B.C.E. "spellbinding" text excavated at Shuihudi (ibid., 354–61). Clearly there was a continuous transmission of these apotropaic texts, even though we remain ignorant of their exact genealogies.

37. *BPZ*, 17.277; a slightly different version of Ge Hong's description appears in *TPYL*, 886.8a–b.

38. *Baize tu*, cited in *TPYL*, 886.7b.

39. *SHJ*, 5.132–33, 14.248; Mathieu 1983, 1: 322–23, 546.

40. The most extensive review of the *kui*/Kui mythology is assembled in Granet 1926, 1: 310–12; 2: 505–15. See also the brief entry in Birrell 1993: 134–35.

41. *Guoyu*, "Luyu xia," 5.69.

42. *SHJ*, 3.60. The close phonetic identity between *hui*[a] and *kui* suggests that the two terms probably stemmed from the same root.

43. See the relevant passage translated in note 24.

44. *SHJ*, 10.219. In addition, virtually identical descriptions of the *xiaoyang* appear in Gao You's (ca. 168–212) commentary on the *Treatises of Huainan*

(which explicitly defines them as "mountain spirits") and in a late chapter of the *Classic of the Mountains and Seas*, where the term is applied to the "Gan giants" *(Gan juren)*, who were said to live in southern China ("Gan" almost certainly denotes the Gan River valley in south-central China). See *HNZ*, 13.458; *SHJ*, 18.296.

45. *Yi Zhou shu*, 59, "Wanghui jie."

46. *Erya*, 2: 30b. Wang Yi's (fl. ca. 125–44) commentary on the *Zhuangzi* also identified the *xiaoyang* with the *feifei* and added that it was a "mountain spirit." Similar descriptions are found for a creature called *feifei*[b] in another Han lexicon, the *Shuowen jiezi*. See *Shuowen jiezi gulin*, 10: 6915a. In more recent times (e.g., in the renowned Ming pharmacopoeia *Bencao gangmu*) the *feifei* has been identified as a species of monkey. The *Classic of the Mountains and Seas* states that the fauna of Mount Yuci in western China included a monkeylike *xiao* (a graph different than but homophonous to *xiaoyang, shanxiao*) and also an owl-like bird with a human face and single foot known as *tuofei*. See *SHJ*, 2.22; Mathieu 1983, 1: 53–54.

47. *Youyang zazu*, 16.161, translated in Schafer 1967: 232. Duan stated that according to old legends *feifei* had inverted feet, whereas hunters claimed the beast had no knees.

48. See *Baize tu*, 4a (monopode); *BPZ*, 17.277 (monopode/antipode).

49. See *SHJ*, 10.219 (country of Xiaoyang); 8.200 (country of Mouli); 18.296 (Gan giants). For another example of monopodes, see the entry on Mount Gang in ibid., 2.37.

50. See Wei Zhao's commentary in *Guoyu*, 5.69; *Xiangzhong ji*, cited in *TPYL*, 886.6a; *Yongjia junji*, cited in *TPYL*, 942.6b.

51. The accounts of the fourth-century B.C.E. Hellenic authors Ctesias and Megasthenes, whose original works survive only in fragments, are preserved in late Roman writings such as Pliny's *Natural History* and Solinus's *Collectanea rerum memorabilium*. For the Latin texts and possible Indian sources for these accounts, see André and Filliozat 1986: 80–81, 152–55, 355n121. On the *ekapada* in Indian legend, see ibid., 355–56n121.

52. *BPZ*, 17.280.

53. *Erya*, 2: 30b.

54. *Nankang ji*, cited in *TPYL*, 884.6b; *Shuyi ji* (Ren Fang), cited in *TPYL*, 884.7a; *SSJ*, 12.94 (no. 313); *Yiwu zhi*, cited in *Hailu suishi*, 22A.24a.

55. *Shuyi ji* (Zu Chongzhi), cited in *TPGJ*, 324.2569–70.

56. *Nankang ji*, cited in *TPYL*, 884.6b–7a.

57. See *Bowu zhi*, 9.2b–3a; *Nankang ji*, cited in *TPYL*, 884.6b–7a; *SSJ*, 12.94 (no. 310).

58. *Xiangzhong ji*, cited in *TPGJ*, 482.3974; *Nankang ji*, cited in *TPYL*, 884.6b–7a.

59. In Tang times, "mute trade" with foreign peoples with whom merchants could not communicate through spoken language was referred to as a "ghost market" *(guishi)*. See Yoshida 1981: 31–36; Sōda 1997: 11–52. The term "ghost market" also alluded to the unintelligible speech of foreign traders. A Tang writer described as a "ghost market" one of the markets in the capital of Chang'an, where the cacophony of traders' cries continued day and night regardless of any

inclement weather. He then went on to say that "during autumn and winter nights one often hears voices hawking firewood; it's said that they come from the specters [*jing*] of dead and fallen trees." *Nianxia suishiji*, cited in Yoshida 1981: 34.

60. *Yudi ji*, cited in *TPYL*, 48.8a.

61. Yet even this distinction was ambiguous. Schafer cites a Tang writer who claimed to have witnessed monkeys in the south expressing grief when one of their kind was injured or killed, observing that "here is a case of man's heart inside the forms of birds and beasts." Quoted in Schafer 1967: 233.

62. "Song of the Mak Yao," translation from Schafer 1967: 51. "Sand mouthers" were fantastic reptilian denizens of the south who spat sand at the shadows of human beings and thereby infected them with a fatal venom.

63. Schafer 1967: 57.

64. *Shenyijing yanjiu*, 49.

65. *Guoyu*, "Luyu xia," 5.69.

66. *Shuyi ji* (Zu Chongzhi), cited in *TPGJ*, 323.2560. The exact same passage appears elsewhere in the same anthology (*TPGJ*, 359.2855–56), where the source given is *SSJ*. However, this passage does not appear in the extant editions of *SSJ*.

67. *Yongjia junji*, cited in *TPYL*, 942.6b.

68. On the simian species of South China and their depictions in Tang literature, see Schafer 1967: 231–33.

69. *Youyang zazu*, 15.144.

70. *Huichang jieyi lu*, cited in *TPGJ*, 361.2870–71; *Jiyi ji* (Xue Yongruo), 16b–17a; *YJZ*, zhijia, 3.734–35.

71. *YJZ*, jiazhi, 14.119.

72. *Guangyun jiaoben*, 1: 149. A tenth-century geographic encyclopedia also identified the *shanxiao* as a conspicuous feature of Tingzhou and adjacent areas. See *Taiping huanyu ji*, 100.11a, 102.6a.

73. *Jiwen*, cited in *Yudi jisheng*, 132.1b. This anecdote is not included among the selections from *Jiwen* in *TPGJ*. A number of Tang-Song stories concerning *shanxiao* are set in Tingzhou. See *Huichang jieyi lu*, cited in *TPGJ*, 361.2870–71; and the *YJZ* tales cited in note 76.

74. *Yudi jisheng*, 32.7a, 9a, 31b.

75. *Linting zhi*, cited in *Yongle dadian*, 7893.15b. See also *Bamin tongzhi*, 38.810. A ninth-century anecdote recounts that when another Tang magistrate of Tingzhou refused to sacrifice an ox to a mountain spirit, the latter caused an outbreak of epidemic disease that cost the life of the magistrate and twenty of his family members. See *Jiwen*, cited in *Taiping huanyu ji*, 102.9a.

76. The cult of the Seven Sisters in Tingzhou is mentioned in three of the anecdotes recorded in *Tales of the Listener*. See *YJZ*, jiazhi, 6.71; yizhi, 7.241; zhijing 8.945–46.

77. *Guixin zashi*, qianji, 19.

78. *Guangyi ji*, cited in *TPGJ*, 428.3840–41. Song authors adopted Dai Fu's account as the authoritative statement about the *shanxiao* and their characteristics. See *Nenggaizhai manlu*, 7.172; *Hailu suishi*, 22A.26a; *Ganzhu ji*, 7.35a. Dai Fu's *Wide World of Marvels* has been the subject of a meticulous study by Dudbridge (1995).

79. On the monstrous caricatures of indigenous peoples constructed by intruding Han settlers, see Schafer 1967: 48–61; von Glahn 1987: 11–16.

80. Thomas Barfield (1989: 8–16) notes that the two roles were inseparable halves of the relationship between steppe nomads and the sedentary Han civilization. The former employed strategies of coercion and extortion to extract trading privileges and indemnities from the latter that provided essential supplements to the material base of steppe society.

CHAPTER 4. PLAGUE DEMONS AND EPIDEMIC GODS

1. Unschuld 1985: 17–28; Harper 1982: 69–70.

2. ZZ, 26.451a–b (Lord Cheng, 10th year). Translated in Watson 1989: 120–21.

3. Kiang 1937: 55.

4. On the range of meanings for *gu,* see Kobayashi Taiichiro 1947: 176–78; Bodde 1975: 100–101; Unschuld 1985: 46–50; Harper 1998: 74–75, 300–302.

5. ZZ, 41.708a–710a (Lord Zhao, 1st year).

6. Loewe 1970, esp. 190–96. On accusations of witchcraft by palace women in the Han period, see also pp. 3–4 above.

7. For example, a medical text of the second century B.C.E. attributed leprosy to a type of boring insect that chewed the flesh of its human host. See Harper 1998: 75, 249–50. See also p. 115 below on the Three Worms.

8. Harper 1998: 148–83; Unschuld 1985: 35–45. On the use of spells in exorcistic healing, see Sawada 1984; Strickmann 2002.

9. These ideas were not entirely new in the Han dynasty; they are also present in the above-mentioned exposition by the physician He in the *Chronicles of Zuo.* He admonished the ruler to moderate his appetites and avoid all forms of excess *(yin),* including food and drink, exposure to the elements, music, and sexual pleasure. See ZZ, 41.708a–709b (Lord Zhao, 1st year). This passage is deeply tinged with Five Phases–*yin/yang* cosmology, which suggests that it reflects ideas prevalent during the fourth century B.C.E., when the work was written, rather than the historical era in which the dialogue was set (sixth century B.C.E.).

10. On the corpus of Mawangdui medical texts, see the study and translation in Harper 1998.

11. Porkert 1974: 140–46.

12. Unschuld 1985: 67–100; see also Schipper 1978.

13. *BPZ,* 18.299 (translation in Sivin 1987: 58–59).

14. On the maturation of *qi* medicine reflected in the textual synthesis of the *Huangdi bashiyi nanjing* (*Resolution of Eighty-one Problems in the Inner Canon of Huangdi;* probably dates from second century C.E.), see Unschuld 1985: 84–85.

15. Hou 1979: 205–9.

16. *LH,* 69, "Lanshi," 23.473; 73, "Nansui," 24.492–98.

17. Unschuld 1985: 68–69.

18. *HNZ,* 17.567.

19. The upper course of the Yangzi River, said to be the homeland of Zhuanxu.

20. *LH,* 65, "Dinggui," 22.450; ibid., 75, "Jiechu," 25.505; *Duduan,*

shang.14b. Wang cites a book entitled *The Rites (Li)* as his source, but this passage appears not in the Confucian classic *Canon of Rites,* but rather in a Han apocrypha, *The Weft of the Rites (Li wei).* See *TPYL,* 530.6a. The same account of the origins of disease is repeated in *SSJ,* 16.116 (no. 376).

21. *Duduan,* shang.14b.

22. For sake of clarity I will refer to the court ritual as the Great Exorcism, and the parallel popular rites as Nuo.

23. Zhang Heng, "Dongjingfu," in *Wenxuan,* 3.123. Among the classes of demons exterminated in this fashion were the *kui* and *wangxiang,* who as we have seen were mountain goblins. The verb "devour" was commonly used to describe both demonic attack and the method of annihilating such demons. The Great Exorcism at the Han court also was described in verses by the classical scholar Ma Rong (79–166), who mentions five classes of demons by name, including the *wangliang,* the Roving Lights plague demons (see below, pp. 106–8), and the *fenyang.* See *Hou Han shu,* 60A.1964.

24. For detailed studies of the Great Exorcism, see Bodde 1975: 75–138; Kobayashi Taiichiro 1947: 117–82; Granet 1926, 1: 298–337.

25. *Zhouli zhengshu,* 31, 1: 851a–b; for tiger skin, see Xue Zong's commentary to Zhang Heng's "Dongjingfu," *Wenxuan,* 3.123.

26. William Boltz 1979: 431.

27. Namely Ode 209, cited in von Falkenhausen 1993: 148–52; *HNZ,* 20.678.

28. Bodde (1975: 112–17) cites the diverse range of demons exterminated by the Great Exorcism as evidence against the claims of Granet (1926) and especially Kobayashi Taiichiro (1947) that the Great Exorcism should be understood principally as an exorcism of pestilence. But virtually all references to the Great Exorcism in Han texts specifically link it to the expulsion of pestilence. See *Hou Han shu,* 95.3127 and the citations in *TPYL,* 530.5a–7a.

29. *LH,* 75, "Jiechu," 25: 505; *Duduan,* shang.14b.

30. *Longyu hetu,* cited in Chen Pan 1991: 414.

31. Éliasberg 1984. On Zhong Kui, see below, pp. 122–28.

32. This name is variously rendered as *yezhong, yezhong*ᵃ, or *yetong.* The latter reading, Wild Youths, seems to make the most sense semantically.

33. Zhang Heng, "Dongjing fu," in *Wenxuan,* 3.124.

34. *Baize jingguai tu,* in *Dunhuang baozang,* 123: 287. A fifth-century lexicon defined the Roving Lights as "apparitions of fire" *(huojing),* but Gan Bao, writing in the fourth century, cites an unidentifiable "Master Wang" in glossing the Roving Lights as "specters of trees." See *Guangya shuzheng,* 9A, 2: 1077–78; *SSJ,* 12.90. The Roving Lights demons also appear in catalogues of demons recorded in Buddhist exorcism manuals from the fifth century. Although these texts only list names of demons without indicating their nature or attributes, they consistently group the Roving Lights with Yinghuo, the baleful aspect of the planet Mars, also a fire demon. See *Foshuo moniluodan jing,* T 1393, 21: 910c; *Foshuo guanding moniluodan da shenzhou jing,* T 1331, 21: 520a.

35. *Dazhidu lun,* T 1509, 25: 165a. The *Recipes for Fifty-Two Ailments* contains an exorcism formula in which the physician-sorcerer constructs a miniature cart (with wheels made of colored gourds and a chassis fashioned from a

winnowing basket) that is pulled through the home of a sick person by a black pig to trap and carry off demons. See Harper 1998: 302 (Recipe 277).

36. *Liji zhengyi,* 16.1370a–b.

37. *Fengsu tongyi jiaoshi,* 414. See Bodde 1975: 302–8 for a translation and discussion of Ying Shao's text.

38. Moriya 1949: 382.

39. Harper 1982: 104–6; Harper 1998: 259–62 (Recipes 118, 120, 125).

40. Berger 1983: 41–43.

41. Lewis 1990: 174–95.

42. Although identification of this scene as a depiction of the Great Exorcism is a subject of much controversy, it remains the most plausible hypothesis. Identification of this scene with the Great Exorcism was made by Kobayashi Tai-ichiro (1947: 119) and later by Sun Zuoyun; see the discussion by Bodde (1975: 117–27), who believes the argument is plausible but not fully convincing. More recently, this hypothesis has been challenged by Hayashi Minao, who instead identifies the scene as an illustration of the myth of Huangdi driving off the Three Barbarians (San Miao), whose profligate use of punishments and violence tormented the people of high antiquity. In his view, the main figure represents not Chiyou but the Emissary of the Celestial Thearch (Tiandi shizhe). See Hayashi 1989: 169–70. Yet, given that Chiyou and the Emissary of the Celestial Thearch functioned in analogous ways in Han religion, the distinction may be immaterial.

43. Bodde 1975: 120–23; Berger 1983: 50.

44. Demon-quelling spirits known as "spouters" *(penzhe)* are invoked in a number of the demonifugic incantations recorded in the *Recipes for Fifty-Two Ailments* (Harper 1998: 164–65). In addition, one therapy requires that the conjurer first chant, "The Thearch possesses the five weapons. You, begone! If you do not go, I will spew knives to coat you." Then he spits on the afflicted portion of the body seven times (fourteen times in the case of women) to drive out the demon. Here, the "five weapons" refer to magical demonifugic weapons like those wielded by Chiyou. See ibid., 294 (Recipe 234). The *Recipes for Fifty-Two Ailments* also advises using menstrual blood in two of five recipes for warding off *gu* sickness; in another recipe for *gu* sickness, a talisman is burned, immersed in water, and then drunk by the patient. Ibid., 300–302. The use of talismans that are burned and immersed in water later was central to the ritual healing practiced by the Great Peace religious sect (see below). On spitting as part of healing therapy in later Daoist ritual, see Strickmann 2002: 29–31, 106–7.

45. Miyashita 1959: 229.

46. The *gangmao* amulets were worn in pairs, hung from silk ribbons that passed through a hole bored lengthwise in the amulet. Sumptuary laws dictated the material from which the *gangmao* were made, but virtually all surviving specimens are jade. The inscriptions on specimens like those shown in figure 15 correspond almost exactly to the ritual formulas preserved in Han records. See *Han shu,* 99B.4109–10; *Hou Han shu,* 30.3673. For a specimen recently excavated from a Han tomb, see Haoxian bowuguan 1974: 190.

47. *Dongxuan lingbao wuyue guben zhenxing tu,* 1a.

48. See Liu Lexian 1993; Harper 1996.

49. Han legends record that Shenshu and Yulü were powerful spirits who bound evil demons with magic cords and fed them to tigers (hence the association of tigers with the devouring of demons). See, for example, *LH*, 65, "Dinggui," 22.452. On the role of these two spirits as household guardians, see Bodde 1974: 127–38; Fong 1989.

50. *LH*, 65, "Dinggui," 22.448. For a similar argument regarding apparitions like mountain goblins, see *HNZ*, 13.458–59, translated in Larre et al. 1993: 190.

51. Cited in *TPYL*, 530.6b–7a. See *Zhuangzi jiaoquan*, 3: 1388.

52. Ironically, the word *fei*, which Wang Chong uses here as a generic term for vermin, also denoted a certain kind of baleful demon. According to the *Classic of the Mountains and Seas*, the *fei* was an oxlike beast with a serpent's tail that causes waters to dry up and plants to wither; its appearance augured the imminent arrival of a great plague. See *SHJ*, 4.100.

53. *LH*, 72, "Biansui," 24.488–89.

54. *LH*, 66, "Duyan," 23.457–58.

55. *LH*, 75, "Jiechu," 25.505.

56. Wang spoke of "disasters and marvels" as "omens of rebuke delivered to the prince of men by the Heavenly Spirit (Tianshen)." See *LH*, 42, "Qiangao," 14.295.

57. Ōfuchi 1991: 87–93, 125–29. Although confession was a fundamental practice in both sects, the Celestial Masters did not use spells and consecrated water in healing as the Great Peace sect did. See Fukui 1952: 88.

58. Kaltenmark 1979: 45. The present text of the *Canon of Great Peace* dates from around the sixth century. There is considerable debate about the relationship of this text to works of the same title, now lost, that circulated among the early Daoist sects (see ibid. and appended discussion). Nonetheless, a recent study concludes that "the arguments in favour of a Han date for the (extant text) outweigh the arguments against it." Beck 1980: 171. However, we cannot be sure that the extant text was utilized by the Celestial Masters in Han times, though there certainly is much evidence that both drew from a common fund of religious and messianic beliefs.

59. *BPZ*, 6.114.

60. Ge Hong also describes the Lord of the Hearth (Zaojun; also known as the Stove God) as a watch-guard spirit who made reports on the conduct of the household's members to Heaven on the final day of each month. But in the esoteric lore of the Han dynasty, the Lord of the Hearth was reviled as a malign entity that brought disease and death down upon the family. See Chard 1995: 5–6. This is yet another example of a noxious demon that is bridled by the forces of moral order and assigned a menial role in the vast edifice of the celestial bureaucracy.

61. In addition to the demon masters, the text also lists plague demons *(wengui)* of individual months, days, and hours, plus a group of nine *gu* (as in *gu* poison) demons, who act at the instruction of the demon masters and inflict illnesses on those who fail to observe the sect's commandments. See *Nüqing guilü*, 6.2a–5b.

62. On exorcistic healing in the *Demon Register of Nüqing*, see Strickmann 2002: 80–87.

63. *Dengzhen yinjue*, xia.11a, 20b–21a.

64. *SSJ*, 5.38.

65. *Zhen gao*, 10.18a–b.

66. Kobayashi Masayoshi 1991: 389–400.

67. *Lishi zhenxian tidao tongjian*, 18.8b–12b. Though a late text manifestly influenced by Song/Yuan developments in Daoism, this hagiography of Zhang Daoling is far more extensive than earlier biographies, and it probably combines a number of long-standing myths about Zhang's exploits.

68. *Taishang dongyuan shenzhou jing*, 7.6b.

69. Ibid., 11.9b.

70. *SSGJ*, xia.128, 125.

71. *Jile bian*, shang.16b. Boat exorcisms are also attested for Changsha (Hunan) in the twelfth century, and the Gan River valley of Jiangxi in the mid-thirteenth century. See *YJZ*, sanbu, 1808–9; *Huangshi richao*, 79.21b–22b.

72. See respectively Katz 1995; Szonyi 1997; Schipper 1985a. Wen Qiong also is discussed below, pp. 128–29.

73. Li Fengmao 1993: 448–50.

74. On the origins and development of the new Daoist ritual traditions of the Song dynasty, see Strickmann 1978; Judith Boltz 1987: 23–49; Davis 2001: 21–44.

75. Davis 2001: 41–42.

76. On the cult of Beidi, see Mollier 1997.

77. On the therapeutic rituals of the Song Thunder Magic traditions, see Davis 2001. On the Four Saints, see ibid., 67–86. Tianpeng originally was the name of an exorcistic spell associated with Beidi, but the name was applied to a de-monifuge divinity by the beginning of the tenth century at the latest. See Liu Zhiwan 1987; Mollier 1997.

78. *Taiyi jieji shizhe dafa*, in *DFHY* 96. Zhang Yuanbo, Liu Yuanda, and several other others (but not Zhao Gongming) also are identified as plague demons serving the Five Thearchs in *Taishang sanwu bangjiu jiao wudi duanwen yi*, 1a.

79. E.g., *Taishang dongyuan ciwen shenzhou miaojing*, dated to Song/Yuan times. See Li Fengmao 1993: 448–49.

80. The use of magic fans to expel plague demons is a common trope in Ming popular literature. See Katz 1995: 57–59.

81. *Zitong dijun huashu*, 1.8b. Cf. the translation in Kleeman 1994a: 108–9. Kleeman speculates that the description of the third of the Five Emissaries as having a "human" *(ren)* head is an error and suggests emending the text to read *quan* (dog). But other depictions of the Five Emissaries confirm that one of the five had a human or at least an anthropomorphic "demonic" face.

82. *Zhengyi longhu xuantan dafa*, in *DFHY*, 236.4a–b.

83. The painting is one scroll from the large set of painted icons preserved at the Baoningsi Monastery in Youyu county in northern Shanxi province. The Baoningsi scrolls probably were composed at the time the monastery was built in 1460, or shortly thereafter. See Shanxisheng bowuguan 1985: 7. On the Land-and-Water Masses, see chapter 5, pp. 145–46.

84. For a review of the fragmentary evidence regarding the origins and religious significance of Zhong Kui, see Éliasberg 1976: 6–42.

85. *Taishang dongyuan shenzhou jing*, 7.12a.

86. *Dongjing menghua lu*, 7.43; translated in Idema and West 1982: 41–42.

87. *Dongjing menghua lu*, 10.61–62; *Mengliang lu*, 6.181.

88. *Dongjing menghua lu*, 10.61; *Mengliang lu*, 6.181; *Suishi guangji*, 40.435–37.

89. Éliasberg 1976: 33–34.

90. *Yeren xianhua*, cited in *Suishi guangji*, 40.436.

91. For discussions of the Zhong Kui theme in literati art, see Fong 1977; Little 1985; Lee 1993.

92. On the perpetuation of Wu Daozi's figurative style in later illustrations of gods and spirits (executed in stone carvings and woodblock prints as well as ink paintings), see Fong 1989. Art historians apparently are unaware of the *SSGJ* depiction of Zhong Kui.

93. The following synopsis of the Wen Qiong cult is based on Katz 1995. The antiquity of the Wen Qiong cult is uncertain. The earliest temple explicitly dedicated to Wen Qiong was founded in Pingyang county, inland from the prefectural capital of Wenzhou, in 1210. A Wen Qiong temple was founded at the capital of Hangzhou in 1264, but the city of Wenzhou did not have a temple until the second decade of the fourteenth century. Nonetheless, the cult seems to have been well established before it began to be housed in its own independent temples.

94. Katz 1995: 104–6.

95. Ibid., 106–14.

96. Cf. Levi 1989: 207.

CHAPTER 5. THE SONG TRANSFORMATION
OF CHINESE RELIGIOUS CULTURE

1. Hartwell 1982; Hymes 1986.

2. Since the Wutong cult from the Song onward developed in the Jiangnan region, and in south China generally, this chapter will focus on the religious culture of the Jiangnan region.

3. The "revolutionary" dimensions of economic change in the Song are described in greater detail in Elvin 1973. Shiba 1968 remains unsurpassed as the finest study of the commercial revolution of Song China. On Song China's crucial place in the world economy of the thirteenth and fourteenth centuries, see Abu-Lughod 1989.

4. *Xu gujin kao*, 18.14a–b.

5. *[Xianchun] Lin'an zhi* (ca. 1270–74), 75.1a.

6. On the significance of temple building to urban development in the Song, see von Glahn 2003b.

7. Hansen 1990.

8. Johnson 1985: 418–24.

9. Dudbridge 1995. The *Guangyi ji* does not survive as an integral text, but some 328 stories from it have been preserved in the early Song anthology *Comprehensive Records of the Taiping Reign (Taiping guangji)* and other texts.

10. Dudbridge 1995: 49.

11. Ibid., 59.

12. Mollier 1997: 336–40; Strickmann 2002: 12–14.

13. Teiser 1994. On Tang antecedents to the Ten Kings mythology, see Mollier 1997: 341–45.

14. Yūsa 1989: 35. For an example of the substitution of Taiyi jiuku tianzun for Kṣitigarbha in Daoist scriptures, see *Taishang jiuku tianzun shuo xiaoqian miezui jing*.

15. On the *bianxiang* genre, see Mair 1986; Wu Hung 1992.

16. For a copiously illustrated study of the Baodingshan Grotto, see Howard 2001. Additional illustrations can be found in Chongqing Dazu shike yishu bowuguan 1991; the epigraphic documents are reproduced in Liu Changjiu 1985. For a study of the representation of the underworld at Baodingshan, see Kucera 1995.

17. Teiser 1994: 44–48.

18. *Daojiao lingyan ji*, 5.1a–3a; translated in Verellen 1992: 240–42. Anecdotes concerning miracles performed by Jiuku tianzun in Du Guangting's *Record of Verified Miracles of the Daoist Teachings* are analyzed in Yūsa 1989: 20–3. On the genre of "verified miracle" anthologies and Du Guangting's work in particular, see Verellen 1992. Verellen observes that Daoist works in this genre display substantial borrowings from Buddhism, yet also are fraught with polemical tensions and sectarian rivalry. See also Campany 1996a for examples of the Guanyin "verified miracle" anthologies on which Du Guangting's and other later Chinese collections were modeled.

19. Makita 1957; Yoshioka 1957.

20. Ebrey 1993: 213.

21. Chikusa 1982: 111–43; Miyamoto 1992.

22. Fang Hui, "Shanying'an ji," *Tongjiang xuji*, 36.10b–12b. On the assimilation of Buddhist and Daoist liturgical practices into ancestor worship at the grave site, see Matsumoto 1983; Ebrey 1991; Miyamoto 1992.

23. Rawson 1996. On tomb construction and furnishings from Han to Tang, see Fong 1991a; Yang Hong 1999. A trend toward more modest tombs had emerged in the third century. Although tomb architecture still imitated actual dwellings, the multichambered tombs of the Han were replaced by single-chambered vaults. By the fifth to sixth century, though, a return to more elaborate tomb architecture and decoration was in full swing.

24. Rawson 1996: 37.

25. Liao 2001: 193–207. Liao observes, however, that although appointment to the infernal bureaucracy was deemed a great honor in the popular mind, Song officials themselves looked upon such a prospect with trepidation and dismay.

26. Kuhn (1994: 102) observes that the simple pit tombs that predominated in south China during the Southern Song "no longer [were] residences in miniature." He attributes this departure from the Northern Song style (which persisted in North China down to the Yuan) to the growing influence of Confucian ritual mores that insisted on frugality and modesty in mortuary practice.

27. Brokaw 1991: 28–52. Accounting systems for calculating the costs and

benefits of evil and good deeds had already become a staple of Daoist practice, at least for initiates, in the fourth century or earlier. See Kohn 1998.

28. Dudbridge 1995: 54–55.

29. Hou 1975.

30. The earliest example of this genre dates to the mid-third century B.C.E. See Harper 1994, and chapter 2, p. 52, above.

31. *YJZ*, bingzhi, 10.448–51.

32. Although this story features Daoist practices, parallel Buddhist celebrants, rites, and doctrines could be readily substituted for the Daoist ones.

33. The text specifically refers to a book entitled *Jiutian shengshen yuzhang*, which is probably a reference to *Dongxuan lingbao ziran jiutian shengshen yuzhang jing* in the Ming Daoist *Canon*.

34. Teiser 1988. For a translation of one of the Dunhuang manuscript versions of the Mulian "transformation scripts," see Mair 1983.

35. See the essays in Johnson 1989.

36. On the rise of Hangzhou as the center of Tiantai Buddhism in the eleventh century and its rivalry with Ningbo, see Satō 1988. Elite patronage of Tiantai in Hangzhou is discussed in Huang Chi-chiang 1999.

37. Getz 1999.

38. Stevenson 1999.

39. Makita 1957: 177. Stories from Hong Mai's *Tales of the Listener* (see Ebrey 1993: 212) confirm this emphasis.

40. On the *shishi egui* ritual, see Yoshioka 1957; Orzech 1996.

41. Makita 1957: 174–76. For eleventh-century testimony by the renowned poet and painter Su Shi about the display of painted icons in the Land-and-Water Mass, see "Shuilufa xiang zan," in *Su Dongpo quanji*, houji, 19.659–61.

42. Surviving examples of painted icons for the Land-and-Water Mass include: 1) a set of one hundred scrolls of the Five Hundred Arhats, originally created from 1178 to the 1190s for a monastery in Ningbo and now dispersed among the collections of the Daitokuji Monastery in Kyoto, the Boston Museum of Fine Arts, and the Freer Gallery (Ide 2001); 2) the temple murals of the Pilusi Monastery (near Shijiazhuang, in Hebei), believed to have been begun in 1342 but modified during the subsequent two centuries (Wang and Chen 1984; Zhongguo meishu quanji bianji weiyuanhui 1988b, plates 159–72); 3) a set of thirty-seven scrolls dated 1454 in the Musée Guimet (Gyss-Vermande 1988, 1991); and 4) a set of 136 scrolls from around 1460 preserved at the Baoningsi Monastery (Shanxi bowuguan 1985; see figure 16).

43. Getz 1999.

44. There is now a considerable literature on the lay Buddhist movements of the Song period. See Ogasawara 1963; Overmyer 1976; Chikusa 1982; and especially ter Haar 1992.

45. On the development of the White Lotus movement in the late Song and Yuan, see ter Haar 1992: 16–113.

46. See examples in Campany 1996a.

47. Stein 1986.

48. Of the forty-nine cases of use of spells in Hong Mai's *Tales of the Lis-*

tener anthology, eleven mention the "invocation of the Great Compassionate Guanyin." In the twelve of Hong Mai's stories wherein the name of a deity is re-cited as an act of exorcism or ritual healing, seven involve Guanyin. See ter Haar 1992: 19.

49. Howard 1990: 56.

50. Yü Chün-fang 2001: 263–91.

51. Stevenson 1999. Hong Mai stated that Yuanjing was "revered and served by the people of Wu [Jiangnan] for curing illness with exorcism water" (*YJZ*, bingzhi, 16.498–99). In this episode Yuanjing sets out an altar on which a statue of Guanyin is placed, and he sprinkles consecrated water on an afflicted boy to drive away the "orphan soul" that had possessed him.

52. Yü Chün-fang 1993.

53. Howard 1990: 55.

54. On the evolution of Guanyin iconography and the emergence of an in-digenous iconography of Guanyin in female forms, see Howard 1990; Yü Chün-fang 1994, 2001: 223–62.

55. This version of the Miaoshan story, recorded by a monk in 1164, is taken from Dudbridge 1978: 25–34.

56. "Chongli Dabei chengdao zhuan," in *Liangzhe jinshi zhi*, 7.6b–11a. The inscription is translated in Dudbridge 1982.

57. The salience of the Miaoshan story within later Guanyin mythology is evidenced by the widely disseminated Ming popular religious tract in which the entry for Guanyin is wholly taken up by a synopsis of the Miaoshan tale. See *Sanjiao yuanliu soushen daquan*, 4.68–72. On the mythology of Miaoshan and other female forms of Guanyin, see Yü Chün-fang 1990, 1994, 2001: 293–486. Dudbridge 1978 relates later versions of the Miaoshan story, many of them richly embellished. Among the later accretions to the Miaoshan myth was a journey to the underworld and her miracle of releasing souls from their purgatorial pun-ishments. In this respect the Miaoshan and Mulian mythologies converged.

58. On the transformation of the god Houtu into a female deity in the Tang-Song period, see Liao Hsien-huei 1996.

59. Yü Chün-fang 1993; Hiraki 1982.

60. Kleeman 1993: 61–64.

61. Hansen 1990.

62. Schipper 1985b: 832–34.

63. On *fashi,* see the authoritative study by Davis 2001.

64. Ibid., 146.

65. Here and subsequently I will render dates in the Chinese lunar calendar using the formula "lunar month/day." Thus 2/19 designates the nineteenth day of the second lunar month.

66. DeBernardi 1992: 256.

67. For a study and translation of this work, see Bokenkamp 1997: 373–438. On its place in the early development of Lingbao Daoism, see also Bokenkamp 1983.

68. Strickmann 1978. Outside clerical circles, the *Duren jing* probably cir-culated in more abbreviated versions. The library of the Southern Song biblio-phile Chao Gongwu (d. 1171), for example, contained a three-chapter edition

and a two-chapter annotated edition. See *Zhaode xiansheng junzhai dushu zhi*, 16.1a, fuzhi, 18a. Beijing National Library contains three copies of a 1499 publication that couples the original one-chapter *Duren jing* with four other short texts that all served as talismans to ward off baleful influences. See Beijing tushuguan n.d., zibu, 1661–62.

69. Yoshioka 1989, 4: 188–89.

70. *Soushen bilan*, shang.22a–23a. Xu Shouxin's fame was spread in part through a hagiography, the *Shengong zhuanji*, that was in circulation at least by 1088. Literati accounts of Xu focus on his encounters with celebrated figures like Su Shi and Wang Anshi. The *Xujing chonghe xiansheng Xu shenweng yulu*, composed by a disciple, showcases these famous encounters, but the majority of its anecdotes concern local people of Xu's native Taizhou (Jiangsu) who sought prophecies from him. An 1187 edition of this text was incorporated into the Daoist *Canon*.

71. Examples can be found in *YJZ*, yizhi, 17.329, and its anonymous Yuan sequel *Huhai xinwen yijian xuzhi*, houji, 1.172.

72. *Daojiao lingyan ji*, 10.1b–2a, 12.8b–9a, 9a–b.

73. *Yuanshi wuliang duren shangpin miaojing zhu*, xia.48a–50a.

74. *YJZ*, zhiyi, 2.804–5, zhijing, 9.953–54.

75. *Wujun zhi*, 31.1a–b. Illustrations of the *Duren jing* date back to the Tang, though these were not specifically referred to as *bianxiang*. A *bianxiang* of the *Duren jing* dating from 1406, originally from a Suzhou temple and now held at the Institute of History and Philology, Academia Sinica, illustrates the majestic splendors of the heavenly paradise on one hand and the "lower three realms," infested with demons, on the other. See Rao 1974: 260–66.

76. *Sanjiao yuanliu soushen daquan*, qianji, 13b–15a. The Zhenwu legend in this text is copied from the Yuan *SSGJ* and ultimately is said to have derived from a Daoist text entitled *Hundong chiwen*.

77. The *Journey to the North (Beiyou ji)*, to use the now more common title of the Ming novel *Beifang Zhenwu zushi xuantian shangdi chushen zhizhuan*. See the translation by Gary Seaman (1987), which is based on Qing editions.

78. Grootaers 1952.

79. Teiser 1994.

80. The title Jade Emperor appears in Tao Hongjing's *Zhen gao*, but not until the tenth century, when Southern Han and subsequently the Song dynasty hailed the Jade Emperor as a champion and protector, did this figure receive recognition as the supreme deity in court religion. See Yamauchi 1981.

81. On the iconography of the Song pantheon, see Jing 1994.

82. On Zhenzong's patronage of Daoism, see Cahill 1980; Jing 1994: 142–44.

83. For official canonization of local gods by the Song government, see Hansen 1990: 79–104; Sue 1994; Mizukoshi 2002. Mizukoshi has shown that the waves of canonization that crested during the reigns of Emperors Shenzong (r. 1068–85), Huizong (r. 1100–25), and Gaozong (r. 1127–1161) were driven by varying political motives. Although Huizong energetically strove to impose central control on local temples and their gods, the large number of canonizations authorized by Shenzong and Gaozong reflected the emperors' political weakness, not their strength.

84. The Yuan court recognized Wenchang as a "divine sovereign" in 1316 (see below), and the Ming elevated Guan Yu (henceforth Guandi) to that rank in 1614. Sue (1994) argues that the rampant award of titles to local gods and their quick promotion to the ranks of "kings" betrayed a marked decline in the central government's control of the canonization process, with the real initiative passing into the hands of local boosters.

85. On the evolution of the cult and mythology of the stove god, see Chard 1995.

86. Evidence from the Song regarding the domestic worship of deities is restricted only to isolated examples. For a description of the contours of domestic worship in a specific locality in the eighteenth century, see von Glahn forthcoming.

87. For Zhenwu, see YJZ, jiazhi, 15.134–35; yizhi, 8.250–51; zhijia, 8.777; zhiding, 3.989; zhixu, 6.1100; zhigui, 2.1231–32; zhigui, 5.1260; sanzhixin, 2.1397; sanzhiren, 9.1538–39; bu, 15.1690–92; bu, 24.1769–70. For Dongyue, see YJZ, jiazhi, 6.47; yizhi, 2.202; yizhi, 16.322–23; yizhi, 17.327–28; bingzhi, 11.458; bingzhi, 17.507–8; dingzhi, 14.656–57; dingzhi, 15.666; zhijia, 1.714–15; zhiyi, 2.804–5; zhiyi, 7.846; zhiyi, 7.847–48; zhijing, 1.883–84; zhiding, 8.1030; zhixu, 3.1074–75; zhixu, 8.1115–16; sanzhisi, 3.1324; sanzhixin, 3.1392–93.

88. For example, it was the local custom *(xiangsu)* in Wuzhou (Zhejiang) to hold a communal Yellow Register Rite on Zhenwu's feast day (3/3) in order to ward off evil and obtain good fortune. See YJZ, zhiwu, 6.1100.

89. YJZ, yizhi, 3.250–51. On this anecdote see also Hansen 1990: 29–31, 171–72.

90. On the contrast between the avowed philosophical secularism of Song Confucianism and the actual religious and ritual conduct of the Song elite, see Ebrey 1991, 1993; Liao 2001.

91. Hansen (1990) emphasizes the commoner status of these cult figures and their origins as identifiable historical figures.

92. Barend ter Haar (1990) has concluded that the majority of local commoner cults in Fujian province emerged from the propitiation of "hungry ghosts," spirits of persons who met untimely deaths and whose worship perhaps was chiefly inspired by fear. In the course of the formation of an enduring cult the malignant features of the hungry ghosts were effaced and the gods were rendered into more acceptable and conventional forms.

93. *Tudi* often is translated as "earth god," but *tudi* were not specifically connected to fertility cults, nor were they an exclusively rural phenomenon.

94. LH, 75, "Jiechu," 25.506. Kitada (1996: 114) interprets *guixing* as denoting the ghosts of the dead, but I believe the term simply means a macabre image.

95. Kitada 1996: 114–15, 124–27.

96. In a series of articles, Kanai Noriyuki (1979, 1980, 1982, 1985) has advanced the argument that the Song period witnessed a dramatic transformation in the character of *tudi* cults. According to Kanai, prior to the Song, rural religion centered on rites of propitiation and thanksgiving addressed to nature deities, collectively represented by the *she* altar. In his view, the *she* rites exclusive to each village promoted communal solidarity and militated against social differentiation. In the Song, however, the *she* atrophied with the rise of the new *tudi*

cults whose anthropomorphic gods became identified with local landowning and merchant elites. Kanai concludes that the *tudi* cults of the Song thus fostered social stratification and elite control of rural society. Yet Kanai's idyllic portrayal of egalitarian village communities in the pre-Song period and his dour view of Song *tudi* cults as tools of social subordination suffer from conceptual rigidity and serious misreadings of evidence. Most problematically, he reads *tudi* as a uniform category at any given point in time and thus fails to recognize the diverse range of deities to whom the designation *tudi* was applied. For pertinent critiques of Kanai's work on both methodological and empirical grounds, see Hamashima 1990b; Matsumoto 1993, 1999.

97. Schipper 1985b. See also Akizuki 1978.

98. On this point see Kitada 1996, who also categorically rejects the view that the nascent *tudi* cults of the Era of Disunion derived from the ancient *she* rites (ibid., 128).

99. Zhou Chu's career (but not his fantastic exploits) were recorded in a memorial stele composed by Lu Yun. See Lu Yun, "Jin Pingxi jiangjun xiaohou Zhou Chu bei," *Lu Shiheng ji*, 10.68–70. The earliest documentation of a cult centered on Zhou Chu is Xu Kai (early tenth century), "Yixing Zhou jiangjun miao ji," in *[Xianchun] Piling zhi* (1268), 21.1a–3b.

100. Hu Jing, "Yingliewang miaoqian ji" (1149), in *Jiangsu jinshi zhi*, 11.38b–40b; Liu Zai, "Yixing fu Zhou xiaogong yingzhao ji" (1223), in *[Xianchun] Piling zhi*, 21.14a–16a. Zhou had received the posthumous honorary title "filial vassal" from the Jin court, but Liu Zai was the first to use the title "filial lord" in relation to his cult.

101. "Chongxiu Yingliemiao ji," in *Jiangsu jinshi zhi*, 13.1a–3b; "Yingliemiao zhitian tanyue timing ji," in ibid., 15.22a–26a. Additional Song epigraphic material regarding the Filial Lord Zhou cult, much of it unfortunately illegible, can be found in Beijing tushuguan 1990, 40: 64; 43: 107; 43: 111; 44: 78.

102. The cult of Filial Lord Zhou in Yixing apparently encouraged imitation in adjacent regions. In Changshu county, across Lake Tai from Yixing, a different Zhou (this one a Changshu native) was also canonized as Filial Lord Zhou. Ming sources claim that Changshu's Filial Lord Zhou cult originated in the thirteenth century. Hamashima Atsutoshi (2001: 47–52) expresses skepticism about these claims and asserts that the Changshu cult was invented in the late Yuan. In my view, the precise details and dating of miracles ascribed to Changshu's Filial Lord Zhou in Ming records suggest that the cult did indeed originate in the Song. Filial Lord Zhou cults also developed in other parts of Suzhou prefecture in Ming-Qing times.

103. "Si Xianying miaoe shangshusheng die" (1209), in *Changxing xianzhi* (1875), 30A.44a–45b. See also ibid., 12.9a–11a; *Changshu xianzhi* (1539), 3.67a–69b; *SSGJ*, houji, 26a–b.

104. Deng Daoshu's sojourn in Changshu is commemorated in a surviving Song inscription. See "Deng Daoshu timing," in *Jiangsu jinshi zhi*, 18.1a–b. The motivation for Deng's founding of the Sire Li shrine is unknown. Reportedly descendants of Sire Li who had migrated to Jiangyin county, adjacent to Changshu, founded a branch temple in the mid-thirteenth century, but it's not clear whether the Jiangyin temple was established before or after the Changshu tem-

ple. On the Jiangyin temple, see Gao Side (d. ca. 1279), "Ti Changxing Liwang xianyingji xu," in *Chitang cungao*, 5.13b; *Jiangyin xianzhi* (1548), 8.7b.

105. *Changshu xianzhi* (1539), 3.67a–69b, 10.92a–b, 12.47a.

106. Yuan inscriptions emphasize, in addition to protection of seafarers, the god's curative powers: incense ashes, candle wax, and even tree leaves from Sire Li's shrine were used to cure fevers, suppurations, ulcers, and dysentery. Yuan sources also state that the god, much like a terrestrial magistrate, seized and prosecuted criminals. See the inscriptions cited in *Chang Zhao hezhi gao* (1904), 15.24b–25b, 45.10a–b.

107. This is one of the major themes of Hansen 1990.

108. *Changshu xianzhi* (1539), 3.69b. Local gazetteers from the early twentieth century list eleven Sire Li temples in the counties (Changshu, Zhaowen, and Taicang) that comprised Changshu in the Song-Yuan period. See *Chang Zhao hezhi gao* (1904), 5.1b–22a, 15.24b; *Taicang zhouzhi* (1918), 2.12a.

109. Another example of the restricted range of local cults was Prince Ming (Mingwang), fourteenth son of the Tang emperor Taizong and once prefect of Suzhou. Prince Ming's cult was confined to the single Suzhou county of Wujiang, which boasted twelve of his temples in the late Northern Song, but failed to attract adherents elsewhere in the prefecture. See the inscription of 1100 cited in *Wujiang xianzhi* (1747), 51.34a–b.

110. For Fujian, see ter Haar 1990; Kojima 1991; Dean 1993; for Jiangnan, see Hamashima 2001; von Glahn forthcoming.

111. *Yufeng zhi* (1251), shang.17b.

112. Von Glahn forthcoming.

113. Ter Haar 1995: 4.

114. Johnson 1985.

115. Hansen (1993) suggests that the original inspiration for the *chenghuang* was Vaiśravaṇa, the Buddhist *deva* king who was invoked as a defender against demonic forces.

116. Hansen 1993: 93.

117. This is the theme of the first story in Hong Mai's anthology. See *YJZ*, jiazhi, 1.1–2; also see ibid., sanzhisi, 10.1383. Johnson (1985: 424, 436–38) also notes that exemplary officials, especially those who died in office, were likely candidates for recognition as *chenghuang*.

118. Johnson 1985, esp. pp. 418–24.

119. The significance of Dongyue temples as the central ritual site in market towns has been noted by Kanai Noriyuki (1987). However, Kanai makes an idiosyncratic and unsubstantiated argument that the Dongyue cult was tied primarily to rural rather than urban communities.

120. Yao Gu, "Da Song Huzhoufu Deqingxian Xinshizhen xinjian Dongyue xinggong ji" (1334), *Xinshi zhenzhi* (1511), 5.13b. On the practice of "attending court" at Dongyue temples in Southern Song Fujian, see Chen Chun, "Shang Zhao sicheng lun yinci," *Beixi daquan ji*, 43.15b–16a. (Chen also mentions the dunning of households for contributions as a heinous feature of this cult.)

121. *Mengliang lu*, 2.150–51.

122. *Xihu laoren fansheng lu*, 117.

123. *Sanshan zhi* (1181), 40.6a, 8.16a.

124. *Mengliang lu,* 19.300. I have not been able to determine the exact significance of the "money banners," though they appear to have been the most distinctive feature of the Dongyue festivals in Song Hangzhou. See also ibid., 2.150; *Xihu laoren fansheng lu,* 117.

125. Von Glahn forthcoming.

126. Goossaert 1998: 56–59.

127. See the text and translation in Chavannes 1910: 354–60. The author also suggested that the sheer volume of icons elicited a much deeper sense of foreboding than the famous murals of the underworld (also referred to as *bianxiang,* i.e., "transformation images") executed by Wu Daozi for Chang'an's Zhao Jinggongsi Monastery in 736. In the great Dongyue temple in Beijing most of the individual shrines of the seventy-six departments of Dongyue's celestial bureaucracy contained statues, reportedly dating from the late Song, of fierce judges and dreadful scenes of punishment. See Goodrich 1964: 23, 242–55.

128. See the sources cited in note 87.

129. *YJZ,* zhijing, 6.927–28.

130. On Song examination cults, see Liao Hsien-huei 2001: 22–84; on the Zitong/Wenchang cult, see Kleeman 1993, 1994a. These gods became specialists in examination prognostication. All six stories concerning the cult of the King of Yangshan in *Tales of the Listener* concern oracles about exam success or failure. See *YJZ,* zhijia, 5.746; zhijia, 5.748; zhijia, 7.768; zhiyi, 2.808; zhiyi, 2.810–11; zhixu, 8.1114–15.

131. Hansen 1990: 128–59.

132. On the origins of the Mazu cult, see Li Xianzhang 1979; Watson 1985; ter Haar 1990: 356–57. Hansen refers to Consort Linghui (the highest title awarded to Lin by the Song court, in 1192) as Heavenly Consort (Tianfei), the name bestowed on her by Khubilai Khan in 1278.

133. Hansen 1990: 151.

134. Sangren 1987: 200–206.

135. Naquin and Yü 1993: 15.

136. On the practice of "dividing the ashes" *(fenxiang)* in the founding of branch temples, see Schipper 1977, 1990.

137. Kleeman (1993: 59) has suggested that Daoist priests played a crucial role in the spread of the Zitong cult to Jiangnan. On the role of Buddhist clergy in the dissemination of the Wutong/Wuxian cult, see chapter 6.

138. See the 1132 inscription in *[Chongxiu] Qinchuan zhi* (1365), 13.46b, and the 1358 inscription in *Changshu xianzhi* (1539), 3.63a–64a.

139. The editor of a Yuan gazetteer in neighboring Kunshan county deplored the enthusiasm of Kunshan people for making pilgrimages to the Dongyue temple at Fushanzhen. See *Kunshan xianzhi* (1344), 1.2b.

140. Huang Jie, "Tong Guanyin xiang ji," *Wujun zhi,* 33.7a–8a.

141. Ibid.; "Guangfusi tong Guanyin xiang ganying shi" (1301), in *Jiangsu jinshi zhi,* 19.25a–27b.

142. "Guangfusi tong Guanyin xiang ji" (1319), in *Jiangsu jinshi zhi,* 21.1a–b.

143. Huang Jie, "Tong Guanyin xiang ji," *Wujun zhi,* 33.7a–8a. Charter myths of sacred sites dedicated to Guanyin typically featured epiphanies of the goddess and miracle-working images. See Yü Chün-fang 1993. The discovery of

the bronze statue of Guanyin at Guangfu was preceded by the miraculous appearance of a wooden Guanyin statue that floated in from the sea in nearby Jiangyin seventeen years earlier. A local man had a dream in which he received instructions from Guanyin to replace the statue's missing right arm. The statue subsequently was installed in Jiangyin's main Buddhist temple (Shoushengyuan Cloister), which, like Guangfu's Guangfusi, attracted large numbers of pilgrims and ample donations. See Wang Xiaojie, "Shoushengyuan fanhai linggan Guanyin ji" (1124), in Beijing tushuguan 1990, 42: 146 (for a translation of part of this stele inscription and an illustration of the Guanyin icon inscribed on it, see Yü Chün-fang 2001: 254–56); *Yudi jisheng,* 9.8b; Hu Yingqing, "Qianming Guangfu chansi chongjian Guanyin dian ji" (1320), in *Jiangsu jinshi zhi,* 20.30a–33b (a rubbing of the obverse side only of this stele is reproduced in Beijing tushuguan 1990, 49: 76).

144. Naquin and Yü 1993: 12.

CHAPTER 6. WUTONG

1. *YJZ,* dingzhi, 19.695–97.

2. Other contemporaries also testify to the belief that *shanxiao* could grant or snatch away wealth. The Southern Song writer Chu Yong scoffed at the entrenched popular belief that the *shanxiao* could "convey treasure and wealth" *(yunzhi baohuo).* See *Quyi shuo,* 15a. Tao Zongyi (fl. ca. 1360), in a satiric poem on the evanescence of wealth, alluded to the same idea, remarking that when the *shanxiao* and *muke* shout and whistle, gold, silver, and coin all vanish. See *Nancun chuogeng lu,* 17.211.

3. Furth 1999: 107–8. Zhu Yu, in a book published in 1119, reported that when deformed infants (he speaks of "demonic forms") are put to death, their spirits will return to the mother and seek to nurse, thus causing the mother's sickness and death. Such spirits were referred to as *hanba,* an ancient term for a drought demon. See *Pingzhou ketan,* 3.58.

4. Nakamura Jihei (1980: 15, 1982: 64) has suggested that the *congci* represented a new type of shrine founded by pioneer settlers who immigrated to south China during the late Tang and Song. In his view, the *congci* embodied values of local identity and community welfare in these newly settled regions, and as such they were the incubators of the *tudi* tutelary spirit cults of the late imperial era. Nakamura also notes that the *congci* were closely associated with female mediums *(wu).* Other scholars have accepted Nakamura's assertion that the *congci* represent a new stage in the formation of *tudi* cults (see Kanai 1982: 353–54; Davis 2001: 12–13), but I have not seen any evidence that connects *congci* to newly settled villages. Indeed, use of the term *congci* was largely restricted to the Jiangdong region and rarely employed in the areas of substantial new settlement and high population growth in the Song (Jiangnan, Fujian, and Jiangxi). In my view Nakamura's hypothesis is untenable, and *congci* more likely had developed since the Era of Disunion in connection with the *shanxiao* cults of south China. Extrapolating from Nakamura's hypothesis, Davis (2001: 12–13, 214) argues that village spirit mediums exercised proprietary control over the *congci* shrines, which became a bulwark of community solidarity against the

outside world. I certainly agree that there was a close relationship between spirit mediums and the *shanxiao* spirits worshiped at *congci* shrines, but such diabolical spirits were unlikely to have served as the nuclei of the *tudi* cults.

5. Su Song, "Runzhou zhouzhai houting ji," *Su Weigong wenji*, 64.6b. Song writers typically associated *congci* and their spirit mediums with worship of grotesque spirits. Hong Mai describes a local official in pursuit of a spirit medium who follows her to a small hut, "no more than knee-high," in which he finds "exceedingly bizarre paintings of ghosts and spirits, such as have never been seen in this world." See *YJZ*, sanzhiren, 4.1498–99. See also the poetry and other texts cited in Nakamura 1978: 66–70.

6. *Kui* and *(shan)sao* of course are familiar terms for wilderness goblins and ogres. *Guimei* is a rare term but like the more typical *chimei* refers to aberrant creatures as a generic category. *Yiyang* and *panghuang* are allusions to the *Zhuangzi*, in which they appear as names for marvelous creatures of remote places and wilderness regions, respectively. See *Zhuangzi jiaoquan*, 19, "Dasheng," 2: 694, 697 (a part of this passage, mentioning the *panghuang*, is translated in this volume, chapter 3, note 24).

7. Wang Ling, "Gumiao," *Guangling ji*, 5.8b–9b.

8. Twice Hong Mai referred to worship of Wulang or Wutong at *congci*. See *YJZ*, dingzhi, 19.695; sanbu, 1803. He also mentions domestic altars dedicated to Wutong. See *YJZ*, zhijia, 7.765; zhijia, 8.773; zhikui, 5.1255–56. On the association of Wutong spirits and *congci* shrines, see also Kanai 1994.

9. Cedzich 1985: 34–35; 1995: 159–61.

10. *Zongjing lu, T* 2016, 15.494b–c.

11. Zhiyuan, "Che tuou wen," *Xianju bian*, 17, in *Dai Nihon zoku zokyo*, 101: 52b–53b. Zhiyuan was a leading ecumenical figure who sought to reconcile Buddhist and Confucian values, and his denunciation of these idols is couched as much in notions of Confucian ritual propriety as in Buddhist theology. "*Wutong xianren*," "*Wutong shenxian*," and "*Wutong daxian*" continued to be used as designations for a category of divine beings summoned to attend the Buddhist Land-and-Water Masses. See Su Shi, "Shuilufa xiang zan," *Su Dongpo quanji*, 1: 660. The temple murals of the Pilusi Monastery near Shijiazhuang include a group of five spirits dressed in officials' robes identified as the *Wutong daxian*. See Zhongguo meishu quanji bianji weiyuanhui 1988b: plate 159.

12. Xing Yuanlong, "Fengxinxian Baoyunsi Shangshantang ji" (1232), *Bianshi guyun hongcheng Xing qingjie gong songyuan wenji*, 5.2b–3b.

13. Cedzich 1985: 37–40.

14. *Taishang zhuguo jiumin zongzhen biyao*, 1.2b.

15. *Taiqing jinque yuhua xianshu baji shenzhang sanhuang neibi wen*, shang, 12a–b; *DFHY*, 104.5a (quoted in Cedzich 1985: 38), 250.1b.

16. *YJZ*, sanzhiren, 3.1484–86; other examples are *YJZ*, bingzhi, 1.364; zhijing, 2.890; zhiwu, 6.1098–1100.

17. *YJZ*, jiazhi, 11.97. Thunder Magic texts in the enormous fourteenth-century ritual compendium *Daofa huiyuan* strictly enjoined Daoist priests not to worship *shanxiao*/Wutong, invoke their aid, serve as wardens of their temples, or organize mass processions in their honor. See Cedzich 1985: 43.

18. *Xiangshi jiashuo*, 8.1b. Tradition attributes the "Nine Songs," a set of

lyric poems on the theme of ecstatic transport and communication with the divine, to Qu Yuan, an ancient poet lionized in Hunan as a native son.

19. Xing Yuanlong, "Fengxinxian Baoyunsi Shangshantang ji" (1232), *Bian-shi guyun hongcheng Xing qingjie gong songyuan wenji*, 5.2b–3b.

20. *YJZ*, zhijing, 2.890; zhikui, 3.1238–39.

21. *Nenggaizhai manlu*, 18.256. Wu places the story in the Jiayou (1056–64) period; however, his fellow Linchuan countryman Yan Shu (d. 1055) figures in the narrative in his capacity as prime minister, an office he held between the seventh month of 1042 and the ninth month of 1044.

22. *YJZ*, dingzhi, 15.667–68.

23. *YJZ*, zhikui, 3.1238–39.

24. *YJZ*, bu, 15.1692–93. The same motifs recur in another story in which a greedy merchant is inveigled by the lure of riches and ends up impoverished, but finally resorts to the services of an adept of the Heavenly Master teachings to exorcise the demon. See *YJZ*, dingzhi, 10.647–48. In another case, a man scrupulously devoted to worship of the Wutong spirits nonetheless suffers repeated thefts until the spirits' statutes are moved to the local *chenghuang* temple, at which point the depredations cease. See *YJZ*, zhijia, 8.773.

25. *YJZ*, bu, 7.1612–13. In the late Ming, the celebrated author Ling Mengchu (1580–1644) included this story as the prologue to one of his own works of fiction. See "Wang Yuweng shejing chong sanbao, Baishui seng daowu sang shuangsheng," *Erke pai'an jingqi*, 36.1a–4a.

26. Li Gou, "Shaoshi shenci ji," *Li Gou ji*, 24.267–68.

27. It should be noted that Jianchang county, part of Nankang prefecture located to the west of Poyang Lake, is a different place than Jiangchangjun, Li Gou's home town, in the western foothills of the Wuyi Mountains.

28. *SSGJ*, qianji, 25b–26a.

29. *YJZ*, zhikui, 10.1295–96. Hong states that the shrine to the Wutong spirits was located in an upper story of the monastery's pagoda. Although the spirits were invisible, they spoke with voices like those of children five or six years of age.

30. Wang Xiangzhi, *Yudi jisheng*, 23.9b. A Qing source places this encounter in the Sui period and claims that Dexing's Wutong first received imperial honors as "Sire Wutong" in 669, before subsequently obtaining official recognition from the Southern Tang and Northern Song. See *Gujin tushu jicheng*, zhifang-dian, 859.4c.

31. All three stories are found in *YJZ*, sanzhisi, 10.1378–80.

32. *SSGJ*, qianji, 26a–b, citing a work entitled *Anthology of Miraculous Responses at the Ancestral Temple (Zudian lingying ji)*, which presumably was a record of the miracles that occurred at the Wuyuan shrine. An alternate history of Wuyuan's Wutong cult recorded on a stele of Song date traced its origins to 627, when five gods appeared (on the thirteenth day of the fifth month, which is celebrated as the feast day of Guandi) to deliver the local community from pestilence. See *Huizhou fuzhi* (1502), 5.32a–b. Another source suggests that Wuyuan's Wutong cult had an even more venerable pedigree. According to a Ming gazetteer, in 503 five brothers from Wuyuan, recently deceased, were believed to have warded off a plague afflicting Huangyan county in Zhejiang. The Liang court

subsequently invested the five as the Five Sagely Divine Agents of Manifest Response (Wusheng yingxian lingguan), a title that prefigures later ones accorded to Wutong. See *Huangyan xianzhi* (1579), 7.8b–9a. Nonetheless, this text is almost certainly spurious, since there are numerous discrepancies between the Huangyan cult and that of Wuyuan (e.g., concerning the surname of the brothers, temple names, and imperial titles). Moreover, the temple identified in this gazetteer is not associated with Wutong in an earlier Song gazetteer, even though many Wutong temples existed in this prefecture in Song times (*[Jiading] Chicheng zhi*, 31.7b, 15b). The Huangyan legend probably reflects a conflation of an older local cult with the flourishing Wuxian cult of late Song or (more likely) post-Song times.

33. *Huizhou fuzhi* (1502), 5.42b. In one story in *Tales of the Listener* Wuyuan's Wutong spirits fulfill the role of tutelary *tudi* gods by barring wandering plague demons from entering the county and spreading epidemic. See *YJZ*, yizhi 17.327–28.

34. *Huizhou fuzhi* (1502), 5.42b; *Song huiyao jigao*, li 20.157b–158a.

35. *Song huiyao jigao*, li 20.14b–15a. Li Zhi, *Huang Song shichao gangyao*, 17.8a, gives a figure of more than 1,380 temples.

36. Mizukoshi 2002: 635–42.

37. Ibid., 645.

38. Zhen Dexiu, "Meishanmiao zhuwen," *Xishan wenji*, 52.10b.

39. *YJZ*, sanzhisi, 10.1379–80. Since Hong Mai was a native of Poyang county, which like Dexing was part of Raozhou prefecture, he may have been partial to the claims of his fellow countrymen.

40. The competition between Dexing and Wuyuan is also mentioned by the compiler of a Wuyuan gazetteer, the *Xingyuan zhi* (1269), cited in *SSGJ*, qianji, 26a–b. By the end of the Song Wuyuan was universally regarded as the original home of the Wuxian cult. See, for examples, Zhu Mu, *Fangyu shenglan*, 16.6b; Wu Zimu, *Mengliang lu*, 14.253. In the early Ming, Wuyuan's claim was also endorsed by no less an authority than Zhang Yuchu (1361–1410), the forty-third patriarch of the Celestial Masters lineage. But Zhang's partisanship is fully evident in his brusque dismissal of claims by his Buddhist rivals that the Wuxian deities had first made an appearance before Daorong at the Yunjusi Monastery. See Zhang Yuchu, "Shangqingshi Wutongmiao tiyuan shu," *Xianquan ji*, 4.60a–b.

41. Zhu Mu, *Fangyu shenglan*, 16.6b.

42. Fang Hui, "Fudemiao bei" (1300), *Tongjiang xuji*, 36.27a.

43. The now-lost 1021 gazetteer for Suzhou mentioned a Wutong temple three *li* outside the city; see *Suzhou fuzhi* (1379), 15.24a. Southern Song and Yuan sources also make reference to Wutong temples dating back to the tenth century in Changzhou and Zhenjiang. See *[Xianchun] Piling zhi* (1268), 14.5b; *[Zhishun] Zhenjiang zhi* (1332), 8.8b–9a.

44. This assertion comes from a now-lost Yangzhou gazetteer, the *Guangling zhi* (1190), which is cited by the Yuan writer Yu Yan in his *Xishang futan*, xia.13b. The spirit residing at this same temple had its diabolic side as well, as seen in an anecdote related by the Southern Song raconteur Guo Tuan about an official's wife who meets an untimely demise when her soul is seized by its Wutong spirit. See *Kuiche zhi*, 5.9b–10a.

45. According to a Southern Song gazetteer, this temple was founded in the tenth century; an inscription dated 1040 is briefly quoted in the same source. See *[Chunxi] Sanshan zhi* (1182), 8.7702.

46. Liu Fu, "Chengong Jingnan," *Qingsuo gaoyi*, buyi, 260.

47. Images of Wutong manufactured at the god's "ancestral home" of Wuyuan played a crucial role in demonstrating the legitimate affiliation of branch temples. In modern Taiwan, branch temples are established by distributing incense ashes from the host temple to the new branch. This distribution of ashes *(fenxiang)* sanctifies its bond with the original cult. See Schipper 1977: 652.

48. Liu Xuan, "Chongjian Wuxianwangci ji"" (1439), *Wu xianzhi* (1642), 21.17b–18a.

49. *Suzhou fuzhi* (1379), 15.24a. This temple, at least during the final days of the Song dynasty, was under the charge of a master of exorcism rites. See *Changzhou xianzhi* (1598), 14.45a–b.

50. *Suzhou fuzhi* (1379), 15.24a; Gu Rubao, "Wanshouci ji," *Wu xianzhi* (1642), 21.19b–21a.

51. *Jiangzhou zhi* (ca. 1240–1279), cited in *Yongle dadian*, 6700.6a; *[Zhiyuan] Jiahe zhi* (1288), 12.4a–b. The temples in Jiaxing bore the name Wusheng rather than Wuxian.

52. *Linchuan zhi* (1263), cited in *Yongle dadian* 10950.8a.

53. Chen Chun, "Shaozhou zhouxue shidaotang ji," *Beixi daquan ji*, 9.6a.

54. Zhang Ning (1454 *jinshi*), "Jurong xian Wuxian lingguanmiao bei," *Fangzhou ji*, 18.7b.

55. The earliest references to Huaguang pavilions are for those founded in Suzhou in 1225 and the 1240s. The Huaguang pavilion at the Rongguosi Monastery was built in 1270. See *[Xianchun] Lin'an zhi* (ca. 1274), 73.14a. One of Wujiang's most prestigious Buddhist monasteries added a Huaguang pavilion in 1283, and the magnificent Wuxian temple in the city of Wujiang included a Huaguang pavilion at the time of its reconstruction in 1385. See *Wujiang xianzhi* (1488), 7.23a; *Wujiang xianzhi* (1747), 11.53b. A Huaguang pavilion of unspecified date was also attached to the Wuxian shrine in Changzhou by 1268 at the latest. See *[Xianchun] Piling zhi* (1268), 14.5b. When a group of sixty-four notables in Jurong (Jiangning) collected tens of thousands of taels through public subscription to refurbish the city's Wuxian temple in 1434, a Huaguang pavilion was built in addition to the main hall. See Zhang Ning, *Fangzhou ji*, 18.7b–8a.

56. *Xianchuang guayi zhi*, 2. Zhu Yunming also described Wuxian as "the one whom Buddhist scriptures refer to as a transformation of the Bodhisattva Flowery Light." See *Zhushi jilüe*, 30.3b.

57. *YJZ*, sanzhisi, 10.1378–79.

58. Wuxian's feast day is given as 9/28 in Zhu Mu, *Fangyu shenglan*, 16.6b; Li Yiji, *Yueling caike* (1619), 3.39b; and *Zhushen shengdanri yuxia ji*, 4b; but (erroneously) as 9/29 in *Mengliang lu*, 19.299; the feast day of Huaguang is given as 9/28 in *Wucheng xianzhi* (1638), 4.28b. The connection between the two figures is also illustrated by a Huaguang temple in Hangzhou in which Wuxian was said to be the focal object of worship. See *Qiantang xianzhi* (1609), jizhi, 25a (on this temple see also p. 219 below).

59. In the Chinese liturgical calendar, on the eighth day of the fourth month Buddhist clergy and laity assembled to bathe images of the Buddha, an extension of the Indian practice of worshiping relics of the Buddha as an especially efficacious means of earning karmic merit.

60. Fang Hui, "Song Xu Ruxin ru Wuyuan sanshi yun," *Tongjiang xuji*, 18.6a–7a. The Huaguang pavilion at the ancestral shrine at Wuyuan is mentioned in a commemoration for the rebuilding of the shrine in 1397. See *Huizhou fuzhi* (1502), 5.42b–44a.

61. *Xingyuan zhi*, in *SSGJ*, qianji, 26a–b; Zhu Mu, *Fangyu shenglan*, 16.6b.

62. Zhipan, *Fozu tongji*, T 2035, 49: 350b–c, under the years 529, 535, and 536.

63. Ōtani 1937: 48–63.

64. YJZ, bu, 15.1692.

65. *Xingyuan zhi*, cited in *SSGJ*, qianji, 26a–b.

66. Huang Zhen, "Shen zhusi qijin shehui zhuang," *Huangshi richao*, 74.27a.

67. Fang Hui, "Raozhoulu zhizhong Wang gong Yuangui muzhiming," *Tongjiang ji*, buyi, 40.

68. *Kunshan xianzhi* (1344), 1.2b.

69. *Yufeng zhi* (1251), xia.20a.

70. *Suzhou fuzhi* (1379), 15.24a–b.

71. *Mengliang lu*, 19.299. The Wuxian temple at Zhili Bridge in Suzhou held monthly convocations for sutra readings and an annual ceremony in honor of the Buddha in the 1260s, if not earlier. See Gu Rubao, "Wanshouci ji," *Wu xianzhi* (1642) 21.19b. Huang Gongshao (1265 *jinshi*), who gave up public life and became a lay Buddhist postulant after the Mongol conquest, observed that "assemblies to honor the Buddha" *(qingfohui)* were held at the Wutong temple in his native Shaowu (Fujian). See Huang Gongshao, "Wutongmiao jieyue bang," *Zaixuan ji*, 29a–30a. A fairly detailed description of the assembly to honor the Buddha held on 4/8 in the city of Fuzhou (Fujian) from 1082 onwards has been preserved in *[Chunxi] Sanshan zhi* (1182), 40.8080. In the mid-twelfth century these assemblies were attended by more than sixteen thousand monks, nuns, Daoist priests, and laity. In 1168, with the city suffering from famine, the provincial governor seized the assembly's assets, some three thousand taels, to provide for public relief. Subsequently the great public festival ceased. Private cult groups continued the tradition, though, attracting as many as several hundred worshipers to temples or homes of the faithful for several days of fasting and admonitory sermons.

72. *Renhe xianzhi* (1687), 29.24b–25b.

73. *Huating xianzhi* (1521), 3.3a. The 1663 edition of the *Songjiang fuzhi*, 5.9a, quotes the text of the 1521 gazetteer but gives no indication that the assemblies were still active.

74. *Dahui jingci miaole tianzun shuo fude wusheng jing* (HY 1183); *Wuxian lingguan dadi dengyi* (HY 206). The earliest datable reference to the title by which Wuxian as a divine agent is known, Wuxian lingguan dadi, appears in a secular work of the 1240s or 1250s. See Lu Yinglong, *Xianchuang guayi zhi*, 2. A Yuan gazetteer from Nanjing notes in connection with an entry for the Huaguang tower of the city's Wuxian temple that this deity "is called Lingguan dadi in Daoist

writings. His shrines and temples are found everywhere, and are especially numerous in Jiangdong." See *[Zhizheng] Jinling xinzhi* (1344), 11.29b.

75. *Taishang dongxuan lingbao wuxianguan huaguang benxing miaojing* (HY 1436).

76. Huang Jin, *Diqi shangjiang Wen Taibao zhuan*, buyi, 1b–2b.

77. Cedzich (1995: 163) asserts that the Wusheng were known and worshiped in Suzhou in the eleventh century, but I do not find her argument persuasive. Her evidence is the existence of a "Wusheng Tower" at the Yunyansi Monastery at Tiger Hill, just outside the city. See *Wujun tujing xuji*, zhong.35. But there is no evidence to link this building to either Wutong or Wuxian, nor is there any mention of "Wusheng Towers" in connection with the cult. The title Wusheng can have many meanings in Buddhist, Daoist, and Confucian mythology apart from this particular cult. Moreover, this monastery is not subsequently associated with the Wutong or Wuxian cults.

78. Hu Sheng, "Ti Wuxian shishi hou," *Xin'an wenxian zhi*, 23.8a.

79. *YJZ*, sanzhisi, 10.1379.

80. *YJZ*, bingzhi, 1.364–69.

81. *SSGJ*, qianji, 25a–26a.

82. *YJZ*, sanzhishi, 8.1364.

83. Yuan Haowen, *Xu Yijian zhi*, 1.17.

84. Tao Zongyi, *Nancun chuogeng lu*, 25.308.

85. Hansen 1990: 133. Hansen's tabulation omits Buddhist and Daoist divinities like Guanyin, Zhenwu, and Dongyue.

86. Wang Yuangui (1233–90), who rebuilt the temple, was appointed district magistrate of his native Wuyuan by the new Yuan dynasty in 1282. Wang's biographer praised him for the restraint he showed in collecting no more than the stipulated commercial fees from the merchants who gathered at Wuyuan for the great temple fair on 4/8. See Fang Hui, "Raozhoulu zhizhong Wang gong Yuangui muzhiming," in *Tongjiang ji*, buyi, 40.

87. Cheng Jufu, "Wuyuan shan Wanshou lingshun wu pusa miaoji," *Chuguo Wenxiangong xuelou Cheng xiansheng wenji*, 13.11a–b.

88. Gu Rubao, "Wanshouci ji," in *Wu xianzhi* (1642), 21.19b–21a.

89. *Huating xianzhi* (1521), 9.6a.

90. Kojima 1990; Hamashima 1992a, 1992b. On Zhu Yuanzhang's religious reforms, see also Taylor 1990.

91. Wada 1985.

92. *Wujiang xianzhi* (1747), 11.51b–52a. On the consolidation of Buddhist temples, see also Hasabe 1993: 7–11.

93. Ter Haar 1992: 166–72.

94. *Ming shi*, 50.1304. The semiannual sacrifices typical of imperial religious ceremonial were performed in Wuxian's case on 4/8 and 9/28, the deity's long-established feast days.

95. Song Na, "Qi jian Wuxian lingshunci ji," *Xiyin ji*, 5.30a–32a.

96. Imperial recognition of the deities honored by inclusion in the Ten Shrines in effect condoned worship of them throughout the empire. Aside from Wuxian, the only other deities of popular origin whose temples were also in-

cluded in the Ten Shrines were King Zhang (in 1388) and King Guan (i.e., Guandi, added in 1394).

97. On popular devotion to Wuxian in the Poyang Lake region, see the dedication for the rebuilding in 1530 of a Wuxian temple next to the Nankang prefectural yamen by the prefect Wang Qin: "Chongxiu Wuxian ci ji," in *Nankang fuzhi* (1515), 8.53a–b. The same gazetteer records the existence of three other Wutong and Wuxian temples in this prefecture: ibid., 7.3b–4b.

98. See the inscription by Cao Tianyou (1550 *jinshi*) in *Fuliang xianzhi* (1783), 10.37a.

99. *Song shi*, 421.12591.

100. *Linting zhi* (ca. 1259), cited in *Yongle dadian* 7892.2b–5b.

101. *Tingzhou fuzhi* (1527), 9.1a–13a.

102. On modern-day worship of Huaguang in this region, see Zhang Hongxiang 1997: 110–13; Zhu Zuzhen 1997: 139–44.

103. On the popularity of this temple in Song times, see *[Chunxi] Sanshan zhi* (1182), 8.7702.

104. Huang Zhongzhao, *Bamin tongzhi* (1491), 58.365. This source clearly connects Fuzhou's Wuxian temples with the Wuxian cult of Wuyuan, but it is not clear whether this connection already existed in Song times.

105. *Fuzhou fuzhi* (1613), 16.9b. The cult, however, was transmitted to Taiwan by immigrants from Fuzhou. A number of Wuxian temples remain in present-day Taiwan, the largest of which, in Tainan, was founded during Koxinga's occupation of the island in the seventeenth century. In Taiwan Wuxian assumes the form of a plague god, specifically identified with immigrants from Fuzhou. See Liu Zhiwan 1983: 228; Lin Hengdao 1974: 38, 43.

106. A local gazetteer of Funing, just to the north of Fuzhou, observed that Wuxian was also known by the names Wusheng and Huaguang, and that the deity's feast day fell on 4/8. See *Funing zhouzhi* (1616), 4.9b–10a. Worship of Wuxian ("colloquially known as Huaguang") also persevered in Youxi, to the west of Fuzhou. See *Youxi xianzhi* (1636), 2.17a. Xie Zhaozhe (1567–1624), a native of Fuzhou, reported in connection with an epidemic that broke out in the region in 1590–91 that "whenever epidemic rages in our prefecture, every family is extremely diligent in their worship of Wusheng." See Xie Zhaozhe, *Wu za zu*, 15.386.

107. Michael Szonyi (1997) argues that Fuzhou's Five Emperors cult was wholly indigenous to Fujian and perhaps descended from a local Wutong cult independent of Wuyuan's Wuxian cult. Yet, given the strong presence of the Wuxian/Huaguang cult not only in the Fujian interior but also in areas around Fuzhou itself, I am inclined to believe that there was a genealogical connection between Wuxian and the Five Emperors cult, as other scholars have argued (see Xu Xiaowang 1994: 81–91). Of course, the more important issue is the distinctive history of the Five Emperors cult, and in that respect I agree with Szonyi that the Five Emperors cult needs to be evaluated in terms of its role in local religious culture, not as an offshoot of the Wuxian cult.

108. See, for example, Lu Can, *Gengsibian*, 5.51; Tian Yiheng, *Liuqing rizha*, 28.11a, 15a.

109. Government surveillance and control at the two main Suzhou temples probably restricted popular worship and encouraged devotees to go elsewhere. The Wuxian temple at Hefengfang was renovated twice by local officials between 1588 and 1594, though it does not figure in any accounts of popular devotion. The temple at Zhili Bridge was converted into a tax office in the early sixteenth century; see *Wu xianzhi* (1642), 21.17b, 19a.

110. Lu Can, *Gengsibian*, 5.51; Yang Xunji, *Suzhoufu zuanxiu shilüe*, 3.9a; Tian Rucheng, *Xihu youlan zhiyu*, 26.476–77; *Gu Su zhi* (1506), 40.27b; Gui Zhuang (1613–73), "Chongjian Wushengmiao men yin," *Gui Zhuang ji*, 10.511–12. A seventeenth-century gazetteer of Hangzhou reported that "from the back alleys of the city to remote hamlets in the countryside, everyone placed shrines, statues, and painted images of Wutong in their homes"; see *Renhe xianzhi* (1687), 5.24b–25a. A Ming ritual manual recommends that devotees of Huaguang/Wuxian should prepare a "thaumaturgical altar to the five gods" in their homes, confess their sins, and invoke blessings through incantatory prayers. See *Taishang dongxuan lingbao wuxianguan huaguang benxing miaojing* (HY 1436), 7a.

111. Wang Shizhen, *Xiangzu biji*, 3.6b–7a; Niu Xiu, *Gusheng*, 1.10a; Di Hao, *Tongsu bian*, 19.14b–15a; Wei Song, *Yishi jishi*, 13.9b–10a.

112. In 1371 Zhu Yuanzhang ordered that altars to provide sacrifices for the untended souls of dead soldiers be raised in every rural community in the empire, but the edict makes no mention of Wutong or any other deity: *Qinding xu wenxian tongkao*, 79.3497a–b.

113. The story of Zhu Yuanzhang's dream was often repeated in Qing works (see the citations in note 111), but its authenticity was challenged by Gu Sizhang, *Tufeng lu*, 18.25b–27b; Gan Xi, *Baixia suoyan*, 4.4b; and Yu Yue (1821–1907), *Quyuan zazuan*, 36.5b–6a.

114. *Wujiang xianzhi* (1488), 6.12b; Huang Wei, *Pengchuang leiji*, 5.49a–b; Lu Can, *Gengsibian*, 5.51–54; Yang Xunji, *Suzhoufu zuanxiu shilüe*, 3.9a.

115. Lu Can, *Gengsibian*, 5.51; Lu Rong (1436–94), *Shuyuan zaji*, 8.94.

116. Huang Wei, *Pengchuang leiji*, 5.49a.

117. This cult centered on the figure of Zhou Que, a Hangzhou native who made a pilgrimage to Wuyuan's Wuxian shrine on 4/8 in 1211, but died, at age twenty-four, while in Wuyuan. In 1235, the magistrate of Dexing (Wuyuan's perennial rival in claiming the Wuxian cult) petitioned the court seeking investiture of Zhou in recognition of his aid in protecting the region from the rebellion that broke out in the Wuyi Mountains in 1231, adding that Zhou's spirit subsequently proved responsive to prayers for relief from plague and drought. The request was granted and Zhou was canonized in the same year. Subsequently, shrines were built in his honor both in Dexing and in Hangzhou, and Zhou's image was also included among Wuxian's retinue at the Wuyuan temple. See Fang Hui, "Fudemiao bei" (1300), *Tongjiang xuji*, 36.26a–29a.

118. Qian Xiyan, *Kuaiyuan*, 10.6b–8a, 12.17b–20b; Feng Menglong, *Zhinang quanji*, 8.377. The figures of Lord Ma and Premier Song continued to be associated with Wutong down to the nineteenth century; see chapter 7.

119. Lu Can, *Gengsibian*, 5.51.

120. According to a hostile critic, the tea séance cost a minimum of ten taels,

or more than the annual income of a typical urban laborer. This sum seems exorbitant. See Li Shaowen, *Yunjian zashi,* 2.1b.

121. *Qiantang xianzhi* (1609), waiji, 29a–b.

122. *Gengsibian* is an anthology of tales about the supernatural that Lu, a Suzhou native, collected between 1511 and 1519 as a student preparing for the civil service exams. Lu's antipathy for the Wutong cult is evident throughout his work. Later in life, according to an anecdote recorded by Feng Menglong, Lu was stricken by an illness that the diviner hired by his family identified as having been inflicted by Wutong. Lu scoffed at his family's pleas that he visit the Wutong temple across the street from his house and beseech the god for forgiveness. Instead, Lu invited the deity to strike him dead, vowing that if he still lived after three days he would destroy the shrine. Lu did recover and carried out his promise. Feng Menglong added that Lu's family "to this day no longer worships Wutong," though the anecdote itself betrays how deeply entrenched the Wutong cult was even within the literati. See Feng, *Zhinang quanji,* 8.380. A similar anecdote wherein a retired official reproves his credulous family and demonstrates the superiority of Confucian skeptical rationalism is found in Huang Wei, *Pengchuang leiji,* 5.49b.

123. See "Miss Zhang," Lu Can, *Gengsibian,* 5.53.

124. See "Shen Ning's Wife," ibid., 5.53.

125. "The Jiangyin Rice Merchant's Daughter," ibid., 6.73.

126. "Shen Sheng's Wife," ibid., 5.53.

127. For examples see Lu Rong, *Shuyuan zaji,* 8.103; Zhu Yunming, *Yuguai lu,* 3b–5a; Lang Ying, *Qixiu leigao,* 2: 703; Tian Yiheng, *Liuqing rizha,* 28.13b–14a.

128. T'ien 1988; Elvin 1984.

129. *Gu Su zhi* (1506), 3.40b, 40.27b; Yang Xunji, *Suzhoufu zuanxiu shilüe,* 3.9a.

130. Lu Rong, *Shuyuan zaji,* 15.183. Lu states that the suppression in Changshu was connected with the efforts of Ma Wensheng to elicit imperial endorsement for a campaign of extermination against "profane cults" *(yinci).* While Ma did indeed ask for such an endorsement, his censure was directed specifically against imperial patronage of the Zhenwu cult; he made no mention of Wutong. See Ma Wensheng, "Chenyan zhensu fengji biyi zhidao shi," *Duansu zouyi,* 3.11b–16b. At least some central government officials did take steps to eradicate Wutong/Wuxian as a deviant cult. In 1491 the president of the Board of Punishments in Beijing ordered the removal of a Wuxian temple from the precincts of the board's administrative offices. See Lin Jun, "Peng Huian gong Shao shendaobei," in Jiao Hong, comp., *Guochao xianzheng lu,* 44.59a.

131. Lu Can, *Gengsibian,* 5.54. According to a later source the deity took revenge on the prefect by possessing his favorite concubine and causing her to fall ill. The prefect was greatly troubled and on the verge of rescinding his order when a doctor came forward who was able to concoct a prescription to cure the woman and drive off the Wutong spirit. See Chu Renhuo, *Jianhu baji,* 4.9b.

132. *Huating xianzhi* (1521), 9.6a.

133. *Jiangyin xianzhi* (1548), 8.3b.

134. Some Jiangnan participants, such as Lu Can, continued to wage one-

man campaigns. Tian Rucheng (*Xihu youlan zhiyu*, 26.477) claimed to have destroyed dozens of Wutong shrines over his lifetime (presumably in his native Hangzhou). To my knowledge the only conversion of a Wuxian temple into a more conventional shrine in late Ming times occurred at Wujiang in 1605. See *Wujiang xianzhi* (1747), 7.13b.

135. *Changshu sizhi* (1618), 6.2b. The epithet Fude was attached to Wusheng in a Daoist tract, the *Dahui jingci miaole tianzun shuo fude wusheng jing* (*HY* 1183).

136. Wang Zhijian, "Wutongwang bian," in *Wu xianzhi* (1642), 21.21a–b. Gui Zhuang identified a Wusheng temple in his native Kunshan as the seat of a "profane cult," but nonetheless succumbed to the urgings of his fellow townsmen and composed a dedicatory inscription for the temple. Gui pronounced himself "unable to contravene the sentiments of the local community." See Gui, "Chongjian Wushengmiao menyin," *Gui Zhuang ji*, 10.511–13.

137. *Gu Su zhi* (1506), 27.25a.

138. *Taixuan fengdu heilü yige*, in *DFHY* 267.14b–15b. On the role of this text in the Daoist elaboration of the Wuxian cult, see Cedzich 1995: 183–84.

139. A heterogenous collection of materials related to Marshal Ma is included in *Lingguan Ma yuanshuai bifa*, in *DFHY, juan* 222–26. These texts make no reference to Wuxian, but the phrase "Huaguang Wutong" appears in the incantation used to summon Marshal Ma. See ibid., 222.4a. Marshal Ma's feast day, like that of Wuxian, fell on 9/28. See *Zhushen shengdanri yuxia ji*, 4b.

140. Cedzich 1995: 184–88. In what is perhaps the earliest datable reference to Marshal Ma, an incident said to have taken place in Jiangxi in 1295, two village ritual masters *(fashi)* summoned Marshal Ma along with Marshal Zhao (i.e., Zhao Gongming) to exorcise a *shanxiao* demon that had taken possession of a young girl. See *Huhai xinwen yijian xuzhi*, houji, 1.165.

141. *Beifang Zhenwu zushi xuantian shangdi chushen zhizhuan*, 3.15a–21b, 4.12b–18b, 4.21b. See also the translation by Seaman 1987: 150–53, 189–90, 200.

142. Liu Ts'un-yan has drawn attention to the fact that General Ma Shan in the sixteenth-century novel *Investiture of the Gods (Fengshen yanyi)* is apparently derived from the character of Huaguang and should be understood as a manifestation of Marshal Ma. See Liu 1962: 176–77.

143. Liu Ts'un-yan, comparing *Journey to the North* and its companion *Journey to the South* to *The Investiture of the Gods*, finds the latter work to be much more sophisticated in its assimilation of Buddhist and Daoist religion. Liu also pronounces *Journey to the South*, in which Huaguang reenacts the extremely popular story of Mulian's rescue of his mother from hell, to be "unrefined both in sense and writing." See Liu 1962: 165–66. Recently Seaman, in confronting the knotty problem of the authorship of *Journey to the North*, has suggested that the book should be understood as a revealed text produced by a spirit-writing cult. See Seaman 1987: 12–39.

144. *Yang Donglai xiansheng piping Xiyou ji*, scene 8, pp. 34–36. Although the extant late Ming edition of this drama claims authorship by a fourteenth-century dramatist, modern scholars consider it a product of the early sixteenth century but think it written no later than 1568. See Dudbridge 1970: 76–80.

145. The authorship and dating of this work, like that of *Journey to the North,* is unclear, but Cedzich (1995: 142) has provided evidence that they were both published before 1590. Subsequently these two works, together with two others, were published together as *The Four Journeys (Siyouji),* but the relationship between them has not yet been studied in any detail. It is possible that the four novels were already published together as *The Four Journeys* in the late Ming, but earliest extant editions of *The Four Journeys* date from the early nineteenth century. The full title of the earliest known copy of *Journey to the South,* the 1631 edition in the British Museum, is *Quanxiang Huaguang tianwang nanyou zhizhuan* (A Fully Illustrated Chronicle of the Journey to the South by the Heavenly King Huaguang). The title page bears the legend *Quanxiang Wuxian lingguan dadi Huaguang tianwang zhuan* (A Fully Illustrated Narrative of the Great Thearch and Divine Agent of Five Manifestations, the Heavenly King Huaguang), which explicitly associates the novel's protagonist with Wuxian, identified by the title by which he is known in contemporary Daoist scriptures. See Liu Ts'un-yan 1967: 64–65, 167, 188–99.

146. *Quanxiang Huaguang tianwang nanyou zhizhuan,* passim. For a detailed study of *Journey to the South* and its relationship to Huaguang and the Wutong/Wuxian cults, see Cedzich 1995.

147. *Xiyou ji,* 96.1088. See the translation in Anthony Yu 1983, 4: 357–58.

148. *Sanjiao yuanliu soushen daquan,* 5.215–17.

149. Shen Defu, *Wanli yehuo bian,* 25.648. See also Zhuang Yifu 1982, 2: 630.

150. See Zhuang Yifu 1982, 3: 1582.

151. "Jia shenxian danao Huaguang miao," in Feng Menglong, *Jingshi tongyan,* 27.411–19.

152. Cedzich 1995: 203–13.

153. *Quanxiang Huaguang tianwang nanyou zhizhuan,* 4.28a.

154. *Sanjiao yuanliu soushen daquan,* 5.217.

155. *Tingzhou fuzhi* (1527), 9.13a; *Guihua xianzhi* (1614), 3.7a; *Ninghua xianzhi* (1684), 7.9b.

156. *Qiantang xianzhi* (1609), waiji, 29a–b.

157. Hansen (1990: 140–43) argues that merchants probably raised Wuxian temples in the trading cities to which they traveled. The actual founders of Wutong and Wuxian temples mentioned in Song sources included monks, officials, prominent local lineages, and ordinary local inhabitants, but merchants are not singled out as patrons of the cult. There is no direct evidence that merchants from Huizhou played any role in the spread of branch temples affiliated with the ancestral shrine at Wuyuan, and in any case belief in Wutong's powers was widespread in south China well before Wutong was canonized as Wuxian.

CHAPTER 7. THE ENCHANTMENT OF WEALTH

1. *She zhi* (1609), 5, fengtu, 12a; subsequently quoted in Gu Yanwu, *Tianxia junguo libing shu,* 9.76a–b.

2. Sakai 1970; Brokaw 1991.

3. Berling 1985.

4. Brief surveys of the gods of wealth can be found in Alexeiev 1928; Day

1940: 113–16; Maspero 1928/1981: 120–21; C. K. Yang 1961: 76–80; Kubō 1986: 236–40.

5. Cammann 1964: 42–43. The triad of the gods of happiness, emolument, and longevity emerged as a distinct configuration by the early Ming. See Fong 1983.

6. Wang Zhijian, "Wutong wang bian," *Wu xianzhi* (1642), 21.21a–b.

7. Hamashima 1983, 1993, 2001; von Glahn forthcoming. Hamashima (2001: 88) has concluded that the *zongguan* cults (he uses *zongguan* as a generic label for local tutelary cults in Jiangnan) emerged only at the very end of the Yuan and especially during the Ming dynasty, contending that claims made in Ming-Qing sources for origins in the Song period are all spurious. However, at least some of these cults (for example, the Sire Li cult, discussed in chapter 5) can indeed be traced back to the Southern Song period.

8. Hamashima 1993: 515–16, 2001: 16–25.

9. Like Wutong, Commandant Jin and his cult were typically classified as "uncanonical," if not "profane." See Lu Can, *Gengsibian*, 2.20; *Wuqing wenxian* (1688), 3 fengsu, 8b; *Wujun Fuli zhi* (1765), 15.6a.

10. The mythology of Fierce General Liu has been explored in depth by Sawada 1982: 118–35; Hamashima 1990a, 2001: 53–65; Che and Zhou 1992.

11. Qian Xiyan, *Kuaiyuan*, 12.16b–17a. On Shutou Wusheng and other appellations for Wusheng, see also Tian Yiheng, *Liuqing rizha*, 28.15a.

12. *Wu xianzhi* (1690), 29.9a. On the incorporation of Wusheng into domestic worship in the Hang-Jia-Hu region, see von Glahn forthcoming.

13. *Tangxi zhilüe* (1767), xia.17a–19a.

14. *Anji zhouzhi* (1750), 7.7b; *Shuanglin xuji* (1819), cited in *Shuanglin zhenzhi* (1917), 15.8a.

15. *Anji zhouzhi* (1750), 7.8a; *Shuanglin xuji* (1819), cited in *Shuanglin zhenzhi* (1917), 15.8a.

16. Qian Xiyan, *Kuaiyuan*, 12.17a–b; Ling Mengchu, "Li Kerang jing da konghan, Liu Yuanpu shuang sheng guizi," *Pai'an jingqi*, 20.341.

17. The earliest reference to Canhua Wusheng is found in *Chongde xianzhi* (1611).

18. *Wujun Fuli zhi* (1703), 5 fengsu, 9a; 5 shenmiao, 3b; *Wujun Fuli zhi* (1765), 15.2b.

19. *Changshu sizhi* (1618), 6.9b–10a. In eighteenth-century Jiangnan Wufang xiansheng temples were in some cases known as Five Transcendents Temples.

20. Wang Zhideng, *Wushe bian*.

21. *Wujun Fuli zhi* (1703), 5 fengsu, 10a.

22. "Li Shaofu simu Fengshi," in *Xiugu chunrong*, "Xinhua zhisui," 859.

23. See *Zhengyi xuantan Zhao Yuanshuai bifa*, DFHY, 232.5b, 233.17a–b; *Zhengyi longhu xuantan dafa*, DFHY, 236.4a–b.

24. *Shenxiao qianwen zhibing juefa*, DFHY, 221.1b.

25. See, for example, the vernacular novel *The Jujube Spell*, a fantastic tale loosely based on the life of the Song Daoist priest Sa Shoujian, published in 1603: *Zhouzao ji*, shang.22a, 23a.

26. Johnson 1989: 9–17.

27. Zhang Dai, *Taoan mengyi*, 6.59. For a translation of the relevant passage, see Johnson 1989: 9.

28. In this instance the people were reading the legend in the literal sense of the word. Actually, the *fu* graph was meant as a place name, indicating that the coins had been minted at the imperial mint in Fuzhou, the capital of Fujian province.

29. *Zidicun xiaozhi* (1718), in *Jiangnan difang xiangtuzhi congbian*, 1: 183.

30. Tian Rucheng, *Xihu youlan zhiyu*, 26.476–77; repeated in his *Youguai lu*, 3b, and *Qiantang xianzhi* (1609), waiji, 31a.

31. *Changzhou xianzhi* (1598), 1.8b.

32. See, for example, Fan Chengda's preface to his set of poems on New Year's festivities among Suzhou peasants: "Layue cuntian yuefu shishou," *Shihu jushi shiji* 30, in *Fan Shihu ji*, 409–10.

33. *Wujiang xianzhi* (1685), 5 fengsu, 15b; *Jiading xianzhi* (1673), 4.14a. This ritual was dedicated to other local tutelary spirits as well, as another contemporary gazetteer from Jiading county, a major cotton-producing district, attests: "Those engaged in trade and commerce make offerings of 'paper horses' [*zhima*] to *tudi* spirits on the days after the new and full moons. A local proverb says, 'Come the month's second and sixteenth day, the *tudi* spirit dines on meat' [*chuer shiliu, tudi chirou*]." See *Zidicun xiaozhi* (1718), 52.

34. In the famous story "The Oil Peddler Courts the Courtesan," a brothel madam greedily sizes up the earning potential of a beautiful young courtesan in terms of *shaoge lishi*. See Feng Menglong, "Maiyoulang duzhan huakui," *Xingshi hengyan*, 3.37. In another story an oil peddler, exultant after discovering a parcel of silver in a privy, exclaims to his mother, "We poor tradesmen, having effortlessly acquired this great fortune, tomorrow will *shaoge lishi*, using it as the capital for our oil-peddling business." See Feng Menglong, "Chen yushi qiaokan jin chaidian," in *Gujin xiaoshuo*, 2.1a.

35. *Changshu sizhi* (1618), 3.31b.

36. Feng Menglong, "Jin lingshi meipai chou xiutong," *Jingshi tongyan*, 15.22a.

37. *Changzhou fuzhi* (1694), 9.8a–b.

38. *Renhe xianzhi* (1687), 5.24b–25a. In Jiaxing, too, offerings were presented to Wutong on the fifth day of the New Year. See *Jiaxing xianzhi* (1637), 15.20a.

39. Tang Bin, "Jinyue shi" (1686), *Tangzi yishu*, 9B.37a–b.

40. The pagoda is all that remains of the Lengqiesi Monastery. The present-day temple buildings date only to the late nineteenth century. For the architectural history of the pagoda, see Wang Deqing 1983.

41. Xu Mingshi, *Hengqi lu* (1629), 4.5a–6a.

42. Qian Xiyan, *Kuaiyuan*, 12.16a–b; see also *Wu xianzhi* (1642), 21.21a.

43. Zhang Shiwei, "Shangfangshan Lengqiesi tabei" (1640) (stele located *in situ* at the Lengqiesi Monastery, Mount Shangfang, Suzhou).

44. Niu Xiu, *Gusheng*, 1.10a; Miao Tong, "Hui Shangfangshan shenmiao ji," *Wu xianzhi* (1690), 29.9b.

45. Miao Tong, "Hui Shangfangshan shenmiao ji," in *Wu xianzhi* (1690), 29.9b.

46. Qian Xiyan, *Kuaiyuan,* 11.30a–b; see also Miao Tong, "Hui Shangfang-shan shenmiao ji," in *Wu xianzhi* (1690), 29.9b. This feature of the cult recalls a story about the Shrine of the God of the Ji River (Jiduci) in Henan related in several early sixteenth-century records. The God of the Ji River had acquired a reputation for making loans to mortals. Those who wished to borrow from the god's hoard first cast divination blocks to determine whether or not the god would grant the request. If a positive answer was received, the supplicant wrote out a loan contract specifying the amount of silver desired and tossed it into the pool before the temple; the correct amount of silver would then float to the surface. This silver, when used in trade, reputedly brought twice the normal profit. At the expiration of the contract the borrower would return the amount of silver he borrowed, plus interest, by throwing it back into the pool. The original contract would float up in return. See Zhu Yunming, *Yuguai lu,* 13b–14a; Lu Can, *Shuoting,* shang.7a–b. An early thirteenth-century account also notes the practice of tossing offerings into the pool at this temple, though the offerings consisted of spirit money and wine rather than silver. But it was also said that silver wine goblets and incense boxes thrown into the pool would float to the surface if the god approved the supplicant's prayer, and that wine drunk from goblets recovered in this fashion would forever taste sweet. The silver wine goblets perhaps inspired the later practice of obtaining silver from the pool. See Yuan Haowen, *Xu Yijian zhi,* 1.22–23.

47. *Yuanbao* (inaugural treasure) refers to the fifty-ounce silver ingot that had become a standard unit for, among other things, forwarding tax receipts from localities to the central government.

48. Cai Limin 1992. This ethnographic report is primarily based on interviews with local inhabitants conducted in 1989.

49. Hou 1975: 35–38, 68–69, 97 ff.

50. Lauwaert 1990.

51. Sakai 1960; Brokaw 1991.

52. See Handlin Smith 1987; Fuma 1997; Liang Qizi 1997.

53. McMahon 1988: 9–10; Berling 1985.

54. I take exception here to the views put forth in Gates 1987.

55. *Yantang jianwen zaji,* 28–29. The author of this work commented that greed and concupiscence prevailed in the realm of the spirits no less than in the world of mortals. Among the gods only Guandi was impervious to the temptations of the flesh.

56. *Shuyi ji* (Dongxuan zhuren), shang, 16b–17a. In another tale, a greedy Fujian fishmonger worshiped an unnamed "evil spirit" *(xieshen)* who brought him great wealth. While the fishmonger was out tending to his business, though, the spirit seduced his wife. Upon discovering her adultery the fishmonger, unwilling to anger the spirit and lose his good fortune, decided to do nothing. The spirit later seduced the wife of the fishmonger's eldest son. When the spirit stole into the bedroom of the younger son's wife, a pious girl who always carried a statuette of Guandi, the warrior god himself appeared in full armor and slew the philandering demon. See Gan Daiyun, comp., *Wudi quanshu,* 7.53b–54a. The compiler of this work noted that in families who worshiped such evil spirits the husband and wife slept in separate rooms in order to provide for the spirits' sexual satisfaction. Ibid., 7.54b–55a.

57. Pu Songling, *Liaozhai zhiyi*, 10.1417–20.

58. Sangren 1987: 150–52.

59. For a more thorough study of Tang Bin's campaign against popular religion in the context of early Qing regulation of religious worship, see Jiang Zhushan 1995a, 1995b.

60. Yao Tinglin (1628–after 1697), *Linian ji*, in *Qingdai riji huichao*, 122; Gu Gongxie, *Danwu biji*, 169–70.

61. Tang Bin, "Qing hui yinci shu," *Tangzi yishu*, 2.78b–81b.

62. Tang Bin, "Qing hui yinci shu," *Tangzi yishu*, 2.78b–81b; "Jin'e xieyin yi zheng renxin yi hou fengsu shi," ibid., 9B.32b; Ye Mengzhu, *Yueshi bian*, 4.98–99; *Changzhou xianzhi* (1765), 31.2a–4a; Niu Xiu, *Gusheng*, 1.10a. The surviving Wuxian temple within the city of Suzhou, tainted by association with the profane popular cult, was also desecrated at this time.

63. *Wuyuan xianzhi* (1694), 5.18a–b; *Gujin tushu jicheng*, zhifangdian, 792.22b.

64. The same two features of the Wutong cult are also stressed in Niu Xiu, *Gusheng*, 1.10a.

65. Miao Tong, "Hui Shangfangshan shenmiao ji," in *Wu xianzhi* (1690), 29.8b–10b.

66. Tang, "Qing hui yinci shu," in *Tangzi yishu*, 2.78b–81b. The willingness of even patrician families to offer daughters to Wutong was later cited as the chief motive behind Tang's suppression of the cult. See Poe shanren (pseud.), *Yehang chuan*, 7.8a.

67. Medical experts regarded dreams of sexual congress with spirits as a result of being deprived of a normal sexual life; thus, ladies of the imperial harem, nuns, and widows were seen as particularly susceptible. However, the range of symptoms associated with this affliction in medical texts generally coincides with the symptoms attributed to possession by Wutong, with one addition: ghost (i.e., false) pregnancies. See Qi Zhongfu, *Nüke baiwen*, shang, 60b–62a. (I am indebted to Charlotte Furth for bringing this work to my attention.) As we have seen (p. 182 and table 2 above), the *shanxiao* and "one-legged Wutong" were blamed for deformed births in Song times, but this particular motif does not appear in the Ming-Qing cult.

68. Lu Can, *Gengsibian*, 5.51.

69. Feng Menglong, *Zhinang quanji*, 7.375.

70. Identical versions of this story are found in Wu Chichang, *Kechuang xianhua*, 8.216–18, and Xuan Ding, *Yeyu qiudeng lu*, sanji, 1.10a–11a.

71. A local historian of Nanjing reported the case of an unmarried daughter of a Nanjing doctor. Soon after dreaming that the city god spoke to her and claimed her as his wife, the young woman died. The townspeople subsequently venerated her as the consort of the city god and placed her statue in the rear vestibule of the city god temple. A similar incident occurred again in 1827, but in this case it was the god of wealth who took a young woman as his bride. See Gan Xi, *Baixia suoyan*, 3.22b. For a general overview of the motif of marriage to the gods, see Sawada 1982: 250–77.

72. Zhao Yi, *Gaiyu congkao*, 35.773–74.

73. Studies of modern female spirit mediums make no reference to sexual

congress with spirits. In Hong Kong, personal tragedy—such as the death of a spouse or children—propels women into the vocation of shamanism; the deceased family members serve as the essential link to the supernatural world. Women who become spirit mediums are believed to retain "fairy bones," ethereal bonds to the realm of spirits that in normal people are ruptured at birth. Interestingly, it is widely feared that unless these bonds are severed before marriage, marriage itself may cause death. See Potter 1974: 225–28.

74. *Wujun Fuli zhi* (1703), 5, "shenmiao," 3b; *Nanxiang zhenzhi* (1782), 12.9a; *Zhixi xiaozhi* (1788), 4.24b.

75. *Changshu xianzhi* (1687), 9.28b–29a.

76. Niu Xiu, *Gusheng*, 1.10a; Ye Mengzhu, *Yueshi bian*, 4.99.

77. Yuan Lian, *Shuyin congshuo*, 1.22b–23a; Qian Siyuan, *Wumen bucheng* (ca. 1771–1803), 8.13b; Zhao Yi, *Gaiyu congkao*, 35.773. *Suzhou fuzhi* (1748), 79.39a–b, quotes Lu Can's description of the cult at length, suggesting that it was still very much alive.

78. Most were converted into shrines dedicated to Wenchang, patron deity of schools and success in the civil service examinations. For a partial list of conversions of Wutong temples in Jiangnan during the late 1680s, see Jiang Zhushan 1995b: 103–4.

79. See von Glahn forthcoming.

80. Xuan Ding, *Yeyu qiudeng lu*, sanji, 1.11b.

81. Gan Xi, *Baixia suoyan*, 1.17b.

82. *Wujiang xianzhi* (1747), 58.31a; *Pingwang zhi* (1840), 5.7b.

83. *Zhenze xianzhi* (1746), 25.6a.

84. *Zhouzhuang zhenzhi* (1882), 6.14b.

85. Zheng Yuanqing, *Hu lu* (ca. 1700), cited in *Wucheng xianzhi* (1746), 13.2b–3a; repeated in *Huzhou fuzhi* (1879), 29.25a. Another nineteenth-century Huzhou gazetteer repeats the same passage and notes that this custom had become even more prevalent in recent times. See *Nanxun zhenzhi* (1840), 23.3b. Yet another Huzhou gazetteer refers to the same sacrifices on the second and sixteenth days of the month in connection with Wutong alone. See *Changxing xianzhi* (1805), 14.8a. Commandant Jin also figured in the worship of wealth gods on the fifth day of the New Year in Wuxi. See Huang Ang, *Xi Jin shi xiaolu* (1752), 1.20b.

86. *Tangxi zhilüe* (1767), xia.17b–19b; *Tangxi zhi* (1881), 6.13a.

87. *Shuanglin xuji* (1819), quoted in *Shuanglin zhenzhi* (1917), 15.8a.

88. Jiang Zhushan (1995b: 110–11; 1997: 207–9), criticizing my earlier article on this subject (von Glahn 1991), argues that state power had a strong influence on curbing the Wutong cult, and emphasizes in this respect the greater power of the Qing state compared to the Ming. I hold to my opinion that although the Qing state had some success in suppressing public temples dedicated to Wutong, it failed to eradicate private worship of and belief in Wutong.

89. Mao Xianglin, *Moyu lu*, 3.7a. A nineteenth-century native of Suzhou observed that anyone who wished to ask favors of the gods invariably included Wutong's subordinates, Lord Ma and Premier Song, in their prayers. Local lore maintained that when Tang Bin destroyed the Wutong temple at Mount Shang-

fang only the images of these two figures remained untouched, reportedly because the temple warden identified them as gods of wealth. The survival of the two cult figures undoubtedly owed more to their status as surrogate gods of wealth than any official dispensation, however. See Qian Yong, *Lüyuan conghua,* 15.399. In recent times Lord Ma has also been called "Commandant Felicitous Ma" (Ma Fu zongguan). See Gu Xijia 1990: 128.

90. *Fenhu xiaozhi* (1847), 6.3a; *Jinshan xianzhi* (1878), 17.3a; *Changhua xianzhi* (1924), 4.4b; *Nanhui xianzhi* (1929), 8.6b. At the turn of the twentieth century the French missionary Henri Doré reported that Wuxian was occasionally given pride of place on domestic altars in the Hangzhou area. See Doré 1916, 4: 418.

91. Gan Xi, *Baixia suoyan,* 6.4b.

92. Stories about Wutong in nineteenth-century anecdotal collections center on the theme of debauchery rather than the attainment of wealth. See, for examples, Zhu Lian, *Mingzhai xiaoshi,* 1.4a–b; Yongna jushi (pseud.), *Zhiwen lu,* 12.10a–11a; Changbai haogezi (pseud.), *Yingchuang yicao,* 4.1a–4b.

93. *Pingwang zhi* (1840), 12.9b–10a; *Yuanhe Weiting zhi* (1848), 3.31a.

94. Jiang Zhushan 1995b: 100–104.

95. Yuan Mei, *Zi buyu,* 8.195.

96. Yuqian, "Jin Wutong yinci bing shiwu xieshuo shi" (1835), in *Mianyizhai xu cungao,* 7.47b–48a; "Jin geshu Wutong dengxiang yinci shi" (1839), in ibid., 15.49a–52a.

97. "Leshi yongjin Lengqie Shan Wutong yinci shi" (1839), in ibid., 16.6a–8b.

98. The primacy of female spirit mediums as intercessors in worship of Wutong is repeatedly stressed in Qing accounts. See, e.g., *Jinshan xianzhi* (1752), 17.3a; *Kun Xin liangxian zhi* (1824), 1.22b; *Fenhu xiaozhi* (1847), 6.3a–b.

99. The *jiaoxi* rite was apparently similar to the "dispelling fright" *(shoujing)* rite that had long been associated with the Wutong cult. See chapter 6.

100. Commenting on Yuqian's campaign against the Wutong cult, Zheng Guangzu likewise observed that the cult encompassed activities like tea séances *(chayan),* offerings of spirit money, dispelling fright *(shoujing),* and borrowing money from the god. See Zheng, *Yiban lu,* zashu, 3.2a–b. Zheng testified that despite repeated prohibitions since Tang Bin's day, secret worship of Wutong cult had continued at the main shrine at Mount Shangfang, and in his native Changshu as well. See *Yiban lu,* 5.2a–3a.

101. Eighteenth-century dedications attest to enthusiastic patronage of the Wuxian God-of-Wealth Temple by the capital's jewelry, antiques, and other guilds as early as the 1730s, but they profess ignorance of when the temple was founded, nor do they mention Wuxian's ambiguous ancestry. See "Wuxian fuwang caishenmiao beiji" (1756), in Beijing tushuguan 1990, 71: 84; "Liuxiangcun caishenmiao beiji" (1780), ibid., 74: 66; "Wuxian caishenmiao bei" (1790), ibid., 75: 146; "Wuxian caishenmiao beiji" (1807), ibid., 78: 2. This temple was still recognized as the principal god of wealth temple in Beijing in the early twentieth century. See Sawada 1982: 48.

102. Yu Jiao, *Mengchang zazhu,* 1.2–3.

103. Berling 1985.

104. Yü Ying-shih 1987b: 136–66.

105. The coalescence of a bourgeois culture that combined mercantile wealth with Confucian ethics and notions of status in the early Qing period has not yet been studied in depth. For preliminary and highly suggestive investigations, see Terada 1972, esp. 283–96; Yü Ying-shih 1987b; Zhang Zhengming 1995: 134–62; Lufrano 1997. The development of a cohesive "urban class" and "guild-centered elite activism" in politics and social welfare in the commercial hub of Hankou during the nineteenth century has been amply documented in Rowe 1984. Rowe refers to this process as "embourgeoisement" (p. 345), and also speaks of the formation of an "urban class" (his translation of the Chinese word *shimin*), but neither term is vested with precise analytical meaning.

106. Guandi, of course, enjoyed widespread homage long before the eighteenth century, but was seen as a special patron of Shanxi and Shaanxi natives. The earliest guildhalls built by Shanxi-Shaanxi merchants usually took the form of temples to Guandi. Shanxi banks explicitly claimed Guandi as their ancestor and patron, though in Qing times Guandi was also the chief cult figure in guildhalls founded by merchants from Huizhou and elsewhere. See Niida 1951: 19, 54, 65, 75, 95. Barend ter Haar suggests that the association of Guandi with Shaanxi merchants originated in patronage of the cult by Xiezhou (Shaanxi) salt merchants in the Song. See ter Haar 2000.

107. Gu Sizhang, *Tufeng lu*, 18.25b–27b.

108. *Shuanglin zhenzhi* (1917), 15.10a. For more detail on the rituals of Greeting the Pathfinder, see Zhang Yongyao et al. 1994: 60–62.

109. Sawada 1969: 94–95. At the end of the Qing worshiping societies in Hangzhou performed the ritual of "borrowing inaugural treasure" from the god of wealth at Mount Wuyun at Qingming, the religious festival marking the beginning of the sericulture season. See *Hangsu yiqing suijin*, 9–10. A slightly later work makes clear that the ritual at Mount Wuyun was addressed to none other than Huaguang. See Hu Puan 1923, 2: 227.

110. Zhang Yongyao et al. 1994: 61; Ou Yue 1992: 131; Wu Zude 1992: 116.

111. Gu Lu, *Qingjia lu*, 1.9a–b. This identification had been advanced by Gu Sizhang at the turn of the century (see *Tufeng lu*, 18.25b–27b), but the compilers of a Nanjing gazetteer had categorically rejected this "recent theory" a half-century before. See *Jiangning xianzhi* (1748), 10.5a. Undoubtedly the effort to connect the Wulu caishen cult to Gu Yewang owed to the fact that Gu's tomb was located at Stone Lake. See Pan Chengzhang, *Songling wenxian*, 1.11b. The cult of the god of wealth was also traced to a number of other historical and pseudo-historical figures from Jiangnan's past in Gu Zhentao, *Wumen biaoyin*, 11.151–52.

112. Scattered references to the founding of god-of-wealth temples during the Ming period appear in Qing gazetteers but cannot be corroborated by contemporary records. Overall, the eighteenth century stands out as a watershed in the founding of god-of-wealth temples. For example, residents of Puyuanzhen (Jiaxing) added a god-of-wealth sanctuary to the town's *tudi* temple in 1749, while the town's cloth merchants pooled funds to build another god-of-wealth sanctuary as part of the reconstruction of the town's main Daoist temple in 1773: *Puchuan suowenji* (1813), 2.15b, 18a.

113. Gu Zhentao, *Wumen biaoyin,* 11.151–52.

114. *Wu xianzhi* (1933), 34.17a.

115. The earliest reference to the god of wealth as central icon of a trade guild appears in an inscription commemorating the construction of a guildhall by Suzhou's Changzhou butchers guild in 1762. See "Zhuhang gongjian Piling gongshu bei," in Suzhou lishi bowuguan, ed., 1981: 250–51. In the relatively few cases where epigraphic records identify the icons housed in the guildhalls of Suzhou and Shanghai, generic gods of wealth are only rarely mentioned (in four out of twenty-three cases in Shanghai, and two of thirty-three cases in Suzhou). Over the course of the nineteenth and early twentieth centuries, as common trade displaced common origin as the organizing principle of merchant guilds, generic gods of wealth appeared more often as objects of worship in guildhalls. Niida Noboru identified the god of wealth, in his various manifestations, as the primary or secondary icon in eleven out of twenty-six Beijing guildhalls he investigated during the 1940s. See Niida 1951: 128–29.

116. *Huangjing zhilüe* (ca. 1790), cited in *Huangjing zhigao* (1940), 1.9a. See also *Zhenyang xianzhi* (1744), 1.9a; *Nanxun zhenzhi* (1859), 23.11b; *Shuanglin zhenzhi* (1917), 9.4a. Wulutang temples are listed, but not explicitly associated with Wutong, in *Shenghu zhi* (1716), shang.53a, *Pingwang zhi* (1840), 5.9a–b, *Wujun Fuli zhi* (1765), 15.5b, *Shatou lizhi* (1740 ms.), 2.12b, *Zhenze zhenzhi* (1844), 6.14b, and *Nanxiang zhenzhi* (1782), 10.12b.

117. In addition to Marshal Ma and Zhao Gongming this quartet included Wen Qiong and Guandi. See *Qingwei Ma Zhao Wen Guan sishuai dafa,* in DFHY (*HY* 1210), 36. Rituals associated with each of the four are recorded in *juan* 222–26, 232–40, 253–54, and 259–60, respectively, of the same work.

118. *Zhengyi xuantan Zhao yuanshuai bifa,* in DFHY, 232.1a–2b. For He He as intercessors in the acquisition of wealth, see the incantations preserved in ibid., 232.14b–15a, 233.8a, 233.12a, 234.18a.

119. *Sanjiao yuanliu soushen daquan,* 3.20a.

120. Xu Zhonglin, *Fengshen yanyi,* 99.994.

121. The earliest reference to worship of Zhao Gongming specifically as a god of wealth dates only from 1830. See Gu Lu, *Qingjia lu,* 3.11b. In this instance Zhao was worshiped on his feast day, the fifteenth day of the third month, rather than at New Year's. Even though Zhao and his assistants later are linked to Wulu caishen, they clearly derived from independent origins. See Nakamura 1983: 374–75.

122. On worship of Zhao Gongming as the Martial God of Wealth in twentieth-century Jiangnan, see Zhang Yongyao et al. 1994: 60; Wu Zude 1992: 115–16; Ou Yue 1992: 130–31.

123. The "precious scroll" of this title denotes a broad genre of religious literature known as "precious scrolls" *(baojuan).* The earliest *baojuan* were products of Buddhist religious sects, and in the late Ming period the genre was closely associated with messianic and prophetic sectarian religion. From the late seventeenth century, though, *baojuan* literature lost contact with its sectarian roots and instead became didactic works for the propagation of conventional ethics and piety compounded from Buddhist, Daoist, and Confucian teachings. *The Precious Scroll of the God of Wealth* clearly belongs to this later phase of the genre.

On the evolution of *baojuan*, see Overmyer 1985; on the early development of the sectarian *baojuan*, see Overmyer 1999.

124. The five sons are born into five different families. Later on, however, they are brought together and recognize themselves as brothers, and the virtuous elderly couple as their real parents.

125. *Caishen baojuan* (undated ms., Beijing University Library). This work is identical to the 1824 manuscript, now held in the Waseda University Library, catalogued in Sawada 1975: 143–44. Other nineteenth- and twentieth-century manuscript copies of this text are catalogued in Li Shiyu 1961: 4, no. 31.

126. On the common trope of dispensing charity to obtain sons in late Ming literature, see Lauwaert 1990.

127. I borrow the term "yangification" from Sangren 1987: 183. Sangren employs the word to describe the process whereby female deities such as Guanyin and Mazu become identified with the established order of society. At the same time, he emphasizes that such female deities occupy an ambiguous position in the patriarchal pantheon and can still serve as vehicles for repudiating the principle of hierarchical subordination. In the case of the modern god of wealth, the disavowal of such ambiguity is more complete.

128. See von Glahn 1996.

129. Von Glahn 2003a.

130. There is a rapidly growing literature on social welfare institutions in the Qing period. See especially Liang Qizi 1997 and Fuma Susumu 1997. The significance of price movements in the Qing is still a subject of much debate, though the stability of secular trends in the eighteenth century in contrast to the sixteenth and seventeenth centuries is generally acknowledged. For a recent review, see Kishimoto 1997: 11–73.

131. Zhejiang minsu xuehui 1986: 66 (in reference to worship of Wusheng in Hangzhou prefecture).

132. Jin 1995: 65–78.

133. *Xiwu canlüe*, cited in *Huzhou fuzhi* (1874), 31.23a. *Shimen xianzhi* (1879), 10.9a, notes that local sericulturalists were extremely diligent in their sacrifices to Canhua wusheng, and went as far as sacrificing a chicken to the deity at the time of the silkworms' "big sleep" *(damian)*.

134. Day 1940: 161–62, 213. The association of these Wusheng deities with the Wutong cult is further substantiated by Day's identification of Huaguang as "Lord of Silkworm Gods." See ibid., p. 212.

135. Jin Tianlin 1990.

136. Gu Xijia 1990: 123, table 1. *Tanfo* is the colloquial name given to these rituals in the Wu dialect of Jiangnan. See Jiang Bin, ed., 1992: 111.

137. Cai Limin 1992; personal observations during my two visits to the Mount Shangfang temple in 1991 and 1998.

138. This manipulation of the symbolism of Tang Bin in service to the Mount Shangfang cult calls into question Jiang Zhushan's contention (1997: 208–9) that popular veneration of Tang Bin in the Qing period should be read as evidence of acceptance of the Confucian tenet that "deviance will never triumph over correctness" *(xie busheng zheng)*.

CONCLUSION

1. This proposition originated with Piet van der Loon (1977: 168). Most scholars of Chinese religion (including myself) abjure shamanism as a useful concept in the context of Chinese religion but nonetheless endorse the essential thrust of van der Loon's argument, which is that the principal function of Chinese religion is to evoke blessings and exorcise demons through ritual action. See Schipper 1985c: 32; Dean 1993: 17; Davis 2001: 1–4

2. Davis 2001: 1–2.

3. Hamashima 2001: 101–3.

4. Davis 2001: 78.

5. Duara 1988.

6. Katz 1995: 113–16.

Bibliography

PRIMARY SOURCES

Anji zhouzhi 安吉州志. 1750.

Baixia suoyan 白下瑣言. Gan Xi 甘熙. 1847. 1926 rpt. of 1890 ed.

Baize jingguai tu 白澤精怪圖. Dunhuang ms., Pelliot no. 2682. In *Dunhuang baozang* 敦煌寶藏, 123: 287–90. Taibei: Xinwenfeng chuban gongsi, 1981–86.

Baize tu 白澤圖. In Ma Guohan 馬國翰, *Yuhan shanfang jiyishu* 玉函山房輯佚書. 1874.

Bamin tongzhi 八閩通志. Huang Zhongzhao 黃仲昭. 1491. Fuzhou: Fujian renmin chubanshe, 1989.

Baopuzi neipian jiaoshi 抱朴子内篇校釋. Ge Hong 葛洪. Ed. Wang Ming 王明. Beijing: Zhonghua shuju, 1980.

Beifang Zhenwu zushi xuantian shangdi chushen zhizhuan 北方真武祖師玄天上帝出身志傳. 1601. Rpt. in *Guben xiaoshuo jicheng* 古本小説集成, vol. 121. Shanghai: Shanghai guji chubanshe.

Beijian ji 北磵集. Jujian 居簡. *SKQS* ed.

Beixi daquan ji 北溪大全集. Chen Chun 陳淳. *SKQS* ed.

Bianshi guyun hongcheng Xing qingjie gong songyuan wenji 編釋古筠洪城幸清節公松垣文集. Xing Yuanlong 幸元龍. 1616 ms.

Bowu zhi 博物志. Zhang Hua 張華. *Longxi jingshe congshu* 龍谿精舍叢書 ed.

Caishen baojuan 財神寶卷. Undated ms. Beijing University Library.

Chang Zhao hezhi gao 常昭合志稿. 1904.

Changhua xianzhi 昌化縣志. 1924.

Changshu sizhi 常熟私志. 1618.

Changshu xianzhi 常熟縣志. 1539.

Changxing xianzhi 長興縣志. 1805.

Changxing xianzhi 長興縣志. 1875.

Changzhou fuzhi 常州府志. 1694.

Changzhou xianzhi 長洲縣志. 1598.

Changzhou xianzhi 長洲縣志. 1765.

[Jiading] Chicheng zhi [嘉定] 赤城志. 1224. *SYDFZ* ed.

Chitang cungao 恥堂存稿. Gao Side 高斯得. *SKQS* ed.

Chongde xianzhi 崇德縣志. 1611.

Chuguo Wenxiangong xuelou Cheng xiansheng wenji 楚國文憲公雪樓程先生
文集. Cheng Jufu 程鉅夫. Facs. of Taoshi sheyuan 陶氏涉園 ed. Rpt. Taibei:
Guoli zhongyang tushuguan, 1970.

Chunqiu zuozhuan zhengyi 春秋左傳正義. *Shisanjing zhushu* 十三經注疏 ed.
Rpt. Shanghai: Shanghai guji chubanshe, 1990.

Dahui jingci miaole tianzun shuo fude wusheng jing 大惠靜慈妙樂天尊説福德
五聖經. *HY* 1183.

Danwu biji 丹午筆記. Gu Gongxie 顧公燮. 1818. Nanjing: Jiangsu guji chubanshe, 1999.

Daofa huiyuan 道法會元. *HY* 1210.

Daojiao lingyan ji 道教靈驗記. Du Guangting 杜光庭. *HY* 590.

Daoyao lingqi shengui pin jing 道要靈祇神鬼品經. Dunhuang ms., Stein no. 986.
In *Dunhuang baozang* 敦煌寶藏, 8: 118–24. Taibei: Xinwenfeng chuban
gongsi, 1981–86.

Dazhidu lun 大智度論 (*Mahāprajñapāramitā-śāstra*). *T* 1509; vol. 25.

Dengzhen yinjue 登真隱訣. Tao Hongjing 陶弘景. *HY* 421.

Diqi shangjiang Wen Taibao zhuan 地祇上將溫太保傳. Huang Jin 黃瑾. 1274.
HY 779.

Dongjing menghua lu 東京夢華錄. Meng Yuanlao 孟元老. 1147. In *Dongjing
menghua lu wai sizhong* 東京夢華錄外四種. Beijing: Zhonghua shuju,
1962.

Dongxuan lingbao wuyue guben zhenxing tu 洞玄靈寶五嶽古本真形圖. *HY* 441.

Dongxuan lingbao ziran jiutian shengshen yuzhang jing 洞玄靈寶自然九天生神
玉章經. *HY* 318.

Duansu zouyi 端肅奏議. Ma Wensheng 馬文升. *SKQS* ed.

Duduan 獨斷. Cai Yong 蔡邕. *SKQS* ed.

Erke pai'an jingqi 二刻拍案驚奇. Ling Mengchu 凌濛初. 1632. Rpt. Shanghai:
Shanghai guji chubanshe, 1985.

Erya 爾雅. *Wuya quanshu* 五雅全書 ed.

Fan Shihu ji 范石湖集. Fan Chengda 范成大. Hong Kong: Zhonghua shuju, 1974.

Fangyu shenglan 方輿勝覽. Zhu Mu 祝穆. Ca. 1240. Facs. of Kongshi yuexuelou
孔氏嶽雪樓 ms. Rpt. Taibei: Wenhai chubanshe, n.d.

Fangzhou ji 方舟集. Zhang Ning 張寧. *SKQS* ed.

Fengshen yanyi 封神演義. Xu Zhonglin 許仲琳. Shanghai: Shanghai guji chubanshe, 1989.

Fengsu tongyi jiaoshi 風俗通義校釋. Ying Shao 應劭. Ed. Wu Shuping 吳樹平.
Tianjin: Tianjin guji chubanshe, 1990.

Fenhu xiaozhi 分湖小志. 1847.

Foshuo guanding moniluodan da shenzhou jing 佛説灌頂摩尼羅亶大神咒經. *T*
1331; vol. 21.

Foshuo moniluodan jing 佛説摩尼羅亶經. *T* 1393; vol. 21.

Fozu tongji 佛祖統紀. Zhipan 志磐. 1269. *T* 2035; vol. 49.

Fuliang xianzhi 浮梁縣志. 1783.

Funing zhouzhi 福寧州志. 1616.

Fuzhou fuzhi 福州府志. 1613.

Gaiyu congkao 陔餘叢考. Zhao Yi 趙翼. 1790. Shanghai: Shangwu yinshuguan, 1957.

Ganzhu ji 紺珠集. Zhu Shengfei 朱勝非. *SKQS* ed.

Gengsibian 庚巳編. Lu Can 陸粲. Ca. 1520. Beijing: Zhonghua shuju, 1987.

Gu Su zhi 姑蘇志. 1506.

Guangling ji 廣陵集. Wang Ling 王令. *SKQS* ed.

Guangya shuzheng 廣雅疏證. Zhang Yi 張揖 Ed. Wang Niansun 王念孫. Hong Kong: Zhongwen daxue chubanshe, 1978.

Guangyi ji 廣異記. Dai Fu 戴孚.

Guangyun jiaoben 廣韻校本. Chen Pengnian 陳彭年. Ed. Zhou Zumo 周祖謨. Beijing: Zhonghua shuju, 1960.

Gui Zhuang ji 歸莊集. Gui Zhuang 歸莊. Beijing: Zhonghua shuju, 1962.

Guihua xianzhi 歸化縣志. 1614.

Guixin zashi 癸辛雜識. Zhou Mi 周密. Ca. 1298. Beijing: Zhonghua shuju, 1988.

Gujin tushu jicheng 古今圖書集成. 1725. Rpt. Beijing: Zhonghua shuju, 1934.

Gujin xiaoshuo 古今小說. Feng Menglong 馮夢龍. Taibei: Dingwen shuju, 1974.

Guochao xianzheng lu 國朝獻徵錄. Jiao Hong 焦竑, comp. 1616.

Guoyu 國語. *CSJC* ed.

Gusheng 觚賸. Niu Xiu 鈕琇. 1700. *BJXS* ed.

Hailu suishi 海錄碎事. Ye Tinggui 葉廷珪. 1149. 1598 ed. Rpt. Taibei: Xinxing shuju, 1974.

Han shu 漢書. Ban Gu 班固. Beijing: Zhonghua shuju ed.

Hanfeizi jishi 韓非子集釋. Ed. Chen Qiyou 陳奇猷. Shanghai: Renmin chubanshe, 1974.

Hangsu yiqing suijin 杭俗怡情碎錦. 1861. Rpt. Taibei: Xuesheng shuju, 1984.

Hengqi lu 橫谿錄. Xu Mingshi 徐鳴時. 1629.

Hou Han shu 後漢書. Fan Ye 范曄. Beijing: Zhonghua shuju ed.

Hu lu 湖錄. Zheng Yuanqing 鄭元慶. Ca. 1700.

Huainan honglie jishi 淮南鴻烈集釋. Ed. Liu Wendian 劉文典. Beijing: Zhonghua shuju, 1989.

Huang Song shichao gangyao 皇宋十朝綱要. Li Zhi 李埴. Ca. 1213. Facs. of Liujingkan congshu 六經勘叢書 ed. Rpt. Taibei: Wenhai chubanshe, 1980.

Huangjing zhigao 璜涇志稿. 1940.

Huangjing zhilüe 璜涇志略. Ca. 1790.

Huangshi richao 黃氏日抄. Huang Zhen 黃震. *SKQS* ed.

Huangyan xianzhi 黃巖縣志. 1579.

Huating xianzhi 華亭縣志. 1521.

Huhai xinwen yijian xuzhi 湖海新聞夷堅續志. Yuan. Beijing: Zhonghua shuju, 1986.

Huichang jieyi lu 會昌解頤錄.

Huizhou fuzhi 徽州府志. 1502.

Huzhou fuzhi 湖州府志. 1874.

Jiading xianzhi 嘉定縣志. 1673.

[Zhiyuan] Jiahe zhi [至元] 嘉禾志. 1288. *SYDFZ* ed.

Jiangning xianzhi 江寧縣志. 1748.

Jiangsu jinshi zhi 江蘇金石志. N.p.: Jiangsu tongzhi ju, 1927. Rpt. *Shike shiliao congshu* 石刻史料叢書. Taibei: Yiwen yinshuguan, 1966.

Jiangyin xianzhi 江陰縣志. 1548.

Jiangzhou zhi 江州志. Ca. 1240–79.

Jianhu baji 堅瓠八集. Chu Renhuo 褚人獲. 1690–1703. *BJXS* ed.

Jiaxing xianzhi 嘉興縣志. 1637.

Jile bian 雞肋編. Zhuang Chuo 莊綽. 1133. Hanfenlou 涵芬樓 ed.

Jingshi tongyan 警世通言. Feng Menglong 馮夢龍. 1624. Rpt. Beijing: Renmin wenxue chubanshe, 1956.

[Zhizheng] Jinling xinzhi [至正] 金陵新志. 1344. *SYDFZ* ed.

Jinshan xianzhi 金山縣志. 1878.

Jiwen 記聞. Niu Su 牛肅.

Jiyi ji 集異記. Xue Yongruo 薛用弱. *SKQS* ed.

Kechuang xianhua 客窗閒話. Wu Chichang 吳熾昌. 1824. Beijing: Wenhua yishu chubanshe, 1988.

Kuaiyuan 獪園. Qian Xiyan 錢希言. 1613. In Qian, *Qian Jianlou gong songshu shijiu shan* 錢蘭樓先生松樞十九山. 1616.

Kuiche zhi 睽車志. Guo Tuan 郭彖. Ca. 1165. *Baihai* 稗海 ed.

Kun Xin liangxian zhi 崑新兩縣志. 1824.

Kunshan xianzhi 崑山縣志. 1344. *SYDFZ* ed.

Li Gou ji 李覯集. Li Gou 李覯. Beijing: Zhonghua shuju, 1981.

Liangzhe jinshi zhi 兩浙金石志. Ruan Yuan 阮元, comp. Hangzhou: Zhejiang shuju, 1890. Rpt. *Shike shiliao congshu* 石刻史料叢書. Taibei: Yiwen yin-shuguan, 1966.

Liaozhai zhiyi 聊齋志異. Pu Songling 蒲松齡. 1679. Shanghai: Shanghai guji chubanshe, 1962.

Liji zhengyi 禮記正義. *Shisanjing zhushu* 十三經注疏 ed. Rpt. Shanghai: Shang-hai guji chubanshe, 1990.

[Chunyou] Lin'an zhi jiyi [淳祐] 臨安志輯逸. 1252. Ed. Hu Jing 胡敬. *Wulin zhanggu congbian* 武林掌古叢編 ed.

[Xianchun] Lin'an zhi [咸淳] 臨安志. Ca. 1265–74. *SYDFZ* ed.

Linchuan zhi 臨川志. 1263.

Lingbao wuliang duren shangpin miaojing 靈寶無量度人上品妙經. *HY* 1.

Lingguan Ma yuanshuai bifa 靈官馬元帥秘法. In *DFHY* (*HY* 1210), 222–26.

Linian ji 歷年記. Yao Tinglin 姚廷遴. In *Qingdai riji huichao* 清代日記匯抄. Shanghai: Shanghai renmin chubanshe, 1982.

Linting zhi 臨汀志. Ca. 1259.

Lishi zhenxian tidao tongjian 歷世真仙體道通鑒. *HY* 296.

Liuqing rizha 留青日札. Tian Yiheng 田藝衡. 1573. Rpt. Shanghai: Shanghai guji chubanshe, 1985.

Longyu hetu 龍魚河圖.

Lu Shiheng ji 陸士衡集. Lu Yun 陸雲. *CSJC* ed.

Lu xiansheng daomen kelüe 陸先生道門科略. Lu Xiujing 陸修靜. *HY* 1119.

Lunheng jijie 論衡集解. Wang Chong 王充. Ed. Liu Pansui 劉盼遂. Beijing: Zhonghua shuju, 1959.

Lüshi chunqiu jiaoshi 呂氏春秋校釋. Lü Buwei 呂不韋. Ed. Chen Qiyou 陳奇猷. Taibei: Huazheng shuju, 1985.

Lüyuan conghua 履園叢畫. Qian Yong 錢泳. 1838. Taibei: Wenhai chubanshe, 1981.

Mengchang zazhu 夢厂雜著. Yu Jiao 余蛟. 1801. *BJXS* ed.

Mengliang lu 夢梁錄. Wu Zimu 吳自牧. 1275. In *Dongjing menghua lu wai sizhong* 東京夢華錄外四種. Beijing: Zhonghua shuju, 1962.

Mianyizhai xu cungao 勉益齋續存稿. Yuqian 裕謙. 1876.

Ming shi 明史. Beijing: Zhonghua shuju ed.

Minggong shupan qingming ji 名公書判清明集. Ming ed. Beijing: Zhonghua shuju, 1987.

Mingzhai xiaoshi 明齋小識. Zhu Lian 諸聯. 1813. *BJXS* ed.

Moyu lu 墨餘錄. Mao Xianglin 毛祥麟. 1870. *BJXS* ed.

Nancun chuogeng lu 南村輟耕錄. Tao Zongyi 陶宗儀. 1366. Beijing: Zhonghua shuju, 1959.

Nanhui xianzhi 南匯縣志. 1929.

Nanjing duchayuan zhi 南京督察院志. Qi Boyu 祁伯裕, ed. 1623.

Nankang fuzhi 南康府志. 1515.

Nankang ji 南康記. Deng Deming 鄧德明.

Nanxiang zhenzhi 南翔鎮志. 1782.

Nanxun zhenzhi 南潯鎮志. 1840.

Nanxun zhenzhi 南潯鎮志. 1859.

Nenggaizhai manlu 能改齋漫錄. Wu Zeng 吳曾. 1157. Shanghai: Shanghai guji chubanshe, 1960.

Nianxia suishiji 輦下歲時記.

Ninghua xianzhi 寧化縣志. 1684.

Nüke baiwen 女科百問. Qi Zhongfu 齊仲甫. 1735 ed. of Song work. Rpt. Shanghai: Shanghai guji chubanshe, 1983.

Nüqing guilü 女青鬼律. HY 789.

Pai'an jingqi 拍案驚奇. Ling Mengchu 凌濛初. 1628. Shanghai: Shanghai guji chubanshe, 1982.

Pengchuang leiji 蓬窗類記. Huang Wei 黃暐. *Hanfenlou biji* 涵芬樓祕笈 ed.

[Xianchun] Piling zhi [咸淳]毘陵志. 1268. *SYDFZ* ed.

Pingwang zhi 平望志. 1840.

Pingzhou ketan 萍洲可談. Zhu Yu 朱彧. 1119. Shanghai: Shanghai guji chubanshe, 1989.

Puchuan suowenji 濮川所聞記. 1813.

Qiantang xianzhi 錢塘縣志. 1609.

[Chongxiu] Qinchuan zhi 重修琴川志. 1365. *SYDFZ* ed.

Qinding xu wenxian tongkao 欽定續文獻通考. 1747. *Shitong* 十通 ed. Shanghai: Shangwu yinshuguan, 1935.

Qingjia lu 清嘉錄. Gu Lu 顧祿. 1830. *BJXS* ed.

Qingsuo gaoyi 青瑣高議. Liu Fu 劉斧. Ca. 1077. Shanghai: Shanghai guji chubanshe, 1983.

Qingwei Ma Zhao Wen Guan sishuai dafa 清微馬趙溫關四帥大法. In *DFHY* (*HY* 1210), 36.

Qixiu leigao 七修類藁. Lang Ying 郎英. 1566. Beijing: Zhonghua shuju, 1961.

Quanxiang Huaguang tianwang nanyou zhizhuan 全像華光天王南游志傳. 1631. Rpt. in *Guben xiaoshuo jicheng* 古本小説集成, vol. 120. Shanghai: Shanghai guji chubanshe.

Quyi shuo 袪疑説. Chu Yong 儲泳. *SKQS* ed.

Quyuan zazuan 曲園雜纂. Yu Yue 俞樾. *Chunzaitang congshu* 春在堂叢書 ed.

Renhe xianzhi 仁和縣志. 1687.

Sanguo zhi 三國志. Chen Shou 陳壽. Beijing: Zhonghua shuju ed.

Sanjiao yuanliu soushen daquan 三教源流搜神大全. Ming ed. Rpt. in *Zhongguo minjian xinyang ziliao huibian* 中國民間信仰資料彙編, vol. 3. Ed. Wang Qiugui 王秋桂 and Li Fengmao 李豐楙. Taibei: Xuesheng shuju, 1989.

[Chunxi] Sanshan zhi [淳熙] 三山志. 1181. *SYDFZ* ed.

Santian neijie jing 三天内解經. *HY* 1196.

"Shangfangshan Lengqiesi tabei" 上方山楞伽寺塔碑. Zhang Shiwei 張世偉. 1640. Stele located *in situ* at the Lengqiesi Monastery, Mount Shangfang, Suzhou.

Shanhaijing jiaozhu 山海經校注. Ed. Yuan Ke 袁珂. Shanghai: Shanghai guji chubanshe, 1980.

Shatou lizhi 沙頭里志. 1740 ms.

She zhi 歙志. 1609.

Shenghu zhi 盛湖志. 1716.

Shenxiao duanwen dafa 神霄斷瘟大法. In *DFHY* (*HY* 1210), 219.

Shenxiao qianwen zhibing juefa 神霄遣瘟治病訣法. In *DFHY* (*HY* 1210), 221.

Shenyijing yanjiu 神異經研究. Ed. Zhou Ciji 周次吉. Taibei: Wenjin chubanshe, 1986.

Shi ji 史記. Sima Qian 司馬遷. Beijing: Zhonghua shuju ed.

Shimen xianzhi 石門縣志. 1879.

Shuanglin xuji 雙林續志. 1819.

Shuanglin zhenzhi 雙林鎮志. 1917.

Shuoting 説聽. Lu Can 陸粲. *Shuoku* 説庫 ed.

Shuowen jiezi gulin 説文解字詁林. Xu Shen 許慎. Ed. Ding Fubao 丁福寶. Rpt. Taibei: Shangwu yinshuguan, 1959.

Shuyi ji 述異記. Dongxuan zhuren 東軒主人 (pseud.). 1701. *BJXS* ed.

Shuyi ji 述異記. Ren Fang 任昉.

Shuyi ji 述異記. Zu Chongzhi 祖沖之.

Shuyin congshuo 書隱叢説. Yuan Lian 袁楝. 1744.

Shuyuan zaji 菽園雜記. Lu Rong 陸容. Beijing: Zhonghua shuju, 1985.

Song huiyao jigao 宋會要輯稿. Facs. of 1809 ms. Rpt. Taibei: Xinwenfeng chuban gongsi, 1976.

Song shi 宋史. Beijing: Zhonghua shuju ed.

Song shu 宋書. Shen Yue 沈約. Beijing: Zhonghua shuju ed.

Songjiang fuzhi 松江府志. 1663.

Songling wenxian 松陵文獻. Pan Chengzhang 潘檉章. 1693.

Soushen bilan 搜神必覽. Zhang Binglin 章炳臨. 1113. *Xu Guyi congshu* 續古逸叢書 ed.

[Xinjiao] Soushen ji [新校] 搜神記. Gan Bao 干寶. Taibei: Shijie shuju, 1962.

Su Dongpo quanji 蘇東坡全集. Su Shi 蘇軾. Taibei: Shijie shuju, 1982.

Su Weigong wenji 蘇魏公文集. Su Song 蘇松. *SKQS* ed.

Suishi guangji 歲事廣記. Chen Yuanjing 陳元靚. Ca. 1230–58. *CSJC* ed.

Suzhou fuzhi 蘇州府志. 1379.

Suzhou fuzhi 蘇州府志. 1748.

Suzhoufu zuanxiu shilüe 蘇州府纂修試略. Yang Xunji 楊循吉. 1506. In Yang, *Yang Nanfeng xiansheng quanji* 楊南峰先生全集. 1609.

Taicang zhouzhi 太倉州志. 1918.

Taiping guangji 太平廣記. Li Fang 李昉, ed. 978. Beijing: Renmin wenxue chubanshe, 1959.

Taiping huanyu ji 太平寰宇記. Yue Shi 樂史. Ca. 980. 1803 ed. Rpt. Taibei: Wenhai chubanshe, n.d.

Taiping yulan 太平御覽. Li Fang 李昉, ed. 983. Song ed. Rpt. Beijing: Zhonghua shuju, 1960.

Taiqing jinque yuhua xianshu baji shenzhang sanhuang neibi wen 太清金闕玉華仙書八極神章三皇內秘文 *HY* 854.

Taishang dongxuan lingbao wuxianguan huaguang benxing miaojing 太上洞玄靈寶五顯官華光本行妙經. *HY* 1436.

Taishang dongyuan ciwen shenzhou miaojing 太上洞淵辭瘟神咒妙經. *HY* 54.

Taishang dongyuan shenzhou jing 太上洞淵神咒經. *HY* 335.

Taishang jiuku tianzun shuo xiaoqian miezui jing 太上救苦天尊說消愆滅罪經. *HY* 378.

Taishang sanwu bangjiu jiao wudi duanwen yi 太上三五傍救醮五帝斷瘟儀. *HY* 808.

Taishang zhuguo jiumin zongzhen biyao 太上助國救民總真秘要. *HY* 1217.

Taixuan fengdu heilü yige 泰玄酆都黑律儀格. In *DFHY* (*HY* 1210), 267.

Taiyi jieji shizhe dafa 太乙捷疾使者大法. In *DFHY* (*HY* 1210), 96.

Tanglü shuyi jianjie 唐律疏議箋解. Ed. Liu Junwen 劉俊文. Beijing: Zhonghua shuju, 1996.

Tangxi zhi 唐棲志. 1881.

Tangxi zhilüe 唐棲志略. 1881 rpt. of 1767 ed.

Tangzi yishu 湯子遺書. Tang Bin 湯斌. 1870 ed.

Taoan mengyi 陶庵夢憶. Zhang Dai 張岱. Shanghai: Xinwenhua shushe, 1933.

Tianxia junguo libing shu 天下郡國利病書. Gu Yanwu 顧炎武. *SBCK* ed.

Tingzhou fuzhi 汀州府志. 1527.

Tongjiang ji 桐江集. Fang Hui 方回. Facs. of Ming ms. Taibei: Guoli zhongyang tushuguan, 1970.

Tongjiang xuji 桐江續集. Fang Hui 方回. *SKQS* ed.

Tongsu bian 通俗編. Di Hao 翟灝. 1751.

Tufeng lu 土風錄. Gu Sizhang 顧思張. 1799. Rpt. in *Min Shin zokugo jisho shūsei* 明清俗語辭書集成, vol. 1. Ed. Nagasawa Kikuya 長澤規矩也. Kyūko shoten, 1974.

Wanli yehuo bian 萬曆野獲編. Shen Defu 沈德符. 1619. Rpt. Taibei: Xinxing shuju, 1983.

Wanshu zaji 宛署雜記. Shen Bang 沈榜. 1592. Beijing: Xinhua shudian, 1980.

Wenxuan 文選. Xiao Tong 蕭統. Shanghai: Shanghai guji chubanshe, 1986.

Wu xianzhi 吳縣志. 1642.

Wu xianzhi 吳縣志. 1690.

Wu za zu 五雜俎. Xie Zhaozhe 謝肇淛. Beijing: Zhonghua shuju, 1959.

Wucheng xianzhi 烏程縣志. 1638.

Wucheng xianzhi 烏程縣志. 1746.

Wudi quanshu 武帝全書. Gan Daiyun 甘岱雲, comp. 1872 rpt. of 1828 ed.

Wujiang xianzhi 吳江縣志. 1488.

Wujiang xianzhi 吳江縣志. 1685.

Wujiang xianzhi 吳江縣志. 1747.

Wujun Fuli zhi 吳郡甫里志. 1703.

Wujun Fuli zhi 吳郡甫里志. 1765.

Wujun tujing xuji 吳郡圖經續記. 1094. Nanjing: Jiangsu guji chubanshe, 1999.

Wujun zhi 吳郡志. Fan Chengda 范成大. 1192, addenda 1229. *SYDFZ* ed.

Wulin jiushi 武林舊事. Zhou Mi 周密. Ca. 1280. In *Dongjing menghua lu wai sizhong* 東京夢華錄外四種. Beijing: Zhonghua shuju, 1962.

Wumen biaoyin 吳門表隱. Gu Zhentao 顧震濤. 1842. Nanjing: Jiangsusheng guji chubanshe, 1986.

Wumen bucheng 吳門補乘. Qian Siyuan 錢思元. Ca. 1771–1803.

Wuqing wenxian 烏青文獻. 1688.

Wushe bian 吳社編. Wang Zhideng 王穉登. *Baoyantang biji* 寶顏堂秘笈 ed.

Wuxian lingguan dadi dengyi 五顯靈官大帝燈儀. *HY* 206.

Wuyuan xianzhi 婺源縣志. 1694.

Xi Jin shi xiaolu 錫金識小錄. Huang Ang 黃卬. 1752.

Xianchuang guayi zhi 閑窗括異志. Lu Yinglong 魯應龍. *CSJC* ed.

Xiangshi jiashuo 項氏家說. Xiang Anshi 項安世. *Wuyingdian juzhen banshu* 武英殿聚珍版書 ed.

Xiangzhong ji 湘中記. Luo Han 羅含.

Xiangzu biji 香祖筆記. Wang Shizhen 王士禛. 1705. *BJXS* ed.

Xianju bian 閑居編. Zhiyuan 智圓. *Dai Nihon zoku zōkyō* 大日本續藏經, vol. 101. Kyoto: Zōkyō shoin, 1905–12.

Xianquan ji 峴泉集. Zhang Yuchu 張宇初. *SKQS* ed.

Xihu laoren fansheng lu 西湖老人繁勝錄. In *Dongjing menghua lu wai sizhong* 東京夢華錄外四種. Beijing: Zhonghua shuju, 1962.

Xihu youlan zhiyu 西湖游覽志餘. Tian Rucheng 田汝成. Ca. 1547. Beijing: Zhonghua shuju, 1965.

Xin'an wenxian zhi 新安文獻志. *SKQS* ed.

Xinbian lianxiang soushen guangji 新編連相搜神廣記. Yuan ed. Rpt. *Zhongguo minjian xinyang ziliao huibian* 中國民間信仰資料匯編, vol. 2. Ed. Wang Qiugui 王秋桂 and Li Fengmao 李豐楙. Taibei: Xuesheng shuju, 1989.

Xingshi hengyan 醒世恆言. Feng Menglong 馮夢龍. 1627. Beijing: Renmin wenxue chubanshe, 1956.

Xingyuan zhi 星源志. 1269.

Xinshi zhenzhi 新市鎮志. 1511.

Xishan wenji 西山文集. Zhen Dexiu 真德秀. *SKQS* ed.

Xishang futan 席上腐談. Yu Yan 俞琰. *SKQS* ed.

Xiugu chunrong 繡谷春容. Ca. 1592. Nanjing: Jiangsu guji chubanshe, 1994.

Xiwu canlüe 西吳蠶略.

Xiyin ji 西隱集. Song Na 宋訥. *SKQS* ed.

Xiyou ji 西游記. Wu Cheng'en 吳承恩. Hong Kong: Zhonghua shuju, 1972.

Xu gujin kao 續古今考. Fang Hui 方回. *SKQS* ed.

Xu yijian zhi 續夷堅志. Yuan Haowen 元好問. Beijing: Zhonghua shuju, 1986.

Xuanyuan benji 軒轅本紀. In *Yunji qiqian,* 100.2b–26b.

Xujing chonghe xiansheng Xu shenweng yulu 虛靖沖和先生徐神翁語錄. *HY* 1241.

Yang Donglai xiansheng piping Xiyou ji 楊東來先生批評西遊記. *Guben xiqu congkan chuji* 古本戲曲叢刊初集. Shanghai: Shangwu yinshuguan, 1954.

Yantang jianwen zaji 研堂見聞雜記. *Tongshi* 痛史 ed.

Yehang chuan 夜航船. Poe shanren 破額山人 (pseud.). 1800. *BJXS* ed.

Yeren xianhua 野人閒話. Jing Huan 景煥.

Yeyu qiudeng lu 夜雨秋燈錄. Xuan Ding 宣鼎. *BJXS* ed.

Yi Zhou shu 逸周書. *CSJC* ed.

Yiban lu 一斑錄. Zheng Guangzu 鄭光祖. 1844. Rpt. Beijing: Zhongguo shudian, 1990.

Yijian zhi 夷堅志. Hong Mai 洪邁. Beijing: Zhonghua shuju, 1981.

Yingchuang yicao 螢窗異草. Changbai haogezi 長白浩歌子 (pseud.). 1905. *BJXS* ed.

Yishi jishi 壹是紀始. Wei Song 魏崧. 1834.

Yiwu zhi 異物志.

Yongjia junji 永嘉郡記.

Yongle dadian 永樂大典. Beijing: Zhonghua shuju, 1960.

Youguai lu 幽怪錄. Tian Rucheng 田汝成. In *Shuofu xu* 説郛續 (1646), *jiu* 46. Ed. Tao Ting 陶挺. Rpt. in *Shuofu sanzhong* 説郛三種. Shanghai: Shanghai guji chubanshe, 1988.

Youxi xianzhi 尤溪縣志. 1636.

Youyang zazu 酉陽雜俎. Duan Chengshi 段成式. Beijing: Zhonghua shuju, 1981.

Yuanhe Weiting zhi 元和唯亭志. 1933 rpt. of 1848 ed.

Yuanshi wuliang duren shangpin miaojing zhu 元始無量度人上品妙經註. *HY* 88.

Yudi ji 輿地記. Gu Yewang 顧野王.

Yudi jisheng 輿地紀勝. Wang Xiangzhi 王象之. Ca. 1221. Yueyatang Wushi 嶽雅堂伍室 ed. Rpt. Taibei: Wenhai chubanshe, n.d.

Yueling caike 月令采可. Li Yiji 李一楫. 1619.

Yueshi bian 閱世編. Ye Mengzhu 葉夢珠. Ca. 1700. Shanghai: Shanghai guji chubanshe, 1981.

Yufeng zhi 玉峰志. 1251. *SYDFZ* ed.

Yuguai lu 語怪錄. Zhu Yunming 祝允明. In *Shuofu xu* 説郛續 (1646), *jiu* 46. Ed. Tao Ting 陶挺 Rpt in *Shuofu sanzhong* 説郛三種. Shanghai: Shanghai guji chubanshe, 1988.

Yunji qiqian 雲笈七籤. Ca. 1029. *HY* 1026.

Yunjian zashi 雲間雜識. Li Shaowen 李紹文 Qing ms. Rpt. Shanghai: Ruihua yinwuju, 1935.

Zaixuan ji 在軒集. Huang Gongshao 黃公紹. *SKQS* ed.

Zhaode xiansheng junzhai dushu zhi 昭德先生郡齋讀書志. Chao Gongwu 晁公武. 1884 ed.

Zhen gao 真誥. Tao Hongjing 陶弘景. *HY* 1010.

Zhengyi hongshen lingguan huoxi daxian kaozhao bifa 正一吽神靈官火犀大仙考召祕法. In *DFHY* (*HY* 1210), 222.

Zhengyi longhu xuantan dafa 正一龍虎玄壇大法. In *DFHY* (*HY 1210*), 236.

Zhengyi wensi bidushen dengyi 正一瘟司辟毒神燈儀. *HY 209*.

Zhengyi xuantan Zhao yuanshuai bifa 正一法玄壇趙元帥祕法. In *DFHY* (*HY 1210*), 232–33.

[Zhishun] Zhenjiang zhi [至順] 鎮江志. 1332. *SYDFZ* ed.

Zhenyang xianzhi 鎮洋縣志. 1744.

Zhenze xianzhi 震澤縣志. 1746.

Zhenze zhenzhi 震澤鎮志. 1844.

Zhinang quanji 智囊全集. Feng Menglong 馮夢龍. 1626. Shijiazhuang: Huashan wenyi chubanshe, 1988.

Zhiwen lu 卮聞錄. Yongna jushi 慵訥居士 (pseud.). 1843. *BJXS* ed.

Zhixi xiaozhi 支溪小志. 1788.

Zhouli zhengshu 周禮正疏. *Shisanjing zhushu* 十三經註疏 ed. Rpt. Shanghai: Shanghai guji chubanshe, 1990.

Zhouzao ji 咒棗記. 1603.

Zhouzhuang zhenzhi 周莊鎮志. 1882.

Zhuangzi jiaoquan 莊子校詮. Ed. Wang Shumin 王叔岷. Taibei: Zhongyang yanjiuyuan lishi yuyan yanjiusuo, 1988.

Zhushen shengdanri yuxia ji 諸神聖誕日玉匣記. Late Ming. *HY 1470*.

Zhushi jilüe 祝氏集略. Zhu Yunming 祝允明. 1557.

Zi buyu 子不語. Yuan Mei 袁枚. Shanghai: Shanghai guji chubanshe, 1986.

Zidicun xiaozhi 紫隄村小志. 1718. In *Jiangnan difang xiangtuzhi congbian* 江南地方鄉土志叢編, vol. 1. Shanghai: Shanghaishi wenwu baoguan weiyuanhui, 1962.

Zitong dijun huashu 梓童帝君化書. *HY 170*.

Zongjing lu 宗鏡錄. Yongming Yanshou 永明延壽. *T 2016*; vol. 15.

SECONDARY WORKS

Ahern, Emily Martin.

1981. *Chinese Ritual and Politics*. Cambridge: Cambridge University Press.

Akatsuka Kiyoshi 赤塚忠.

1977. *Chūgoku kodai no shūkyō to bunka: In ōchō no saiji* 中国古代宗教と文化：殷王朝の祭事. Tokyo: Kadokawa shoten.

Akizuki Kan'ei 秋月観映.

1978. *Chūgoku kinsei dōkyō no keisei: Jōmeidō no kisōteki kenkyū* 中国近世道教の形成：浄明道の基礎的研究. Tokyo: Sōbunsha.

Alexeiev, Basil M.

1928. *The Chinese Gods of Wealth*. London: School of Oriental Studies and the China Society.

Allan, Sarah.

1991. *The Shape of the Turtle: Myth, Art, and Cosmos in Early China*. Albany: State University of New York Press.

1993. "Art and Meaning." In Whitfield, ed., 1993: 9–33.

André, Jacques, and Jean Filliozat.

> *1986. L'Inde vue de Rome: textes latins de l'antiquité relatifs à l'Inde.* Paris: Société d'édition "Les belles lettres."

Bagley, Robert.

> *1987. Shang Ritual Bronzes in the Arthur M. Sackler Collections.* Washington, D.C.: Arthur M. Sackler Foundation.

> *1993. "Meaning and Explanation." In Whitfield, ed., 1993: 34–55.

Bakhtin, Mikhail.

> *1968. Rabelais and His World.* Cambridge, Mass.: MIT Press.

Baojishi bowuguan 宝鸡市博物馆.

> *1981. "Baojishi Chanchechang Han mu 宝鸡市铲车厂汉墓." Wenwu 文物 1981.3: 46–52.

Barfield, Thomas J.

> *1989. The Perilous Frontier: Nomadic Empires and China, 221 B.C. to A.D.1757.* Cambridge, Mass.: Blackwell.

Beck, B. J. Mansvelt.

> *1980. "The Date of the Taiping Jing." T'oung Pao 66.4–5: 149–82.

Beijing tushuguan 北京图书馆.

> *1990. Beijing tushuguan cang Zhongguo lidai shike tuoben huibian 北京图书馆藏中国历代石刻拓本汇编.* Zhengzhou: Zhongzhou guji chubanshe.

> N.d. *Beijing tushuguan guji shanben shumu 北京图书馆古籍善本书目.* Beijing: Shumu wenxian chubanshe.

Bell, Catherine.

> *1989. "Religion and Chinese Culture: Toward an Assessment of 'Popular Religion.'" History of Religions 29.1: 37–57.

Berling, Judith A.

> *1985. "Religion and Popular Culture: The Management of Moral Capital in the Romance of Three Teachings." In Johnson et al., ed., 1985: 188–218.

Berger, Patricia.

> *1983. "Pollution and Purity in Han Art." Archives of Asian Art 36: 40–58.

Bijutsu kenkyūjo 美術研究所.

> *1932. Shina ko hanga zuroku 支那古版畫圖録.* Tokyo: Ōtsuka kōgei sha.

Birrell, Anne.

> *1993. Chinese Mythology: An Introduction.* Baltimore, Md.: Johns Hopkins University Press.

Bodde, Derk.

> *1961. "Myths of Ancient China." In Mythologies of the Ancient World, pp. 369–408.* Ed. Samuel N. Kramer. New York: Doubleday.

> *1975. Festivals in Classical China: New Year and Other Annual Observances

During the Han Dynasty, 206 B.C.–A.D. 220. Princeton, N.J.: Princeton University Press.

Bokenkamp, Stephen R.

1983. "Sources of the Ling-pao Scriptures." In *Tantric and Taoist Studies in Honour of R. A. Stein*, 2: 434–86. Ed. Michel Strickmann. Bruxelles: Institut Belge des Hautes Études Chinoises.

1989. "Death and Ascent in Ling-pao Taoism." *Taoist Resources* 1.2: 1–17.

1997. *Early Daoist Scriptures.* Berkeley: University of California Press.

Boltz, Judith M.

1987. *A Survey of Taoist Literature: Tenth to Seventeenth Centuries.* Berkeley: Institute of East Asian Studies, University of California, Berkeley.

Boltz, William G.

1979. "Philological Footnotes to the Han New Year Rites." *Journal of the American Oriental Society* 99.2: 423–39.

1981. "Kung Kung and the Flood: Reverse Euhemerism in the *Yao Tien.*" *T'oung Pao* 67.3–5: 141–53.

Brashier, K. E.

1995. "Longevity Like Metal and Stone: The Role of the Mirror in Han Burials." *T'oung Pao* 81.4–5: 201–29.

1996. "Han Thanatology and the Division of 'Souls.'" *Early China* 21: 125–58.

Brokaw, Cynthia J.

1991. *The Ledgers of Merit and Demerit: Social Change and Moral Order in Late Imperial China.* Princeton, N.J.: Princeton University Press.

Burkert, Walter.

1985. *Greek Religion.* Cambridge, Mass.: Harvard University Press.

Cahill, Susanne E.

1980. "Taoists at the Sung Court: The Heavenly Text Affair of 1008." *Bulletin of Sung-Yuan Studies* 16: 23–44.

1993. *Transcendence and Divine Passion: The Queen Mother of the West in Medieval China.* Stanford, Calif.: Stanford University Press.

Cai Limin 蔡利民.

1992. "Shangfangshan jie yinzhai—Suzhou minjian xinyang huodong diaocha 上方山借阴债—苏州民间信仰活动调查," *Zhongguo minjian wenhua* 中国民间文化 6: 239–56.

Cammann, Schuyler.

1964. "A Ming Dynasty Pantheon Painting." *Archives of the Chinese Art Society of America* 18: 38–47.

Campany, Robert F.

1991. "Ghosts Matter: The Culture of Ghosts in Six Dynasties *Zhiguai.*" *Chinese Literature: Essays, Articles, Reviews* 13: 15–34.

1996a. "The Earliest Tales of the Bodhisattva Guanyin." In Lopez, ed., 1996: 82–96.

1996b. *Strange Writing: Anomaly Accounts in Early Medieval China*. Albany: State University of New York Press.

Cedzich, Ursula-Angelika.

1985. "Wu-t'ung: Zur bewegeten Geschichte eines Kultes." In *Religion und Philosophie in Ostasien: Festschrift für Hans Steininger zum 65. Geburtstag*, pp. 33–60. Ed. Gert Naundorf et al. Wurzburg: Konigshausen und Neumann.

1993. "Ghosts and Demons, Law and Order: Grave Quelling Texts and Early Taoist Liturgy." *Taoist Resources* 4.2: 23–35.

1995. "The Cult of the Wu-t'ung / Wu-hsien in History and Fiction: The Religious Roots of the *Journey to the South*." In Johnson, ed., 1995: 137–218.

Chang, K. C. (Kwang-chih).

1980. *Shang Civilization*. New Haven, Conn.: Yale University Press.

1983. *Art, Myth, and Ritual: The Path to Political Authority in Ancient China*. Cambridge, Mass.: Harvard University Press.

1990. "The 'Meaning' of Shang Bronze Art." *Asian Art* 3.2: 9–18.

Chard, Robert.

1995. "Rituals and Scriptures of the Stove Cult." In Johnson, ed., 1995: 3–54.

Chavannes, Edouard.

1910. *Le T'ai chan: essai de monographie d'un culte chinois*. Paris: Ernest Leroux.

Che Xilun 车锡伦 and Zhou Zhengliang 周正良.

1992. "Quhuangshen Liu Mengjiangde laili he liubian 驱蝗神刘猛将的来历和流变." *Zhongguo minjian wenhua* 中国民间文化 5: 1–21.

Chen Pan 陳槃.

1991. *Gu chenwei yantao jiqi shulu jieti* 古讖緯研討及其書録解題. Taibei: Guoli bianyiguan.

Chikusa Masaaki 竺沙雅章.

1982. *Chūgoku bukkyō shakaishi kenkyū* 中国仏教社会史研究. Kyoto: Dōhōsha.

Childs-Johnson, Elizabeth.

1998. "The Metamorphic Image: A Predominant Theme in the Ritual Art of Shang China." *Bulletin of the Museum of Far Eastern Antiquities* 70: 5–171.

Chongqing Dazu shike yishu bowuguan 重庆大足石刻艺术博物馆.

1991. *Zhongguo dazu shike* 中国大足石刻. Chongqing: Wanli shudian.

Creel, Herrlee G.

1970. *The Origins of Statecraft in China*. Chicago: University of Chicago Press.

Davis, Edward L.

    2001. *Society and the Supernatural in Song China.* Honolulu: University of Hawaii Press.

Day, Clarence B.

    1940. *Chinese Peasant Cults.* Shanghai: Kelly & Walsh.

Dean, Kenneth.

    1993. *Taoist Ritual and Popular Cults of Southeast China.* Princeton, N.J.: Princeton University Press.

DeBernardi, Jean.

    1992. "Space and Time in Chinese Religious Culture." *History of Religions* 31.3: 247–68.

Dohrenwend, Doris J.

    1975. "Jade Demonic Images from Early China." *Ars Orientalis* 60: 55–78.

Doré, Henri.

    1916. *Researches into Chinese Superstitions.* Shanghai: T'usewei.

Duara, Prasenjit.

    1988. "Superscribing Symbols: The Myth of Guandi, Chinese God of War." *Journal of Asian Studies* 47.4: 778–95.

Dudbridge, Glen.

    1970. *The* Hsi-yu-chi: *A Study of Antecedents to the Sixteenth-Century Chinese Novel.* Cambridge: Cambridge University Press.

    1978. *The Legend of Miao-shan.* London: Ithaca Press.

    1982. "Miao-shan on Stone: Two Early Inscriptions." *Harvard Journal of Asiatic Studies* 42.2: 589–614.

    1995. *Religious Experience and Lay Society in T'ang China: A Reading of Tai Fu's* Kuang-i chi. Cambridge: Cambridge University Press.

Ebrey, Patricia Buckley.

    1991. *Confucianism and Family Rituals in Imperial China: A Social History of Writing about Rites.* Princeton, N.J.: Princeton University Press.

    1993. "The Response of the Sung State to Popular Funeral Practice." In Ebrey and Gregory, ed., 1993: 209–39.

Ebrey, Patricia Buckley, and Peter N. Gregory.

    1993. "The Religious and Historical Landscape." In Ebrey and Gregory, ed., 1993: 1–44.

Ebrey, Patricia Buckley, and Peter N. Gregory, ed.

    1993. *Religion and Society in Tang and Sung China.* Honolulu: University of Hawaii Press.

Éliasberg, Danielle.

    1976. *Le Roman du pourfendeur de démons: traduction annotée et commentaires.* Paris: Collège de France, Institut des Haut Études Chinoises.

1984. "Quelques aspects du grand exorcisme *no* à Touen-houang." In *Contributions aux études de Touen-houang,* 3: 237–53. Ed. Michel Soymié. Paris: École Française d'Extrême-Orient.

Elvin, Mark.

1973. *The Pattern of the Chinese Past.* Stanford, Calif.: Stanford University Press.

1984. "Female Virtue and the State in China." *Past and Present* 104: 111–52.

Eno, Robert.

1990a. *The Confucian Creation of Heaven.* Albany: State University of New York Press.

1990b. "Was There a High God *Ti* in Shang Religion?" *Early China* 15: 1–26.

1996. "Deities and Ancestors in Early Oracle Inscriptions." In Lopez, ed., 1996: 41–51.

Erickson, Susan N.

1994. "Money Trees of the Eastern Han Dynasty." *Bulletin of the Museum of Far Eastern Antiquities* 66: 5–115.

Feuchtwang, Stephan.

1992. *The Imperial Metaphor: Popular Religion in China.* London: Routledge.

Fong, Mary H.

1977. "A Probable Second 'Chung K'uei' by Emperor Shun-chih of the Ch'ing Dynasty." *Oriental Art* 23.4: 423–37.

1983. "The Iconography of the Popular Gods of Happiness, Emolument, and Longevity (Fu Lu Shou)." *Artibus Asiae* 44: 159–99.

1989. "Wu Daozi's Legacy in the Popular Door Gods (Menshen) Qin Shubao and Yuchi Gong." *Archives of Asian Art* 42: 6–24.

1991a. "Antecedents to Sui-Tang Burial Practices in Shaanxi." *Artibus Asiae* 51.2: 147–98.

1991b. "Tomb Guardian Figures: Their Evolution and Iconography." In Kuwayama, ed., 1991: 84–105.

Fracasso, Riccardo.

1983. "Teratoscopy or Divination by Monsters: Being a Study on the *Wu-tsang shan-ching.*" *Hanxue yanjiu* 漢學研究 1.2: 657–700.

1988. "Holy Mothers of Ancient China: A New Approach to the Hsi-wang-mu Problem." *T'oung Pao* 74.1: 1–48.

Freedman, Maurice.

1974. "On the Sociological Study of Chinese Religion." In Wolf, ed., 1974: 19–41.

Fukui Kōjun 福井康須.

1952. *Dōkyō no kisōteki kenkyū* 道教の基礎的研究. Tokyo: Shorui bunbutsu ryūtsūkai.

Fuma Susumu 夫馬進.

1997. *Chūgoku zenkai zendō shi kenkyū* 中国善会善堂史研究. Kyoto: Dōhōsha.

Furth, Charlotte.

1999. *A Flourishing Yin: Gender in China's Medical History, 960–1665.* Berkeley: University of California Press.

Gao Guofan 高国藩.

1989. *Dunhuang minsu xue* 敦煌民俗学. Shanghai: Shanghai wenyi chubanshe.

Gates, Hill.

1987. "Money for the Gods." *Modern China* 13.3: 259–77.

Getz, Daniel.

1999. "T'ien-t'ai Pure Land Societies and the Creation of the Pure Land Patriarchate." In Gregory and Getz, ed., 1999: 477–523.

Ginzburg, Carlo.

1980. *The Cheese and the Worms: The Cosmos of a Sixteenth-Century Miller.* Baltimore, Md.: Johns Hopkins University Press.

Goodrich, Anne S.

1964. *The Peking Temple of the Eastern Peak.* Nagoya: Monumenta Serica.

Goossaert, Vincent.

1998. "Portrait epigraphique d'un culte: les inscriptions des dynasties Jin et Yuan de temples du Pic de l'Est." *Sanjiao wenxian: Matériaux pour l'étude de la religion chinoise* 2: 41–83.

Graham, A. C.

1989. *Disputers of the Tao: Philosophical Argument in Ancient China.* LaSalle, Ill.: Open Court.

Granet, Marcel.

1926. *Danses et légendes de la chine ancienne.* Paris: Librairie Félix Alcan.

Gregory, Peter N., and Daniel A. Getz, Jr., ed.

1999. *Buddhism in the Sung.* Honolulu: University of Hawaii Press.

Grootaers, William A.

1952. "The Hagiography of the Chinese God Chen-wu." *Folklore Studies* 12.2: 139–82.

Gu Xijia 顾希佳.

1990. "Taihu liuyu minjian xinyangzhongde shenling tixi 太湖流域民间信仰中的神灵体系." *Shijie zongjiao* 世界宗教 1990.4: 123–33.

Gyss-Vermande, Caroline.

1988. "Démons et merveilles: vision de la nature dans une peinture liturgique du XVe siècle." *Arts Asiatiques* 43: 106–22.

1991. "Les Messagers divins et leur iconographie." *Arts Asiatiques* 46: 96–110.

Hamashima Atsutoshi 浜島敦俊.

1983. "Chūgoku sonbyō zakkō 中国村廟雑考." *Kindai Chūgoku kenkyū ippō* 近代中国研究彙報 5: 1–21.

1990a. "Kōnan Ryūseishin zakkō 江南劉姓神雑考." *Machikaneyama ronsō* 待兼山論叢 *(Shigaku hen* 史学篇*)* 24: 1–18.

1990b. "Min Shin jidai Kōnan nōson no sha to tochibyō 明清時代江南農村の 社と土地廟." In *Yamane Yukio kyōju taikyū kinen Mindaishi ronsō* 山根幸 夫教授退休記念明代史論叢, 2: 1325–57. Tokyo: Kyūko shoin.

1992a. "The City-god Temples (ch'eng-huang-miao) of Chiang-nan in the Ming and Ch'ing Dynasties." *Memoirs of the Research Department of the Tōyō Bunko* 50: 1–27.

1992b. "Min Shin Kōnan jōko kō hōkō 明清江南城隍考補考." In *Chūgoku no toshi to nōson* 中国の都市と農村, pp. 495–527. Ed. Tōdaishi kenkyūkai 唐 代史研究会. Tokyo: Kyūkō shoin.

1993. "Kinsei Kōnan Riō kō 近世江南李王考." In *Chūgoku kinsei no hōsei to shakai* 中国近世の法制と社会, pp. 511–41. Ed. Umehara Kaoru 梅原郁. Kyoto: Kyoto daigaku jimbun kagaku kenkyūjo.

2001. *Sōkan shinkō: Kinsei Kōnan nōson shakai to minkan shinkō* 総管信仰 ：近世江南農村社会と民間信仰. Tokyo: Kembun shuppan.

Handlin Smith, Joanna F.

1987. "Benevolent Societies: The Reshaping of Charity during the Late Ming and Early Ch'ing." *Journal of Asian Studies* 46.2: 309–37.

Hansen, Valerie.

1990. *Changing Gods in Medieval China, 1127–1276.* Princeton, N.J.: Princeton University Press.

1993. "Gods on Walls: A Case of Indian Influence on Chinese Lay Religion?" In Ebrey and Gregory, ed., 1993: 75–113.

Haoxian bowuguan 亳县博物馆.

1974. "Haoxian Fenghuangtai yihao Han mu qingli jianbao 亳县凤凰台一号 汉墓清理简报." *Kaogu* 考古 1974.3: 187–90.

Harper, Donald.

1982. "The *Wu Shih Erh Ping Fang:* Translation and Prolegomena." Ph.D. diss., University of California, Berkeley.

1985. "A Chinese Demonography of the Third Century B.C." *Harvard Journal of Asiatic Studies* 45.2: 459–98.

1994. "Resurrection in Warring States Popular Religion." *Taoist Resources* 5.2: 13–28.

1996. "Spellbinding." In Lopez, ed., 1996: 241–50.

1998. *Early Chinese Medical Literature: The Mawangdui Medical Manuscripts.* London: Kegan Paul.

1999. "Warring States Natural Philosophy and Occult Thought." In Loewe and Shaughnessy, ed., 1999: 813–84.

2000. "The Taiyi Cult as an Example of Early Chinese Common Religion." Paper presented at the International Conference on Religion and Chinese Society. Chinese University of Hong Kong, Hong Kong, May 29–June 2.

Hartwell, Robert M.

1982. "Demographic, Political, and Social Transformations of China, 750–1550." *Harvard Journal of Asiatic Studies* 42.2: 365–442.

Hasabe Yūkei 長谷部幽蹊.

1993. *Min Shin Bukkyō kyōdan shi kenkyū* 明清仏教教団史研究. Kyoto: Dōhōsha.

Hayashi Minao 林巳奈夫.

1988. "Chūgoku kodai no gyokki sō ni tsuite 中国古代の玉器琮について." *Tōhō gakuhō* 東方学報 60: 1–72.

1989. *Kandai no kamigami* 漢代の神々. Kyoto: Rinsen shoten.

1990. "On the Chinese Neolithic Jade *Tsung/Cong*." *Artibus Asiae* 50.1/2: 5–22.

Hiraki Kōhei 平木康平.

1982. "Jōjōshin seiritsu kō: Chūgoku boshin no kenkyū 娘娘神成立考：中国母神の研究." *Tōhō shūkyō* 東方宗教 60: 48–68.

Hou Ching-lang.

1975. *Monnaies d'offrande et la notion de trésorie dans la religion chinoise.* Paris: Institut des Hautes Études Chinoises.

1979. "The Chinese Belief in Baleful Stars." In Welch and Seidel, ed., 1979: 193–228.

Howard, Angela F.

1990. "Tang and Song Images of Guanyin from Sichuan." *Orientations* 21.1: 49–57.

2001. *Summit of Treasures: Buddhist Cave Art of Dazu, China.* Trumbull, Conn.: Weatherhill.

Hu Puan 胡朴安.

1923. *Zhonghua quanguo fengsu zhi* 中華全國風俗志. Rpt. Shijiazhuang: Hebei renmin chubanshe, 1988.

Huang Chi-chiang.

1999. "Elite and Clergy in Northern Sung Hang-chou: A Convergence of Interest." In Gregory and Getz, ed., 1999: 295–339.

Hulsewé, Anthony F. P.

1955. *Remnants of Han Law,* vol. 1, *Introductory Studies and Annotated Translation of Chapters 22 and 23 of the History of the Former Han Dynasty.* Leiden: E. J. Brill.

Hunansheng bowuguan 湖南省博物馆.

    1973. *Changsha Mawangdui yihao Han mu* 长沙马王堆一号汉墓. Beijing: Wenwu chubanshe.

Hymes, Robert P.

    1986. *Statesmen and Gentlemen: The Elite of Fu-chou, Chiang-hsi, in Northern and Southern Sung.* Cambridge: Cambridge University Press.

Ide Seinosuke 井手誠之輔.

    2001. "Daitokuji denrai no gohyaku rakan zu to Tōsenko no shiji suiriku dōjō 大徳寺伝来の五百羅漢図と東銭湖の四時水陸道場." Paper presented at the 46th International Conference of Eastern Studies. Tokyo, May 18.

Idema, Wilt, and Stephen H. West.

    1982. *Chinese Theater, 1100–1450: A Sourcebook.* Wiesbaden: Franz Steiner.

Inahata Kōichirō 稲畑耕一郎.

    1979. "Shimei shinzō no tenkai 司命信像の展開." *Chūgoku bungaku kenkyū* 中国文学研究 5: 1–12.

Inoue Ichii 井上以智為.

    1926. "*Gogaku shinkei zu* ni tsuite 五岳真形図について." In *Naitō Konan hakase kanreki shukuga Shinagaku ronsō* 内藤湖南博士還暦祝賀支那学論叢, pp. 43–100. Kyoto: Kobundo shobō.

Ivanits, Linda J.

    1989. *Russian Folk Belief.* Armonk, N.Y.: M. E. Sharpe.

James, Jean M.

    1995. "An Iconographic Study of Xiwangmu During the Han Dynasty." *Artibus Asiae* 55.1/2: 17–41.

    1996. *A Guide to the Tomb and Shrine Art of the Han Dynasty, 206 B.C.–A.D. 220.* Lewiston, N.Y.: Edwin Mellen Press.

Jiang Bin 姜彬, ed.

    1992. *Wu Yue minjian xinyang minsu* 吴越民间信仰民俗. Shanghai: Shanghai wenyi chubanshe.

Jiang Zhushan 蔣竹山.

    1995a. *Cong daji yiduan dao suzao zhengtong—Qingdai guojia yu Jiangnan cishen xinyang* 從打擊異端到塑造正統－清代國家與江南祠神信仰. M.A. thesis, Guoli Taiwan shifan daxue.

    1995b. "Tang Bin jinhui wutongshen: Qingchu zhengzhi jingying daji tongsu wenhuade gean 湯斌禁毀五通神：清初政治菁英打擊通俗文化的個案." *Xin shixue* 新史學 6.2: 67–110.

    1997. "Song zhi Qingdaide guojia yu cishen xinyang yanjiude huigu yu taolun 宋至清代的國家與祠神信仰研究的回顧與討論." *Xin shixue* 新史學 8.2: 187–219.

Jiangsusheng wenwu guanli weiyuanhui 江苏省文物管理委员会.

    1960. "Jiangsu Gaoyou Shaojiagou Handai yizhide qingli 江苏高邮邵家沟汉代遗址的清理." *Kaogu* 考古 1960.10: 18–23.

Jin Tianlin 金田麟.

    1990. "Zhejiang Jiashan Wangjiadaicun 'zhaitian' de diaocha 泰浙江嘉善王家埭村《斋天》的调查." *Minjian wenyi jikan* 民间文艺季刊 1990.1: 135–59.

    1995. "Zhejiang Jiashanxian difangshen jilüe." 浙江嘉善呆地方神记略 *Zhongguo minjian wenhua* 中國民間文化 18: 64–91.

Jing, Anning.

    1994. "Buddhist-Daoist Struggle and a Pair of 'Daoist Murals.'" *Bulletin of the Museum of Far Eastern Antiquities* 66: 117–81.

Johnson, David.

    1980. "The Wu Tzu-hsu *Pien-wen* and Its Sources." *Harvard Journal of Asiatic Studies* 40.1: 93–156; 40.2: 465–505.

    1985. "The City God Cults of T'ang and Sung China." *Harvard Journal of Asiatic Studies* 45.2: 363–457.

    1989. "Actions Speak Louder Than Words: The Cultural Significance of Chinese Ritual Opera." In Johnson, ed., 1989: 1–45.

Johnson, David, ed.

    1989. *Ritual Opera, Operatic Ritual: "Mu-Lien Rescues His Mother" in Chinese Popular Culture*. Berkeley: Chinese Popular Culture Project, University of California, Berkeley.

    1995. *Ritual and Scripture in Chinese Popular Religion: Five Studies*. Berkeley: Chinese Popular Culture Project, University of California, Berkeley.

Johnson, David, Andrew J. Nathan, and Evelyn S. Rawski, ed.

    1985. *Popular Culture in Late Imperial China*. Berkeley: University of California Press.

Kaltenmark, Max.

    1979. "The Ideology of the *T'ai P'ing Ching*." In Welch and Seidel, ed., 1979: 19–45.

Kamitsuka Yoshiko.

    1996. "The Concept of Māra and the Idea of Expelling Demons." *Taoist Resources* 6.2: 30–50.

Kanai Noriyuki 金井德幸.

    1979. "Sōdai no sonsha to shashin 宋代の村社と社神." *Tōyōshi kenkyū* 東洋史研究 38.2: 219–45.

    1980. "Sōdai no gyōsha to tochishin 宋代の郷社と土地神." In *Nakajima Satoshi sensei koki kinen ronshū* 中嶋敏先生古希記念論集, 1: 385–407. Tokyo: Kyūko shoin.

    1982. "Sōdai no sonsha to sōzoku 宋代の村社と宗族." In *Rekishi ni okeru*

minshū to bunka: Sakai Tadao sensei koki shukuga kinenshū 歴史におけ
る民衆と文化：酒井忠夫先生古希祝賀記念集, pp. 351–67. Tokyo: Koku-
sho kankōkai.

1985. "Sōdai Sessai no sonsha to toshin: Sōdai gyōson shakai no shūkyō kōzō
宋代浙西の村社と土神：宋代郷村社会の宗教構造." In *Sōdai no shakai to
shūkyō* 宋代の社会と宗教, pp. 81–118. Ed. Sōdaishi kenkyūkai 宋代史
研究会. Tokyo: Kyūko shoten.

1987. "Nan-Sō jidai no shichin tōgakubyō 南宋時代の市鎮東岳廟." *Rissei shigaku* 立正史学 61: 21–39.

1994. "Sōdai no gotsūshin shinkō to baibyō 宋代の五通神信仰と売廟." *Rissei shigaku* 立正史学 76: 21–40.

Katz, Paul R.

1995. *Demon Hordes and Burning Boats: The Cult of Marshal Wen in Late
Imperial Chekiang.* Albany: State University of New York Press.

1999. *Images of the Immortal: The Cult of Lü Dongbin at the Palace of Eternal Joy.* Honolulu: University of Hawaii Press.

Keightley, David N.

1976. "Late Shang Divination: The Magico-Religious Legacy." In *Explorations
in Early Chinese Cosmology,* pp. 11–34. Ed. Henry Rosemont, Jr. Chico,
Calif.: Scholars Press.

1978a. "The Religious Commitment: Shang Theology and the Genesis of Chinese Political Culture." *History of Religions* 17.3–4: 211–25.

1978b. *Sources of Shang History.* Berkeley: University of California Press.

1982. "Akatsuka Kiyoshi and the Culture of Early China: A Study in Historical Method." *Harvard Journal of Asiatic Studies* 42.1: 267–320.

1983. "The Late Shang State: When, Where, and What?" In *The Origins of
Chinese Civilization,* pp. 523–64. Ed. David N. Keightley. Berkeley: University of California Press.

1991. "The Quest for Eternity in Ancient China: The Dead, Their Gifts, Their
Names." In Kuwayama, ed., 1991: 12–25.

1998. "Shamanism, Death, and the Ancestors: Religious Mediation in Neolithic and Shang China (ca. 5000–1000 B.C.)." *Asiatische Studien* 52.3:
765–831.

1999. "The Shang: China's First Historical Dynasty." In Loewe and Shaughnessy, ed., 1999: 232–91.

2001. *The Ancestral Landscape: Time, Space, and Community in Late Shang
China (ca. 1200–1045 B.C.).* Berkeley: Institute of East Asian Studies, University of California, Berkeley.

Kesner, Ladislav.

1991. "The *Taotie* Reconsidered: Meanings and Functions of Shang Theri-
omorphic Imagery." *Artibus Asiae* 51.1: 29–53.

Kiang, Shao-yuan (Jiang Shaoyuan).

　1937. *Le voyage dans la chine ancienne, considéré principalement sous son aspect magique et réligieux.* Shanghai: Commission mixte des oeuvres franco-chinoises.

Kishimoto Mio 岸本美緒.

　1997. *Shindai Chūgoku no bukka to keizai hendō* 清代中国の物価と経済変動. Tokyo: Kembun shuppan.

Kitada Hideto 北田英人.

　1996. "Ichi-roku seiki ni okeru tochishin seisei no shosō 1–6 世紀における土地神生成の諸相." *Chūgoku shigaku* 中国史学 6: 109–30.

Kleeman, Terry F.

　1993. "Expansion of the Wen-ch'ang Cult." In Ebrey and Gregory, ed., 1993: 45–73.

　1994a. *A God's Own Tale:* The Book of Transformations of Wenchang, the Divine Lord of Zitong. Albany: State University of New York Press.

　1994b. "Mountain Deities in China: Domestication of the Mountain God and the Subjugation of the Mountains." *Journal of the American Oriental Society* 114.2: 226–38.

　1994c. "Licentious Cults and Bloody Victuals: Standards of Religious Orthodoxy in Traditional China." *Asia Major,* 4th series, 7.1: 185–211.

　1998. *Great Perfection: Religion and Ethnicity in a Chinese Millennial Kingdom.* Honolulu: University of Hawaii Press.

Kobayashi Masayoshi 小林正美.

　1991. *Rikuchō dōkyōshi kenkyū* 六朝道教史研究. Tokyo: Sobunsha.

Kobayashi Taiichirō 小林太一郎.

　1947. *Kan Tō kozoku to myōki dōgu* 漢唐古俗と明器道具. Kyoto: Ijo shobō.

Kohn, Livia.

　1998. "Counting Good Deeds and Days of Life: The Quantification of Fate in Medieval China." *Asiatische Studien* 52.3: 833–70.

Kojima Tsuyoshi 小島毅.

　1990. "Seikobyō seido no seiritsu 城隍廟制度の成立." *Shisō* 思想 792: 197–212.

　1991. "Seishi to inshi: Fukken no chihoshi ni okeru kijutsu to ronri 正祠と淫祠：福建の地方志における記述と論理." *Tōyō bunka kenkyūjo kiyō* 東洋文化研究所紀要 114: 87–213.

Kominami Ichirō 小南一郎.

　1987. "Sha no saiji no shokeitai to sono kigen 社の祭事の諸形態とその起源." *Koshi shunjū* 古史春秋 4: 17–37.

　1994. "Kandai no sōrei kannen 漢代の宗礼観念." *Tōhō gakuhō* 東方学報 66: 1–62.

Kubō Noritada 窪德忠.

1986. *Dōkyō no kamigami* 道教の神々. Tokyo: Hirakawa shuppansha.

Kucera, Karil J.

1995. "Lessons in Stone: Baodingshan and its Hell Imagery." *Bulletin of the Museum of Far Eastern Antiquities* 67: 79–157.

Kuhn, Dieter.

1994. "Decoding Tombs of the Song Elite." In *Burial in Song China,* pp. 11–159. Ed. Dieter Kuhn. Heidelberg: Edition Forum.

Kuwayama, George, ed.

1991. *Ancient Mortuary Traditions of China: Papers on Chinese Ceramic Funerary Sculptures.* Los Angeles: Los Angeles County Museum of Art.

Lagerwey, John.

1987. *Taoist Ritual in Chinese Society and History.* New York: Macmillan.

Larre, Claude, Isabelle Robinet, and Elisabeth Rochat de la Vallée.

1993. *Les grands traités du Huainan zi.* Paris: Editions du Cerf.

Lauwaert, Françoise.

1990. "Comptes des dieux, calculs des hommes: essai sur la notion de retribution dans les contes en langue vulgaire du 17ᵉ siècle." *T'oung Pao* 76.1–3: 62–94.

Le Blanc, Charles.

1985–86. "A Re-Examination of the Myth of Huang-ti." *Journal of Chinese Religions* 13/14: 45–63.

Lee, Sherman E.

1993. "Yan Hui, Zhong Kui, Demons and the New Year." *Artibus Asiae* 53.1–2: 211–27.

Levenson, Joseph R., and Franz Schurmann.

1969. *China: An Interpretive History, From the Beginnings to the Fall of Han.* Berkeley: University of California Press.

Levi, Jean.

1989. *Les Fonctionnaires divins: politique, despotisme, et mystique en chine ancienne.* Paris: Editions du Seuil.

Lewis, Mark Edward.

1990. *Sanctioned Violence in Early China.* Albany: State University of New York Press.

1999. *Writing and Authority in Early China.* Albany: State University of New York Press.

Li Fengmao 李豐楙.

1993. "*Daozang* suoshou zaoqi daoshude wenyiguan—yi *Nüqing guilü* ji *Dongyuan shenzhou jing* xi wei li 道藏所收早期道書的瘟疫觀－以女青鬼

律及洞源神咒經析為例." *Zhongguo wenzhe yanjiu jikan* 中國文哲研究集刊 3: 417–54.

Li Ling.

　1995–96. "An Archaeological Study of Taiyi (Grand One) Worship." *Early Medieval China* 2: 1–39.

Li Shiyu 李世瑜.

　1961. *Baojuan zonglu* 寶卷綜錄. Beijing: Zhonghua shuju.

Li Xianzhang 李獻璋.

　1979. *Boso shinkō no kenkyū* 媽祖信仰の研究. Tokyo: Taizan bunbutsusha.

Li Xueqin.

　1993. "Liangzhu Culture and the Shang *Taotie* Motif." In Whitfield, ed., 1993: 56–66.

Liang Qizi 梁其姿.

　1997. *Shishan yu jiaohua: Ming Qingde cishan zuzhi* 施善與教化：明清的慈善組織. Taibei: Lianjing chuban gongsi.

Liao Hsien-huei (Liao Xianhui) 廖咸惠.

　1996. "Tang Song shiqi nanfang houtu xinyangde yanbian—yi Yangzhou houtu chongbai wei li 唐宋時期南方后土信仰的演變—以揚州后土崇拜為例." *Hanxue yanjiu* 漢學研究 14.2: 103–34.

　2001. "Popular Religion and the Religious Beliefs of the Song Elite, 960–1276." Ph.D. diss., University of California, Los Angeles.

Liaoningsheng bowuguan 辽宁省博物馆.

　1988. *Gusu xihua tu* 姑蘇繫華圖. Hong Kong: Shangwu yinshuguan.

Lin Hengdao 林衡道.

　1974. *Taiwan simiao daquan* 台灣寺廟大全. Taibei: Qingwen chubanshe.

Little, Stephen.

　1985. "The Demon Queller and the Art of Ch'iu Ying." *Artibus Asiae* 46.1–2: 1–128.

Liu Changjiu 刘长久 et al., ed.

　1985. *Dazu shike yanjiu* 大足石刻研究. Chengdu: Sichuansheng shehui kexueyuan chubanshe.

Liu Lexian 刘乐贤.

　1993. "Shuihudi Qinjian rishu 'Jiejiu pian' yanjiu" 睡虎地秦简日书《诘咎篇》研究. *Kaogu xuebao* 考古学报 1993.4: 435–54.

Liu Ts'un-yan.

　1962. *Buddhist and Taoist Influences on Chinese Novels*. Wiesbaden: Otto Harrassowitz.

　1967. *Chinese Popular Fiction in Two London Libraries*. Hong Kong: Lung Men Bookstore.

Liu Zhiwan 劉枝萬.

1983. "Taiwan zhi wenshen xinyang" 台灣之瘟神信仰. In Liu, *Taiwan min-jian xinyang lunji* 台灣民間信仰論集, pp. 225–34. Taibei: Lianjing chuban shiye gongsi.

1987. "Tenhōshin to tenhōju ni tsuite 天蓬神と天蓬呪について." In *Dōkyō to shūkyō bunka* 道教と宗教文化, pp. 403–24. Ed. Akizuki Kan'ei 秋月観映. Tokyo: Hirakawa shuppansha.

Loewe, Michael.

1970. "The Case of Witchcraft in 91 B.C.: Its Historical Setting and Effect on Han Dynastic History." *Asia Major,* 3rd series, 15.2: 159–96.

1971. "K'uang Heng and the Reform of Religious Practices (31 B.C.)." *Asia Major,* 3rd series, 17.1: 1–27.

1978. "Man and Beast: The Hybrid in Early Chinese Art and Literature." *Numen* 25.2: 97–117.

1979. *Ways to Paradise: The Chinese Quest for Immortality.* London: George Allen & Unwin.

1982. *Chinese Ideas of Life and Death: Faith, Myth, and Reason in the Han Period (202 B.C.–A.D. 220).* London: George Allen & Unwin.

Loewe, Michael, and Edward L. Shaughnessy, ed.

1999. *The Cambridge History of Ancient China: From the Origins of Civilization to 221 B.C.* Cambridge: Cambridge University Press.

Lopez, Donald S., Jr., ed.

1996. *Religions of China in Practice.* Princeton, N.J.: Princeton University Press.

Lufrano, Richard John.

1997. *Honorable Merchants: Commerce and Self-Cultivation in Late Imperial China.* Honolulu: University of Hawaii Press.

McMahon, Keith.

1988. *Causality and Containment in 17ᵗʰ-Century Chinese Fiction.* Leiden: E. J. Brill.

Mair, Victor.

1983. *Tun-huang Popular Narratives.* Cambridge: Cambridge University Press.

1986. "Records of Transformation Tableau (Pien-Hsiang)." *T'oung Pao* 72.3: 3–43.

Major, John S.

1993. *Heaven and Earth in Early Han Thought: Chapters Three, Four, and Five of the* Huainanzi. Albany: State University of New York Press.

Makita Tairyō 牧田諦亮.

1957. "Suirikkai shokō 水陸会小考." In Makita, *Chūgoku kinsei bukkyōshi kenkyū* 中国近世仏教史研究, pp. 169–93. Kyoto: Heirakuji shoten.

Maruyama Hiroshi 丸山宏.

1986. "Sei'ichi dōkyō no jōshō girei ni tsuite: 'chōshōshō' o chūshin to shite" 正一道教の上章儀礼について：《冢訟章》を中心として. *Tōhō shūkyō* 東方宗教 68: 44–64.

Maspero, Henri.

1924. "Légendes mythologiques dans le *Chou king*." *Journal Asiatique* 204: 11–100.

1928/1981. "Mythologie de la Chine moderne." In *Mythologie asiatique illustré*. Paris: Libraire de France. Translated as "The Mythology of Modern China," in Maspero, *Taoism and Chinese Religion*, pp. 75–196. Amherst: University of Massachusetts Press, 1981.

Mathieu, Remi.

1983. *Étude sur la mythologie et l'ethnologie de la chine ancienne*. Paris: Institut des Hautes Études Chinoises.

Matsumoto Kōichi 松本浩一.

1983. "Sōrei, sairei ni miru Sōdai shūkyōshi no ichi keikō 葬礼祭礼にみる宋代宗教史の一傾向." In *Sōdai no shakai to bunka* 宋代の社会と文化, pp. 169–94. Ed. Sōdaishi kenkyūkai 宋代史研究会. Tokyo: Kyūko shoten.

1993. "Chūgoku sonraku ni okeru shibyō to sono hensen: Chūgoku no shibyō ni kansuru kenkyū dōkō to mondaiten 中国村落における祠廟とその変遷：中国の祠廟に関する研究動向と問題点." *Shakai bunka shigaku* 社会文化史学 31: 27–43.

1999. "Sōdai no sha to shibyō 宋代の社と祠廟." *Shikyō* 史境 38–39: 1–15.

Miyakawa Hisayuki 宮川尚志.

1964. *Rikuchō shi kenkyū: shūkyō hen* 六朝史研究：宗教篇. Kyoto: Heirakuji shoten.

Miyamoto Noriyuki 宮本則之.

1992. "Sō Gen jidai ni okeru fun'an to sosen saishi 宋元時代における墳庵と祖先祭祀." *Bukkyō shigaku kenkyū* 仏教史学研究 35.2: 112–34.

Miyashita Saburō 宮下三郎.

1959. "Chūgoku kodai no shippeikan to ryōhō 中国古代の疾病観と療法." *Tōhō gakuhō* 東方学報 30: 227–52.

Mizukoshi Tomo 水越知.

2002. "Sōdai shakai to shibyō shinkō no tenkai: chiikikaku to shite no shibyō no shutsugen 宋代社会と祠廟信仰の展開：地域核としての祠廟の出現." *Tōyōshi kenkyū* 東洋史研究 60.4: 629–66.

Mollier, Christine.

1991. *Une apocalypse taoiste du Ve siècle: Le Livre des Incantations Divines des Grottes Abyssales*. Paris: Collège de France / Institut des Hautes Études Chinoises.

1997. "La Méthode de l'Empereur du Nord du Mont Fengdu: une tradition exorciste du taoisme médiéval." *T'oung Pao* 83.4–5: 329–85.

Mori Yasutarō 森安太郎.

　1970. *Kōtei densetsu: kodai Chūgoku shinwa no kenkyū* 黄帝伝説：古代中国神話の研究. Kyoto: Kyoto joshi daigaku jimbun gakkai.

Moriya Mitsuo 守屋美都雄.

　1949. *Chūgoku ko saijiki no kenkyū* 中国古歳事記の研究. Tokyo: Teikoku shoin.

Nagahiro Toshio 長広敏雄.

　1969. "Kishinzū no keifu 鬼神図の系譜." In Nagahiro, *Rikuchō jidai bijutsu no kenkyū* 六朝時代美術の研究, pp. 105-41. Tokyo: Bijutsu shuppansha.

Nakamura Hiroichi 中村裕一.

　1983. "Dōkyō to nenchū gyōji 道教と年中行事." In *Dōkyō* 道教, 2: 371-411. Ed. Fukui Kōjun 福井康須 et al. Tokyo: Hirakawa shuppansha.

Nakamura Jihei 中村治兵衛.

　1978. "Hoku-Sōcho to fu 北宋朝と巫." *Chūo daigaku bungakubu kiyō, shigakka* 中央大学文学部紀要史学科 23: 63-78.

　1980. "Chūgoku shūraku shi kenkyū no kaiko to tembō: tokuni sonraku shi o chūshin to shite 中国聚落史研究の回顧と展望：とくに村落史を中心として." In *Chūgoku shūraku shi no kenkyū: shūhen shochiiki to no hikaku o fukumete* 中国聚落史の研究：周辺諸地域との比較を含めて, pp. 5-22. Tōdaishi kenkyūkai 唐代史研究会, ed. Tokyo: Katanamizu shobō.

　1982. "Sōdai no fu no tokuchō: nyūfu katei no kyūmei o fukumete 宋代の巫の特徴：入巫過程の究明を含めて." *Chūo daigaku bungakubu kiyō, shigakka* 中央大学文学部紀要史学科 27: 51-75.

Naquin, Susan, and Chün-fang Yü.

　1993. "Introduction: Pilgrimage in China." In Naquin and Yü, ed., 1993: pp. 1-38.

Naquin, Susan, and Chün-fang Yü, ed.

　1993. *Pilgrimage and Sacred Places in China*. Berkeley: University of California Press.

Needham, Joseph.

　1974. *Science and Civilisation in China*, vol. 5, *Chemistry and Chemical Technology*, pt. 2: *Spagyrical Discovery and Invention: Magisteries of Gold and Immortality*. Cambridge: University of Cambridge Press.

Nickerson, Peter.

　1994. "Shamans, Demons, Diviners and Taoists: Conflict and Assimilation in Medieval Chinese Ritual Practice (c. A.D. 100-1000)." *Taoist Resources* 5.1: 41-66.

　1996. "Abridged Codes of Master Lu for the Daoist Community." In Lopez, ed., 1996: 347-59.

　2000. "The Ritual of 'Petitioning Celestial Officials' in Celestial Master Taoism: A Re-examination of the Problem of Taoism and Popular Religion." Paper presented at the International Conference on Religion and Chinese Society. Chinese University of Hong Kong, Hong Kong, May 29–June 2.

Niida Noboru 仁井田陞.

1951. *Chūgoku no shakai to girudo* 中国の社会とギルド. Tokyo: Iwanami shoten.

Ōfuchi Ninji 大淵忍爾.

1964. "*Sankōbun* yori *Dōshinkei* e 三皇文より洞神経へ." In Ōfuchi, *Dōkyō-shi no kenkyū* 道教史の研究, pp. 277–343. Okayama: Okayama daigaku kozaikai shosekibu.

1991. *Shoki no Dōkyō* 初期の道教. Tokyo: Sobunsha.

Ogasawara Senshū 小笠原宣秀.

1963. *Chūgoku kinsei jōdokyō shi no kenkyū* 中国近世浄土教史の研究. Kyoto: Hōzōkan.

Orzech, Charles.

1996. "Saving the Burning Mouth Hungry Ghost." In Lopez, ed., 1996: 278–83.

Ōtani Kōshō 大谷光照.

1937. *Tōdai no bukkyō girei* 唐代の仏教儀礼. Tokyo: Yukosha.

Ou Yue 欧粤.

1992. "Shanghai shijiao suishi xinyang xisu diaocha 上海市郊岁时信仰习俗调查." *Zhongguo minjian wenhua* 中国民间文化 5: 127–50.

Overmyer, Daniel.

1976. *Folk Buddhist Religion of China.* Cambridge, Mass.: Harvard University Press.

1985. "Values in Chinese Sectarian Literature: Ming and Ch'ing Pao-chüan." In Johnson et al., ed., 1985: 219–54.

1999. *Precious Volumes: An Introduction to Chinese Sectarian Scriptures of the Sixteenth and Seventeenth Centuries.* Cambridge, Mass.: Council on East Asian Studies, Harvard University.

Paper, Jordan.

1995. *The Spirits Are Drunk: Comparative Approaches to Chinese Religion.* Albany: State University of New York Press.

Parry, Jonathan, and Maurice Bloch, ed.

1989. *Money and the Morality of Exchange.* Cambridge: Cambridge University Press.

Po, Sung-nien, and David Johnson.

1992. *Domesticated Deities and Auspicious Emblems: The Iconography of Everyday Life in Village China.* Berkeley: Chinese Popular Culture Project, University of California, Berkeley.

Poo, Mu-chou.

 1998. *In Search of Personal Welfare: A View of Ancient Chinese Religion.* Albany: State University of New York Press.

Porkert, Manfred.

 1974. *The Theoretical Foundations of Chinese Medicine: Systems of Correspondence.* Cambridge, Mass.: MIT Press.

Potter, Jack M.

 1974. "Cantonese Shamanism." In Wolf, ed., 1974: 207–32.

Powers, Martin J.

 1991. *Art and Political Expression in Early China.* New Haven, Conn.: Yale University Press.

Puett, Michael.

 1998. "Sages, Ministers, and Rebels: Narratives from Early China Concerning the Initial Creation of the State." *Harvard Journal of Asiatic Studies* 58.2: 425–79.

Rao Zongyi 饒宗頤.

 1969. "Ba Dunhuang ben *Baize jingguai tu* liang canjuan (P. 2682, S. 6261) 跋敦煌本白澤精怪圖兩殘卷." *Zhongyang yanjiuyuan lishi yuyan yanjiusuo jikan* 中央研究院歷史語言研究所集刊 21.4: 539–43.

 1974. "Wuxian Xuanmiaoguan shichu huaji 吳縣玄妙觀石礎畫跡." *Zhongyang yanjiuyuan lishi yuyan yanjiusuo jikan* 中央研究院歷史語言研究所集刊 25.2: 255–309.

Rawski, Evelyn S.

 1985. "Economic and Social Foundations of Late Imperial Culture." In Johnson et al., ed., 1985: 3–33.

 1988. "A Historian's Approach to Chinese Death Ritual." In *Death Ritual in Late Imperial and Modern China,* pp. 20–34. Ed. James L. Watson and Evelyn S. Rawski. Berkeley: University of California Press.

Rawson, Jessica.

 1996. "Changes in the Representation of Life and Afterlife as Illustrated by the Contents of Tombs of the Sung and Yüan Periods." In *Arts of the Sung and Yüan,* pp. 23–43. Ed. Maxwell K. Hearn and Judith G. Smith. New York: Metropolitan Museum of Art.

 1999a. "The Eternal Palaces of the Western Han: A New View of the Universe." *Artibus Asiae* 49.1/2: 1–35.

 1999b. "Western Zhou Archaeology." In Loewe and Shaughnessy, ed., 1999: 352–449.

 2000. "Religious Change as Seen in the Material Record, 500 BC–AD 200: The Changes in Offerings to the Ancestors." Paper presented at the International Conference on Religion and Chinese Society. Chinese University of Hong Kong, Hong Kong, May 29–June 2.

Robinet, Isabelle.

    1984. *La révélation du Shangqing dans l'histoire du taoisme*. Paris: École Française d'Extrême Orient.

    1997. *Taoism: Growth of a Religion*. Stanford, Calif.: Stanford University Press.

Rowe, William.

    1984. *Hankow: Commerce and Society in a Chinese City, 1796–1889*. Stanford, Calif.: Stanford University Press.

Rudova, Maria, ed.

    1988. *Chinese Popular Prints*. Leningrad: Aurora Art Publishers.

Sabean, David Warren.

    1984. *Power in the Blood: Popular Culture and Village Discourse in Early Modern Germany*. Cambridge: Cambridge University Press.

Sakai Tadao 酒井忠夫.

    1960. *Chūgoku zensho no kenkyū* 中国善書の研究. Tokyo: Kōbundō.

    1970. "Confucianism and Popular Educational Works." In *Self and Society in Ming Thought*, pp. 331–66. Ed. Wm. Theodore de Bary. New York: Columbia University Press.

Sangren, Steven P.

    1987. *History and Magical Power in a Chinese Community*. Stanford, Calif.: Stanford University Press.

Satō Seijun 佐藤成順.

    1988. "Hoku-Sō jidai no Kōshū to jōdokyō 北宋時代の杭州と浄土教." In *Kamata Shigeo hakushi kanreki kinen ronshū Chūgoku no bukkyō to bunka* 鎌田茂雄博士還暦紀念論集中国の仏教と文化, pp. 457–82. Tokyo: Ōkura shuppan.

Sawada Mizuho 沢田瑞穂.

    1969. "Kami ni shakkin suru hanashi 神に借金する話." *Tenri daigaku gakuhō* 天理大学学報 61: 85–96.

    1975. *[Zōhō] Hōkan no kenkyū* [増補] 宝巻の研究. Tokyo: Kokusho kankōkai.

    1982. *Chūgoku no minkan shūkyō* 中国の民間宗教. Tokyo: Kōsakusha.

    1984. *Chūgoku no juhō* 中国の呪法. Tokyo: Hirakawa shuppansha.

Schaberg, David.

    1999. "Travel, Geography, and the Imperial Imagination in Fifth-Century Athens and Han China." *Comparative Literature* 55.2: 152–91.

Schafer, Edward H.

    1967. *The Vermillion Bird: T'ang Images of the South*. Berkeley: University of California Press.

Schipper, Kristofer.

1971. "Démonologie chinoise." In *Sources orientales,* vol. 8, *Génies, anges, et démons,* pp. 405–29. Paris: Éditions du Seuil.

1977. "Neighborhood Cult Associations in Traditional Tainan." In *The City in Late Imperial China,* pp. 651–76. Ed. G. William Skinner. Stanford, Calif.: Stanford University Press.

1978. "The Taoist Body." *History of Religions* 17.2: 355–87.

1985a. "Seigneurs royaux, dieux des épidemies." *Archives sciences sociales des religions* 59.1: 31–40.

1985b. "Taoist Ritual and Local Cults in the T'ang Dynasty." In *Tantric and Taoist Studies in Honour of R. A. Stein,* 3: 812–34. Ed. Michel Strickmann. Bruxelles: Institut Belge des Hautes Études Chinoises.

1985c. "Vernacular and Classical Religion in Taoism." *Journal of Asian Studies* 45.1: 21–57.

1990. "The Cult of Baosheng Dadi and its Spread to Taiwan—A Case of *Fenxiang.*" In *Development and Decline of Fukien Province in the Seventeenth and Eighteenth Centuries,* pp. 397–416. Ed. E. B. Vermeer. Leiden: E. J. Brill.

Schwartz, Benjamin I.

1985. *The World of Thought in Ancient China.* Cambridge, Mass.: Harvard University Press.

Seaman, Gary.

1987. *Journey to the North: An Ethnohistorical Analysis and Annotated Translation of the Chinese Folk Novel* Pei-yu chi. Berkeley: University of California Press.

Seidel, Anna.

1969. *Le divinisation de Lao tseu dans le taoisme des Han.* Paris: École Française d'Extrême Orient.

1983. "Imperial Treasures and Taoist Sacraments: Taoist Roots in the Apocrypha." In *Tantric and Taoist Studies in Honour of R. A. Stein,* 2: 291–371. Ed. Michel Strickmann. Bruxelles: Institut Belge des Hautes Études Chinoises.

1987a. "Post-mortem Immortality—or: the Taoist Resurrection of the Body." In *Gilgul: Essays on Transformation, Revolution, and Permanence in the History of Religions Dedicated to R. J. Zwi Werblowsky,* pp. 223–37. Ed. S. Shaked, D. Shulman, and G. G. Stroumsa. Leiden: E. J. Brill.

1987b. "Traces of Han Religion: In Funerary Texts Found in Tombs." In *Dōkyō to shūkyō bunka* 道教と宗教文化, pp. 21–57. Ed. Akizuki Kan'ei 秋月観映. Tokyo: Hirakawa shuppansha.

Shahar, Meir, and Robert Weller.

1996. "Introduction: Gods and Society in China." In Shahar and Weller, ed., 1996: 1–36.

Shahar, Meir, and Robert Weller, ed.

　1996. *Unruly Gods: Divinity and Society in China*. Honolulu: University of Hawaii Press.

Shanghai bowuguan qingtongqi yanjiuzu 上海博物馆青铜器研究组.

　1984. *Shang Zhou qingtongqi wenshi* 商周青铜器文饰. Beijing: Wenwu chubanshe.

Shanxisheng bowuguan 山西省博物馆.

　1985. *Baoningsi Mingdai shuiluhua* 宝宁寺明代水陆画. Beijing: Wenwu chubanshe.

Shaughnessy, Edward L.

　1991. *Sources of Western Zhou History: Inscribed Bronze Vessels*. Berkeley: University of California Press.

　1999. "Western Zhou History." In Loewe and Shaughnessy, ed., 1999: 292–351.

Shen Zongxian 沈宗憲.

　1995. "Songdai minjian cisi yu zhengfu zhengce 宋代民間祠祀與政府政策." *Dalu zazhi* 大陸雜誌 91.6: 23–41.

Shiba Yoshinobu 斯波義信.

　1968. *Sōdai shōgyōshi kenkyū* 宋代商業史研究. Tokyo: Kazama shobō.

Shinohara Hisao 篠原寿雄.

　1977. "Dōkyōteki kishin: oni ni kansuru oboegaki 道教の鬼神：鬼に関する覚書." In *Yoshioka hakase kanreki kinen Dōkyō kenkyū ronshū* 吉岡博士還暦記念道教研究論集, pp. 225–47. Tokyo: Kokusho kankōkai.

Sivin, Nathan.

　1987. *Traditional Medicine in Contemporary China*. Ann Arbor: University of Michigan Center for Chinese Studies.

Sōda Hiroshi 相田弘.

　1997. *Ijin to ichi: kyōkai no Chūgoku kodai shi* 異人と市：境界の中国古代史. Tokyo: Kenbun shuppan.

Stein, Rolf.

　1979. "Religious Taoism and Popular Religion from the Second to the Seventh Centuries." In Welch and Seidel, ed., 1979: 53–81.

　1986. "Avalokiteśvara/Kouan-yin: exemple de transformation d'un dieu en déese." *Cahiers d'Extrême-Asie* 2: 17–80.

Stevenson, Daniel B.

　1999. "Protocols of the Gods: Tz'u-yun Tsun-shih (964–1032) and T'ien-t'ai Lay Buddhist Ritual in the Sung." In Gregory and Getz, ed., 1999: 340–408.

Strickmann, Michel.

　1977. "The Mao Shan Revelations: Taoism and the Aristocracy." *T'oung Pao* 63: 1–64.

　1978. "The Longest Taoist Scripture." *History of Religions* 17.2: 331–54.

1981. *Le Taoisme du Mao Chan, chronique d'une révélation.* Paris: Presses Universitaires de France.

2002. *Chinese Magical Medicine.* Stanford, Calif.: Stanford University Press.

Sue Takashi 須江隆.

1994. "Tō-Sōki shibyō no byōgaku, hōgo no kashi ni tsuite 唐宋期の廟額, 封号の下賜について." *Chūgoku—shakai to bunka* 中国--社会と文化 9: 96–119.

Suzhou lishi bowuguan 苏州历史博物馆, ed.

1981. *Ming Qing Suzhou gongshangye beike ji* 明清苏州工商业碑刻集. Nanjing: Jiangsu renmin chubanshe.

Szonyi, Michael.

1997. "The Illusion of Standardizing the Gods: The Cult of the Five Emperors in Late Imperial China." *Journal of Asian Studies* 56.1: 113–35.

Taylor, Romeyn.

1990. "Official and Popular Religion and the Political Organization of Chinese Society in the Ming." In *Orthodoxy in Late Imperial China,* pp. 126–57. Ed. Kwang-ching Liu. Berkeley: University of California Press.

Teiser, Stephen F.

1988. *The Ghost Festival in Medieval China.* Princeton, N.J.: Princeton University Press.

1994. *The Scripture of the Ten Kings and the Making of Purgatory in Medieval Chinese Buddhism.* Honolulu: University of Hawaii Press.

ter Haar, Barend.

1990. "The Genesis and Spread of Temple Cults in Fukien." In *Development and Decline of Fukien Province in the Seventeenth and Eighteenth Centuries,* pp. 349–95. Ed. E. B. Vermeer. Leiden: E. J. Brill.

1992. *The White Lotus Teachings in Chinese Religious History.* Leiden: E. J. Brill.

1995. "Local Society and the Organization of Cults in Early Modern China: A Preliminary Study." *Studies in Central & East Asian Religions* 8: 1–43.

2000. "The Rise of the Guan Yu Cult: The Taoist Connection." In *Linked Faiths: Essays on Chinese Religions and Traditional Culture in Honour of Kristofer Schipper,* pp. 184–204. Ed. Jan A. M. de Meyer and Peter M. Engelfriet. Leiden: E. J. Brill.

Terada Takanobu 寺田隆信.

1972. *Sansei shōnin no kenkyū* 山西商人の研究. Kyoto: Dōhōsha.

Thomas, Keith.

1971. *Religion and the Decline of Magic.* New York: Scribner's.

Thorp, Robert.

1991. "Mountain Tombs and Jade Burial Suits: Preparations for Eternity in the Western Han." In Kuwayama, ed., 1991: 26–39.

Thote, Alain.

Forthcoming. "Burial Practices as Seen in Rulers' Tombs of the Eastern Zhou Period: Patterns and Regional Traditions." In *Chinese Religion and Society: The Transformation of a Field*, vol 1. Ed. John Lagerwey. Hong Kong: Chinese University of Hong Kong and École Française d'Extrême-Orient.

Tianjinshi yishu bowuguan 天津市艺术博物馆.

1993. *Tianjinshi yishu bowuguan cang yu* 天津市艺术博物馆藏玉. Beijing: Wenwu chubanshe.

T'ien Ju-k'ang.

1988. *Male Anxiety and Female Chastity: A Comparative Study of Chinese Ethical Values in Ming-Ch'ing Times*. Leiden: E. J. Brill.

Unschuld, Paul U.

1985. *Medicine in China: A History of Ideas*. Berkeley: University of California Press.

van der Loon, Piet.

1977. "Les Origines rituelles de théâtre chinoise." *Journal Asiatique* 265: 141–68.

Verellen, Franciscus.

1992. " 'Evidential Miracles in Support of Taoism': The Inversion of a Buddhist Apologetic Tradition in Late Tang China." *T'oung Pao* 78: 217–63.

von Falkenhausen, Lothar.

1993. "Issues in Western Zhou Studies: A Review Article." *Early China* 18: 139–226.

1994. "Sources of Taoism: Reflections on Archaeological Indicators of Religious Change in Eastern Zhou China." *Taoist Resources* 5.2: 1–12.

1999. "The Waning of the Bronze Age: Material Culture and Social Developments, 700–481 B.C." In Loewe and Shaughnessy, ed., 1999: 450–544.

Forthcoming. "Mortuary Behavior in Pre-Imperial Qin: A Religious Interpretation." In *Chinese Religion and Society: The Transformation of a Field*, vol 1. Ed. John Lagerwey. Hong Kong: Chinese University of Hong Kong and École Française d'Extrême-Orient.

von Glahn, Richard.

1987. *The Country of Streams and Grottoes: Expansion, Settlement, and the Civilizing of the Sichuan Frontier in Song Times*. Cambridge, Mass.: Council on East Asian Studies, Harvard University.

1991. "The Enchantment of Wealth: The God *Wutong* in the Social History of Jiangnan." *Harvard Journal of Asiatic Studies* 51.2: 651–714.

1996. *Fountain of Fortune: Money and Monetary Policy in China, 1000–1700*. Berkeley: University of California Press.

2003a. "Money-Use in China and Changing Patterns of Global Trade in Monetary Metals, 1500–1800." In *Global Connections and Monetary History,*

1470–1800, pp.187–205. Ed. Dennis Flynn, Arturo Giráldez, and Richard von Glahn. Aldershot, UK: Ashgate.

2003b. "Towns and Temples: Urban Growth and Decline in the Yangzi Delta, 1200–1500." In *The Song-Yuan-Ming Transition in Chinese History*, pp. 176–211. Ed. Paul Jakov Smith and Richard von Glahn. Cambridge, Mass.: Council on East Asian Studies, Harvard University.

Forthcoming. "The Sociology of Local Religion in the Lake Tai Basin." In *Chinese Religion and Society: The Transformation of a Field*, vol. 2. Ed. John Lagerwey. Hong Kong: Chinese University of Hong Kong and École Française d'Extrême-Orient.

Wada Hironori 和田博徳.

1985. "Rikōsei to rishadan gyōreidan: Mindai no gyōson shihai to saishi 里甲制と里社壇郷厲壇：明代の郷村支配と祭祀." In *Nishi to higashi to: Maejima Shinji sensei tsuitō ronbunshū* 西と東と：前島信次先生追悼論文集, pp. 413–32. Tokyo: Kyūko shoin.

Wang Deqing 王徳庆.

1983. "Suzhou Lengqiesi ta 苏州楞伽寺塔." *Wenwu* 文物 1983.10: 83–85.

Wang Haihang 王海航 and Chen Yaolin 陈耀林.

1984. *Pilusi he Pilusi bihua* 毗庐寺和毗庐寺壁画. Shijiazhuang.

Watson, Burton.

1989. *The Tso Chuan: Selections from China's Oldest Narrative History*. New York: Columbia University Press.

Watson, James L.

1976. "Anthropological Analyses of Chinese Religion." *China Quarterly* 66: 355–64.

1985. "Standardizing the Gods: The Promotion of T'ien Hou ('Empress of Heaven') Along the South China Coast, 960–1960." In Johnson et al., ed., 1985: 292–324.

1988. "The Structure of Chinese Funerary Rites: Elementary Forms, Ritual Sequence, and the Primacy of Performance." In *Death Ritual in Late Imperial and Modern China*, pp. 3–19. Ed. James L. Watson and Evelyn S. Rawski. Berkeley: University of California Press.

Weber, Charles D.

1968. *Chinese Pictorial Bronze Vessels of the Late Chou Period*. Ascona: Artibus Asiae.

Weber, Max.

1951. *The Religion of China*. New York: Free Press.

1978. *Economy and Society*. Ed. Guenther Roth and Claus Wittich. Berkeley: University of California Press.

Welch, Holmes, and Anna Seidel, ed.

1979. *Facets of Taoism: Essays in Chinese Religion*. New Haven, Conn.: Yale University Press.

Weller, Robert.

   1987. *Unity and Diversity in Chinese Religion*. Seattle: University of Washington Press.

Wheatley, Paul.

   1971. *The Pivot of the Four Quarters: A Preliminary Enquiry into the Origins and Character of the Ancient Chinese City*. Edinburgh: Edinburgh University Press.

Whitfield, Roderick, ed.

   1993. *The Problem of Meaning in Early Chinese Ritual Bronzes*. London: School of Oriental and African Studies, University of London.

Wolf, Arthur P.

   1974. "Gods, Ghosts, and Ancestors." In Wolf, ed., 1974: 131–82.

Wolf, Arthur P., ed.

   1974. *Religion and Ritual in Chinese Society*. Stanford, Calif.: Stanford University Press.

Wu Hung.

   1988. "From Temple to Tomb: Ancient Chinese Art and Religion in Transition." *Early China* 13: 78–115.

   1989. *The Wu Liang Shrine: The Ideology of Early Chinese Pictorial Art*. Berkeley: University of California Press.

   1992. "What is *Bianxiang*? On the Relationship Between Dunhuang Art and Literature." *Harvard Journal of Asiatic Studies* 52.1: 111–92.

   1995. *Monumentality in Early Chinese Art and Architecture*. Stanford, Calif.: Stanford University Press.

Wu Rongzeng 吴荣曾.

   1981. "Zhenmuwen zhong suojiandaode Dong Han daowu guanxi 镇墓文中所见到的东汉道巫关系." *Wenwu* 文物 1981.3: 56–63.

Wu Zude 吴祖德.

   1992. "Shangpin jingji chongji xiade dushi jieri: Shanghai shiqu suishi xinyang xisu 商品经济下的都市节日：上海市区岁时信仰习俗." *Zhongguo minjian wenhua* 中国民间文化 5: 114–26.

Xu Xiaowang 徐晓望.

   1994. *Fujian minjian xinyang yuanliu* 福建民间信仰源流. Fuzhou: Fujian jiaoyu chubanshe.

Yamauchi Kōichi 山内弘一.

   1981. "Hoku-Sō kokka to gyokkō: Shinrei kyōsha tenchi o chūshin ni 北宋国家と玉皇：新礼恭謝天地を中心に." *Tōhōgaku* 東方学 62: 83–97.

Yang, C. K.

   1961. *Religion in Chinese Society*. Berkeley: University of California Press.

Yang Hong 杨泓.

    1999. "Tan Zhongguo Han Tang zhi jian zangyide yanbian 谈中国汉唐之间葬仪的演变." *Wenwu* 文物 1999.10: 60–68.

Yang Xiaoneng.

    1999. *The Golden Age of Chinese Archaeology: Celebrated Discoveries from the People's Republic of China.* New Haven, Conn.: Yale University Press.

Yoshida Ryūei 吉田隆英.

    1981. "Kishi to ijin 鬼市と異人." *Tōhō shūkyō* 東方宗教 58: 30–47.

Yoshioka Yoshitoyo 吉岡義豊.

    1957. "Segaki shisō no Chūgokuteki jūyō 施餓鬼思想の中国的受容." In Yoshioka, *Dōkyō to bukkyō* 道教と仏教, 1: 369–411. Tokyo: Nihon gakujutsu shinko kai.

    1989. *Dōkyō nyūmon* 道教入門. Rpt. in *Yoshioka Yoshitoyo chosakushū* 吉岡義豊著作集, vol. 4. Gogatsu shobō, 1989.

Yu, Anthony.

    1983. *The Journey to the West.* Chicago, Ill.: University of Chicago Press.

Yü Chün-fang.

    1990. "Images of Kuan-yin in Chinese Folk Literature." *Hanxue yanjiu* 漢學研究 8.1: 221–85.

    1993. "P'u-t'uo Shan: Pilgrimage and the Creation of the Chinese Potalaka." In Naquin and Yü, ed. 1993: 190–245.

    1994. "Guanyin: The Chinese Transformation of Avalokiteśvara." In *Latter Days of the Law: Images of Chinese Buddhism, 850–1850,* pp. 151–81. Ed. Marsha Weidner. Lawrence: Spencer Museum of Art, University of Kansas.

    2001. *Kuan-yin: The Chinese Transformation of Avalokiteśvara.* New York: Columbia University Press.

Yü, Ying-shih (Yu Yingshi 余英時).

    1987a. " 'O Soul, Come Back!' A Study in the Changing Conceptions of the Soul and Afterlife in Pre-Buddhist China." *Harvard Journal of Asiatic Studies* 47.1: 363–95.

    1987b. *Zhongguo jinshi zongjiao lunli yu shangren jingshen* 中國近世宗教倫理與商人精神. Taibei: Lianjing chuban shiye gongsi.

Yūsa Noboru 遊佐昇.

    1989. "Tōdai ni mirareru Kyūku tenson shinkō ni tsuite 唐代に見られる救苦天尊信仰について." *Tōhō shūkyō* 東方宗教 73: 19–40.

Zhang Hongxiang 張鴻祥.

    1997. "Tingzhou chengqude miaohui daguan 汀州城區的廟會大觀." In *Minxide chengxiang miaohui yu cunluo wenhua* 閩西的城鄉廟會與村落文化, pp. 80–113. Ed. Yang Yanjie 楊彥潔. Hong Kong: International Hakka Studies Association and École Française d'Extrême-Orient.

Zhang Yongyao 张永尧 et al.

1994. "Jiaxing mishi xisu diaocha 嘉兴米市习俗调查." *Zhongguo minjian wenhua* 中国民间文化 14: 48–65.

Zhang Zhengming 张正明.

1995. *Jin shang xingshuai shi* 晋商兴衰史. Taiyuan: Shanxi guji chubanshe.

Zhejiang minsu xuehui 浙江民俗学会.

1986. *Zhejiang minsu jianzhi* 浙江民俗简志. Hangzhou: Zhejiang renmin chubanshe.

Zhongguo meishu quanji bianji weiyuanhui 中国美术全集编辑委员会.

1988a. *Zhongguo meishu quanji* 中国美术全集, *Huaxiangshi huaxiangzhuan bian* 画像石画像砖编. Shanghai: Shanghai renmin meishu chubanshe.

1988b. *Zhongguo meishu quanji* 中国美术全集, *huihua bian* 绘画编, vol. 15, *Siguan bihua* 寺观壁画. Shanghai: Shanghai renmin meishu chubanshe.

Zhu Zuzhen 朱祖振.

1997. "Xiaogu Zhuxing fazhan jiqi minsu 小姑朱姓發展及其民俗." In *Gannan diqude miaohui yu zongzu* 贛南地區的廟會與宗祖, pp. 139–73. Ed. LuoYong 羅勇 and John Lagerwey. Hong Kong: International Hakka Studies Association and École Française d'Extrême-Orient.

Zhuang Yifu 莊一拂.

1982. *Gu xiqu cunmu huikao* 古戲曲存目彙考. Shanghai: Shanghai guji chubanshe.

Zürcher, Eric.

1959. *The Buddhist Conquest of China*. Leiden: E. J. Brill.

1980. "Buddhist Influence on Early Taoism: A Survey of Scriptural Evidence." *Toung Pao* 66.1–3: 84–147.

1982. "Prince Moonlight: Messianism and Eschatology in Early Medieval Chinese Buddhism." *Toung Pao* 68.1–3: 1–75.

Glossary

Amituofo 阿彌陀佛
An Lushan 安祿山
Anlegong 安樂公
bai lishi 拜利市
Baidi 白帝
Bailianshe 白蓮社
Baiyi Guanyin 白衣觀音
baojuan 寶卷
Baoningsi Monastery 寶寧寺
Baoshanyuan Cloister 寶山院
baoying 報應
Baoyunsi Monastery 寶雲寺
Beidi 北帝
Beigaofeng 北高峰
Beixinguan 北新關
Bencao gangmu 本草綱目
benming 本命
Biancai Yuanjing 辯才元淨
bianwen 變文
bianxiang 變相
Bifang 畢方
bin 賓
bingshe weihui 並社為會
Bixia Yuanjun 碧霞元君
Bohai 渤海
Boqi 伯奇
Boyou 伯有

budao 不道
buyun 補運
Cai Yong 蔡邕
caishen 財神
Canhua Wusheng 蠶花五聖
Cao Cao 曹操
Cao Tianyou 曹天祐
Changsha 長沙
Changshu 常熟
Changxing 長興
Changzhou 常州
chao Dongyue 朝東嶽
chaoshan jinxiang 朝山進香
chaoxian 朝獻
chayan 茶筵
chenghuang 城隍
Chengyang Jing wang 城陽景王
Chetou Wusheng 車頭五聖
chimei 魑魅
Chixian Shenzhou 赤縣神州
Chiyou 蚩尤
Chizhou 池州
chong 衝
Chu 楚
chuer shiliu, tudi chirou 初二十六，
　土地喫肉
Ciyun Zunshi 慈雲尊式

congci 叢祠
Dabei Guanyin zhou 大悲觀音咒
Dabei jiuku Guanyin pusa 大悲救苦
　觀音菩薩
daiyan 待筵
damian 大眠
Dan 丹
Dao De Jing 道德經
Daomin 道民
Daorong 道瑢
daoshi 道士
Dazu 大足
De 德
Deng Daoshu 鄧道樞
Dexing 德興
di 帝
dijun 帝君
Diqiu 帝丘
ding 鼎
diyu 地獄
Dizang 地藏
Dongfang Shuo 東方朔
Dongfangjun 東方君
Dongyue 東嶽
Dongyue qitian dasheng di 東嶽齊
　天大聖帝
Du Yu 杜預
Duanwu 端午
dujiao wutong 獨腳五通
Fang La 方臘
fangliang 方良
Fangsheng 放生
fangshi 方士
fangxiang 方相
fashi 法師
fei 蜚
feifei 狒狒
feifei[a] 費費
fenan 墳庵
Fengbo 風伯
Fenghuasi Monastery 奉化寺
fengjian 封建
fenxiang 分香
fenyang 羵羊
fenyang[a] 墳羊
fohui 佛會
fu 福

Fu Qian 服虔
Fude Wutong 福德五通
fujun 符君
Fushanzhen 福山鎮
Fuzhou (Fujian) 福州
Fuzhou (Jiangxi) 撫州
Gan juren 贛巨人
Gan River 贛水
gangmao 剛卯
ganqing 感情
ganying 感應
Ganzhou 贛州
Gao You 高誘
Gaozong, Emperor of Song 宋高宗
ge 閣
Ge Chaofu 葛巢甫
gengshen 庚申
gong 公
Gong Kai 龔開
gongguoge 功過格
gu 蠱
Gu Yewang 顧野王
guai 怪
Guandi 關帝
Guang'an Gate 廣安門
Guangde 廣德
Guangfu 光福
Guangfusi 光福寺
Guangling zhi 廣陵志
Guangong 關公
Guangxiao Abbey 光孝觀
Guangyou wang 廣佑王
Guanyin 觀音
Guanyin jing 觀音經
gui (ghost, demon) 鬼
gui (tureen) 簋
guidao 鬼道
Guiji 會稽
guimei 傀魅
guishen 鬼神
guishi 鬼市
guiwei 鬼位
guixiang 鬼相
guixing 鬼形
Guixishe 歸西社
Guo Pu 郭璞
Gusu xihua tu 姑蘇繫華圖

Haishen Li wang 海神李王
Han Yu 韓愈
hanba 旱魃
Hangzhou 杭州
Hankou 漢口
He He Erxian 和合二仙
He Xiangu 何仙姑
Heisha 黑煞
Hengtang 橫塘
Hou 侯
Hou Ji 后稷
Hou Yi 后羿
Houchao Gate 候潮門
Houtu 后土
hu 壺
Huaguang 華光
Huaguang tianwang 華光天王
Huaguang xiansheng 華光顯聖
Huaguang zangwang miaojixiang
    pusa 華光藏王妙吉祥菩薩
Huajiu Ma Lingguan 花酒馬靈官
Huangdi (Yellow Thearch) 黃帝
Huangdi*ª* (Resplendent Thearch)
    皇帝
Huangdi bashiyi nanjing 黃帝八十
    一難經
Huangdi neijing 黃帝內經
Huangjing 璜涇
Huanglu zhai 黃籙齋
Huangshen 黃神
huashen 化身
hui (creature) 暉
huiª (creature) 揮
huiᵇ (assembly) 會
Huizhou 徽州
Huizong, Emperor of Song 宋徽宗
hun 魂
Hundong chiwen 混洞赤文
huo 惑
huojing 火精
huqielan shen 護伽藍神
Huzhou 湖州
Ji (surname) 姬
Ji (God of Grains) 稷
Ji Huanzi 季桓子
Jianchang 建昌
Jianchangjun 建昌軍

Jiang Ziwen 蔣子文
Jiangling 江陵
Jiangnan 江南
Jiangyin 江陰
Jiangzhou 江州
Jiankang 建康
jiao (music) 角
jiaoxi 叫喜
Jiashan 嘉善
jiatang 家堂
Jiaxiang 嘉祥
Jiduci 濟瀆祠
jie lutou 接路頭
jie yinzhai 借陰債
jie yuanbao 借元寶
jieshe jianxian 結社薦獻
Jin Chang 金昌
Jin Yuanqi 金元七
Jin Zongguan 金總管
jing 精
Jingangjing 金剛經
Jingdezhen 景德鎮
jingqi 精氣
jinshi 進士
Jingtu 淨土
Jingtushe 淨土社
Jinguangchan 金光懺
Jining 濟寧
Jishen Wusheng 機神五聖
Jiuding ji 九鼎記
Jiuqucheng 九曲城
Jiutian shengshen yuzhang 九天生
    神玉章
Jiuyou zhai 九幽齋
Jizhou 驥州
jubaopen 聚寶盆
junzhu 郡主
Jurong 句容
Kaifeng 開封
Kelong Wusheng 窠籠五聖
kui 夔
Kunlun 崑崙
Kunshan 崑山
La 臘
Langye 琅耶
Laojun 老君
Lengqie, Mount 楞伽山

Lengqiesi Monastery 楞伽寺
Li 禮
Li Congzhi 李從智
Li Hou 李侯
Li wei 禮緯
Li Zeng 李繪
Liangzhu 良渚
Lianshe 蓮社
liming 立命
Lin Lingsu 林靈素
ling 靈
Ling, Lord of Qin 秦靈公
Lingbao 靈寶
linggan 靈感
Linggansi Monastery 靈感寺
lingguan 靈官
Linghui fei 靈惠妃
Lingjian 靈鑑
Lingshun 靈順
lingyan 靈驗
lingyanji 靈驗集
Lingyinsi Monastery 靈隱寺
lishi 利市
lishi fan 利市飯
Lishi xianguan 利市仙官
Liu Hai 劉海
Liu Mengjiang 劉猛將
Liu Song 劉宋
Liu Yuanda 劉元達
Liu Yuxi 劉禹錫
Liu Zhang 劉章
Liuheta 六合塔
liutian xieqi 六天邪氣
Lizhou 澧州
Lizong, Emperor of Song 理宗
lu 祿
Lü Dongbin 呂洞賓
Lu Ji 陸機
Lu Xiujing 陸修靜
Lü Xu 呂需
Lu Yun 陸雲
Lu Zhi 陸贄
Lüxing 呂刑
Luzhizhen 甪直鎮
Ma Fu zongguan 馬福總管
Ma Rong 馬融
Ma Shan 馬善

Ma Yuanshuai 馬元帥
Ma'anshan 馬鞍山
Maershan wang 馬耳山王
Magong 馬公
Mak Yao (Mo Yao) 莫猺
Manao'yuan Cloister 瑪瑙院
Mao Shan 茅山
Mao Ziyuan 茅子元
Matouniang 馬頭娘
Mazu 媽祖
Miaojixiang pusa 妙吉祥菩薩
Miaoshan 妙善
mingqi 冥器，明器
Mingwang 明王
Moling 秣陵
mowang 魔王
muke 木客
Mulian 目連
mushi zhi guai 木石之怪
muxia sanlang 木下三郎
Nangaofeng 南高峰
Nanjing 南京
Nankang 南康
Nanling 南嶺
Nanxiang 南翔
Nanxun 南潯
nazhai 納債
Nazhen tianzun 納珍天尊
nianfo 念佛
niangniang 娘娘
niangzi 娘子
Ningbo 寧波
Ningwu 寧武
nuegui 瘧鬼
Nuo 儺
panghuang 彷徨
penzhe 噴者
Pilusi Monastery 毘盧寺
ping'an xi 平安戲
Pingchangwan 瓶場灣
Pingwang 平望
Pingyang 平陽
po 魄
Poyang 鄱陽
Poyang Lake 鄱陽湖
Pujisi Monastery 普濟寺
pusa 菩薩

Putian 莆田
Putuo, Mount 普陀山
Puyuanzhen 濮院鎮
qi (vapor) 氣
Qi (state) 齊
qi[a] (creature) 蚑
qian 韱
Qian erbai guanyi 千二百官儀
Qian Yueyou 潛説友
qianfanshe 錢幡社
Qiantang Gate 錢塘門
qielanshen 伽藍神
Qiguzi 七姑子
Qin 秦
Qin Shihuangdi 秦始皇帝
qingfohui 慶佛會
Qinglongzhen 青龍鎮
qingmiaoshe 青苗社
Qingming 清明
Qingwei 清微
Qingzhou 青州
qisi 奇祀
Qu Yuan 屈原
quan 犬
*Quanxiang Wuxian lingguan dadi
Huaguang tianwang zhuan* 全像
五顯靈官大帝華光天王傳
quji jiangfu 趨吉降福
Raozhou 饒州
ren 人
renshen 人參
Rongguosi Monastery 榮國寺
roushendeng 肉身燈
ru 儒
rulai 如來
Ruo River 若水
Sa Shoujian 薩守堅
San Miao 三苗
Sanguan 三官
Sanhuangwen 三皇文
Sanjiao 三教
Sanshi 三尸
shandu 山都
Shang shu 尚書
Shang Tianzhusi Monastery 上天
竺寺
Shangdi 上帝

Shangfang, Mount 上方山
Shangjunshu 商君書
Shangluo, Mount 上洛山
shangong 山公
Shangqing 上清
Shangshantang 上善堂
shangu 山姑
shanhui 山揮
shanjing 山精
shansao 山臊，山塀
Shanshen 山神
shanshu 善書
shanxiao 山魈
Shanxiao Wulang 山魈五郎
shanzao 山繰
shao lishi 燒利市
shaoge lishi 燒個利市
Shaohao 少昊
Shaowu 邵武
Shaxizhen 沙溪鎮
She, *she* 社
Sheji 社稷
shemo 社陌
shen (spirit, divinity) 神
shen[a] (creature) 宰
Shengong zhuanji 神公傳記
shenhebing 神合病
shenjun 神君
Shennong 神農
shenshi 神師
Shenshu 神荼
Shenxiao 神霄
Shenyijing 神異經
Shenzhuan 神傳
Shenzong, Emperor of Song 宋神宗
shidafu 士大夫
Shihu 石湖
shijing xiaoren 市井小人
shimin 市民
shiniang 師娘
shishi egui 施食餓鬼
Shizhouji 十洲記
Shou shangui laomi zhi xiejing jing
收山鬼老魅治邪精經
shoujing 收驚
Shoushengyuan Cloister 壽聖院
Shuanglinsi Monastery 雙林寺

Shuanglinzhen 雙林鎮
Shuifu 水府
Shuilu zhai 水陸齋
shuilu'an 水陸庵
Shuiyue Guanyin 水月觀音
Shutou Wusheng 樹頭五聖
sidian 祀典
Siming 司命
Sisheng 四聖
Siyouji 四遊記
Song, Mount 嵩山
Songxiang 宋相
Songzi Guanyin 送子觀音
Su Hanchen 蘇漢臣
sui 祟
Sun Quan 孫權
Sun Wukong 孫無空
Suzhou 蘇州
Tai, Mount 泰山
Taicang 太倉
Taifeng Ward 泰豐坊
Taima 太媽
Taimu 太姆
Taimu chan 太母懺
Taipingjing 太平經
Taishan fujun 泰山府君
Taisui 太歲
Taiyi 太乙
Taiyi jiuku tianzun 太乙救苦天尊
Taizhou (Jiangsu) 泰州
Taizhou (Zhejiang) 台州
Taizu, Emperor of Ming 明太祖
tanfo 賧佛
Tangxizhen 唐棲鎮
tangzi 堂子
Tao Hongjing 陶弘景
taotie 饕餮
Tian 天
Tiandi 天帝
Tiandi shizhe 天帝使者
Tianfei 天妃
Tianguang 天光
Tianhou 天后
tianming 天命
Tianpeng 天蓬
tianren shuo 天人説
tianshen 天神

Tianshidao 天師道
Tiantai 天台
tianxia 天下
Tianxian 天仙
Tianxin 天心
Tianyou 天猷
Tingzhou 汀州
tong 通
tudi 土地
tuofei 橐甚
turen sici 土人私祠
wang 王
Wang Jie 王捷
Wang Qin 王溱
Wang Yi 王逸
Wang Yuangui 汪元圭
Wang Zhijian 王志堅
wangliang 罔魎
wangxiang 罔象
Wangye 王爺
Wanshou lingshun wu pusa 萬壽靈
順五菩薩
Wei (kingdom) 衛
Wei Liangchen 魏良臣
Wei Zhao 韋昭
weishe 委蛇
Wen, Emperor of Wei 魏文帝
Wen Qiong 溫瓊
Wenchang 文昌
wengui 瘟鬼
Wenzhou 溫州
Wu (kingdom) 吳
wu (spirit medium) 巫
Wu caishen 武財神
Wu Daozi 吳道子
Wu, Emperor of Han 漢武帝
Wu, King of Zhou 周武王
Wu-Yue 吳越
Wu Zixu 伍子胥
wuaihui 無礙會
wubing 五兵
wubing zhi gui 五兵之鬼
Wuchanggui 五猖鬼
Wudao jiangjun 五道將軍
wude 五德
Wudi 五帝
Wudi shizhe 五帝使者

Wudoumi jiao 五斗米教

wufang guizhu 五方鬼主

Wufang xiansheng 五方賢聖

wufang yigui 五方疫鬼

Wugemiao 五哥廟

wugu 巫蠱

Wulang 五郎

Wulu caishen 五路財神

Wulu da jiangjun 五路大將軍

Wulu dashen 五路大神

wulutang 五路堂

wumu zhi gui 五墓之鬼

wushang guijing 五傷鬼精

Wusheng yingxian lingguan 五聖應
顯靈官

Wushengtai 五聖臺

wushenren 五神人

Wusong River 吳淞江

Wutong 五通

Wutong daxian 五通大仙

Wutong shenxian 五通神仙

Wutong xianren 五通仙人

Wutong xiansheng 五通賢聖

Wuwen shizhe 五瘟使者

Wuwenmiao 五瘟廟

Wuwenshe 五瘟社

Wuwenshen 五瘟神

Wuxi 無錫

Wuxian (Five Manifestations) 五顯

Wuxian[a] (Five Transcendents) 五仙

Wuxian chanye ta 五顯懺業塔

Wuxianmiao 五仙廟

Wuxiansheng 五顯聖

wuxianwang qingfohui 五顯王慶
佛會

wuxing 五行

Wuyi Mountains 武夷山

Wuyuan 婺源

Wuyue 五嶽

Wuyun, Mount 五雲山

wuzhehui 無蔗會

Wuzhou 婺州

Xia 夏

Xia Song 夏竦

Xia Tianzhusi Monastery 下天竺寺

xiagui 下鬼

xian 仙

Xiang (Xia king) 相

Xiang, Lord of Qin 秦襄公

Xiang Qianqiu 享千秋

Xiang Yu 項羽

xiangsu 鄉俗

xiao 嚻

xiaoyang 梟陽

xie busheng zheng 邪不勝正

xieqi 邪氣

xieshen 邪神

Xiezhou 解州

xinggong 行宮

Xinjing 心經

Xinshi 新市

Xiwangmu 西王母

Xizishe 西資社

Xu (surname) 許

Xu (village) 徐村

Xu Mi 許謐

Xu Shouxin 徐守信

Xu Wentai 胥文泰

Xu Yang 徐揚

xuan 玄

Xuantan zhenjun 玄壇真君

Xuanyuan 軒轅

Xuanzang 玄藏

Xuanzong, Emperor of Tang
唐玄宗

Xue Zong 薛綜

xueshi 血食

Yan (state) 燕

Yan Shu 晏殊

Yandi 炎帝

yang 陽

Yang Xi 楊羲

Yangzhou 揚州

Yanqingsi Monastery 延慶寺

Yanshan wang 仰山王

yaoguai 妖怪

yaojing 妖精

yaotong 妖通

ye (bird) 冶鳥

yezhong 野仲

yezhong[a] 野重

yezhong youguang 野仲游光

yezhong you xiongdi baren 野仲游
兄弟八人

yetong 野童
Yichun 宜春
yin (female principle) 陰
yin (excess) 淫
Yin Jishan 尹繼善
yinci 淫祠
Yinghuo 熒惑
yinjiao 陰教
yinzhai 陰債
yisi 乙巳
Yixing 宜興
yiyang 汱陽
Yong 雍
Yongle, Emperor of Ming 明永樂
Youshengguan Abbey 祐聖觀
Youyu 右玉
Yu the Great 大禹
yuanbao 元寶
Yuanshi tianzun 元始天尊
Yuanshuai 元帥
Yuantong chan'an Convent 圓通
   禪菴
Yuci, Mount 郁次山
yue (marchmont) 嶽
Yue (region) 越
Yueling 月令
Yugong 禹貢
Yuhuang dadi 玉皇大帝
Yulü 鬱壘
yun 運
Yunju, Mount 雲居山
Yunjusi Monastery 雲居寺
Yunxiao Wulang 雲霄五郎
Yunyansi Monastery 雲岩寺
yunzhi baohuo 運致寶貨
Yushi 雨師
Zao 竈
Zaojun 竈君
zhaihui 齋會
Zhang Daoling 張道陵
Zhang Dayou 張大酋
Zhang Heng 張衡
Zhang Jue 張角
Zhang Lu 張魯
Zhang Renbiao 張仁表
Zhang Yuanbo 張元伯
Zhangwang 張王

Zhangyi Gate 彰義門
Zhao Gongming 趙公明
Zhao Jinggongsi Monastery 趙景
   公寺
Zhao Wufang egui 招五方惡鬼
Zhao Wuguan 趙五官
Zhaobao tianzun 招寶天尊
Zhaocai shizhe 招財使者
Zhaowen 昭文
zhen (fevers) 疹
zhen (market town) 鎮
zheng (correctness) 正
Zheng (kingdom) 鄭
Zheng, King of Qin 秦政王
Zheng Qingzhi 鄭清之
zhengdao 正道
zhengshen 正神
Zhengshou Miaojixiang tianwang
   正受妙吉祥天王
Zhengyi Lingguan Ma Yuanshuai
   正一靈官馬元帥
Zhenjiang 鎮江
zhenren 真人
Zhenwu 真武
Zhenze 震澤
Zhenzong, Emperor of Song 宋真宗
zhi 治
Zhi Miaojixiang rulai 至妙吉祥如來
zhiguai 志怪
Zhili (monk) 智禮
Zhili Bridge 織里橋
zhima 紙馬
zhishan wuai dazhai 至善無礙大齋
Zhong Kui 鐘馗
Zhong Shan 鐘山
Zhong Shiji 鐘士季
Zhongguo 中國
zhongkui 終葵
zhongmin 種民
zhongqiu jiasuoshe 重囚枷鎖社
Zhongshi dasheng 終始大聖
zhongsong 冢訟
Zhou Chu 周處
Zhou, King of Shang 商紂王
Zhou Que 周確
Zhou Xiaogong 周孝公
Zhou Xuan lingwang 周宣靈王

Zhouzhuang　周莊

zhouzu　咒詛

Zhu Conglong　朱從龍

Zhu Yuanzhang　朱元璋

zhuangyuan　狀元

Zhuangzi　莊子

Zhuanxu　顓頊

zhuhe　祝劾

zhuli　逐癘

zhuyi　逐疫

Zichan　子產

Zitong　梓橦

Zongdao　宗道

Zongguan, *zongguan*　總管

Zou Yan　騶衍

Zudian lingying ji　祖殿靈
　　　　　應集

zuodao　左道

Index

Compositor:	Integrated Composition Systems
Text:	10/13 Sabon
Display:	Sabon
Printer and binder:	Thomson-Shore